The HEALTHY HEART Cookbook

OVER 650 RECIPES FOR EVERY DAY AND EVERY OCCASION

The HEALTHY HEART Cookbook

OVER 650 RECIPES FOR EVERY DAY AND EVERY OCCASION

Joseph C. Piscatella
and Bernie Piscatella

BLACK DOG
& LEVENTHAL
PUBLISHERS
NEW YORK

Acknowledgements

It takes a team of dedicated people to put together a book. In particular we are grateful to many people who gave of their time and expertise, providing information and insight, offering valuable suggestions and testing recipes. These include our daughter, Anne Vaughan, and our son, Joe Piscatella, and our friends Nancy Weaver, Sue Black and Mike McGowan. Special thanks to Bev Utt, R.D., MPH, for her nutritional calculations.

We wish to thank our friends at Black Dog and Leventhal Publishers, especially J.P. Leventhal for his commitment to our work, and Dinah Dunn for her patience, understanding and skill in guiding the book to completion. We also want to thank our friend Peter Workman and the team at Workman Publishing Company, our partners for 30 years, for their dedicated support.

Library of Congress Cataloguing in Publication Data available on file

Published by
Black Dog & Leventhal Publishers
151 West 19th Street
New York, NY 10011

Distributed by
Workman Publishing Company
225 Varick Street
New York, NY 10014

This material was originally published in the following books:
CHOICES FOR A HEALTHY HEART
FAT PROOF YOUR CHILD
DON'T EAT YOUR HEART OUT COOKBOOK
CONTROLLING YOUR FAT TOOTH
THE FAT TOOTH FAT GRAM COUNTER

The material in this book is provided for information only and should not be construed as medical advice or instruction. Always consult with your physician or other appropriate health professionals before making any changes in diet, physical activity, and/or drug therapy.

Manufactured in the United States

Jacket and interior design by Red Herring Design.

ISBN: 978-1-57912-925-5
h g f e d c b a

Contents

Preface

At the age of thirty-two, I underwent coronary bypass surgery. On the thirty-fifth anniversary of that surgery, I celebrated my survival by hiking on Mount Rainier with my wife, Bernie. I could not have climbed from an operating table to a mountaintop without changing my dietary lifestyle. And I could not have changed my dietary lifestyle without the recipes in this book.

THE HEALTHY HEART COOKBOOK presents over 600 delicious, quick-to-fix recipes developed by Bernie, tested by our family and friends, and enjoyed by millions of people over the past three decades in books such as *DON'T EAT YOUR HEART OUT COOKBOOK, CHOICES FOR A HEALTHY HEART* and *CONTROLLING YOUR FAT TOOTH*. Her underlying principle, "good food and good health go together"—and her commitment to practicality, simplicity, and convenience—is reflected in every recipe.

Cooking and eating to promote cardiac health is not about dieting. It's about establishing eating habits for a lifetime. During the past thirty-five years, many diets have been promoted, been the rage, and then faded away. They fail because they tout unrealistic solutions that might be successful in the short term, but cannot be sustained for a lifetime. This is particularly critical for heart patients and others interested in cardiac health. The fundamental question for someone who wants to control cholesterol, keep cardiac risks in check, and manage weight, once and for all, is not "how do I eat for the next week?" but "how do I eat for the rest of my life?" Short-term diets provide no viable answer.

Experts agree that the starting point for changing your eating habits is credible science. Fortunately, the American Heart Association, the surgeon general, and others have compiled a wide body of scientific information on which to base sound dietary decisions.

But eating healthy in the real world takes more than science. It takes common sense, practicality, and talent to turn those recipes into delicious meals. Taste and convenience are as critical to success as cutting-edge science. Experts tell us, for example, that your family should eat less fat—particularily saturated and trans fat—to promote weight loss and cholesterol reduction. That is fine in principle, but in reality, fat tastes good and satisfies, and it's found in many familiar foods that your family likes. Serving a steady diet of "no-fat" and "low-fat" recipes may provoke a rebellion. In addition, many no-and low-fat versions of prepared foods are made with a long list of additives that I'd rather do without. It makes more sense to strike a compromise, one that creates healthier, lower-fat meals that still taste great. This is a critical balance, because if the recipe isn't tasty and appealing, it will be a hard sell to your family no matter what the health consequences.

The recipes in this book, made in the Mediteranean diet style, *are* delicious, but they are heart-healthy as well. I should know. These recipes have helped me to eat a healthy, balanced diet for more than three decades. By doing so, they literally have saved my heart and my life.

I was not always interested in healthy eating. Indeed, I learned of its importance the hard way. Coronary-bypass surgery was a rude awakening to the fact that a poor diet could penalize the health of my heart and put my life in jeopardy. Luckily, I also learned that a balanced diet could promote cardiac health.

Discovering diet as a key to good health while at the same time experiencing a major disease might seem contradictory on the surface, but in reality this is the way that most people come to practical terms with the subject. Good health is usually not a true concern until it is threatened. As long as physical problems or ailments are not evident, most of us take our health for granted and treat it as if it were a permanent state. We forget that many diseases take a long time to manifest themselves in pain or other symptoms, and that being healthy isn't automatic.

That's the way it was with me. For most of my life, good health was not a high priority. A consciously healthy lifestyle took a back seat to other seemingly more important things: Bernie and our children Anne and Joe, my work, and our community. Besides, I'd always been healthy. There were no major illnesses or conditions in my life, and no reason for that to change. Ominous diseases like cancer and heart disease were things that happened to other people. For me, they simply weren't real.

Not that everything was perfect, of course. Sure, my cholesterol was high (about 250 mg/dl, but many doctors in those days considered this "average" for Americans and not a cause for alarm), and I could stand to lose a few pounds. But I was too busy to take action. There would be plenty of time tomorrow, I reasoned, to eat healthier, exercise more regularly, and take better care of my health. Then I found out that you can't have a tomorrow if you don't have a today. Here is my story.

For about a month, I had noticed a nagging pain in my chest when playing tennis. It was a dull pain, more like a feeling of fullness or pressure. I would "work through it" during the warmup, and the pain would gradually dissipate. At first I simply ignored it, hoping it would go away. When it didn't, and in fact became more intense, I made an appointment with my doctor. I had seen him just four months earlier for a complete physical exam, so I wasn't expecting any surprises now. "It's probably bronchitis," I told myself. "You'll be out of his office in thirty minutes with a prescription."

The exam indicated no problem existed with my lungs. Instead, his concern was with my heart, or more accurately, my coronary arteries, the blood vessels that curl around the surface of the heart and supply blood to it. He suggested an electrocardiogram (EKG). "The arteries are the pipeline for blood to reach the heart," he explained. "Unfortunately, these arteries are very small, approximately an eighth of an inch in diameter, or about as wide as a piece of cooked spaghetti. As long as they are open, Joe, your heart can receive sufficient blood to do its job: pumping about 100,000 times a day to move blood throughout the body. But the EKG suggests that your coronary arteries may have become nar-

rowed with layers of cholesterol, much as rust accumulates in an old water pipe. The chest pain you felt on the tennis court may be the result of impeded blood flow to your heart. If that's the case, you could be at risk for a heart attack. You need to see a cardiologist right away . . . I mean today!"

An appointment was made for that same afternoon for a full cardiac exam. The cardiologist also was concerned about the external indicators. He suggested an angiogram, a procedure to X-ray the coronary arteries. It would give the doctors and me more information. The procedure was performed the next morning. The results indicated three arterial blockages ranging from 50 to 95 percent. The doctors were extremely concerned about a high heart-attack risk. Bypass surgery, they said, not only must be done, it must be done immediately.

I found it hard at first to identify with their concern. What could heart attack have to do with me, a thirty-two-year-old guy in the prime of life? As their diagnosis finally sank in—they were talking about *my heart*, *my heart disease*, and *my life*—the age of innocence (and perhaps ignorance as well) ended for me. Heart disease was no longer someone else's problem. Suddenly, the alarm clock of reality rang, the result of a time bomb in my chest, and I understood.

So instead of being sent home with an antibiotic for my lungs, I was wheeled into the operating room to have bypass surgery for my heart. In a five-hour operation, a piece of vein was taken from my leg and used to create a new arterial channel around the blocked area (literally "bypassing" it) so that blood could once again flow freely to my heart.

Returning home about a week after the surgery, I experienced a wide range of emotional ups-and-downs. I was elated to have survived, avoided a heart attack, and be back with my family again. I fully understood how lucky I was that my condition was diagnosed quickly and that bypass surgery was an available option. Had it been ten years earlier, I probably would have died on the tennis court.

At the same time I was worried about my future. Bypass surgery had circumvented the immediate problem, having a heart attack, but it had not taken away the disease. It did not "cure" me.

One doctor even predicted that I would probably not live to age forty, and that the chance to see my children graduate from high school was a slim one. I could not bear the thought that Anne and Joe would not know their father or that I would not grow old together with Bernie. His comments angered and upset me, but they were the catalyst for an increased resolve.

There were many things about coronary heart disease that I did not know. But there were some things that I did know. I knew that I did not want the disease to progress in me. I knew that I did

not want to die a premature death from heart attack. I knew that I did not want to live the half-life of a coronary victim.

I felt stressed and was unable to move forward until Bernie put the situation into perspective: "Heart disease could have killed you, Joe, but it didn't. You are alive and recuperating, thanks to the surgery. Avoiding a heart attack was the first step. But the surgery is in the past. We now need to focus on the second step: making lifestyle changes to reduce your future risk. You may have a genetic leaning toward high cholesterol and heart disease, but it may also be a product of your lifestyle, particularly your diet. The bottom line is that you can't change the cards you were dealt, but you can play those cards the best you can."

She was supported by my doctor, who told me, "My advice is to focus on making healthy dietary changes. The typical American diet is a cardiac risk, but it wasn't always that way. One hundred years ago Americans ate a different diet, one with less fat and more fruits, vegetables, and whole grains. The incidence of coronary heart disease then was low. But our modern diet has driven up cholesterol levels. Today, arterial blockages are evident in virtually all American adults and in many children as well, and millions of people have coronary heart disease. Improving your diet can help to lower your future cardiac risk by improving your cholesterol, triglycerides, blood pressure, glucose, and weight. Forget about your

DNA; you can't change your parents! Instead, focus on changing your food habits."

This advice became a turning point in my life. I had reached what health professionals term "a teachable moment," a time when one is ready to listen, learn, and take action to foster good health. Bernie and I became focused on the future, not the past, and on what we could do rather than on what genetic weakness I might have. We were ready to make healthy lifestyle changes, but first we needed information and a clear direction. What should we do? How should we do it? We needed a plan.

We began by dedicating six months to learn about diet and cardiac health.

My job was to sift through the data. I didn't want some pop-science diet that might work for a few weeks. What was needed was a way of living based on accepted nutritional principles that could last for a lifetime. I examined medical texts and journals about cholesterol, coronary heart disease, and healthy eating.

I attended lectures and clinics from coast to coast and interviewed numerous doctors, registered dieticians, and other health professionals. My intention was not to discover something new, but instead to evaluate current findings and to arrive at a rational conclusion as to what was the best, most healthful diet pattern for my family and me.

Meanwhile, we still had to eat, and hopefully to do so without penalizing health. Bernie's job was to give practical application to the science of healthy eating—otherwise known as cooking! She searched through stacks of cookbooks looking for ways to make healthier meals. It was often frustrating. The quick weight-loss diet books were generally useless. Some of the medically sound cookbooks counseled diets so low in fat as to be unrealistic. And most of the so-called "healthy-heart" cookbooks told how to prepare a recipe but not how to maintain a permanent change in dietary habits.

But from each she gleaned information and insight. She tried new recipes and adapted old ones. Her focus was on what we could eat, not on what we couldn't have. This was neither an easy nor a quick effort. Progress was measured in small increments. Trial and error ruled. Some meals were excellent; others were disasters. Some new cooking techniques worked well; others did not and had to be abandoned. Some days I was well satisfied with Bernie's healthy meals; other days I experienced cravings for pizza, pastrami, and chocolate.

But we kept at it. We knew that returning to our old diet was not the answer. Finally, progress started to take root and, thanks to Bernie's ever-increasing trove of recipes, a new way of eating—a healthy diet pattern—began to take shape for our family. And we've never looked back.

Through the years, as science has moved

forward and cooking techniques improved, we've made changes. Today, we subscribe to the Mediteranean-style dietary pattern that emphasizes fresh, in season, and local whole foods. It is the best balance, in our opinion, of good taste and good health.

Bernie's work in the kitchen provided another benefit: It taught us how to better handle eating in a restaurant. Eliminating restaurant meals makes little sense. Even though generally higher in fat, sodium, and calories than home-cooked food, restaurant meals are part of the fabric of modern life. In fact, about 50 percent of the U.S. food budget is now spent in restaurants. It makes more sense to learn how to make the healthiest choices when in a restaurant. Eating healthy recipes at home provided us with a blueprint for ordering successfully in restaurants.

An added benefit has been the impact on my now-grown children. One of my concerns was that they might have a genetic makeup that placed them at higher risk for heart disease. So the recipes I ate for rehabilitation, they ate for prevention, and it worked. Now grown, neither has heart problems, illustrating how healthy lifestyle habits can be taught to children and can offset family genes to a great extent.

Bernie's more than 600 recipes were born out of the frustration of trying to eat and to live a healthy lifestyle and still be a part of the real world. They must work.

It is now more than thirty-five years since my coronary bypass surgery, and my biometric measurements reflect a lifetime of her delicious, healthy food.

Critical markers such as weight, cholesterol, triglycerides, and blood pressure show that I'm in better health now than in 1977.

Tests show not only that my heart disease has been stabilized, but also that I actually have less disease today than in 1977, a condition called coronary regression.

More importantly, I've watched my children graduate from high school, college, graduate school and law school, have walked my daughter down the aisle, played baseball with my four grandchildren, and have celebrated with Bernie our forty-fifth wedding anniversary.

THE HEALTHY HEART COOKBOOK blends current science with practical application. The recipes, tips, and techniques are designed to help families eat healthy food every day without sacrificing taste or time. We hope you enjoy it.

—Joe Piscatella
Gig Harbor, Washington

Introduction

WHY MAKE DIETARY CHANGES?

ost people love eating foods typically found in the American diet, from fried chicken to prime rib, Thanksgiving gravy to Super Bowl snacks, McDonald's hamburgers to Krispy Kreme doughnuts.

Whatever the occasion, food is enjoyed and celebrated. Why then should we change our dietary habits? Perhaps the best reason can be best summarized by a quote from the German poet Goethe, made more than two centuries ago: "You are what you eat." That concept is more clearly understood today in light of the established relationship between nutrition and health.

Unfortunately, the makeup of our modern diet has little to do with our knowledge about its impact on good health. In fact, a CNN poll found that 33 percent of men and 23 percent of women believe you can eat badly and stay healthy! "That misconception is certainly reflected in our typical diet," says Bev Utt, R.D., M.P.H.. "What we eat is the result of daily decisions based on impulse, advertising, convenience, economics, status, taste,

and cravings—on influences other than positive nutrition." Says Dr. Mark Hegsted, former director of the federal government's Human Nutrition Center, "The menu we happen to eat today—high in fat, sugar, salt, and calories, and low in fiber and complex carbohydrates—was never planned on the basis of health. It just grew as the result of our affluence, the efficiency of American farmers, the growth of the processed food and fast-food industries, the emergence of sophisticated advertising techniques, and the increased pace of modern life. The fact that we consume it today is no indication that it is balanced or desirable."

Our national eating pattern was not always so unbalanced. A comparison of foods consumed in 1910, when the U.S. Department of Agriculture first started to keep figures on the food supply, with those consumed today shows a dramatic shift in calorie sources. Dietary fat then made up just 27 percent of calories; today, it accounts for about 35 percent, reflecting a love of red meat and other animal foods, whole milk dairy products, fast foods, fried foods, baked goods, convenience foods, cooking and salad oils, snacks, and restaurant meals. As a result, each person in the United States consumes about 100 pounds of fat annually. Unfortunately, much of it comes in the form of saturated fat and trans fat, which can raise LDL cholesterol, the type that sticks to artery walls, and increases heart-attack risk. Excessive dietary fat is also linked to an increased risk for weight gain, high blood pressure, and diabetes.

In that same period, the yearly consumption of sugar has more than doubled to 150 pounds for adults and 275 pounds for children. Sugar now constitutes more than a quarter of calories eaten. Soft drinks, candy, and highly refined carbohydrates such as cake, doughnuts, and other commercially baked goods are the leading sources. One of the worst offenders is fat-free baked goods that, while free of fat, are high in sugar and total calories. The impact of a sweet tooth on health is twofold: Sugar can raise triglyceride levels and contribute to weight gain.

Salt and sodium intake have also increased dramatically. It is estimated that Americans currently consume two to four teaspoons of salt daily, or about fifteen pounds a year. This is a reflection of food choices that include a steady diet of convenience foods, snack foods, and restaurant foods (takeout and sit-down.) The high consumption of salt and sodium has helped to make high blood pressure a health risk for millions of people.

At the same time as we've experienced sharp increases in fat, salt, and sugar, there has been a dangerous decrease in the consumption of complex carbohydrates—fruits, vegetables, beans, and whole grains. These foods are rich in cardioprotective elements such as fiber, antioxidants, and phytochemicals. They are critical to cardiac risk

In the late 1970s, fat constituted 40 percent of calories in our diet. Today it is about 35 percent. Isn't that progress? "Not so," says Bonnie Liebman, a registered dietitian at the Center for Science in the Public Interest. "Fat reduction is a myth. What we're eating is not a lower-fat diet. It's a higher-calorie diet. We are actually eating slightly more fat than in the past, but we're eating a lot more calories. So, the percentage looks better, but the actual amount of fat eaten has not fallen."

IT'S A FACT

reduction and weight control.

Unfortunately, only one in five Americans eats the recommended daily servings of fruits and vegetables. Some 20 percent eat no fruit in any given day, and about 25 percent eat no vegetables. But it gets worse. Of those who do eat vegetables, French fries constitute one-quarter of all vegetables eaten!

And to top if off, we're eating more, period. Super-sized servings generate about 150 more calories per day than was eaten twenty years ago. This amount may not seem significant, but it could add up to a weight gain of fifteen pounds in one year. It's easy to overeat when cookies are the size of pancakes, bagels look like life rafts, muffins are bigger than baseballs, and sodas are large enough to drown in. No wonder, according to some experts, the United States is "the most overfed and under-nourished country in the world."

HEALTH CONSEQUENCES

Public interest in diet and health has existed since the early 1900s, when there was widespread concern about contamination of foods and alteration of food products. "Germs" were in their heyday. In books and newspapers, reformers brought attention to unsanitary conditions and methods of handling foods. The government responded by creating the Food and Drug Administration, which was responsible for great improvements in food inspection, sanitation, and uniform standards of identity.

In the late 1930s and early 1940s, interest in food was again peaked by the discovery of vitamins and essential elements. At this time, deficiency diseases such as rickets, scurvy, and beriberi, arising from inadequate diets, were a significant public health problem. This led to the establishment of "Recommended Dietary Allowances," the creation of the Food and Nutrition Board, and widespread programs of food fortification and enrichment.

Today the emphasis has changed. Says former surgeon general C. Everett Koop, "As the diseases of nutritional deficiency have diminished, they have been replaced by diseases of dietary excess and imbalance. After smoking, the choice of diet can influence long-term health prospects more than any other factor."

In the United States an unbalanced diet contributes to an imposing list of typical American diseases:

Heart Disease

If four fully loaded 747s were to crash tomorrow, by nightfall newspapers throughout the country would carry four-inch headlines shouting about the 1,500 people killed. CNN and every other television network would preempt regular programming to bring on-the-spot special reports. And for weeks afterward, radio talk-show hosts would interview anyone remotely connected to the tragedies. No two ways about it, when more than a thousand people die from a single cause in one day, it's big news. Or is it?

The fact is, about 1,500 Americans die every day, 365 days a year, from a single cause —heart disease. By far the number-one killer of Americans, this disease is rampant throughout the country.

- According to the American Heart Association, almost 100 million Americans have cardiovascular disease.

- Each year some 1.5 million Americans are struck by heart attacks, causing 600,000 to 800,000 deaths.

- Heart disease causes almost 45 percent of all deaths in the United States each year—more than cancer, AIDS, auto accidents, floods, and airplane disasters combined.

- Women make up 50 percent of heart-attack victims.

For many years, coronary heart disease and heart attacks were regarded as a natural part of the degenerative process, the inevitable consequences of aging and genetics. Now, after more than a half-century of sustained investigation, certain aspects of lifestyle have been identified as cardiac risk factors. Says Dr. William Roberts, editor-in-chief of the American Journal of Cardiology, "For every one person with heart disease because of family genes, there are 499 people who have it because of lifestyle decisions. None is more important than diet. The modern American diet is a significant factor in total cholesterol, LDL cholesterol, and triglycerides, blood lipids that are the building blocks of arterial blockages, and in other risk factors such as [being] overweight, high blood pressure, and diabetes."

In America, because of our eating habits, virtually no family escapes heart disease. Says Dr. Edward Schneider of the University of Southern California, "A hundred years from now, people will look back on the twentieth century and realize there was an epidemic of coronary heart disease in the Western world that was unique in history. The tragedy is that much of it was—and is—preventable."

IT'S A FACT

Enough people die every year of heart disease to equal ten Vietnam Wars!

> " It is estimated that the world's population is overweight by 300 million tons. Americans are 100 million tons overweight. So, with 6% of the world's population, we make up 33% of the world's overweight population."

IT'S A FACT

Stroke

A heart attack occurs when blood flow to the heart is cut off. A stroke occurs when blood flow to the brain is cut off. The underlying condition in both instances is arterial blockages. Because the similarities between heart attack and stroke are so great, many physicians now refer to stroke as a "brain attack."

Each year over 500,000 Americans suffer a stroke, and 144,000 of them die. Stroke has now become the third leading cause of death in the United States. Some of the most common results include speech impairment, paralysis, memory loss, and visual disorders.

As with heart attack, stroke is a product of both genetic makeup and lifestyle habits. An eating pattern that promotes high cholesterol, elevated blood pressure, and obesity can increase stroke risk.

Being Overweight or Obese

The American diet produces, on average, some 2,200 calories per person each day, and bears much of the responsibility (along with sedentary habits such as television watching) for the United States' ranking as the fattest nation in the world. About 65 percent of Americans are currently overweight or obese, a figure expected to increase in the future unless food habits change. Indeed, the typical man now weighs 20 to 30 pounds too much and the typical woman is overweight by 15 to 30 pounds. To make matters worse, the obesity rate in children ages six to eleven has doubled in the past twenty years. Obesity is overtaking smoking as the nation's leading cause of preventable death.

Costing an estimated 300,000 lives yearly in the United States, excess weight is linked to an increased risk for high blood pressure, stroke, and Type 2 diabetes. It is also one of the top three or four risk factors for heart disease. Studies suggest that people as little as 5 percent overweight are 30 percent more likely to develop heart disease than their leaner counterparts.

The link between being overweight or obese and having heart disease is particularly strong if the excess weight is carried around the middle. Abdominal fat (otherwise known as a "potbelly") is a characteristic of a serious cardiac risk called metabolic syndrome. This condition occurs when triglyceride level is too high and HDL level is too low. Says Dr. William Castelli, former director of the Framingham Heart Study, "People with wide hips and flat bellies may be overweight, but the extra weight does not seem to increase their cardiac risk as much as that of people with narrow hips and potbellies. Abdominal obesity is predictive of heart disease."

Diabetes

About 16 million Americans have diabetes, a condition that often results in stroke, high blood pressure, blindness, kidney disease, amputation, and heart attack. About 75 percent of diabetics die from heart attack or stroke.

Non-insulin-dependent diabetes, also called Type 2 diabetes, is an important risk factor for both coronary heart disease and high blood pressure. Diabetes increases heart-disease risk in men by 2 to 3 percent, but in women by three to seven times.

Type 2 diabetes accounts for 90 to 95 percent of all cases of diabetes. Unlike Type 1 diabetes, which has a strong genetic component, Type 2 diabetes can be triggered by poor lifestyle habits. Being overweight or obese are particular risks. Indeed, about 85 percent of all Type 2 diabetics are overweight. Burgeoning obesity is the main reason why more Americans are contracting Type 2 diabetes at an earlier age. Historically, children and teens made up just 2 percent of the 300,000 new Type 2 cases yearly; now they make up almost 40 percent. The typical American diet constitutes a risk for Type 2 diabetes.

High Blood Pressure

Blood pressure is the force needed to move blood through the vascular system. The condition in which blood pressure exceeds an upper limit for an extended period of time is called hypertension, or high blood pressure. Blood pressure is measured when the heart beats (systolic pressure) and rests between beats (diastolic pressure), and this is expressed as two numbers representing millimeters of mercury. A systolic pressure of 120 mm Hg and a diastolic pressure of 80 mm Hg are commonly expressed as 120/80, or "120 over 80."

Recently, new guidelines recommend that "normal" systolic pressure be less than 120 and diastolic pressure be less than 80. "Pre-hypertension" is defined as a range of 120– 139/80–89, while "hypertension" is considered to begin at 140/90.

Afflicting about 63 million Americans, high blood pressure greatly increases the risk of heart disease, stroke, diabetes, and kidney failure. People with high blood pressure are up to five times more likely to have a heart attack and more than twice as likely to have a stroke than people with normal blood pressure. The condition kills an estimated 45,000 people outright and contributes to the deaths of an additional 210,000. While genetic makeup may play a role in the development of this condition, a diet pattern rich in sodium and high in calories (which leads to becoming overweight) dramatically increased risk.

Cancer

Across America, there is an impression that the "war against cancer" is being won. It is not. Despite the billions of dollars spent on cancer research, the incidence of the disease is on the rise. Currently, there are about one million new cancer cases a year. By 2050, according to estimates by the National Cancer Institutes, there will be 1.9 million new cases of cancer per year.

Why such a continuous rise in this dreaded disease? The causes of cancer are many and complex. However, scientists believe that the majority of cases can be attributed to just two environmental factors—smoking and eating habits. According to Dr. Oliver Alabaster of George Washington University, "There is evidence that 60 percent of cancer in women and 40 percent of cancer in men is triggered by diet.

The American diet—rich in fat and calories, low in fiber—promotes cancer in a variety of ways:

- Excessive dietary fat can act as a cancer-causing agent (much like tobacco smoke) to initiate cells for cancer growth.

- Overweight and obesity, products of excessive calories, increase the risk of certain cancers.

- And a diet low in complex carbohydrates and fiber promotes certain cancers.

The cancer risks associated with eating the American diet are demonstrably large. The question to be asked, therefore, is not why we should change our diet, but why not?

IT'S A **FACT**

An estimated 90,000 Americans die each year of cancer caused by obesity and excess weight, according to a report in the New England Journal of Medicine.

GOOD NEWS

It is well accepted that what and how much you eat can have a direct impact on health, appearance, and longevity. In light of its connection to many dangerous and debilitating diseases and conditions, the American diet can certainly be considered a hazard to your health. In particular, many experts consider it to be the single greatest contributing factor to the enormous incidence of heart disease and heart attack in this country.

But it doesn't have to be that way.

Research suggests that at least 90 percent of premature heart attacks and strokes are preventable. Modify your diet, and you can reduce cholesterol and triglycerides, manage weight, and lower blood pressure to prevent, halt, and even reverse heart disease. A twelve-year study on 100,000 people conducted at Harvard University found that those who ate a healthy diet had 30 to 40 percent less heart disease than those who did not.

There is great consensus among nutritional experts on what is recommended for positive cardiac health:

■ Eat a variety of foods. Center your selection on fresh, local, and in season whole foods and reduce refined packaged foods, particularly those containing numerous additives.

■ Eat a diet moderate in total fat. When you do eat fat, choose healthy ones such as olive oil, canola oil, and seafood rich in Omega-3 fatty acids such as salmon.

■ Avoid unhealthy fats—such as saturated fat and trans fat—and dietary cholesterol. Saturated fats are found in meat, whole milk dairy products, and lard. Trans fats are found in products with hydrogenated oils, such as stick margarine and shortening.

■ Eat more foods rich in complex carbohydrates and fiber such as fruits, vegetables, whole grains, legumes, and nuts. Avoid refined carbohydrates such as white bread, muffins, doughnuts, and bagels.

■ Eat low-fat protein such as lean meat, poultry and fish, fat-free milk, eggs, beans and legumes, soy and fat-reduced yogurt.

■ Avoid food and drinks with added sugars. Read labels carefully and remember that four grams of sugar equals one teaspoon.

■ Avoid foods high in salt and sodium. Again, read food labels so you know what is in the food.

■ Stay hydrated with 5 to 8 glasses of water a day.

■ Drink and eat fat-free and low-fat dairy foods rich in calcium and vitamin D.

■ If you drink alcoholic beverages, do so in moderation.

■ Use portion control.

(And although not technically a dietary principle, I'd add regular physical activity to the list of recommendations.)

BEFORE YOU GET STARTED

Making healthy changes to your family's eating habits are simple. Not easy, but simple. However, before you get started, it makes sense to have a sense of perspective to help with the process of change.

Think long-term

For most people, the word "diet" has a singular connotation. It's a short-term weight reduction program, a means of shedding excess pounds rapidly by controlling calories. People who want to lose weight quickly (often magically) periodically go "on" then "off" a diet, much like Toynbee's cyclical theory of history, until either the "on" or more likely the "off" eventually wins.

There are many good reasons not to diet, but the most obvious one is that diets don't work. Research shows that while weight (much of it body fluids rather than body fat) may be lost in the short term, few dieters keep the lost weight off in the long term. One study of "high protein, low carbohydrate" diets suggests that 94 percent of participants not only regained their lost weight after one year, they put on a few extra pounds. Over the last fifty years, thousands of quick weight-loss diets have been promoted. (Remember the "grapefruit and cigarette diet?") If any one of them had been effective, we'd be a nation of skinny folks. But we

are not. And we are not because diets do not work.

In addition, there is little relationship between dieting and good health. You don't need a "diet" to manage cardiac and other health risks; you need a "diet pattern," a long-term manner of eating that will produce positive health results.

Anyone can change the way he eats for a week. The real goal is to change your eating habits for a lifetime.

Base your actions on sound nutritional science.

There are no magic foods or quick-fix solutions for eating healthy, reducing cholesterol, or losing weight. Base your dietary decisions on science from credible sources such as the American Heart Association, the American Dietetic Association, and the National Cancer Institute. Stick with the basics: more fruit, whole grains, vegetables, legumes, and cardioprotective foods such as fish, olive oil, and oat bran; moderate fat, saturated fat, trans fat, sodium, and added sugars; choose lean proteins, use healthy cooking methods; and moderate your intake of calories.

Be aware that bogus nutritional claims are all over the Internet. Lose Weight Fast! Cure Arthritis! Rotor-Root Your Arteries! A good tip-off to such claims is if they are selling a product.

Magazine racks and bookstores are not immune either, offering pop-science diets with regularity. According to Dr. David Katz of Yale University School of Medicine, avoid diets that ban certain foods, promote food-combining, promise a quick fix, offer enticing testimonials, or are based on the defiant claims of a renegade genius. If their dietary advice cures every health problem known to man, run—do not walk—away as fast as you can.

Be realistic

If your new diet pattern forbids favorite foods and indulgences, depends on spending long hours in the kitchen, and involves complicated record keeping, it will not work. Eating healthy is about moderation, and balance, not undue sacrifice. Simply put, your new way of eating must be in tune with your lifestyle. For example, we liked eating together as a family, taking the time to talk with our children. So our new diet pattern centered on family meals that satisfied our nutritional as well as our emotional needs.

Make good taste a priority

Almost everyone today knows that food choices are linked to their cholesterol number and pant size. Despite the knowledge that Americans are gobbling themselves into the grave (according to the surgeon general, diet is linked to five of the ten leading causes of death), our national diet continues to be unbalanced. It is a strange dichotomy. We know about diet and health, but we do not put that knowledge to work for us. People with high cholesterol still eat cheeseburgers and French fries; overweight folks still find the candy store. Why is this the case? A great part of the answer centers on taste.

Despite lethal doses of fat, salt, and calories, the undisputed fact is that French fries taste good. And therein lies the problem. In order to compete with such foods, healthy meals must be delicious and quick-to-fix. Unfortunately, many so-called "healthy" cookbooks too often provide recipes that result in bland, dull meals. These foods may be healthy, but they skimp on taste. In addition, many use ingredients that may be hard to find in a grocery store and cooking methods that take hours to prepare. It is no wonder when faced with the choice of bland, healthy food or delicious, unhealthy food, most people choose the latter, cholesterol be damned! While it is critical to put together a dietary pattern based on nutritional science, don't lose sight of the fact that eating is about real food for real people. If experience regarding food behavior has taught us anything, it is this: People will eat healthy food only when it tastes good.

With taste a high priority, we made two con-

The larger the serving size, the more you are likely to eat. In a study at Penn State University, men and women in their twenties were given as much macaroni and cheese as they wanted. When the portions served were large (35 ounces), the group on average ate 30 percent more calories than when portions were small (18 ounces). The group reported no change in feeling of fullness with one portion size over the other.

IT'S A FACT

scious decisions. First, we based our eating plan on the Mediteranean diet. It is, we believe, the best balance of taste and health. Next, we always used the best ingredients, such as extra virgin olive oil and Kosher salt. So not only are these recipes healthy, they are delicious as well.

Have a reasonable timeline

Research estimates that it takes about one to three months to change a lifestyle habit. So, give yourself enough time to institute important changes. Start slow and make changes to your eating habits over time. There is no need to do everything at once. If you're drinking whole milk, for instance, and want to move to fat-free milk, don't think it will happen overnight. Take five or six weeks to move gradually from whole to 2-percent milk, then to 1-percent and finally to fat-free. The gradual reduction of fat will allow your taste buds to adapt.

Use portion control

A healthy diet pattern isn't just about what you eat, but how much you eat as well. It's easy to overeat in a super-sized society. Restaurant foods and convenience foods do not come in realistic serving sizes. Make certain you are not getting too much of a good thing. A good example is pasta, a healthy food choice. But the average individual serving size in the United States would, according to the Food and Drug Administration, feed a family of three.

Portion control is more easily achieved with some sense of serving size. After all, it's easy to overeat if you don't know what a cup, an ounce, or a teaspoon looks like in practical terms. A good method is to use your own palm, fist, and thumb:

- **1 Palm = 3 Ounces.** The size of your palm is about the size of a 3-ounce serving of meat, fish, or poultry.

- **1 Fist = 1 Cup.** One cup of cereal, spaghetti, vegetables, or cut fruit is about the size of your closed fist.

- **1 Thumb = 1 Ounce of Cheese.** As a general rule, a chunk of cheese the size of your thumb is about one ounce.

- **1 Thumb = 1 Teaspoon.** One teaspoon of butter, peanut butter, mayonnaise, or sugar is about the size of the top joint of your thumb. Three such portions make up about one tablespoon.

- **1 or 2 Handfuls = 1 Ounce of Snack Food.** For nuts or small candies, one handful equals about one ounce. For chips or pretzels, two handfuls is about one ounce.

Another tip is to use smaller plates and glasses. It will create an environment that can curtail overeating naturally.

Learn to read food labels

If you live in the real world, there are times when you eat packaged foods. It is essential to know what is in the food, and that's where reading food labels can help. Skip the advertising hype and go directly to the section of the label called "Nutrition Facts." The information in "Nutrition Facts" is the key to knowing what is contained in the food. In particular, take note of the following:

- **Serving size and calories** How many servings in the container and how many calories per serving? If you eat a can of chili with 100 calories per serving, but there are four servings in the can, you've just consumed 400 calories.

- **Fat-grams** Be sure to keep fat content moderate. (Many experts counsel no more than 3 grams of fat per 100 calories of food.)

- **Saturated and trans fats** Keep these cholesterol-raising fats low. Watch out for heavily hydrogenated ingredients.

- **Fiber** The recommended level is 20 to 35 grams of fiber a day.

- **Cholesterol** The guideline is for no more than 300 milligrams daily.

- **Sugars** Sugars are expressed in grams. Remember, 4 grams equals a teaspoon.

- **Sodium** Sodium is expressed in milligrams. The recommendation is to consume less than 2,300 milligrams of sodium daily. No more than 1,500 milligrams daily if you are over age 50, African American of any age, or already have hypertension and/or heart disease.

LAST WORD

t is important to get organized before you start making healthy changes. It's too easy to go off in all directions, like a Ping-Pong ball in a boxcar. Remember, "activity" is not necessarily "productivity." Know your goals and have a clear focus before you begin. For us, it took about six months to prepare ourselves for taking action. It will not take you that long if you use the suggestions in this chapter.

INGREDIENTS FOR A HEART-HEALTHY DIET

A healthy, balanced diet is a key to lasting cardiac health. You don't have to be a doctor or a dietitian to understand the truth in this statement. But having that knowledge is one thing; putting it to work every day is quite another. That's where the recipes in this book will help. They will not only provide your family with healthy, tasty food. They will give you the building blocks for permanent dietary change.

Moderate dietary fat

Dietary fat is one of the three components of all foods, the others being protein and carbohydrate. Starting with the cholesterol-mania brought on in the mid-1980's, dietary fat has been considered the villain of the American diet. It does not deserve this reputation. Fat gives food taste, promotes satiety, and is necessary for the transportation of important vitamins. In truth, dietary fat *per se* is not harmful.

However, only a small amount— about one tablespoon of vegetable oil a day—is needed for good health. But thanks to a prevalence of high-calorie fatty foods on the American diet, the average person consumes eight times that amount, some 800 to 1,000 calories daily. Because of its caloric density—fat contains nine calories per gram, while the same amount of protein or carbohydrate has just four calories—a diet rich in fat can produce excessive calories and lead to added pounds or even obesity.

Cardiac experts recommend a moderate fat intake. That does not mean that you have to eat a "no-fat" or extremely "low-fat" diet. Indeed, in the face of healthy evidence about olive oil, canola oil, and fish oil, even the American Heart Association has increased its guideline. The diet pattern we follow, the Mediterranean diet, meets the "moderate" description and emphasizes healthy oils.

This style of cooking and eating is reflected in our recipes. They average about 25 to 35 percent of calories from fat, moderate enough to support good health, fat enough for delicious taste. (Each recipe includes a nutritional analysis, so you will know how much fat comes in a serving.) Used in the right amount and with the right type, fat can be a culinary ally. Note: Estimate your daily fat budget with the chart on page 27.

Choose heart-healthy oils

The amount of fat consumed is one consideration in the quest for healthy eating. The type of fat consumed is another. From a cardiac standpoint, not all fats are created equal.

The best choice for heart health are monounsaturated fats such as olive oil, canola oil, olives, peanuts, peanut butter, avocados, almonds, almond oil, and cashews. Studies by Dr. Scott Grundy of the University of Texas Southwestern Medical Center found that these fats reduce artery-clogging LDL and total cholesterol, reduce the risk of blood-clot formation, and minimize decreases in protective HDL cholesterol. As Dr. Grundy has observed, "While olive oil may explain the low incidence of heart problems among Mediterranean populations, canola oil may explain it for Asian populations. In both cases, the monounsaturated oils are used as replacements for saturated fats."

The next best choice is polyunsaturated fats including safflower oil, soybean oil, sunflower oil, corn oil, cottonseed oil, and sesame oil. These fats tend to lower total cholesterol and LDL cholesterol, and reduce the risk of blood-clot formation. However, they also lower levels of beneficial HDL cholesterol, which is why they are considered secondary to monounsaturated fats.

Mono- and polyunsaturated fats, the primary oils used in our recipes, stay liquid at room temperature.

Avoid unhealthy fats

Fats that penalize heart health include saturated fats and trans fats. These fats cause cholesterol, particularly LDL cholesterol, to increase dramatically. However, the opposite is also true. Reducing these fats can cause LDL cholesterol to fall. Animal foods are the primary source of saturated fat. Good examples are the visible fat on red meat, poultry skin, cheese, cream, bacon drippings, lard, and butter. A characteristic of saturated fat is that it stays solid at room temperature.

A second source of saturated fats is "tropical oils" —palm oil, palm kernal oil, and coconut oil. Tropical oils are found in nondairy creamers, potato chips, salad dressings, and crackers.

The American Heart Association has two recommendations for saturated fat:

■ For heart patients and those with cardiac risks, saturated fats should make up no more than 7 percent of total calories daily. So, for a person who consumes 2,000 calories daily, the limit for saturated fat is 15.5 grams.

■ For a person without heart disease or cardiac risks, saturated fat should make up no more than 10 percent of total calories daily. So, for a person who consumes 2,000 calories daily, the limit for saturated fat is 22 grams.

Trans fats also increase total and LDL cholesterol, and reduce HDL cholesterol. In the Harvard Nurses Health Study, women who ate lots of foods rich in trans fats had a 66 percent higher risk of heart disease than those who did not. Trans fats are created when polyunsaturated oils are hardened or stiffened into a solid or semisolid state in a process known as hydrogenation. A good example is hardening liquid corn oil into stick margarine. Trans fats are also found in solid shortenings, potato chips, crackers, commercially prepared baked goods such as cookies and muffins, and fried fast foods such as French fries and chicken nuggets.

The American Heart Association recommends no more than 2 grams of trans fat per day. Since most trans fat comes in prepared foods, it is important to read the food label to understand how much you are eating. The problem is that the nutrition information on the label may be misleading. That's because food manufacturers are allowed to "round down" on food labels to "0 grams" if a serving of the food has .49 grams or less. That spread you think is 0 grams might actually contain almost .5 grams. Eat it three times a day and you are perilously close to the daily maximum.

Increase complex carbohydrates

Healthy eating advice often focuses on foods we should limit or eliminate altogether. While such advice is valid (limiting foods rich in cholesterol-raising saturated fat, for example, certainly makes sense), this "exclusionary view" of eating for good health is often discouraging. It places too much emphasis on foods to be avoided. It makes more sense to concentrate on foods that should be eaten for heart health. The recipes in this book illustrate this "inclusionary view."

Experts counsel that foods rich in complex carbohydrates—fruits, vegetables, whole grains,

IT'S A FACT

Many physicians recommend a diet with 25 to 35 percent of calories from fat. Here is what it looks like in grams of fat, an easier measurement to manage:

TOTAL CALORIES PER DAY	GRAMS OF TOTAL FAT PER DAY		
	25%	30%	35%
1,000	27	33	39
1,100	30	36	43
1,200	33	40	46
1,300	36	43	50
1,400	39	47	54
1,500	42	50	58
1,600	44	53	62
1,700	47	57	66
1,800	50	60	70
1,900	53	63	73
2,000	56	67	77
2,100	58	70	81
2,200	61	73	85
2,300	64	77	89
2,400	67	80	93
2,500	69	83	97
2,600	72	87	101
2,700	75	90	105
2,800	77	93	109
2,900	80	96	112
3,000	83	100	116

beans, nuts, and legumes—are the building blocks of a heart-healthy diet. Numerous worldwide studies suggest that people who consume a diet rich in plant food have a low risk of coronary heart disease because of what they do consume (soluble fiber, antioxidants, unsaturated oils, fiber, and other nutrients) and because of what they do not consume (saturated fat from animal foods and trans fats from convenience foods). The Harvard Nurses Study, with some 95,000 participants, found that those who ate fruits and vegetables daily lowered their risk of heart attack by 25 percent. Experts advise eating two to three cups of fruit and vegetables daily.

Another study found that men who ate whole grain products—brown rice, oats, corn, and barley—were less likely to get diabetes than their counterparts who ate refined grain products. Whole grains also reduce inflamation and lower cholesterol.

The cardioprotective evidence is so overwhelming that experts advise complex carbohydrates should make up at least 55 percent of total calories. According to the National Research Council's Committee on Diet and Health, all Americans should consume "nine or more servings of vegetables and fruit, and at least three servings of whole-grains each day."

What constitutes "a serving"? It's not as much as most people would think, making this recommendation relatively easy to accomplish.

- A serving of fruits or vegetables is one medium piece of fruit, half a cup of cooked or canned fruits/vegetables, or one cup of leafy vegetables.

- A serving of grains is one slice of bread, or half a cup of cooked cereal, rice, or pasta, or one cup of cold cereal.

It is especially important to eat deeply colored fruits and vegetables, particularly green, red, and yellow ones. "Dark" foods contain more vitamins, phytochemicals, minerals, and antioxidants than lightly colored foods. In our house, we consume at least two cups of dark vegetables daily.

From a practical standpoint, there are three compelling reasons to make complex carbohydrates the centerpiece of your diet. First, they aid in weight control. These foods generally contain mass, bulk, and fiber, but are not calorically dense. For example, I doubt if anyone could eat

IT'S A FACT

According to the Food and Drug Administration, if the U.S. food industry removed 100 percent of trans fats from margarine and just 3 percent from baked goods, it would prevent more than 17,000 heart attacks and 5,000 deaths annually.

an entire pound of apples because their bulk would cause your stomach to distend and make you feel too full. But if you did, you'd have taken in just 242 calories. Compare that with eating a pound of chocolate-covered peanut candies (which, by the way, many people would find easy to do). You'd take in 2,240 calories, but an hour later you would be hungry all over again. In addition, certain of these foods—whole fruits, raw vegetables, beans, whole grains and cereals, and nuts—are rich in fiber. Since fiber passes through the digestive system intact, not all the calories consumed stay with the body, which aids in weight control. Experts recommend we should eat 20 to 35 grams of fiber a day. Complex carbohydrate foods help to realize that goal while filling you up, not out.

Next, some complex carbohydrates contain soluble fiber, which helps the body clear total and LDL cholesterol. Soluble fiber—found in oat bran, oatmeal, barley, apples, oranges, strawberries, prunes, carrots, corn, broccoli, navy beans, pinto beans, and lentils—is particularly effective in people with cholesterol levels over 200. Experts advise at least 3 grams of soluble fiber a day.

And finally, complex carbohydrate foods are rich in protective phytonutrients and antioxidant vitamins, particularly beta-carotene (good sources include carrots, sweet potato, cantaloupe, and spinach), and vitamin C (good sources include cantaloupe, grapefruit, oranges, strawberries, broccoli, red and green peppers, and raspberries.)

IT'S A FACT

"Dark" fruits and vegetables promote cardiac health. Look for:

Red: tomatoes, pink grapefruit, watermelon;

Red/Purple: red and blue grapes, blueberries, strawberries, beets, eggplant, red cabbage, red peppers, plums, red apples;

Orange: carrots, mangoes, cantaloupe, winter squash, sweet potato;

Green: broccoli, Brussels sprouts, cabbage, kale, bok choy;

Orange/Yellow: oranges, peaches, papaya, nectarines;

White/Green: onions, leeks, garlic, celery, asparagus, pears, green apples.

While much research still needs to be done, evidence to date suggest that antioxidant vitamins can protect coronary artery health. Research by Dr. JoAnn Manson of Harvard Medical School found that women who ate at least five servings a day of deeply colored fruits and vegetables lowered their risk of heart attack by 33 percent

> **I**f you see any of these ingredients listed on a food label, there is added sugar in the product: beet sugar, brown sugar, cane sugar, confectioner's sugar, crystallized cane juice, dextrose, fructose, evaporated cane juice, high fructose corn syrup, honey, invert sugar, malto dextrin, maple syrup, molasses, raw sugar, sucrose, turbinado, white sugar.

IT'S A FACT

and their risk of stroke by 71 percent.

Avoid added sugars

Like dietary fats, not all carbohydrates are created equal. While complex carbohydrates are recommended for heart health, it's not so for refined carbohydrates, especially those high in added sugars.

In an effort to eat less fat, Americans have increased the consumption of carbohydrates. Unfortunately, that increase has come mostly from refined carbohydrates, foods rich in added sugars such as muffins, cookies, white bread, white rice, pasta, potatoes, and soft drinks. High in calories, low in fiber, and lacking in mass (which produces satiety), refined carbohydrates are quickly digested and send blood sugar (glucose) into the bloodstream. This causes the pancreas to release insulin and absorb the sugar, and the resulting sudden drop in glucose can increase hunger.

Some doctors believe these fluctuations in blood sugar are a significant cause of obesity. Says Walter C. Willett, a professor at the Harvard School of Public Health, "There is growing evidence that these rapid swings up and down in blood sugar do stimulate the appetite and make it harder for some people to control and lose weight." Experts think that a diet high in highly refined carbohydrates may also reduce protective HDL cholesterol and raise levels of artery-clogging triglycerides. And because we like the taste of sugar, it can often displace more nutritious food choices.

Two sources of sugar and calories may not readily come to mind. The first is fat-free and low-fat baked goods. These items are generally loaded with sugar to boost flavor. "If you don't have a weight problem when you start eating low-fat and fat-free muffins, you may have one afterward," says Netty Levine, R.D., at Cedars-Sinai Medical Center in Los Angeles. "They may take out some fat, but they add more sugar, which jacks up calories. And watch out for the portions. The calorie figure on the label is for one serving, but a big muffin may be three or more servings.

That could make it a four hundred and fifty–calorie muffin!"

The second source is soft drinks. There is an incredible amount of sugar—and calories —that can be crammed into a can or bottle. Twelve ounces of cola, for example, contain ten teaspoons of sugar and 158 calories, making it more calorically dense than a bottle of beer. "Supersize" varieties can contain 40 or more teaspoons of sugar. Our advice is "don't drink your calories.

Eat more fish and seafood

The oil in fish and seafood are rich in omega-3 fatty acids, which are beneficial to heart health and protect against heart disease. Research suggests that omega-3 fatty acids reduce cholesterol and triglycerides, prevent clotting and promote the health of coronary artery walls. In its latest dietary guidelines the American Heart Association recommends that everyone eat at least two three-ounce servings of fatty fish each week, more if possible. Some of the best choices are salmon, trout, herring, tuna, sardines, and mackerel. One major study, published in the New England Journal of Medicine, concluded that eating "as little as 7.5 ounces of fish a week may cut the risk of dying from heart attack in half." That recommendation is easily met with our many recipes for fish and seafood. We use a variety of types of fish, including shellfish. Once banned for high cholesterol content, shellfish in

moderation is now acceptable.

Another source of omega-3 is the oil in flaxseed. Studies demonstrate that flaxseed consumption is linked with a reduction of LDL in people with elevated cholesterol. Many experts advise adding about two tablespoons of ground flaxseed to your daily diet. Sprinkle it on yogurt, cereal, or salads, mix it with juice, or add it to baked goods.

And finally, do not overlook nuts and seeds as good sources of omega-3 fatty acids. Almonds and walnuts are particularly nutritious. In one study, women who ate more than 5 ounces of nuts a week had a 35% reduction in heart attack risk compared with women who ate only 1 ounces a week or none at all.

Eat lean protein

Protein is an important part of a healthy diet. It is essential to renew and repair cells, build muscle, and meet 10 to 15% of your body's energy needs. It may also help to lower the blood sugar impact of a meal. And finally, because protein satisfies, it is a key to weight control.

Unfortunately, some sources of protein are high in fat and in the past that was enough to give protein a bad rap. No more. Today experts recognize the need for lean protein in our diet, foods that provide a rich source of protein but little, if any, harmful fat.

Good sources of lean protein include fish and seafood, eggs, oatmeal, beans, peas, legumes, nuts, seeds and fat-free and low-fat dairy foods. But what about red meat and poultry as sources of protein?

Red meat is a two-edged sword. As an important supplier of protein, iron, and B vitamins in the diet, it contributes to good health. However, red meat comes with a downside—saturated fat. Because it causes a rise in both total and LDL cholesterol, people who consume large amounts of saturated fat are at increased cardiac risk. But the opposite is also true. Studies found that people who reduced saturated fat experienced a lowering of total and LDL cholesterol.

A number of our recipes use red meat and poultry. We are able to do so because of three techniques.

First, we use leaner cuts. While spareribs, prime rib, and T-bone steak can have 20 to 30 grams of fat in a 3.5-ounce serving, many leaner cuts of red meat contain just 6 to 9 grams. When selecting beef, look for cuts labeled *loin* or *round*. Some good examples are top round, eye of round, round tip, top sirloin, top loin, and tenderloin. For pork, lamb, and veal, the leanest cuts are labeled *loin* or *leg*. Good choices include pork tenderloin, Canadian bacon, extra-lean canned ham, pork center loin, fresh ham, lamb loin chop, lamb leg, veal leg, and veal loin.

Read labels to determine the leanest available ground beef. Don't go by descriptions like "lean" or "extra lean." Instead, look for labels with a high lean-to-fat ratio. The leanest is "95% lean/5% fat."

For poultry, employ a simple rule: Choose a skinless white breast. Unlike red meat, poultry is not marbled with fat; instead, the fat is concentrated just beneath the skin. Most of the fat is removed if you take off the skin before cooking.

Next, we cut down on portion size. A 3- to 4-ounce serving of red meal is often less than 200 calories. But if the portion size is too large, even a lower-fat cut can end up supplying too many calories. In our recipes a serving of meat is about 3.5 ounces—the size of a woman's palm, or an audiocassette (not a videocassette), or a standard deck of cards. The serving for poultry should be

IT'S A FACT

Once condemned for high cholesterol content, eggs are now viewed as part of a healthy diet. That is because science suggests that the dietary cholesterol found in eggs has less to do with the level of cholesterol in your bloodstream than it does saturated fat and trans fat. While still counseling keeping dietary cholesterol to under 300 milligrams a day, the American Heart Association says that 3 to 4 eggs per week is not out of line.

three or four ounces.

And finally, we employed heart-healthy cooking methods. It makes little sense to fry meat or chicken, or cover turkey in fatty gravy. Instead, we roast, broil, grill, bake, and stew.

Use dairy products wisely

Milk and cheese are favorite foods of Americans. Rich in vitamins, minerals, protein, and calcium, these dairy products make an important contribution to balanced nutrition. However, they can also come with too much heavily saturated fat. The challenge is to choose milk and cheese that do not penalize cardiac health.

Milk is easy. The best choice is fat-free (also called nonfat and skim). Only 2 percent of its calories come from fat, yet is has all the calcium and protein benefits of whole milk. Fat-free buttermilk and 1% "light" milk are also good choices. Whole milk is the worst choice, with a staggering 8 grams of fat per 8 ounces. Also, be aware that so-called 2% milk is not a low-fat choice. The term "2%" refers to what fat weighs in the carton. It has little to do with real fat content. At almost 5 grams of fat per 8 ounces, it is practically full fat.

Cheese is a more complicated decision. Like whole milk, full-fat cheese is also a concentrated source of fat, saturated fat, and calories. Most regular cheese is about 60 to 80 percent fat, two-thirds of which is saturated. This means that a typical 1.5-ounce serving, about one-and-a-half slices of American cheese, contains as much fat as three-and-a-half pats of butter.

Our first inclination when faced with this quandary was to choose fat-free and low-fat cheeses. While full-fat cheddar, for instance is 10 grams of fat per ounce; you can buy a low-fat cheddar at 4 grams and a fat-free cheddar at 0 grams.

The problem is that we found many of the low-fat varieties to be virtually tasteless and that many of the fat-free types were made with so many additives and chemicals that we didn't want to eat them. So, being faithful to our mantra of "good taste and good health," we often skipped the fat-free and lower-fat varieties in favor of smaller amounts of the full-fat version. (We did the same with butter. If a pan needed greasing, we'd use a bit of real butter rather than margarine filled with additives.) You will see this in our recipes. Where we could use fat-free cream cheese, for example, we instead would use fat-reduced or maybe even full fat—but less of it.

Another technique is to "stretch" cheese by grating and sprinkling it over vegetables, soups, salads, and pasta. This will bring added flavor to the food but will hold down fat content.

Reduce salt and sodium

Americans consume about 15 pounds of sodium a year, or some 60 times more than is necessary for good health. About 35 percent comes in the form of salt (and salt derivatives such as celery salt and onion salt) used in cooking and as a table condiment. Unfortunately, for the 10 to 30 percent of the population estimated to be salt-sensitive, these levels can trigger high blood pressure.

An effective way to limit sodium is to avoid the saltshaker in favor of non- or low-sodium spices. Good choices include black pepper, garlic powder, tarragon, chili flakes, chili powder, lemon juice, and homemade or commercial dried herbs and seasoning combinations. To reduce salt in cooking, simply reduce the amount called for by one-fourth to one-half. Your family will not notice the difference.

We took two actions in our recipes to reduce sodium. First we opted for Kosher, or coarse, salt. With more exposed surfaces, Kosher salt goes futher in flavoring food with less sodium. Compared with regular salt, a teaspoon of Kosher salt has 400 milligrams less sodium.

Next, whenever a recipe called for canned

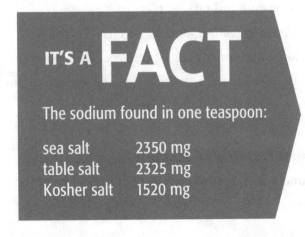

IT'S A FACT

The sodium found in one teaspoon:

sea salt	2350 mg
table salt	2325 mg
Kosher salt	1520 mg

beans, we made sure to rinse and drain them. This can reduce the sodium of the beans by 40%.

Also, remember that most salt and sodium on the American diet comes from processed foods, so opt for fresh foods whenever possible.

Include cardioprotective foods.

There is no such thing as a magic food for cardiac health. However, research suggests that some foods—such as olive oil and fish—benefit the heart more than other foods.

Soy foods such as soymilk, tofu, and soybeans are also heart-healthy. This may explain in part why heart disease is less prevalent in Asian populations that consume soy products regularly. Research indicates that substituting soy products for animal foods could lower LDL cholesterol by 8 percent.

Good sources of soy protein include soybeans, soy milk on cereal and in hot cocoa, tofu in salads and stir-fries, soy nuts, veggie burgers, soy flour, breakfast cereals fortified with soy, textured vegetable protein (TVP) used as a substitute for ground beef, and sports bars that contain soy. We have come to enjoy Japanese soybeans, called edamame, eaten as a snack food. A half-cup serving contains 16 grams of soy protein.

Beans and legumes provide protection because they are great sources of complex carbohydrates, fiber, folate, protein, phytochemicals, and other nutrients, yet contain little or no fat and no cholesterol. In particular, they contain soluble fiber that is effective in lowering blood cholesterol. A half-cup serving of kidney or lima beans has twice the soluble fiber as 3/4-cup of oat bran or oatmeal.

A new generation of margarine made from plant stanol esters can lower cholesterol in much the same way as oat bran. Two brands, Benecol and Taking Control, have been found to reduce LDL cholesterol by 7 to 14 percent. One caution, however. A pat of regular Benecol or Taking Control contains 80 calories. If you add cholesterol-lowering margarine to your diet, be sure it is in lieu of—not in addition to—other fats.

A number of studies have also found that people who eat nuts regularly cut their risk of heart attack by as much as half, compared with those who rarely or never eat nuts. One to three ounces a day of walnuts or almonds, in particular, can lower cholesterol. Many experts believe small amounts should be part of a daily diet. Nuts are rich in mono- and polyunsaturated fats, fiber, and protective phytochemicals. The downside is that they are high in calories, so don't go overboard.

Finally, research suggests that taken regularly in moderate amounts, alcohol can provide cardiac protection. Alcohol works to improve heart health by increasing HDL, decreasing LDL, reducing the blood's propensity to clot, and reducing arterial inflammation. Some types of alcohol, notably red wine, also contain powerful antioxidants. Health

IT'S A FACT

One ounce of nuts means:

22 whole almonds (170 calories)
18 medium cashews (165 calories)
20 hazelnuts (178 calories)
33 peanuts (165 calories)
14 walnut halves (185 calories)

experts define "moderate" as no more than two drinks per day for men and one per day for women. But nondrinkers should not take up drinking for health reasons.

Stay hydrated

A number of Americans simply do not drink enough water, having traded it for soft drinks, tea, coffee, and sports drinks. One result is that dehydration negatively impacts snacking habits. When dehydrated, your brain receives a message that your body needs more water. But this message may be interpreted as a hunger cue. So instead of drinking a glass of water, you make a sandwich, eat a peach, or down a bag of chips. Drinking the recommended five to eight glasses of water daily can help you stick with a healthy, balanced diet. Experts recommend drinking one glass of water upon waking and one glass before each meal.

Be physically active

Okay, I know this is not a "nutritional principle" in the strictest sense of the term. But it should be. The impact of regular exercise on health is so positive that Dr. Robert Butler, former director of the National Institute on Aging, says, "If exercise could be packaged into a pill, it would be the single most widely prescribed—and beneficial—medicine in the nation."

The cardiac benefits of regular exercise are widely accepted. It improves protective HDL cholesterol, strengthens the heart muscle, contributes to weight control, and reduces the risk of high blood pressure and diabetes. A study of almost 17,000 Harvard alumni found that the active men in the group had 35 percent fewer heart attacks and lived about two and a half years longer than their sedentary counterparts.

What is less known is that regular exercise can also exert a positive influence on dietary habits. There can be many reasons why a person abandons a healthy diet. One of the most important, however, is daily stress. Living in our modern society usually means that you are hurried, harried, and constantly out of time. In a word, you're under chronic stress, and as the axiom says, "When you are under stress, all roads lead to the refrigerator." People under pressure tend to overeat, binge, or live on a diet of fast food and snacks. Experts today recognize excessive stress as a serious factor in dietary noncompliance.

Regular physical activity, nature's own tranquillizer, can help you to better manage stress and, in doing so, more effectively control your eating habits. Scientists believe that exercise promotes the production of endorphins by the brain. Acting as natural painkillers, endorphins generate a happy, self-satisfied attitude and are associated with feelings of increased self-esteem and control. A calm, relaxed person is less likely to pig out on brownies or ice cream. Recent studies also suggest that endorphins may inhibit or neutralize stress hormones, such as cortisol, that may promote overeating.

So, when contemplating your new, healthy diet, don't restrict your thoughts to fruits, vegetables, and fish. Consider regular physical activity as an ingredient for success.

Nutritional Analysis

**A** nutritional analysis is provided for each recipe, usually on a per-serving basis and listing number of calories, grams of total fat, grams of saturated fat, milligrams of cholesterol, grams of carbohydrates, grams of dietary fiber, grams of protein, and milligrams of sodium.

In the interest of consistency and clarity, the analyses were based on the following factors:

- When a range is given for an ingredient, the mid-point amount is analyzed.

- When the ingredients listing gives one or more options, the first ingredient is the one analyzed.

- Figures are rounded off to whole numbers, so there might be slight discrepancies between an analysis for a whole meal and the sum of its parts.

- Fat-grams are rounded off to whole numbers. A total of less than 0.5 grams of fat is considered a trace amount.

- In many cases, salads and dressings have been analyzed separately. The amount of dressing, which is an individual choice, can greatly alter the calories and fat content of a salad.

- We have used the leanest ground beef that is 90% lean/10% fat, which according to USDA has no more than 11 grams of fat per 3.5 ounces, cooked.

- Recipes that call for "light" soy sauce use a soy sauce yielding 600 milligrams of sodium per tablespoon (about half that of regular soy sauce).

- Recipes using a "reduced-fat" cheese call for a cheese containing 5 grams of fat and 80 calories per ounce.

- Recipes that call for "fat-free" cheese use a cheese containing 0 grams of fat and 40 calories per ounce.

- In recipes using oil-based marinades, only a quarter to a half of the marinade was used in the nutritional analysis if the marinade is drained off before cooking.

- Portions are based realistically on average-size servings and have not been shaved to make the number appear more favorable.

■ For most recipes, the decision was made not to measure the amount cup by cup since this is not the way most families eat. The analysis per serving is to be understood as an approximation since serving size most likely varies among family members.

The menus and recipes in this book are designed to ensure that meals fall well within the American Heart Association's guidelines for fat, cholestero,l and sodium. Bear in mind that on occasion, in order to give a particular recipe the proper taste and texture, more fat is used. The great majority of recipes, however, are significantly below the fat content of conventional recipes. It is our intent to accommodate as healthy a diet as possible with foods that give pleasure as well, rather than simply adhere to strict numerical rules.

Whatever health guideline you use regarding fat, keep in mind it is all about how you eat for the day. It is not the fat count of every recipe or single food that is important. How the meal or the foods for the day go together is more to the point. Thus a low-fat meal might be capped off with a dessert that is relatively higher in fat. The more important perspective is how many grams of fat you're eating for the day, and whether or not that figure falls within your fat budget.

Every effort has been made to ensure the accuracy of nutritional data information; however, we cannot guarantee suitability for specific, medically imposed diets. People with special dietary needs should consult their physician and/ or a registered dietitian. Recipes have been analyzed for nutritional content using The Food Processor, Version 10.10 by ESHA. The nutrient information in the database is from the latest USDA data, manufacturer's data, and reference data comprising more than 1700 sources. Each analysis is based on the entry of nutritional data for all ingredients in each recipe. In the few cases where data are incomplete or unavailable, substitutions of similar ingredients have been made.

Comments from the Cook

'll never forget the day my husband, Joe, underwent bypass surgery. Nor will I ever forget the day, two weeks later, when he came home from the hospital and I realized that I had no idea how I was going to cook for him…and our family of four.

Since then I've co-authored 12 books and written over 2000 recipes and here's what I've discovered: Healthy eating isn't about rigid nutritional rules or depriving yourself of your favorite foods. Healthy eating is about expanding your food choices to achieve that balance of good health and great taste. It's about creating recipes that are not only good for you, but will keep your family running to the table at mealtime. Real food without the fuss. That's been my goal since the day Joe came home from the hospital over 35 years ago and that's why we put this book together.

My underlying theme was to balance the use of fiber-rich complex carbohydrates (such as whole grains, fruits, vegetables, beans, and legumes), lean protein (such as meat, poultry, nuts, and dairy products), and healthy fats (such as olive oil and fish) and minimize foods high in fat, saturated fat, trans fat, sodium, added sugars and calories. (See the end of this chapter for examples of foods in each category.) All of my recipes adhere to the USDA's ChooseMyPlate recommendations.

You don't have to rule out your favorite foods and favorite meals. You just have to find balance in the menu. Pair higher fat foods with lower fat foods. Pair a serving of meat with greater amounts of rainbow-colored vegetables, whole grains and fruits.

Planning Ahead

Joe always says, "Dinner shouldn't come as a surprise. We eat it every night." And yet between work and raising a family, dinner does sneak up on us. The key to healthy eating is planning ahead. For our family, Joe and I used Plan A and Plan B.

Plan A is to simply spend a few minutes each week making a meal plan. Take into account the menu, preparation time and the schedule of family members. Stick to the basics. We liked to use a weekly format as a guide: pasta on Monday, chicken on Tuesday, soup on Wednesday, main-meal salad on Thursday, and so on. If you plan to have French Market Soup on Wednesday, for instance, cook a ham for a weekend meal and use the leftover ham bone to make the stock. If the beans need to be soaked overnight, make sure it is on your "to do" list on Tuesday. Being organized and planning ahead saves time in the end. It can also be the difference between stopping for take-out and having a nutritional dinner at home.

Plan B (otherwise known as Fast Food at Home) is for when life gets in the way of Plan A. You are running late, you're too tired…fill in the blank.

Our fallback Plan B is to already have on hand the ingredients for 10 simple, easy and quick-to-fix, tasty meals that your family will love. Here are a few examples of our favorites:

Tortellini Chicken Soup
Pasta with Marinara Sauce
Three Bean Chili
Chicken Taco Salad
Combination Pizza

Here is how it works. Take Pasta Marinara, for example. Most of the ingredients (a good olive oil, a brand of quality canned tomatoes, a package of pasta) are easy to have on hand. Served with a green salad and a loaf of French bread, it offers a simple alternative and is much healthier than picking up fast food or cooking hot dogs.

Over the years of cooking for my family, I've found that the trick to making Plan B work is to replenish your Plan B supplies quickly, so that they will be there for the next time. If you make Pasta and Marinara sauce for dinner on Tuesday, replenish those ingredients on your next grocery store run.

Another trick is to carry at least two menus on your mobile phone (or if you're like me, in your purse or briefcase) so that you can still make good choices at the grocery store, even on those it's-5 P.M.-and-I-don't-know-yet-what's-for-dinner grocery store stops.

My final planning tip: be realistic about the needs of each family member. If your daughter has soccer practice and won't be home until late, and your son has band practice, serve a soup or make chili that can be prepared ahead and has holding power. This is a better choice than grilled steak, which tastes best just after it's been cooked. With flexible meal planning, you can meet each family's member's needs.

Change Your Favorite Recipe

The day Joe came home from the hospital I realized that I simply could not cook one meal for him and a second meal for the rest of the family. So I learned to make healthy meals that the entire family enjoyed. Planning means choosing your family's favorite meals and then becoming an expert at modifying them to be more heart healthy. Research shows that most American families prepare 12 recipes 80% of the time. So, if you identify your family's favorites and modify them to be healthier without sacrificing taste, you get the best of both worlds: familiar food that is healthy.

Kids like their favorites like pizza, fried chicken and spaghetti. Instead of throwing away your old recipes, analyze them for ways to reduce fat and increase fiber without sacrificing taste. To modify a recipe, first identify the sources of excessive fat and ask two key questions: "Why is this ingredient in the recipe?" and "How can I reduce the fat in this dish without sacrificing taste?"

Use Low-Fat Substitutes

Switching to low-fat versions of the foods in your own recipes is one of the easiest modification strategies. This involves simple "one-for-one" exchanges of lower-fat foods for those higher in fat. If, for instance, your favorite chili recipe calls for hamburger, substitute extra-lean ground round or shredded chicken breast. There will be very little change in taste from the original recipe, but the fat content will plummet. Choose the leanest cuts of meat, poultry and fish, and look for the lowest-fat dairy products that will satisfy your taste buds.

A second method involves more use of low-fat ingredients. For example, if your child's favorite lunch is a tuna sandwich, make it with "light" mayonnaise instead of the regular full-fat version. You'll get half the fat and more than enough "real" mayonnaise flavor to keep his or her taste buds happy. If a salami sandwich is a favorite, try Black Forest ham instead.

Check the labels for products that are low in fat. If one brand of fat-free sour cream doesn't meet your taste requirements, try others. Keep looking until you find one that works for you and your family. Constantly check the ingredient list. Sometimes fat-free and reduced-fat versions of a food contain so many unfamiliar and undesired food additives that a high-fat version, with fewer additives, is a better choice. There's a whole new world of products available in the grocery store these days to help in healthy low-fat cooking and eating.

Cooking Without Extra Fat

How you cook is as important as what you cook. Look for ways to cook without added fat. A well-made, heavy-gauge nonstick skillet is indispensable for stir-frying or sautéing in minimal fat. You can use one tablespoon of olive oil, for example rather than an inch of oil to "fry" potatoes. Or cook your pancakes in a nonstick pan rather than the traditional skillet with added fat. There will be no change in taste, but the fat content will be cut substantially. Grilling fish is more flavorful (and healthful) than frying in deep fat. If you're using ground beef, brown, drain, and pat dry with paper towels before adding it to your recipe. Learn to use fresh herbs and spices like fresh rosemary, thyme and Kosher salt to add flavor to food without added fat. Fresh herbs and the good taste from using quality ingredients (such as extra-virgin olive oil) will help you to rely less on large amounts of fat to carry the taste. Change your focus to make whole grains, beans, legumes, fruit, nuts and vegetables the center of your meals.

We all know that vegetables are one of the keys to a healthy diet. Unfortunately, the American diet is woefully short of them. We need to make an effort to include them at every meal, use them as snacks, and eat from a rainbow of colors—red, yellow, orange, and green. Vegetables are important for two health reasons. First, they are not calorically dense. You can eat a lot of them without taking in too many calories. In a society where 67% of adults are overweight or obese, this is an important tool in losing weight and keeping it off.

Next, vegetables are a powerhouse of vitamins, minerals, fiber, phytochemicals, folate, potassium, and other nutrients found to reduce the risk of heart disease, stroke, and diabetes. Look for ways to go beyond the traditional green salad, such as roasted Brussels sprouts, grilled heirloom tomatoes, and edamame as a snack food. Vegetables need to become our "go-to" food group.

A Last Word

Lasting change to your dietary habits only takes place over time. It is an evolutionary, not revolutionary, action. That is why we stress starting slowly to make changes and let them happen over time. We recognize that some people are ready to move from French fries to brown rice, while for others, white rice is the best that they can do right now. It's not a race. It's about small steps that over time result in big changes. My advice: eat like it matters—it does.

COMPLEX CARBOHYDRATES

Grapefruit
Apples
Prunes
Dried apricots
Pears
Plums
Strawberries
Oranges
Peaches
Papaya
Pineapple
Blueberries
Raspberries
Cantaloupe
Honeydew
Watermelon

Turnip Greens
Lettuce
Water Cress
Zucchini
Asparagus
Artichokes
Spinach
Okra
Cabbage
Yams
Celery
Carrots
Cucumbers
Potatoes
Radishes
Broccoli
Brussels Sprouts
Cauliflower
Eggplant

Buckwheat
Buckwheat bread
Oat bran bread
Oatmeal
Oat bran cereal
Museli
Wild rice
Brown rice
Multi-grain bread
Whole meal bread

Pinto beans
Lentils
Soybeans
Navy beans
Garbanzo beans
Kidney beans
Split peas
Whole Barley

SIMPLE CARBOHYDRATES

Table sugar
Corn syrup
Fruit juice
Candy
Cake
Cookies
Chips
Bread from white flour
Pasta from white flour

Soda pop
All baked goods made
    with white flour
Most packaged cereals
Honey
Jam
Chocolate
Biscuits

HEALTHY FATS

Olive oil
Canola oil
Sunflower oil
Peanut oil
Sesame oil
Soybean oil
Safflower oil
Nuts (*almonds, peanuts, macadamia nuts, hazelnuts, pecans, cashews*)

Peanut butter
Avocadoes
Olives
Fatty fish (*salmon, tuna, mackerel, herring, trout, sardines*)
Soymilk and Tofu

FATS TO AVOID

High-fat cuts of meat (*beef, lamb, pork*)
Chicken with the skin
Whole-fat dairy products (*milk and cream*)
Butter
Cheese
Ice cream
Palm and coconut oil
Lard
Commercially-baked pastries, cookies, doughnuts, muffins, cakes, pizza dough
Packaged snack foods (*crackers, microwave popcorn, chips*)
Stick margarine
Vegetable shortening
Fried foods (*French fries, fried chicken, chicken nuggets, breaded fish*)
Candy bars

LEAN PROTEIN

Eggs
Fat-free milk
Fat-free and low-fat cheese and yogurt
Fish and seafood (*halibut, rockfish, tuna, salmon, flounder, sole, cod, scrod, sardines, clams, sea bass, shrimp and scallops*)
Lean beef (*top round, top sirloin and flank steak*)
Lamb shoulder

Skinless chicken breast
Pork (*shoulder, loin, tenderloin and ham*)
Beans (*navy, white, red, black, lima, pinto, cannelloni and kidney*)
Lentils and peas
Soy foods (*tofu, veggie burgers, tempeh, texturized vegetable protein, soy milk*)
Nuts (*almonds, cashews, peanuts, walnuts*)

Table of Low-Fat Ingredient Substitutions

INSTEAD OF	USE
DAIRY PRODUCTS	
Sour cream	Low-fat or nonfat sour cream or yogurt
Yogurt	Low-fat or nonfat yogurt
Whipping cream	Pressurized light whipped cream—use sparingly
Milk, whole or 2%	Fat-free or 1% milk
1% buttermilk	1% buttermilk
Evaporated milk	Light (1%) evaporated milk
American, cheddar, Colby, Havarti, Edam, Swiss	Cheeses with 5 grams of fat or less per ounce
Mozzarella	Part-skim mozzarella; mozzarella with 5 grams of fat or less per ounce
Cottage cheese	Nonfat or 1% cottage cheese
Cream cheese	Nonfat or light processed cream cheese
Ricotta cheese	Nonfat, light or part-skim ricotta cheese
Ice cream	Low-fat, light or reduced-fat ice cream; nonfat or low-fat frozen yogurt or sherbet; sorbet; frozen fruit bars
Frozen yogurt	Reduced-fat or nonfat frozen yogurt
FATS AND OILS	
Butter and/or margarine	Reduced-calorie tub-style margarine made with water; whipped butter;
	Reduced-calorie tub-style margarine made with safflower, soybean, corn, canola or peanut oil; reduced-calorie stick margarine (made with safflower oil) in baked products
Mayonnaise	Nonfat or reduced-calorie mayonnaise
Oil	Olive oil; safflower, soybean, corn, canola or peanut oil in reduced amounts

INSTEAD OF	USE
MEATS AND POULTRY	
Bacon	Canadian bacon, lean ham
Beef, veal, lamb, pork	Skinless chicken or turkey breast; lean cuts of meat trimmed of all visible fat
Ground beef	Leanest ground beef
Luncheon meats	Sliced skinless turkey or chicken breast; lean cooked Black Forest ham; lean roast beef
Poultry	Skinless breast
Turkey, self-basting	Turkey basted with fat-free broth
Tuna packed in oil	Tuna packed in water
MISCELLANEOUS	
Fudge sauce	Fat-free fudge sauce or chocolate syrup
Nuts	One-third to one-half less, toasted
Soups, canned	Reduced-fat or fat-free condensed cream soups
Soy sauce	Reduced-sodium light soy sauce

Beverages

Iced Tea

4 servings

Boiling water

6 to 8 tea bags, or 6 to 8 teaspoons loose tea measured into a tea ball

4 cups boiling water

Fresh mint for garnish

Sugar (optional)

Fresh lemon slices (optional)

Fill a teapot with rapidly boiling water; let stand a few minutes, then empty teapot. Add tea bags or tea ball, then 4 cups boiling water. Cover; let steep 3 to 5 minutes, or until tea is desired strength. Remove tea bags. (For best results, judge the strength by the taste not by the color.) Stir. Let cool at room temperature for 2 hours. Serve over ice. Garnish with mint. Pass sugar and lemon slices, if desired.

Note: Tea that has been steeped too long or refrigerated will become cloudy. To make clear again, pour a small amount of boiling water into the tea.

For Sun Tea: Prepare as above using 6 to 8 tea bags and 1½ quarts cold water. Cover and let stand in full sun or at room temperature for 2 to 3 hours, or until tea reaches desired strength. Remove tea bags. Serve over ice.

Scientific studies have shown that both black teas and green teas increase the body's antioxidant activity by up to 45%. They are also said to have antibacterial powers against cavities and gum disease.

APPROXIMATE NUTRITIONAL INFORMATION PER SERVING

Calories: 5
Total fat: trace
Saturated fat: 0 g
Dietary fiber: 0 g
Carbohydrate: 2 g
Protein: 0 g
Cholesterol: 0 mg
Sodium: 5 mg

Fresh Lemonade

4 servings

1 cup fresh lemon juice

4 cups cold water

½ cup superfine sugar, or to taste

1 lemon, sliced into rings

1 thin orange slice, quartered

4 fresh strawberries

4 fresh mint sprigs

Combine lemon juice, water, and sugar in a large pitcher; stir to dissolve sugar. Add lemon slices to mixture. Chill. Pour into 4 ice-filled glasses. Put an orange quarter, a strawberry and a sprig of mint into each glass for garnish.

APPROXIMATE NUTRITIONAL INFORMATION PER SERVING

Calories: 120
Total fat: trace
Saturated fat: 0 g
Dietary fiber: 0 g
Carbohydrate: 32 g
Protein: 1 g
Cholesterol: 0 mg
Sodium: 8 mg

Hot Cider

4 1-cup servings

1 quart apple juice

2 cloves

1 cinnamon stick

Heat apple juice, cloves, and cinnamon over medium heat until juice is piping hot; do not boil. Serve at once.

APPROXIMATE NUTRITIONAL INFORMATION PER SERVING

Calories: 116
Total fat: trace
Saturated fat: 0 g
Dietary fiber: 0 g
Carbohydrate: 2 g
Protein: 0 g
Cholesterol: 0 mg
Sodium: 7 mg

Fruit Shake

2 servings

2 cups chilled strawberries, raspberries, or blackberries*

½ small ripe banana

¼ cup low-fat vanilla frozen yogurt

Frost tall glasses in the freezer for 30 to 60 minutes. Purée fruits in a food processor or blender until smooth. Add frozen yogurt and whirl to combine.

Note: Plums, oranges, peaches, melon, papaya, or pineapple may be used in place of berries.

*Nutritional anaylsis is for blackberries

APPROXIMATE NUTRITIONAL INFORMATION PER SERVING

Calories: 130
Total fat: 1 g
Saturated fat: 0 g
Dietary fiber: 8 g
Carbohydrate: 27 g
Protein: 5 g
Cholesterol: 10 mg
Sodium: 15 mg

Papaya Smoothie

4 servings

**1 ripe papaya,
peeled and seeded**

½ small ripe banana

**¼ cup low-fat vanilla frozen
yogurt**

In a blender or food processor, purée papaya and banana. Add frozen yogurt. Whirl to combine. Pour into stemmed glasses.

**APPROXIMATE
NUTRITIONAL
INFORMATION
PER SERVING**

Total calories: 160
Total Fat: 0
Saturated Fat: 0 g
Dietary Fiber: 2 g
Carbohydrates: 14 g
Protein: 2 g
Cholesterol: 5 mg
Sodium: 10 mg

Pineapple Smoothie

4 servings

**1 fresh pineapple, peeled
and cored**

**¼ cup low-fat vanilla frozen
yogurt**

whole orange slices, for garnish

fresh mint sprigs, for garnish

In a blender or food processor, purée pineapple. Add frozen yogurt. Whirl to combine. Pour into stemmed glasses. Cut a slit halfway through the orange slices and hook one over the edge of each glass. Garnish with fresh mint.

**APPROXIMATE
NUTRITIONAL
INFORMATION
PER SERVING**

Total calories: 140
Total Fat: 1 g
Saturated Fat: 0 g
Dietary Fiber: 3 g
Carbohydrates: 33 g
Protein: 2 g
Cholesterol: 5 mg
Sodium: 10 mg

Strawberry Frost

2 servings

2 cups strawberries

Juice of 2 oranges

Juice of 1/2 lemon

1/4 cup apple juice

5 to 8 ice cubes

Whole berries for garnish

Purée strawberries in a blender; add juices. Add ice cubes one at a time; crush. Pour into tall glasses. Garnish with whole berries.

Variation: For a creamier taste, fold in $1/2$ to 1 cup plain low-fat yogurt. For a sweeter taste, add $1/2$ papaya.

APPROXIMATE NUTRITIONAL INFORMATION PER SERVING

Calories: 80
Total fat: trace
Saturated fat: 0 g
Dietary fiber: 2 g
Carbohydrate: 19 g
Protein: 1 g
Cholesterol: 0 mg
Sodium: 3 mg

Awesome Strawberry Shakes

4 servings

1 10-ounce package sliced, fresh-frozen strawberries with sugar, thawed

1/4 cup nonfat milk

1 quart light, half the fat, slow-churned vanilla ice cream

You might be surprised at how much ice cream it takes to make a shake. However, when you taste this creamy milk shake, I think you'll find it very satisfying.

Put $1/2$ cup of the thawed berries in a blender; add milk and blend 30 seconds. Add ice cream and blend until nearly smooth. Stir and pour into glasses. (Reserve remaining $1/2$ cup berries to serve over ice cream at a later meal.)

APPROXIMATE NUTRITIONAL INFORMATION PER SERVING

Calories: 305
Total fat: 1 g
Saturated fat: 0 g,
Cholesterol" 0 mg
Carbohydrates: 68 g
Dietary fiber: 4 g
Protein: 7 g
Sodium: 168 mg.

Guiltless Chocolate Milkshake

1 cup

1 cup light, ½ the fat, slow-churned chocolate ice cream

⅓ cup nonfat milk

1½ tablespoons chocolate syrup

⅛ teaspoon vanilla extract

Combine ice cream, milk, chocolate syrup, and vanilla in a blender. Whirl 2 to 3 minutes.

Note: Some brands of light or nonfat ice cream are better than others. Keep tasting them until you find one you like.

Serving Suggestion: A favorite quick-to-fix guiltless dinner is Grilled Chicken Burgers (page 303), Jumbo Oven Fries (page 379), with a Guiltless Chocolate Milkshake.

APPROXIMATE NUTRITIONAL INFORMATION PER 1-CUP SERVING

USING LIGHT ICE CREAM	**USING NONFAT ICE CREAM**
Calories: 297	Calories: 297
Total fat: 8 g	Total fat: trace
Saturated fat: 5 g	Saturated fat: 0 g
Dietary fiber: 0 g	Dietary fiber: 0 g
Carbohydrate: 49 g	Carbohydrate: 67 g
Protein: 9 g	Protein: 9 g
Cholesterol: 51 mg	Cholesterol: 1 mg
Sodium: 155 mg	Sodium: 245 mg

Best-Ever Chocolate Shakes

4 servings

¼ cup nonfat milk

¼ cup Hershey's Chocolate Syrup

1 quart light, ½ the fat, slow-churned vanilla ice cream, softened

¾ teaspoon pure vanilla extract

Fat-free ice cream in combination with chocolate syrup makes a smooth and creamy shake. The integrity of the shake is not compromised by substituting leaner ingredients.

Combine milk, chocolate syrup, and ice cream in a blender and blend until nearly smooth. Add vanilla and blend until smooth, about 30 seconds longer. Stir and pour into glasses.

APPROXIMATE NUTRITIONAL INFORMATION PER SERVING

Calories: 253
Total fat: 0 g
Saturated fat: 0 g
Cholesterol: 0 mg
Carbohydrates: 57 g
Dietary fiber: 0 g
Protein: 7 g
Sodium: 197 mg

Breads, Pancakes & Waffles

Italian Bread

Two 18-inch loaves

2 cups warm water (100°–105°F.)

½ teaspoon granulated sugar

2 packages active dry yeast

5 cups unbleached bread flour

1 teaspoon Kosher salt

Dab of olive oil

Cornmeal

1 egg white, slightly beaten

1 tablespoon cold water

In a small bowl, combine water and sugar; sprinkle yeast over top. Let stand 10 minutes. In a large mixing bowl, combine 2 cups of the flour, salt and dissolved yeast. Mix with a wooden spoon about 30 seconds to combine ingredients. Gradually add 2 more cups of the flour.

Knead by hand or by machine, gradually adding remaining 1 cup flour, until dough is smooth and elastic. Put dough in a bowl greased with olive oil, turning once to coat top. Cover and let rise in a warm place until double in size, about 1½ hours.

Punch dough down. Turn out onto lightly floured surface and divide in half. Cover and let rest 10 minutes. Roll each half into 15–10-inch rectangles. Roll up from long sides and seal well. Taper ends. Using a very sharp knife, make 3 or 4 diagonal cuts about ¼ inch deep across loaves. Place seam side down on nonstick bread pans greased with olive oil and lightly sprinkle cornmeal over top. Cover and let rise until nearly double, about 1 hour. To check if the dough has risen sufficiently, poke your finger in about 2 inches. If hole remains and does not close up when you remove your finger, the dough has risen enough.

Bake in a 375°F. oven 20 minutes. Push loaves out of pans and onto oven racks. Bake 10 minutes longer. Combine egg white and cold water, and brush loaves. Bake on oven racks 10–15 minutes longer or until loaves sound hollow when tapped. Cool on wire racks.

APPROXIMATE NUTRITIONAL INFORMATION PER ½-INCH SLICE

Total calories: 33
Total fat: trace
Saturated fat: trace
Dietary fiber: trace
Carbohydrates: 6 g
Protein: 1 g
Cholesterol: 0 mg
Sodium: 31 mg

Country Italian Bread

Two 18-inch loaves (20 slices per loaf)

2 cups warm water (100°–105°F.)

¼ teaspoon granulated sugar

1½ teaspoons active dry yeast

5 cups unbleached bread flour

1 tablespoon Kosher salt

2 tablespoons olive oil

In a bowl, combine water and sugar; sprinkle yeast over top. Let stand 10 minutes. In a mixing bowl, combine flour, salt, and olive oil. Add dissolved yeast and mix with a wooden spoon to form a soft dough.

Knead by hand or by machine until smooth and elastic. Put dough in a bowl greased with olive oil, turning once to coat top. Cover and let rise in a warm place until double in size, about 1½ hours.

Punch dough down. Cover and return to warm place. Let rise until double in size, about 1 hour. Punch down again. Divide dough in half. Roll each half into a loaf shape. Place in non-stick bread pans. Return to warm place and let rise until nearly double in size, about 1 hour.

Bake in a 450°F. oven 15–20 minutes. (Bake on a pizza stone if available.) Remove loaves from pans. Reduce heat to 375°F. and continue baking about 30 minutes or until loaves sound hollow when tapped.

APPROXIMATE NUTRITIONAL INFORMATION PER SLICE

Total calories: 63
Total fat: 1 g
Saturated fat: trace
Dietary fiber: trace
Carbohydrates: 12 g
Protein: 1 g
Cholesterol: 0 mg
Sodium: 150 mg

Grilled Garlic Bread

1 loaf (15 slices per loaf)

1 12-inch loaf skinny French baguette

8 teaspoons olive oil

5 cloves garlic, finely minced

chopped fresh Italian parsley

Warm oil in a small saucepan. Turn off heat. Add garlic. Allow garlic to sit at least 15 minutes—the longer the better.

Just before serving, slice the baguette in half lengthwise. Lightly brush the cut side with the garlic oil. Sprinkle with parsley.

Put the bread on a foil-lined pan. Place in a preheated broiler 2-3 inches from the heat until the bread is lightly browned.

APPROXIMATE NUTRITIONAL INFORMATION PER SLICE

Total calories: 108
Total fat: 3 g
Saturated fat: 0 g
Dietary fiber: 1 g
Carbohydrates: 17 g
Protein: 3 g
Cholesterol: 0 mg
Sodium: 223 mg

Roasted Garlic Bread

1 loaf (12 slices per loaf)

1 head garlic, cloves separated but not peeled

1 tablespoon olive oil

½ teaspoon Kosher salt

1 12-inch fresh, thin French baguette

Arrange garlic in a 9 x 13 x 2-inch non-stick baking dish. Add olive oil, salt and pepper. Bake at 350°F. 30–40 minutes or until garlic is soft. Release garlic from peels right into the baking dish by pressing with a fork. Stir garlic into the oil and sprinkle with salt.

Slice the baguette in half lengthwise. Rub each half with the garlic oil, then cut into slices. Delicious!

Variation: Place the garlic-oil mixture in the center of the table and let each person dip bread into the warm oil.

Note: It doesn't seem possible that only one tablespoon of oil could be enough, but it is!

APPROXIMATE NUTRITIONAL INFORMATION PER SLICE

Total calories: 111
Total fat: 2 g
Saturated fat: trace
Dietary fiber: 1 g
Carbohydrates: 18 g
Protein: 3 g
Cholesterol: 0 mg
Sodium: 216 mg

Soft Pretzels

1 dozen

1 package active dry yeast

1½ cups lukewarm water (not to exceed 105°F)

1 teaspoon Kosher salt

1 tablespoon sugar

4 cups all-purpose flour

1 egg, beaten

Dissolve yeast in water; add salt, sugar, and flour. Knead 5 to 10 minutes, adding more flour as necessary to reduce stickiness. Divide dough into 12 pieces. Twist dough into the shape of pretzels, cars, trucks, airplanes, flowers, trees, gingerbread boys, numerals, or circles. Place on a nonstick baking sheet. Brush with beaten egg. Bake at 425°F for 15 minutes, or until lightly browned.

APPROXIMATE NUTRITIONAL INFORMATION PER PRETZEL

Calories: 159
Total fat: trace
Saturated fat: 0 g
Dietary fiber: 2 g
Carbohydrate: 33 g
Protein: 5 g
Cholesterol: 0 mg
Sodium: 150 mg

Italian Breadsticks

20 breadsticks

¼ **teaspoon granulated sugar**

1½ **cups warm water (100°–105°F.)**

1½ **teaspoons active dry yeast**

3¾ **cups unbleached flour**

2 **teaspoons Kosher salt**

2 **tablespoons olive oil**

Dab of olive oil

In a small bowl, combine sugar and water; sprinkle yeast over top. Let stand 10 minutes.

In a mixing bowl, combine flour, salt, and olive oil. Add dissolved yeast and mix with a wooden spoon to form a soft dough.

Knead by hand or by machine until dough is smooth and elastic. Put dough in a bowl rubbed with olive oil, turning once to coat top. Cover and let rise in a warm place until double in size, about 1½ hours. Punch dough down and divide into 4 parts. Roll each part into a 5 x 8-inch rectangle. Cut each rectangle crosswise into 5 pieces.

Roll each piece between palms to a ¾ x 4-inch rope. (Be sure to keep standing dough covered while working.) Arrange on nonstick baking pans, cover and let rest 10 minutes.

Bake in a 400°F. oven 20–25 minutes or until lightly browned. Remove to napkin-lined basket and serve at once.

Shortcut Suggestion: In place of homemade dough, use a heart-healthy frozen bread dough. Read the label to be sure it is made with olive oil or an unsaturated, nonhydrogenated oil such as safflower, soybean or corn oil. Do not use a brand made with hydrogenated shortening, lard, palm oil or coconut oil.

Serving Suggestion: Good with soups and stews and for after-school snacks.

APPROXIMATE NUTRITIONAL INFORMATION PER BREADSTICK

Total calories: 98
Total fat: 2 g
Saturated fat: trace
Dietary fiber: trace
Carbohydrates: 18 g
Protein: 2 g
Cholesterol: 0 mg
Sodium: 175 mg

Cheese Bread

2 loaves (15 slices per loaf)

2 packages active dry yeast

2 cups warm water (100°–105°F.)

2 tablespoons sugar

1 tablespoon Kosher salt

¼ cup canola oil

6 cups all-purpose flour

1 cup whole-wheat flour

¾ cup grated, reduced-fat Cheddar cheese

Dissolve yeast in water, add sugar, salt, oil, and 3 cups of the flour. Mix. Add remaining flour; knead into a soft dough, about 5 minutes. Divide bread into two loaves; knead one half of the cheese into each loaf. Shape into round loaves; flatten slightly. Bake on a nonstick baking sheet or in individual loaf pans at 375°F. for 30 to 35 minutes. (You may have to coat baking sheet with olive oil spray as cheese can cause sticking even on nonstick baking sheets.

Note: Since this bread is higher in fat than most we recommend, serve it with a low-fat soup such as Manhattan Clam Chowder (page 133).

APPROXIMATE NUTRITIONAL INFORMATION PER SLICE

Total calories: 146
Total fat: 4 g
Saturated fat: 2 g
Dietary fiber: 1 g
Carbohydrates: 20 g
Protein: 7 g
Cholesterol: 9 mg
Sodium: 290 mg

Bread Stuffing

26 ½-cup servings (enough to accompany a 10- to 14-pound turkey)

1 large onion, chopped

3 celery stalks, chopped

2 tablespoon olive oil

½ pound fresh mushrooms, sliced

10 cups dried bread cubes

2½ cups chicken broth, preferably homemade (page 143)

1¼ teaspoons sage

½ teaspoon or less Kosher salt

¼ teaspoon pepper

Sauté onion and celery in olive oil until tender. Add mushrooms; cook 2 to 3 minutes. Remove from heat. Add bread cubes. Gradually moisten with broth, adding a little more or less as necessary. Season and toss. Bake covered at 350°F for 30 to 40 minutes, or until piping hot.

APPROXIMATE NUTRITIONAL INFORMATION PER ½-CUP SERVING

Calories: 94
Total fat: 2 g
Saturated fat: 0 g
Dietary fiber: 1 g
Carbohydrate: 16 g
Protein: 3 g
Cholesterol: 0 mg
Sodium: 230 mg

Cheese and Herb Flatbread

14 slices

¾ **teaspoon active dry yeast**

1 cup warm water (100°–105°F.)

2½ cups unbleached flour

½ **teaspoon Kosher salt**

Dab of olive oil

2 teaspoons olive oil

3 tablespoons freshly grated Parmesan cheese

1 teaspoon fresh basil, chopped

Dissolve yeast in the cup of warm water. In a bowl, combine flour and salt; add dissolved yeast; Knead by hand or by machine until smooth. (If dough is sticky, gradually add up to ½ cup additional flour.) Place in a bowl greased with olive oil. Turn dough once to coat top. Cover and let rise in a warm place 1½ hours or until double in size.

Punch dough down. Put back in bowl and let rise again until double in size, about 1 hour. Punch down again. Roll dough out to ½-inch thickness. Transfer to nonstick pizza pan. Drizzle olive oil over dough's surface and spread oil with hands to coat evenly. Sprinkle with Parmesan and basil.

Bake in a 400°F. oven 20–25 minutes or until crust is cooked. (Bake on a pizza stone if available.) Slice into wedges.

Shortcut Suggestion: In place of homemade dough, use a heart-healthy, uncooked crust purchased from a local pizza parlor. Be sure it's made with olive oil or an unsaturated, nonhydrogenated oil such as safflower, soybean, or corn oil. Do not use a crust made with hydrogenated shortening, lard, palm oil, or coconut oil. Consider purchasing several crusts at one time to keep in the freezer.

Serving Suggestion: Especially good with soups.

APPROXIMATE NUTRITIONAL INFORMATION PER SLICE

Total calories: 94
Total fat: 1 g
Saturated fat: trace
Dietary fiber: trace
Carbohydrates: 17 g
Protein: 3 g
Cholesterol: 1 mg
Sodium: 91 mg

Cajun Flatbread

14 slices

¾ teaspoon active dry yeast

1 cup warm water (100°–105°F.)

2½ cups unbleached flour

½ teaspoon Kosher salt

Dab of olive oil

2 teaspoons olive oil

Black pepper

Kosher salt

Cayenne pepper

Paprika

Dissolve yeast in the cup of warm water. In a bowl, combine flour and salt; add dissolved yeast. Knead by hand or by machine until smooth. Place dough in a bowl greased with olive oil, turning once to coat top. Cover and let rise in a warm place 1½ hours or until double in size.

Punch dough down. Put back in bowl and let rise again until double in size, about 1 hour. Punch down again. Roll dough out to ½-inch thickness. Transfer to nonstick pizza pan. Drizzle olive oil over pizza. Sprinkle lightly with seasonings (about ⅛ teaspoon of each). Spread oil and seasonings with hands to coat evenly.

Bake in a 400°F. oven 20–25 minutes or until crust is cooked. (Bake on a pizza stone if available.) Slice into wedges.

Shortcut Suggestion: In place of homemade dough, use a heart-healthy, uncooked crust purchased from a local pizza parlor. Be sure it's made with olive oil or an unsaturated, nonhydrogenated oil such as safflower, soybean, or corn oil. Do not use a crust made with hydrogenated shortening, lard, palm oil, or coconut oil. Consider purchasing several crusts at one time to keep in the freezer.

Serving Suggestion: Especially good with soups and Creole dishes.

APPROXIMATE NUTRITIONAL INFORMATION PER SLICE

Total calories: 88
Total fat: 1 g
Saturated fat: trace
Dietary fiber: trace
Carbohydrates: 17 g
Protein: 2 g
Cholesterol: 0 mg
Sodium: 73 mg

Pan Rolls

20 rolls

1½ teaspoons active dry yeast

2 cups warm water (100°–105°F.)

5 cups unbleached bread flour

1 teaspoon Kosher salt

Dab of olive oil

Sprinkle yeast over the warm water. Let stand 5 minutes.

In a bowl, combine flour with salt; add dissolved yeast. Mix with a wooden spoon to form a soft dough.

Knead dough by hand or by machine until smooth and elastic. Place in a bowl greased with olive oil, turning once to coat top. Cover and let rise in a warm place 1½ hours or until double in size.

Punch dough down. Form into a ball. Divide dough in half; then each half into 10 equal pieces. Shape 10 pieces into balls and place close together in a nonstick 9-inch round pan. Repeat with second 10 pieces. Cover and return to a warm place. Let rise until double in size, about 1 hour.

Bake at 400°F. for20 minutes. Reduce heat to 350°F. and bake 10–15 minutes longer.

Shortcut Suggestion: In place of homemade dough, use a heart-healthy frozen bread dough. Read the label to be sure it is made with olive oil or an unsaturated, nonhydrogenated oil such as safflower, soybean or corn oil. Do not use a brand made with hydrogenated shortening, lard, palm oil or coconut oil.

APPROXIMATE NUTRITIONAL INFORMATION PER ROLL

Total calories: 105
Total fat: trace
Saturated fat: trace
Dietary fiber: 1 g
Carbohydrates: 22 g
Protein: 3 g
Cholesterol: 0 mg
Sodium: 98 mg

Warm Tortillas

4 servings

4 7-inch flour or corn tortillas

Both flour and corn tortillas are available. Always buy flour tortillas that are made with soybean oil, not with lard. Corn tortillas, generally made without oil or shortening, are more healthful and lower in fat and calories.

Oven Method: Wrap tortillas in aluminum foil and heat in a 325°F. oven until warm, about 15 minutes.

Microwave Method: Place tortillas between 2 slightly dampened paper towels. Microwave on high for 1 to 2 minutes, or until warm. Keep wrapped until ready to serve.

Easiest Method: Invest in an inexpensive terra-cotta tortilla warmer available at your local kitchen store or by mail order.

APPROXIMATE NUTRITIONAL INFORMATION PER TORTILLA

Calories: 114
Total fat: 2.5 g
Saturated fat: 0 g
Cholesterol: 0 mg
Carbohydrates: 20 g
Dietary fiber: 1 g
Protein: 3 g
Sodium: 167 mg

Easy Pizza Crust

1 pizza crust (10 slices per crust)

1 heaping teaspoon active dry yeast

2 tablespoons warm water (110°–115°F.)

½ teaspoon salt

1 tablespoon olive oil, plus 1 teaspoon

1½ teaspoons honey

6 tablespoons cool water

1½ cups all-purpose flour

Dab of olive oil

Dissolve yeast in the warm water. Let stand 10 minutes.

In a small bowl, combine salt, 1 tablespoon olive oil, honey, and cool water; add dissolved yeast. In a mixing bowl or food processor, combine the honey-yeast mixture and flour. Knead by hand or by machine until dough is smooth and elastic. If dough is too sticky, add up to ½ cup additional flour.

Place dough in a bowl that has been greased with olive oil, turning once to coat top. Cover and let rest for 30 minutes.

Using a rolling pin, flatten dough into a circle about 12 inches in diameter. Slide onto a nonstick pizza pan. Brush dough with 1 teaspoon olive oil.

Bake in a 500°F. oven that has been preheated for 30 minutes with a pizza stone inside. (Pizza stone is optional.) Bake 8 minutes or until golden brown.

APPROXIMATE NUTRITIONAL INFORMATION PER SLICE

Total calories: 88
Total fat: 2 g
Saturated fat: trace
Dietary fiber: 1 g
Carbohydrates: 14 g
Protein: 2 g
Cholesterol: 0 mg
Sodium: 112 mg

Pizza

2 crusts; 1 9-inch pizza (8 slices)

CRUST:

1 package active dry yeast

¾ cup warm water

4 cups all-purpose flour

½ teaspoon sugar

½ teaspoon salt

2 tablespoons olive oil

1 egg, beaten

Dab of olive oil

SAUCE PER CRUST:

1 14½-ounce can plum tomatoes

1 tablespoon tomato paste

1 tablespoon olive oil

½ teaspoon minced fresh oregano or ¼ teaspoon dried

2 fresh basil sprigs or ¼ teaspoon dried

¼ teaspoon pepper

½ pound grated part skim mozzarella cheese

TOPPING SUGGESTIONS:

1 cup fresh ripe tomatoes

½ cup sautéed onions

1 cup fresh mushrooms, sliced

½ cup sliced green onions

½ cup jalapeno chili peppers, sliced

2 ounces sliced prosciutto

½ pound sauteed extra-lean ground round

½ pound sauteed extra lean Italian sausage

½ cup Kalamata olives

Dissolve yeast in warm water. Mix flour with sugar and salt; add to yeast along with oil and egg, and stir until mixed. Knead on a heavily floured board until smooth and elastic. (Add additional water if needed for moisture.) Put dough in a bowl greased with olive oil; cover, and let rise in a warm place for 1 hour. Punch down. Knead slightly. Let rise 1 hour more. Punch down. Knead slightly. Let rise 1 hour more. Divide dough in half. (Dough may be frozen.) Roll into two 9-inch crusts.

Drain tomatoes; dice. Reserve ½ cup of the juice and mix with diced tomatoes, tomato paste, and olive oil. Spread over crust; sprinkle with oregano, basil, and pepper. Add choice of toppings. Sprinkle with cheese. Bake at 450°F. for 20 minutes, or until crust is done and cheese is melted.

APPROXIMATE NUTRITIONAL INFORMATION PER SLICE (WITH CHEESE AND VEGETABLE TOPPINGS)

Calories: 202
Total fat: 6 g
Saturated fat: 2 g
Dietary fiber: 2 g
Carbohydrate: 28 g
Protein: 8 g
Cholesterol: 21 mg
Sodium: 171 mg

Breakfast Pizza

1 pizza (10 slices per pizza) servings

1 Easy Pizza Crust (page 62)

1 teaspoon olive oil

⅔ cup finely chopped white onion

⅛ teaspoon cumin

½ teaspoon fresh thyme

⅔ cup shredded part-skim mozzarella cheese

3 eggs

½ cup commercial tomato salsa

SALSA CRUDA:

4 large ripe tomatoes, diced

2 cups finely chopped white onion

2 jalapeño peppers, chopped

½ cup fresh lime juice

3 tablespoons extra-virgin olive oil

½ teaspoon black pepper

1 teaspoon Kosher salt

Prepare pizza crust and bake 8 minutes according to instructions.

Meanwhile, in a medium bowl, prepare Salsa Cruda by combining tomatoes, onion, jalapeño peppers, lime juice, olive oil, black pepper, and salt; set aside.

In a nonstick skillet, heat the olive oil. Add onion and sauté 4–5 minutes or until onion is tender. Sprinkle with cumin and thyme.

When crust is lightly browned, sprinkle with half the mozzarella cheese, then some of the diced tomatoes and onions from the Salsa Cruda. Break one egg over each third of the pizza. Prick yolk with a fork to break. Sprinkle remaining cheese over top. Bake in 350°F. oven about 20 minutes or until eggs are cooked. (Use a pizza stone if available.) Top each slice of pizza with Salsa Cruda, then with the commercial tomato salsa.

Note: Serve this pizza with fresh fruits or other low-fat accompaniments to reduce percentage of calories from fat in the total meal.

Shortcut Suggestion: In place of homemade dough, purchase a heart-healthy, uncooked crust from a local pizza parlor. Be sure it's made with olive oil or an unsaturated, nonhydrogenated oil such as safflower, soybean, or corn oil. Do not use a crust made with hydrogenated shortening, lard, palm oil, or coconut oil.

APPROXIMATE NUTRITIONAL INFORMATION PER SLICE

Calories: 217
Total fat: 11 g
Saturated fat: 2 g
Dietary fiber: 2 g
Carbohydrates: 22 g
Protein: 9 g
Cholesterol: 72 mg
Sodium: 378 mg

Combination Pizza

6 servings

¼ pound extra-lean Italian sausage (as lean as you can find)

1 12-inch commercially prepared pizza crust*

2 teaspoons extra-virgin olive oil

10 fresh basil leaves, chopped

1 16-ounce can crushed tomatoes

1 7-ounce can mushroom stems and pieces, drained

1 4-ounce can sliced black Kalamata olives, drained

½ cup shredded mozzarella cheese

3 ounces part-skim mozzarella cheese, very thinly sliced or ⅔ cup shredded

*When selecting a pizza crust, be sure to read labels. Some crusts have little or no fat, while others may be very high in fat. Once the crust is loaded with cheese and toppings, the low-fat crusts will taste just as good as the high-fat crusts.

You can get all these pizzas on the table in less time than it takes to order a pie and have it delivered.

Preheat the oven to 450° or 500° F. (the highest setting, but not broil). Move oven rack to highest position. (If using a baking stone, place stone on rack and heat for at least 30 minutes.)

Slit open, remove, and discard the casing on the Italian sausage. Preheat a nonstick skillet over medium-high heat. Add sausage and brown 6 to 8 minutes or until cooked, breaking the sausage apart as it browns. Drain on paper towels and pat dry with additional paper toweling to remove all excess fat. Set aside.

Slide the crust onto a nonstick pizza pan. Rub crust with olive oil, but do not dampen the edges with the oil. Combine basil and tomatoes. Spread crust with ⅓ to ½ cup of the sauce, again taking care not to dampen the edges. (Reserve remaining sauce for pizza at a later date, or serve it over pasta.) Sprinkle pizza evenly with sausage, mushrooms, and olives. Top with shredded mozzarella cheese and then the slices of part-skim mozzarella cheese. Bake 12 to 15 minutes, or until crust is golden brown.

Vegetarian Mexican Pizza: Drain and rinse one 15-ounce can black beans. Toss beans with 1 teaspoon extra-virgin olive oil, 1 tablespoon chili powder, and salt to taste; set aside. Combine one 8-ounce can tomato sauce, ½ teaspoon ground cumin (use 1 teaspoon for a more spicy flavor), ¼ teaspoon chili powder, ¼ teaspoon salt and ¼ teaspoon pepper; spread over pizza dough. Sprinkle black beans over top. Add the shredded and sliced mozzarella cheese and bake as directed above. Top baked pizza with cherry tomato halves and avocado slices, if desired.

Pizza Garlic Bread: Rub pizza crust with 1 tablespoon extra-virgin olive oil. Sprinkle with 1 teaspoon minced garlic and 2 teaspoons fresh rosemary. Sprinkle lightly with salt. Bake on pizza stone for 7 to 8 minutes.

APPROXIMATE NUTRITIONAL INFORMATION PER SERVING

Calories: 294
Total fat: 12 g
Saturated fat: 2 g
Cholesterol: 23 mg
Carbohydrates: 31 g
Dietary fiber: 1 g
Protein: 16 g
Sodium: 771 mg

VEGETARIAN MEXICAN PIZZA

Calories: 297
Fat: 8 g
Sodium: 650 mg
Other amounts remain the same.

PIZZA GARLIC BREAD

Calories: 154
Fat: 4 g
Sodium: 225 mg
Other amounts remain the same.

Italian Pizza Bread with Garlic and Rosemary

10 slices

¾ teaspoon active dry yeast

1 cup warm water (100°-105°F.)

2½ cups unbleached flour

¾ teaspoon Kosher salt

Dab of olive oil

5 cloves garlic, minced

⅓ cup fresh sprigs rosemary

2 teaspoons olive oil

¼ teaspoon black pepper

Dissolve yeast in the cup of warm water. In a bowl, combine flour and ½ teaspoon of the salt; add dissolved yeast. Knead by hand or by machine until smooth. Place dough in a bowl greased with olive oil, turning once to coat top. Cover and let rise in a warm place 1½ hours or until double in size.

Punch dough down. Put it back in bowl and let rise again until double in size, about 1 hour.

Punch down. Roll dough out to ½-inch thickness. Transfer to nonstick pizza pan. Make indentations at frequent intervals over the surface of dough. Insert a slice of garlic and a sprig of rosemary into each indentation. Drizzle olive oil over dough's surface and spread oil with hands to coat evenly. Sprinkle with remaining ¼ teaspoon salt and pepper.

Bake in a 400°F. oven 20–25 minutes or until crust is cooked and golden brown. (Bake on a pizza stone if available.) Remove garlic and rosemary. Slice into wedges. Serve at once.

Shortcut Suggestion: In place of homemade dough, use a heart-healthy, uncooked crust purchased from a local pizza parlor. Be sure it's made with olive oil or an unsaturated, nonhydrogenated oil such as safflower, soybean, or corn oil. Do not use a crust made with hydrogenated shortening, lard, palm oil, or coconut oil. Consider purchasing several crusts at one time to keep in the freezer.

APPROXIMATE NUTRITIONAL INFORMATION PER SLICE

Total calories: 128
Total fat: 1 g
Saturated fat: trace
Dietary fiber: 1 g
Carbohydrates: 24 g
Protein: 3 g
Cholesterol: 0 mg
Sodium: 133 mg

Taco Pizza

8 servings

1 white onion, chopped

1 pound extra-lean ground round

1 tablespoon chili powder

¼ teaspoon garlic, minced

⅛ teaspoon ground cumin

⅛ teaspoon cayenne pepper

¼ teaspoon black pepper

½ teaspoon paprika

½ teaspoon Kosher salt

½ cup commercial or homemade tomato salsa

⅓ cup Red Bean Dip (see page 91)

1 Easy Pizza Crust (page 62)

2 medium tomatoes, diced

1½ cups lettuce, shredded

½ cup grated low-fat Cheddar cheese

In a nonstick skillet, sauté onion and ground round. Season with chili powder, garlic powder, cumin, cayenne pepper, black pepper, paprika, and salt. Add salsa and toss.

Spread Red Bean Dip over cooked pizza crust. Top with ground round mixture. Arrange diced tomatoes over top. Cover with lettuce and sprinkle with cheese. Place under the broiler for 1–2 minutes or just until cheese begins to melt.

Shortcut Suggestion: In place of homemade dough, purchase a heart-healthy, uncooked crust from a local pizza parlor. Be sure it's made with olive oil or an unsaturated, nonhydrogenated oil such as safflower, soybean, or corn oil. Do not use a crust made with hydrogenated shortening, lard, palm oil, or coconut oil. (You may wish to purchase several crusts at one time to keep on hand in the freezer.)

Serving Suggestion: Serve with seasonal fruits.

APPROXIMATE NUTRITIONAL INFORMATION PER SERVING

Total calories: 249
Total fat: 10 g
Saturated fat: 4 g
Dietary fiber: 3 g
Carbohydrates: 25 g
Protein: 14 g
Cholesterol: 32 mg
Sodium: 432 mg

Shallot-Basil Bread

1 loaf (15 slices per loaf)

1 12-inch loaf French bread

3 tablespoons olive oil

3 shallots, thinly sliced

3 tablespoons chopped fresh basil

2 tablespoons grated Parmesan cheese

Slice French bread in half lengthwise. Spread with olive oil. Sprinkle with shallots and basil, then with Parmesan. Place bread on a foil-lined pan in a preheated broiler 2–3 inches from heat 3–4 minutes, or until bread begins to brown and cheese melts.

Serving Suggestion: This bread is great for dipping into Seafood Stew (page 136).

APPROXIMATE NUTRITIONAL INFORMATION PER SLICE

Total calories: 132
Total fat: 3 g
Saturated fat: trace
Dietary fiber: 1 g
Carbohydrates: 17 g
Protein: 4 g
Cholesterol: 1 mg
Sodium: 247 mg

Oat-Bran Bread

2 loaves (20 slices per loaf)

½ cup warm water (100°-105°F.)*

3 cups unbleached bread flour

2 packages active dry yeast

2 cups whole-wheat flour

1 cup rolled oats

⅓ cup wheat germ

½ cup oat bran

1½ cups water

½ cup molasses

2 tablespoons safflower oil

1 egg white, lightly beaten

1 tablespoon salt

olive oil for greasing

Make a poolish with 1 cup of warm water, ¾ cup of unbleached bread flour, and 1 package of yeast. Mix all ingredients with a whisk. Cover with plastic wrap for 4 to 24 hours at room temperature. When poolish bubbles, it is ready.

Add remaining bread flour, whole-wheat flour, oats, wheat germ and oat bran. Add water, molasses, safflower oil, and salt. Mix with a wooden spoon. Put mixture into table top mixer with a dough hook or mix by hand with wooden spoon. Knead on a lightly floured surface until smooth and elastic. Place in a mixing bowl greased with olive oil. Cover with a kitchen towel and let rise in a warm place 2 hours. Punch down; knead lightly. Cover and let rise 1½- 2 hours. Punch down.

Divide dough in half. Roll each half into a rectangle and place in a non-stick loaf pan. Cover and let rise in a warm place 1½ - 2 hours. Score the top with a sharp knife when ready to bake. Bake at 375°F. 30 minutes, or until bread pulls away from edges of the pans. Remove from pan and let cool on wire racks.

Variation: To make rolls, divide dough into 4 dozen equal-size balls, keeping dough thoroughly covered at all times. Place 3 balls into each cup of non-stick muffin pan. Brush tops with egg whites. Bake at 375°F. 12-15 minutes or until done.

*Water temperature above 105°F. kills yeast.

APPROXIMATE NUTRITIONAL INFORMATION PER SLICE

Total calories: 94
Total fat: 1 g
Saturated fat: 0 g
Dietary fiber: 2 g
Carbohydrates: 18 g
Protein: 3 g
Cholesterol: 0 mg
Sodium: 297 mg

Old-Fashioned Wheat Bread

2 loaves (20 slices per loaf)

¼ cup warm water (100°-105°F.)*

3 cups unbleached white flour

1 package active dry yeast

½ cup cornmeal

¾ cup cold water

1½ cups water

3 tablespoons olive oil

½ cup dark molasses

3 cups whole-wheat flour

⅓ cup 1% buttermilk

2 tablespoons salt

olive oil for greasing

Make a poolish with 1 cup of warm water, ¾ cup of unbleached bread flour, and 1 package of yeast. Mix all ingredients with a whisk. Cover with plastic wrap for 4 to 24 hours at room temperature. When poolish bubbles, it is ready.

Meanwhile, put cornmeal into a small bowl; cover with ¾ cup cold water. Soak 5 minutes; stir. Bring 1½ cups water to a boil; gradually add cornmeal. Cook and stir over low heat until mixture comes to a boil. Remove from heat. Add to poolish along with olive oil, molasses, and whole-wheat flour. Using a wooden spoon, gradually blend in remainder of unbleached white flour, buttermilk, and salt.

Put into table top mixer with a dough hook or mix by hand with wooden spoon. Knead on a lightly floured surface until smooth and elastic. If dough seems dry, add additional water, one tablespoon at a time. (This dough has a dry, heavy consistency; however, it will not be that way once it is baked.)

Turn dough into a mixing bowl greased with olive oiL Cover with a kitchen towel and let rise in a warm place 3 hours. (It may not double in size.) Punch down; knead lightly. Divide dough in half. Roll each half into a cylinder; turn each cylinder into a non-stick loaf pan. Cover and let rise in a warm place for 1½ hours.

Score the top with a sharp knife when ready to bake. Bake at 400°F. 15 minutes. Reduce heat to 350°F. and bake 20-30 minutes longer, or until bread pulls away from edges of the pans. Remove from pans and let cool on wire racks.

*Water temperature above 105°F. kills yeast.

APPROXIMATE NUTRITIONAL INFORMATION PER SLICE

Total calories: 90
Total fat: 1 g
Saturated fat: 0 g
Dietary Ffber: 1 g
Carbohydrates: 17 g
Protein: 2 g
Cholesterol: trace
Sodium: 473 mg

Multi-Grain Bread

3 loaves (15 slices per loaf)

2 packages active dry yeast

3 cups warm water (100°-105°F.)

2 tablespoons honey

2⅓ cups whole-wheat flour

2½ cups semolina flour

1¾ cups unbleached bread flour

½ cup soy flour

¾ cup non-fat milk powder

1 tablespoon Kosher salt

1 tablespoon olive oil

1 tablespoon safflower oil

3 tablespoons wheat germ

In a mixing bowl, dissolve yeast in 3 cups warm water; stir in honey. Let stand 5 minutes. Combine flours with milk powder; add 3 cups of the flour mixture to the dissolved yeast. Add salt and stir with a wooden spoon to form a soft dough. Stir in olive oil, safflower oil, wheat germ, and remaining flour. Knead on a lightly floured surface until smooth and elastic. Turn dough into a bowl greased with olive oil. Cover and let rise in a warm place until double in size. Punch down. Return dough to warm place; let rest 15 minutes.

Knead lightly. Divide dough into thirds and roll into rectangles; place each in a nonstick bread pan. Cover and let rise until bread comes over the top of pan.

Bake at 350°F. 30 minutes, or until bread pulls away from edges of the pans. Remove from pans and let cool on wire racks.

Variation: Prepare part of the bread as indicated above and the other part as raisin bread (see Multi-grain Raisin Bread below).

APPROXIMATE NUTRITIONAL INFORMATION PER SLICE

Total calories: 91
Total Fat: 1 g
Saturated Fat: 0 g
Dietary Fiber: 1 g
Carbohydrates: 17 g
Protein: 3 g
Cholesterol: trace
Sodium: 216 mg

Multi-Grain Raisin Bread

3 loaves (20 slices per loaf)

1 recipe Multi-grain Bread (above)

3 cups raisins

Prepare Multi-Grain Bread according to instructions until the last paragraph. Then divide dough into 3 loaves. Knead 1 cup of raisins into each loaf. Turn dough into non-stick loaf pans. Cover. Let rise in warm place until dough comes over the top of pan. Bake at 350°F. 30 minutes, or until bread pulls away from edges of the pans. Remove from pans and let cool on wire racks.

APPROXIMATE NUTRITIONAL INFORMATION PER SLICE

Total calories: 120
Total Fat: 1 g
Saturated Fat: 0 g
Dietary Fiber: 2 g
Carbohydrates: 25 g
Protein: 4 g
Cholesterol: 0 mg
Sodium: 226 mg

Oatmeal Bread

2 loaves (20 slices per loaf)

1 cup rolled oats

2 cups hot water (100°-105°F.)

½ cup molasses

2 teaspoons olive oil

2 teaspoons canola oil

1½ teaspoons Kosher salt

1 package active dry yeast

¼ cup warm water

6 cups unbleached white flour

Pour rolled oats into a mixing bowl; add 2 cups hot water. Stir slightly. Let stand 10 minutes. Stir in molasses, olive oil, canola oil, and salt.

Dissolve yeast in ¼ cup warm water; add to oat mixture. Add flour and mix with a wooden spoon to form a soft dough. Remove to a heavily floured surface. Knead 3–4 minutes, or until smooth and elastic.

Place dough in a mixing bowl greased with olive oil. Cover with a kitchen towel. Let dough rise in a warm place until double in size, about 2 hours. Punch down. Divide in half. Turn into 2 nonstick loaf pans. Cover and let rise until double in size, about 1½ hours.

Bake at 350°F. oven 45 minutes, or until bread pulls away from edges of the pans. Remove from pans and let cool on wire racks.

APPROXIMATE NUTRITIONAL INFORMATION PER SLICE

Total calories: 97
Total Fat: 1 g
Saturated Fat: 0 g
Dietary Fiber: 1 g
Carbohydrates: 19 g
Protein: 3 g
Cholesterol: 0 mg
Sodium: 312 mg

Cranberry Bread

1 loaf (20 slices per loaf)

1¼ cups unbleached white flour

¾ cup whole-wheat flour

⅔ cup granulated sugar

1½ teaspoons baking powder

½ teaspoon baking soda

1 teaspoon Kosher salt

2 tablespoons canola oil

¾ cup freshly squeezed orange juice

1 tablespoon grated orange peel

1 egg, beaten

1 12-ounce package fresh cranberries, coarsely chopped

In a mixing bowl, combine flours, sugar, baking powder, baking soda, and salt. Stir in oil, orange juice, orange peel, and egg, mixing just to moisten. Fold in cranberries. Pour into a nonstick loaf pan.

Bake at 350°F. 50 minutes, or until toothpick inserted into center comes out clean. Cool on wire rack for 15 minutes. Remove bread from pan and continue cooling on wire rack.

APPROXIMATE NUTRITIONAL INFORMATION PER SLICE

Total calories: 99
Total Fat: 2 g
Saturated Fat: 0 g
Dietary Fiber: 2 g
Carbohydrates: 19 g
Protein: 2 g
Cholesterol: 9 mg
Sodium: 269 mg

Honey Oat Bread

2 loaves (10 slices per loaf)

⅓ cup honey

2 cups warm water (100°-105°F.)

3 packages active dry yeast

1½ cups rolled oats

¼ cup olive oil or canola oil

1 egg

1 tablespoon Kosher salt

2 cups whole-wheat flour

3¼ cups all-purpose flour

Dab of olive oil for greasing

Combine honey with water; add yeast. Let stand 5 minutes.

In a mixing bowl, combine oats, olive oil, egg, salt, whole-wheat flour, and all but 2 cup of the all-purpose flour. Mix with wooden spoon to form a soft dough.

Knead the dough by hand or by machine, gradually adding remaining 1 cup all-purpose flour, until smooth and elastic. Place dough in a 2½-quart bowl greased with olive oil, turning once to coat top. Cover and let rise in a warm place until double in size, about 1½ hours. Dough is ready if indentation remains when touched.

Punch dough down; divide into halves. Let rest 5 minutes. Flatten each half with hands or rolling pin into an 18 x 9-inch rectangle. Roll into a cylinder. Place seam side down in nonstick loaf pans. Cover and let rise until double in size, about 1 hour.

Bake in a 350°F. oven 20–30 minutes. When dough is set, remove from pans to oven rack and cook 10–15 minutes longer or until bread sounds hollow when tapped. Cool on wire racks.

APPROXIMATE NUTRITIONAL INFORMATION PER SLICE

Total calories: 92
Total Fat: 2 g
Saturated Fat: 0 g
Dietary Fiber: 1 g
Carbohydrates: 16 g
Protein: 2 g
Cholesterol: 5 mg
Sodium: 142 mg

English Muffin Bread

2 loaves (10 slices per loaf)

3 cups unbleached white flour

2 cups whole-wheat flour

1½ teaspoons active dry yeast

1½ teaspoons salt

1 tablespoon granulated sugar

2 teaspoons safflower oil

2 cups very warm water

Dab of olive oil for greasing

cornmeal

In a large mixing bowl, combine flours, yeast, salt, sugar, and safflower oil; add warm water. Stir with a wooden spoon until ingredients are moistened. Mix with an electric mixer, on low speed, 1–2 minutes, just long enough to mix thoroughly. Place dough in a bowl greased with olive oil. Cover with a kitchen towel. Let rise in a warm place 6 hours.

Grease 2 nonstick loaf pans with olive oil; sprinkle pans with cornmeal. Divide dough in half; roll each half into a loaf-shaped cylinder. Put dough into nonstick pans. Sprinkle top of each loaf with cornmeal. Cover with kitchen towel. Let rise in warm place 2 hours.

Bake at 350°F. 30–40 minutes, or until bread pulls away from edges of the pans. Remove from pans and cool on wire racks.

APPROXIMATE NUTRITIONAL INFORMATION PER SLICE

Total calories: 116
Total Fat: 0 g
Saturated Fat: 0 g
Dietary Fiber: 2 g
Carbohydrates: 23 g
Protein: 4 g
Cholesterol: 0 mg
Sodium: 168 mg

Blueberry Muffins

16 muffins

¼ cup canola oil

¾ cup brown sugar

1 cup unbleached white flour

2 teaspoons baking powder

1 teaspoon baking soda

¼ teaspoon salt

1 cup 1% buttermilk

1 egg

⅓ cup oat bran

⅓ cup oatmeal

⅓ cup wheat germ

1⅓ cups blueberries

In a mixing bowl, combine oil, brown sugar, flour, baking powder, baking soda, and salt. Add buttermilk, egg, oat bran, oatmeal, and wheat germ; mix lightly with a wooden spoon to moisten. Stir in blueberries. Fill paper-lined muffin tins ¾ full with batter. Bake at 400°F. 20 minutes, or until toothpick inserted into center comes out dry. Remove muffins from tins and cool on wire racks.

Variation: Substitute raisins for blueberries.

APPROXIMATE NUTRITIONAL INFORMATION PER MUFFIN

Total calories: 127
Total Fat: 5 g
Saturated Fat: 1 g
Dietary Fiber: 2 g
Carbohydrates: 20 g
Protein: 3 g
Cholesterol: 12 mg
Sodium: 299 mg

Banana Currant Muffins

18 muffins

1 cup unbleached bread flour

1¼ cups whole-wheat flour

⅓ cup granulated sugar

2 teaspoons baking powder

½ teaspoon baking soda

2 teaspoons cinnamon

½ teaspoon nutmeg

½ cup 1% buttermilk

½ cup canola oil

2 ripe bananas, mashed

1 egg

1 cup currants

In a mixing bowl, combine flours, sugar, baking powder, baking soda, cinnamon and nutmeg. In a smaller bowl, combine buttermilk, oil, bananas, and egg; add to dry ingredients. Stir with a wire whisk just until all ingredients are moistened. Fold in currants. Fill paper-lined muffin cups ¾ full with batter. Bake at 375°F. 15–20 minutes, or until toothpick inserted into center comes out dry. Remove muffins from tins and cool on wire racks.

APPROXIMATE NUTRITIONAL INFORMATION PER MUFFIN

Total calories: 161
Total Fat: 7 g
Saturated Fat: 1 g
Dietary Fiber: 2 g
Carbohydrates: 24 g
Protein: 3 g
Cholesterol: 11 mg
Sodium: 189 mg

Overnight Oatmeal Muffins

14 muffins

½ cup unbleached bread flour

½ cup whole-wheat flour

¼ cup oat bran

1 cup rolled oats

⅓ cup brown sugar

½ teaspoon baking powder

½ teaspoon baking soda

½ teaspoon cinnamon

¼ teaspoon salt

¾   cup 1% buttermilk

¼ cup canola oil

1 egg

½ cup puréed apricots*

½ cup raisins

In a mixing bowl, combine flours, oat bran, rolled oats, brown sugar, baking powder, baking soda, cinnamon, salt, buttermilk, oil, egg, and apricots. Stir in raisins. Cover and refrigerate overnight or bake at once. Fill paper-lined muffin cups 3/4 full with batter. Bake at 400°F. 20–25 minutes, or until toothpick inserted into center comes out dry. Remove muffins from tins and cool on wire racks.

*If using canned apricots, use unsweetened. Three apricots yield ½ cup puréed apricots. If using fresh, wash, halve, and seed 3 whole apricots. Simmer, covered, in a saucepan, with 3 tablespoons water 5–10 minutes, or until apricots soften. Purée in blender or food processor.

APPROXIMATE NUTRITIONAL INFORMATION PER MUFFIN

Total calories: 155
Total Fat: 5 g
Saturated Fat: 1 g
Dietary Fiber: 3 g
Carbohydrates: 24 g
Protein: 4 g
Cholesterol: 14 mg
Sodium: 181 mg

Oat-Bran Muffins

18 muffins

¼ **cup canola oil**

¾ **cup brown sugar**

1 **cup unbleached bread flour**

2 **teaspoons baking powder**

¼ **teaspoon salt**

1 **cup 1% buttermilk**

1 **egg**

1 **teaspoon baking soda**

1 **cup oat bran**

1 **cup raisins**

In a mixing bowl and with a wire whisk, combine oil, brown sugar, flour, baking powder, and salt. Add remaining ingredients and stir just until moistened. Fill paper-lined muffin cups ¾ full with batter. Bake at 400°F. 20 minutes, or until toothpick inserted into center comes out dry. Remove muffins from tins and cool on wire racks.

APPROXIMATE NUTRITIONAL INFORMATION PER MUFFIN

Total calories: 120
Total Fat: 4 g
Saturated Fat: 0 g
Dietary Fiber: 2 g
Carbohydrates: 22 g
Protein: 3 g
Cholesterol: 11 mg
Sodium: 267 mg

Apple Oat Bran Muffins

18 muffins

3 **cups oat bran**

2½ **cups whole-wheat flour**

½ **teaspoon Kosher salt**

2 **teaspoons baking soda**

2 **eggs**

¼ **cup molasses**

¼ **cup canola oil**

2 **cups apple juice concentrate**

2 **cups nonfat milk**

2½ **cups chopped Granny Smith apples (about 2 large apples)**

1½ **cups raisins (optional)**

½ **cup chopped walnuts (optional)**

In a small bowl, combine oat bran, whole-wheat flour, salt, and baking soda; set aside. In a large mixing bowl, beat eggs; stir in molasses. Mix in olive oil, apple juice concentrate, and milk. Gradually add flour mixture using a wire whisk. Mix ingredients just until moistened. Stir in chopped apples and raisins and walnuts, if desired. Pour into paper-lined muffin pans. Bake at 350°F. 20–25 minutes or until toothpick inserted into center comes out dry.

APPROXIMATE NUTRITIONAL INFORMATION PER MUFFIN

Total calories: 201
Total fat: 4 g
Saturated fat: 1 g
Dietary fiber: 4 g
Carbohydrates: 39 g
Protein: 5 g
Cholesterol: 23 mg
Sodium: 150 mg

Applesauce Oatmeal Muffins

24 muffins

2½ cups applesauce

2 eggs

¾ cup brown sugar

¼ cup canola oil

1½ cups rolled oats

1 cup whole-wheat flour

1 cup all-purpose flour

1 teaspoon baking soda

1 teaspoon baking powder

1½ teaspoons Kosher salt

2 teaspoons cinnamon

1½ cups raisins

In a large bowl, combine applesauce, eggs, brown sugar, and oil; set aside. In a medium bowl, combine oats, flours, baking soda, baking powder, salt, and cinnamon. Add to applesauce mixture. Stir with wire whisk just until dry ingredients are moistened. Stir in raisins. Pour into paper-lined muffin pans. Bake at 350°F. 15–20 minutes or until toothpick inserted into center comes out dry.

APPROXIMATE NUTRITIONAL INFORMATION PER MUFFIN

Total calories: 154
Total fat: 3 g
Saturated fat: trace
Dietary fiber: 2 g
Carbohydrates: 30 g
Protein: 3 g
Cholesterol: 18 mg
Sodium: 199 mg

Hot Cross Buns

18 buns

5 cups unbleached flour

2 ¼ -ounce packages regular or quick-rising active dry yeast

⅓ cup granulated sugar

¼ teaspoon ground nutmeg

½ teaspoon salt

1 ½ teaspoons cinnamon

¾ cup non-fat milk

¼ cup canola oil

½ cup water

3 eggs

1 ¾ cups raisins

1 egg white, lightly beaten

1 tablespoon cold water

Vanilla Glaze (page 399)

In a large mixing bowl, combine 1½ cups of the flour, undissolved yeast, sugar, nutmeg, salt, and cinnamon. Set aside.

In a 1-quart saucepan, heat milk, oil, and water to 125°F.; gradually add to dry ingredients. Beat 2 minutes at medium speed of electric mixer. Add eggs and ¾ cup of the flour; beat 2 minutes at high speed. Using dough hook or wooden spoon, gradually add remaining 2¾ cups of flour to make a soft dough. Knead by hand on a lightly floured surface or by machine until dough is smooth and elastic. Cover and let rest 20 minutes.

Punch dough down. Knead in raisins. Divide dough into 18 equal pieces. Roll into smooth balls. Arrange rolls in 2 nonstick 8 x 8 inch-square nonstick baking pans. Cover and let rise in a warm place 30–60 minutes or until nearly double in size.

Bake in a 350°F. oven 10 minutes. Meanwhile, combine egg white and cold water; brush over rolls. Bake 5-10 minutes longer or until done. When done, rolls will pull away easily from edges of pan. Remove rolls from pans. Cool on wire racks. Drizzle glaze in a cross shape over tops.

Variation: Substitute Orange Glaze (page 399) for Vanilla Glaze or drizzle half the buns with Orange and half with Vanilla.

APPROXIMATE NUTRITIONAL INFORMATION PER BUN

Total calories: 262
Total fat: 4 g
Saturated fat: 0 g
Dietary fiber: 2 g
Carbohydrates: 51 g
Protein: 6 g
Cholesterol: 35 mg
Sodium: 92 mg

Buttermilk Pancakes

20 pancakes

2 cups sifted unbleached white flour

½ teaspoon salt

1¼ teaspoons baking soda

¾ teaspoon baking powder

1 egg

2¼ cups 1% buttermilk

2 teaspoons nonfat milk

1 tablespoon canola oil

In a mixing bowl, blend ingredients with a wire whisk, just enough to moisten. Dip up batter with a large serving spoon. Bake on a preheated nonstick griddle. Turn pancakes when top side is bubbly and a few bubbles have broken. Flip only once.

APPROXIMATE NUTRITIONAL INFORMATION PER PANCAKE

Total calories: 63
Total Fat: 1 g
Saturated Fat: 0 g
Dietary Fiber: 0 g
Carbohydrates: 10 g
Protein: 2 g
Cholesterol: 14 mg
Sodium: 149 mg

Sour Cream Pancakes

18 pancakes

4 eggs

½ cup all-purpose flour, sifted

¼ teaspoon salt

1 teaspoon baking soda

2 cups nonfat sour cream

Lightly beat eggs. In a seperate bowl, combine dry ingredients; blend with eggs and sour cream, using a wire whisk.

Pour enough batter for each pancake onto a preheated nonstick griddle. Cook until top side is bubbly and a few bubbles have broken. Turn and brown other side.

Note: If batter is too thick, add up to 2 tablespoons of water.

APPROXIMATE NUTRITIONAL INFORMATION PER PANCAKE

Calories: 50
Total fat: 1 g
Saturated fat: 0 g
Dietary fiber: 0 g
Carbohydrate: 6 g
Protein: 3 g
Cholesterol: 40 mg
Sodium: 160 mg

Crêpes

15 crêpes

2 eggs

½ cup nonfat milk

½ cup cold water

1 cup all-purpose flour, sifted

2 tablespoons canola oil

½ teaspoon sugar

⅛ teaspoon salt

Lightly beat eggs, milk, and water. Add remaining ingredients; blend with a wire whisk. Pour enough batter into a preheated 5-inch nonstick crêpe pan to coat bottom; tilt pan to spread batter. Cook 1 minute, or just until set. Turn. Cook 1 minute longer, or until browned.

Notes: Crêpes may be prepared in advance, layered between wax paper, and wrapped in aluminum foil for freezing. Bring to room temperature for easy separation before using. To reheat, remove wax paper layers; wrap stack of crêpes in aluminum foil. Heat in a 200°F. oven for about 10 minutes, or until warm.

Some crêpe fillings may be prepared in advance and refrigerated or frozen for later use.

Serving Suggestion: Especially good with fresh strawberries and whipped cream.

APPROXIMATE NUTRITIONAL INFORMATION PER CRÊPE

Total calories: 60
Total fat: 3 g
Saturated fat: 0 g
Dietary fiber: 0 g
Carbohydrates: 7 g
Protein: 2 g
Cholesterol: 29 mg
Sodium: 31 mg

French Toast

6 slices

2 eggs

⅓ cup nonfat milk

¼ teaspoon sugar

½ teaspoon cinnamon

1 tablespoon olive oil

6 slices day-old crusty French bread

Beat eggs; add milk, sugar, and cinnamon. Blend. Heat olive oil on a nonstick griddle over medium-high heat. Dip bread one slice at a time into egg mixture, coating both sides evenly, and place on the griddle. Brown, about 2 to 3 minutes. Turn and brown other side, 2 to 3 minutes longer.

APPROXIMATE NUTRITIONAL INFORMATION PER SERVING

Calories: 82
Total fat: 2 g
Saturated fat: 1 g
Dietary fiber: 1 g
Carbohydrate: 12 g
Protein: 4 g
Cholesterol: 71 mg
Sodium: 177 mg

French Omelet

2 omelets

1 teaspoon olive oil

2 teaspoons chopped onion

¼ cup sliced mushrooms

1 teaspoon minced green pepper

OMELET:

4 whole eggs

2 tablespoons water

Dash of salt and pepper

4 slices tomato for garnish

Fresh Italian parsley for garnish

FILLINGS:

**2 tablespoons grated
reduced-fat cheddar cheese**

1 teaspoon minced fresh chives

2 teaspoons chopped Italian parsley

**2 teaspoons diced green chilies or
jalapeno peppers**

2 tablespoons chopped tomato

2 tablespoons crabmeat

Heat olive oil in a nonstick skillet over medium heat. Sauté onion, mushrooms, and green pepper until tender. Set aside.

Beat eggs, water, salt, and pepper with a fork until mixture is well blended but not frothy. Heat an 8-inch nonstick skillet over medium heat until a drop of water sizzles when sprinkled on the pan. Pour in egg mixture. Tilt pan to spread evenly throughout and at an even depth.

Using a fork, stir rapidly through top of uncooked eggs. Shake pan frequently to keep eggs moving. When egg is set but still shiny, remove pan from heat. Spoon desired fillings across center. Flip sides of omelet over, envelope style, to hold in filling. Tilt pan and roll omelet over onto plate. Garnish with sliced tomatoes and fresh parsley.

**APPROXIMATE NUTRITIONAL
INFORMATION PER OMELET**

Calories: 160
Total fat: 11 g
Saturated fat: 3 g
Dietary fiber: 1 g
Carbohydrate: 3 g
Protein: 15 g
Cholesterol: 325 mg
Sodium: 190 mg

Huevos Rancheros

4 servings

**1 4-ounce can whole
green chilies, drained**

**3 tablespoons grated reduced-fat
Monterey Jack cheese**

6 whole eggs, beaten

**2 tablespoons grated reduced-fat
cheddar cheese**

4 6-inch corn tortillas

**½ cup Tomato Salsa,
preferably homemade (page 214)**

1 slice tomato for garnish

Gently slit each chili lengthwise and remove seeds. Stuff with Jack cheese. Press slit edges together to hold cheese in. Cut stuffed chilies into bite-size pieces.

Heat a nonstick skillet over medium heat. Arrange chilies in pan. When cheese begins to melt, pour in beaten eggs. When eggs start to firm, lift chilies slightly to allow uncooked eggs to run underneath. When almost fully cooked, sprinkle grated cheddar cheese on top. When cheese melts, remove skillet from heat.

Serve with corn tortillas and salsa. Garnish with sliced tomato.

Variation: Sprinkle with black or Kalamata olives and a dollop of sour cream.

**APPROXIMATE
NUTRITIONAL
INFORMATION
PER SERVING**

Total calories: 190
Total fat: 8 g
Saturated fat: 3 g
Dietary fiber: 3 g
Carbohydrates: 159 g
Protein: 12 g
Cholesterol: 250 mg
Sodium: 470 mg

Buttermilk Waffles

10 6-inch waffles

3 eggs

2 cups 1% buttermilk

1¼ cups unbleached white flour

¾ cup whole-wheat flour

2 teaspoons granulated sugar

2 teaspoons baking powder

1 teaspoon baking soda

¼ teaspoon salt

2 tablespoons canola oil

In a mixing bowl, lightly beat eggs with a wire whisk. Add buttermilk and beat. Add remaining ingredients. Beat until smooth. Bake in a nonstick waffle iron until waffles are golden brown.

Serving Suggestion: In place of high-calorie syrup, serve puréed fresh or frozen strawberries, raspberries, blueberries or blackberries with waffles, pancakes, and French toast.

**APPROXIMATE
NUTRITIONAL
INFORMATION
PER WAFFLE**

Total calories: 200
Total fat: 6 g
Saturated fat: 1 g
Dietary fiber: 2 g
Carbohydrates: 28 g
Protein: 18 g
Cholesterol: 165 mg
Sodium: 460 mg

Sesame Waffles

10 6-inch waffles

1 cup unbleached flour

1 cup whole-wheat flour

1 cup non-fat milk

2 tablespoons sugar

1 tablespoon baking powder

1 teaspoon salt

2 eggs, slightly beaten

2 tablespoons canola oil

½ cup water

¼ cup sesame seeds

1 teaspoon vanilla extract

In a large mixing bowl, combine flours, milk, sugar, baking powder, and salt. In a small mixing bowl, combine eggs, olive oil, and water.

Make a well in the flour mixture; add egg mixture and blend. Fold in sesame seeds and vanilla extract. Pour ⅔ cup of mix into a waffle iron and bake 3 minutes.

Note: Instead of the traditional butter and syrup, try topping waffles with a mixture of puréed and whole fresh strawberries, raspberries or blueberries, powdered sugar, and a dollop of Greek non-fat yogurt.

APPROXIMATE NUTRITIONAL INFORMATION PER WAFFLE

Total calories: 160
Total fat: 5 g
Saturated fat: trace
Dietary fiber: 2 g
Carbohydrates: 23 g
Protein: 5 g
Cholesterol: 35 mg
Sodium: 430 mg

Popovers

8 popovers

2 eggs, room temperature

1 egg white, room temperature

1¼ cups nonfat milk

1¼ cups unbleached white flour

¼ teaspoon salt

In a mixing bowl, beat eggs and egg white with a rotary beater until lemon colored and frothy; add milk. Beat 1 minute. Add flour and salt; beat 1–2 minutes, or until batter is smooth and foamy on top.

Pour mixture into nonstick popover or muffin pan. Fill each cup ⅔ full with batter. (If using standard muffin pans, grease and fill alternating cups to prevent sides of popovers from touching.)

Bake at 450°F. 15 minutes (do not open oven). Reduce heat to 350°F.; bake 20–25 minutes, or until high, hollow, and golden brown. Remove from oven. Insert a sharp knife into each popover to allow steam to escape. Remove from pan. Serve hot.

Note: The eggs and milk must be at room temperature or the popovers will not rise. It is also essential that the custard cups or the muffin pan (including the tops) be very well greased or the popovers will stick.

Serving Suggestion: Serve with warm Apple Butter (page 219).

APPROXIMATE NUTRITIONAL INFORMATION PER POPOVER

Total calories: 120
Total fat: 2.5 g
Saturated fat: 1 g
Dietary fiber: 1 g
Carbohydrates: 18 g
Protein: 6 g
Cholesterol: 45 mg
Sodium: 125 mg

Cheese Popovers

8 popovers

2 eggs, room-temperature

1 egg white, room-temperature

1¼ cups nonfat milk

1¼ cups unbleached white flour

¼ teaspoon salt

½ cup shredded reduced-fat Cheddar cheese

In a mixing bowl, beat eggs and egg white with a rotary beater until lemon-colored and frothy. Add milk and beat 1 minute. Add flour and salt, and beat 1–2 minutes or until batter is smooth and foamy on top.

Pour mixture into nonstick popover or muffin pan. (You may need to coat with olive oil spray as cheese can cause sticking even in nonstick pans). Fill each cup ⅓ full with batter. Sprinkle with 1 tablespoon cheese. Top with ⅓ cup more batter. (If using a standard muffin pan, grease and fill alternating cups to prevent sides of popovers from touching.)

Bake at 450°F. 15 minutes (do not open oven). Reduce heat to 350°F. and bake 20–25 minutes or until high, hollow and golden brown. Remove from oven. Insert a sharp knife into each popover to allow steam to escape. Remove from pan. Serve hot.

Note: The eggs and milk must be room-temperature or the popovers will not rise.

APPROXIMATE NUTRITIONAL INFORMATION PER POPOVER

Total calories: 130
Total fat: 3 g
Saturated fat: 1.5 g
Dietary fiber: 1 g
Carbohydrates: 18 g
Protein: 7 g
Cholesterol: 45 mg
Sodium: 170 mg

Appetizers

Bruschetta

16 servings (1 slice bread with 1/4 cup tomato mixture)

1 pound fresh, ripe plum tomatoes, chopped

3 garlic cloves, finely chopped

2 tablespoons extra-virgin olive oil

1 12-inch loaf Italian, Tuscan, or peasant bread

16 kalamata olives, pitted and chopped

¼ cup chopped fresh basil

2 tablespoons chopped fresh Italian parsley

Combine tomatoes, garlic, and olive oil. Let stand at room temperature for 1 hour.

Meanwhile, slice bread into approximately 16 half-inch slices. Toast under a preheated broiler or in a toaster oven for 2 to 3 minutes, or until brown on both sides.

Just before serving, add olives, basil, and parsley to tomato mixture. Spoon mixture into a medium-size bowl and place in center of a basket or serving tray. Ring with toasted bread.

Variation: Lightly spread bread with Garlic Olive Oil (page 210) before or after toasting. Pour some oil into a spray bottle and spray it on the bread. (Spraying allows a lot of flavor while using a very small amount of oil.)

Serving Suggestion: Bruschetta works well as an appetizer or first course, especially with pasta, and is great on a picnic with roast or grilled chicken.

APPROXIMATE NUTRITIONAL INFORMATION PER SERVING

Total calories: 95
Total fat: 3 g
Saturated fat: 0 g
Dietary fiber: 0 g
Carbohydrates: 15 g
Protein: 3 g
Cholesterol: 0 mg
Sodium: 239 mg

Mediterranean Antipasto

6 servings

⅓ pound fresh asparagus

⅓ pound fresh green beans

¼ cup fresh lemon juice

2 tablespoons extra-virgin olive oil

½ teaspoon Kosher salt or to taste

¼ teaspoon black pepper

1 head red leaf lettuce

1 8-ounce can garbanzo beans, drained and rinsed

2 ounce buffalo mozzarella, cut into julienne strips

In a steamer over boiling water, steam asparagus and then green beans until just crisp-tender. In a jar with cover, combine lemon juice, olive oil, salt, and pepper. Pour over asparagus and green beans while vegetables are still warm.

Just before serving, drain marinade from vegetables. Arrange leaf lettuce over small serving platter. Mound asparagus, green beans, garbanzo beans, and cheese over top.

APPROXIMATE NUTRITIONAL INFORMATION PER SERVING

Total calories: 92
Total fat: 4 g
Saturated fat: 1 g
Dietary fiber: 2 g
Carbohydrates: 9 g
Protein: 5 g
Cholesterol: 5 mg
Sodium: 159 mg

The Easiest Vegetable Antipasto

10 servings

1 15-ounce jar pickled beans

1 15-ounce jar pickled asparagus

1 15-ounce jar pickled snap peas

1 15-ounce can water-packed baby ears of corn

1 14½ -ounce can water-packed artichoke hearts

1 15-ounce can pitted black olives

Chill vegetables in their individual jars or cans. When ready to assemble the hors d'oeuvre, thoroughly drain vegetables. Pat dry with paper towels, if necessary. Arrange beans, asparagus, snap peas, baby corn, and artichoke hearts in individual vegetable mounds on a serving platter or tray. Tuck olives among the mounds.

Serving Suggestion: Goes well with a heaping platter of shrimp cocktail.

APPROXIMATE NUTRITIONAL INFORMATION PER SERVING

Total calories: 63
Total fat: 2 g
Saturated fat: 0 g
Dietary fiber: 1 g
Carbohydrates: 11 g
Protein: 2 g
Cholesterol: 2 mg
Sodium: 306 mg

Vegetable and Black Bean Antipasto

6 servings

3 carrots

3 stalks celery

2 jicama

1 bunch radishes, trimmed

1 English cucumber

1 head red leaf lettuce

1 cup Black Bean Dip, preferably homemade (page 91)

Slice carrots, celery, jicama, radishes, and cucumber diagonally into sticks. Place lettuce on chilled salad plates and arrange vegetables on lettuce. Serve with a dollop of Black Bean Dip.

Serving Suggestion: An excellent accompaniment to a soup meal. Also good as an appetizer.

APPROXIMATE NUTRITIONAL INFORMATION PER SERVING

Total calories: 43
Total fat: trace
Saturated fat: 0 g
Dietary fiber: 3 g
Carbohydrates: 10 g
Protein: 1 g
Cholesterol: 0 mg
Sodium: 45 mg

Antipasto

12 servings

1 15-ounce jar pickled beans

1 15-ounce jar pickled asparagus

1 15-ounce jar pickled snap peas

1 15-ounce can whole spears baby corn on the cob

1 15-ounce can water-packed artichoke hearts, drained

1 15-ounce jar pepperoncini peppers (optional)

1 15-ounce can garbanzo beans, drained

1 15-ounce can black Kalamata olives

2 bunches carrots

2 bunches radishes

2 cups ripe cherry tomatoes

1 bunch red leaf lettuce

It's good to have the ingredients on hand for this easy salad or quick-to-fix hors d'oeuvre.

Chill beans, asparagus, snap peas, baby corn, artichoke hearts, peppers, garbanzo beans, and olives in their individual jars or cans. Wash carrots; trim, peel and slice on the diagonal. Trim and wash radishes. Put carrots and radishes into a bowl of ice water and place in refrigerator to crisp. Wash tomatoes and lettuce.

Just before serving, thoroughly drain vegetables. Pat dry with paper towels. Arrange beans, asparagus, snap peas, corn, artichoke hearts, peppers, garbanzo beans, carrots, radishes, and tomatoes in mounds in a lettuce-lined basket. Tuck olives among the mounds.

*Sodium Alert: Choose low-sodium foods at other meals throughout the day to offset the high sodium in this recipe.

Variation: Add ¼ pound thinly sliced lean Prosciutto Di Parma (be sure to cut away any visible fat.) Roll each slice like a cigar. Tuck around the edge of the platter.

APPROXIMATE NUTRITIONAL INFORMATION PER SERVING

Total calories: 154
Total fat: 2 g
Saturated fat: 0 g
Dietary fiber: 5 g
Carbohydrates: 26 g
Protein: 6 g
Cholesterol: 0 mg
Sodium: 837 mg

Caponata

8 1/2-cup servings

1 large eggplant (about 2 pounds)

1 8-ounce can tomato sauce

3 garlic cloves, minced

1 green pepper, seeded and chopped

1 to 2 teaspoons cumin

¼ teaspoon cayenne

¾ teaspoon Kosher salt

1 teaspoon sugar

¼ cup red wine vinegar

Dice unpeeled eggplant; place in a 4-quart saucepan. Add remaining ingredients. Cover and cook over medium heat for 20 minutes, stirring frequently. Uncover and cook 30 minutes more, or until thick.

Serving Suggestions: Serve hot or cold with crusty French bread; or as a side dish to roast chicken or beef; or over pasta. Especially nice on a picnic with roast chicken.

APPROXIMATE NUTRITIONAL INFORMATION PER SERVING

Total calories: 31
Total fat: 0 g
Saturated fat: 0 g
Dietary fiber: 3 g
Carbohydrates: 8 g
Protein: 1 g
Cholesterol: 0 mg
Sodium: 299 mg

Spring Rolls

24 servings

2 dozen spring roll (lumpia) wrappers

¾ pound pork loin, ground

2 tablespoons ginger juice*

1 teaspoon sake

1 teaspoon reduced-sodium soy sauce

1 tablespoon olive oil

¼ pound bamboo shoots, washed and cut into 2-inch lengths

3 to 4 green onions, cut into thin 2-inch lengths

5 to 6 shiitake mushrooms, thinly sliced

½ teaspoon potato starch

½ cup water

Olive oil

Fresh Italian parsley for garnish

⅓ cup Soy Sauce and Rice Vinegar Sauce (page 217)

Thaw spring roll wrappers. Sprinkle pork with ginger juice,* sake, and soy sauce; let stand 20 minutes. Brown pork in a nonstick skillet over medium heat; set aside.

Sauté bamboo shoots and onions in olive oil using a wok or heavy skillet; when barely tender, add mushrooms; cook 2 to 3 minutes. Cool to room temperature.

In a small saucepan, bring potato starch and water to a boil. Remove from heat; cool to room temperature.

Separate spring roll wrappers and lay them flat. Toss vegetables with pork; place 3 to 4 tablespoons of mixture in the center of each wrapper. Brush outside edges of wrappers with potato-starch mixture and fold edges over, envelope style. Seal outside seam with potato-starch mixture.

Brown spring rolls in a nonstick skillet over medium heat for 10 minutes, or until very hot, or brown in a heavy skillet using a very small amount of olive oil—just enough to coat bottom of pan. Arrange spring rolls on a bed of fresh parsley and serve with Soy Sauce and Rice Vinegar Sauce.

Note: Spring roll (lumpia) wrappers are available in Asian markets and in the Asian section of many supermarkets.

*To make ginger juice, purée a 2½-inch piece of peeled fresh ginger in a food processor, squeeze the pulp to obtain the ginger juice.

APPROXIMATE NUTRITIONAL INFORMATION PER SERVING

Total calories: 273
Total fat: 2 g
Saturated fat: 0 g
Dietary fiber: 0 g
Carbohydrates: 61 g
Protein: 16 g
Cholesterol: 13 mg
Sodium: 197 mg

Mini Cheese Burritos

4 servings

4 6-inch corn or flour tortillas

⅓ cup grated reduced-fat cheddar cheese

2 tablespoons chopped green chilies or jalapenos peppers

2 tablespoons finely chopped tomato

2 tablespoons finely chopped onion

¼ cup Tomato Salsa, preferably homemade (page 214)

¼ cup nonfat sour cream

Lay tortillas flat; sprinkle with cheese, chilies, tomato, and onion. Roll each into a tight roll. Heat at 350°F. for 5 to 6 minutes. Serve with salsa and sour cream.

APPROXIMATE NUTRITIONAL INFORMATION PER SERVING

Total calories: 98
Total fat: 2 g
Saturated fat: 1 g
Dietary fiber: 1 g
Carbohydrates: 15 g
Protein: 5 g
Cholesterol: 7 mg
Sodium: 237 mg

Appetizer Cheese Tostados

4 servings

4 6-inch corn or flour tortillas

½ cup grated reduced-fat cheddar cheese

½ cup Tomato Salsa, preferably homemade (page 214)

½ cup Black Bean Dip (page 91)

2 cups shredded lettuce

1 ripe tomato, diced

Place tortillas on a nonstick baking sheet; sprinkle with cheese. Bake at 350°F. until cheese is melted and tortilla is crisp. Serve with salsa, bean dip, lettuce, and tomato.

APPROXIMATE NUTRITIONAL INFORMATION PER SERVING

Total calories: 97
Total fat: 3 g
Saturated fat: 2 g
Dietary fiber: 1 g
Carbohydrates: 12 g
Protein: 6 g
Cholesterol: 10 mg
Sodium: 153 mg

Nachos

2 servings

20–22 heart-healthy tortilla chips*

2 tablespoons chopped green chilies

½ cup grated reduced-fat cheddar cheese

¼ cup Tomato Salsa, preferably homemade (page 214)

Arrange chips on a nonstick baking sheet. Sprinkle with green chilies. Top with cheese. Bake at 350°F. for 6 to 8 minutes, or until cheese is melted. Serve with salsa for dipping.

* Look for tortilla chips made with heart-healthy oils, such as sunflower, corn, soybean, or canola oil

APPROXIMATE NUTRITIONAL INFORMATION PER SERVING

Calories: 147
Total fat: 6 g
Saturated fat: 3 g
Dietary fiber: 0 g
Carbohydrate: 16 g
Protein: 11 g
Cholesterol: 20 mg
Sodium: 326 mg

Black Bean Dip

10 servings

1 15-ounce can black beans, drained but not rinsed

1 tablespoon chili powder

½ teaspoon ground cumin

¼ teaspoon Kosher salt

Combine all ingredients in a food processor and process until smooth, 2 to 3 minutes. Taste. Add additional salt if needed. Accompany with salsa.

Serve with cut-up celery, carrots, cucumber and jicama sticks, heart-healthy tortilla chips, or warm flour tortillas.

Red Bean Dip: Substitute red kidney beans for black beans.

APPROXIMATE NUTRITIONAL INFORMATION PER TABLESPOON

Total calories: 24
Total fat: 0 g
Saturated fat: 0 g
Dietary fiber: 2 g
Carbohydrates: 4 g
Protein: 4 g
Cholesterol: 0 mg
Sodium: 126 mg

Layered Bean Dip

10 servings

1 15-ounce can red kidney beans, drained but not rinsed

1 tablespoon chili powder

½ teaspoon ground cumin

¼ teaspoon Kosher salt

⅓ cup nonfat sour cream

¾ cup shredded lettuce

⅓ chopped white onion

1 ripe tomato, diced

¼ cup grated reduced-fat cheddar cheese

1½ cups Tomato Salsa, preferably homemade (page 214)

Purée kidney beans in food processor. Add chili powder, cumin, and salt, and whirl 1 minute longer. Chill for at least 1 hour. Spread onto a 10-inch serving tray. Top with sour cream. Sprinkle with lettuce, then onion, tomato, and cheddar cheese. Accompany with salsa.

Serving Suggestion: Ring with heart-healthy tortilla chips and carrot and celery sticks to scoop up the dip.

APPROXIMATE NUTRITIONAL INFORMATION PER SERVING

Total calories: 80
Total fat: 1 g
Saturated fat: 0 g
Dietary fiber: 4 g
Carbohydrates: 13 g
Protein: 5 g
Cholesterol: 0 mg
Sodium: 330 mg

White Bean and Garlic Dip

1 1/2 cups

1 15-ounce can cannellini beans, drained and rinsed

2–3 large cloves garlic, peeled

1 tablespoon fresh lemon juice

1 tablespoon extra-virgin olive oil

½ teaspoon Kosher salt

¼ teaspoon white pepper

Here's another dip for your vegetables, and because it's made with beans, you get some fiber.

Combine all ingredients in a food processor and process 2 to 3 minutes until smooth.

Serve with cut-up celery and carrot sticks, radishes, broccoli and cauliflower florets, warm breadsticks or pita bread, or sliced and toasted bagels.

APPROXIMATE NUTRITIONAL INFORMATION PER TABLESPOON

Total calories: 20
Total fat: 5 g
Saturated fat: 0 g
Dietary fiber: 1 g
Carbohydrates: 3 g
Protein: 1 g
Cholesterol: 0 mg
Sodium: 51 mg

Hummus

Makes 2 3/4 cups

⅓ cup sesame paste (tahini)

¼ cup fresh lemon juice

1 tablespoon extra-virgin olive oil

2 tablespoons water

4 cloves garlic

½ teaspoon salt

½ teaspoon cumin

½ teaspoon black pepper

1 20-ounce can garbanzo beans (chick peas), drained and rinsed

1 bunch watercress

½ red onion, coarsely chopped

1½ white onion, coarsely chopped

In a food processor, process sesame paste until smooth. Add lemon juice, olive oil, water, garlic, salt, cumin, black pepper, and garbanzo beans. Blend until beans are puréed and mixture is smooth.

Arrange watercress on a serving platter. Mound dip in center and garnish with red and white onion.

Serving Suggestion: Serve with carrots, celery, radishes, and homemade warm breadsticks or toasted pita bread, toasted English muffins or toasted bagels.

APPROXIMATE NUTRITIONAL INFORMATION PER TABLESPOON

Total calories: 19
Total fat: 1 g
Saturated fat: trace
Dietary fiber: trace
Carbohydrates: 2 g
Protein: trace
Cholesterol: 0 mg
Sodium: 61 mg

Artichoke Dip

1 cup

1 15-ounce can artichoke bottoms, drained

3 tablespoons extra-virgin olive oil

3 large cloves garlic, peeled

2 tablespoons freshly grated Parmesan cheese

½ teaspoon Kosher salt

¼ teaspoon white pepper

Great with raw vegetables or as a spread on grilled or toasted French or Tuscan bread.

Combine artichoke bottoms, olive oil and garlic in a food processor and process until smooth. Add cheese, salt and pepper and process until combined, about 30 seconds.

Variation: Double the recipe and stir in ¼ cup cooked Dungeness crabmeat. Serve with pretzel chips.

APPROXIMATE NUTRITIONAL INFORMATION PER TABLESPOON

Total calories: 33
Total fat: 3 g
Saturated fat: 0 g
Dietary fiber: 1 g
Carbohydrates: 1 g
Protein: 1 g
Cholesterol: 1 mg
Sodium: 125 mg

Quick Avocado Dip

1 cup

1 ripe avocado

1 tablespoon fresh lime juice

⅛ teaspoon Kosher salt

1 tablespoon grated onion (optional)

Use this dip in moderation with fresh vegetables such as fresh carrots and radishes, or as a complement to Mexican food.

In a small bowl, mash avocado with a fork. Add lime juice and salt. Stir with fork until avocado is smooth. Add onion, if desired.

Avocado Shrimp Dip: Add ½ cup cooked shrimp to mixture above.

APPROXIMATE NUTRITIONAL INFORMATION PER TABLESPOON

Total calories: 26
Total fat: 3 g
Saturated fat: 0 g
Dietary fiber: 0 g
Carbohydrates: 2 g
Protein: 1 g
Cholesterol: 8 mg
Sodium: 28 mg

Sour Cream Dip

2 cups

1 cup nonfat sour cream

1 cup nonfat cottage cheese

2 tablespoons light mayonnaise

1 0.4-ounce package Hidden Valley Ranch Original Ranch Salad Dressing Mix (Buttermilk Recipe)

You may want to serve this dip as a condiment for baked potatoes, chili or Jumbo Oven Fries (page 379). It works equally well as a fresh vegetable dip.

Combine sour cream, cottage cheese, mayonnaise, and salad dressing mix. Chill.

APPROXIMATE NUTRITIONAL INFORMATION PER TABLESPOON

Total calories: 13
Total fat: 0 g
Saturated fat: 0 g
Dietary fiber: 0 g
Carbohydrates: 0 g
Protein: 1 g
Cholesterol: 1 mg
Sodium: 44 mg

Italian Eggplant Dip

1 1/2 cups

1 1½ -pound eggplant

1½ tablespoons fresh lemon juice

3 cloves garlic

1½ tablespoons sesame paste (tahini)

1 tablespoon olive oil

½ teaspoon Kosher salt

¼ teaspoon black pepper

2 tablespoons minced Italian parsley

2 tablespoons pine nuts

Pierce eggplant all over with a fork. Place in a foil-lined ovenproof dish. Broil about 4 inches from heat, turning frequently, 20–30 minutes or until skin is charred and eggplant is mushy and falling apart. Remove from heat. Place eggplant in a colander. Slit one side and let drain ½ hour.

Scoop out the eggplant pulp (should yield about 1 cup). Put pulp into a blender or food processor; add lemon juice and purée. Add garlic, sesame paste, olive oil, salt, and pepper. Process until smooth. Add minced parsley and pine nuts. Process 1 minute more. Chill, the longer the better. (Flavor is even better the second day.)

Serving Suggestion: Serve with Cajun Flatbread still warm from the oven (page 60) and plenty of celery, carrots, and crispy vegetables for dipping. Also excellent with toasted bagels or toasted English muffins.

APPROXIMATE NUTRITIONAL INFORMATION PER TABLESPOON

Total calories: 21
Total fat: 1 g
Saturated fat: 0 g
Dietary fiber: 1 g
Carbohydrates: 2 g
Protein: trace
Cholesterol: 0 mg
Sodium: 45 mg

Vegetable Crudités with Tomato and Chili Salsa

4 servings

2 large carrots

2 stalks celery

1 turnip

½ English cucumber

1 bunch radishes

1 cup Tomato and Chili Salsa (page 217)

Cut carrots, celery, turnip, and English cucumber into sticks. Cut radishes into flowers. Serve with Tomato-and-Chili Salsa.

Add 20 calories per ¼ cup of salsa.

APPROXIMATE NUTRITIONAL INFORMATION PER SERVING WITHOUT SALSA

Total calories: 39
Total fat: 0 g
Saturated fat: 0 g
Dietary fiber: 2 g
Carbohydrates: 8 g
Protein: 1 g
Cholesterol: 0 mg
Sodium: 55 mg

Stuffed Mushrooms

28 mushrooms

1 pound large fresh mushrooms (about 28)

½ cup Italian Vinaigrette (page 204)

1 bunch fresh spinach leaves, about 3 cups

2 teaspoons light mayonnaise

2 tablespoons grated onion

1 tablespoon lemon juice

6 ounces crabmeat

¼ cup grated reduced-fat cheddar cheese

Clean and stem mushrooms. Marinate in dressing for 1 hour; drain on paper towels. Use additional papertowels to blot extra oil. Wash spinach leaves; shake, but do not dry. Cook covered in a heavy skillet for 2 to 3 minutes, or until spinach is wilted. Drain, squeeze out excess moisture, and chop. Combine mayonnaise, onion, and lemon juice. Toss with crab and spinach. Stuff mushrooms; sprinkle with cheese. Bake at 375°F. for 15 minutes.

APPROXIMATE NUTRITIONAL INFORMATION PER MUSHROOM

Total calories: 20
Total fat: 0 g
Saturated fat: 0 g
Dietary fiber: 0 g
Carbohydrates: 1 g
Protein: 2 g
Cholesterol: 5 mg
Sodium: 45 mg

Marinated Mushrooms

28 mushrooms

1 pound fresh mushrooms (about 28)

1 cup Italian Vinaigrette (page 204)

2 garlic cloves

1 bunch fresh Italian parsley for garnish

1 lemon, cut into thin rounds

Clean and stem mushrooms. Place in a large saucepan, and toss with viniagrette and garlic. Cook over medium-high heat for 20 to 30 minutes, stirring frequently. Remove from heat; cool to room temperature. Drain. *Chill.

Cover a serving plate with fresh parsley; top with lemon rounds. Spoon mushrooms over lemons.

Note: Marinated mushrooms will keep several days in the refrigerator.

*Remaining liquid may be used as a marinade for another batch of mushrooms. It also works well as a marinade for artichoke hearts, or as a salad dressing.

APPROXIMATE NUTRITIONAL INFORMATION PER MUSHROOM

Total calories: 15
Total fat: 1 g
Saturated fat: 0 g
Dietary fiber: 0 g
Carbohydrates: 1 g
Protein: 0 g
Cholesterol: 0 mg
Sodium: 15 mg

Little Red Potato Appetizers

10 servings (1 whole potato each)

10 bite-sized red potatoes

¼ cup reduced-fat cream cheese

¼ cup nonfat sour cream

3 green onions with tops, finely chopped

2 tablespoons grated reduced-fat cheddar cheese

2 tablespoons Tomato Salsa, preferably homemade (page 214)

Cut potatoes in half; microwave or steam until just tender. Cool. Using a grapefruit spoon, scoop out about one third of flesh from center of each potato half (reserve for another use).

Combine cream cheese with sour cream. Add green onions.

Just before serving, place about 1 teaspoon of cream cheese mixture in center of each potato. Dot half the potatoes with cheese and the other half with salsa. Arrange on a round serving tray. Serve cold or at room temperature.

Variation: Top some of the potatoes with pitted black olive halves.

APPROXIMATE NUTRITIONAL INFORMATION PER SERVING

Total calories: 80
Total fat: 1 g
Saturated fat: trace
Dietary fiber: 1 g
Carbohydrates: 15 g
Protein: 3 g
Cholesterol: 5 mg
Sodium: 65 mg

Oysters Rockefeller

6 servings

12 cups trimmed fresh spinach (about 2 bunches)

1 tablespoon extra-virgin olive oil

2 tablespoons dry bread crumbs

1 tablespoon grated onion

½ teaspoon chervil (optional)

½ teaspoon salt

1 fresh tarragon sprig or ¼ teaspoon dried (optional)

⅛ teaspoon pepper

2 to 3 drops Tabasco sauce

30 extra-small oysters

¼ cup grated part-skin mozzarella cheese

Steam spinach 2 to 3 minutes; squeeze dry and chop. Toss with olive oil. Combine bread crumbs, olive oil, onion, and seasonings; toss with spinach. Divide well-drained oysters into 6-inch ramekins and broil or grill 5 to 7 minutes, or until very hot; drain excess liquid. Top oysters with spinach mixture; broil 3 to 4 minutes. Sprinkle with cheese; broil 2 to 3 minutes longer, or until cheese is melted and mixture is piping hot.

Note: If using unshucked oysters, thoroughly wash them. Open shells with an oyster knife or other blunt-tipped knife. Remove oysters and dry. Discard flat-top shells; wash deep-bottom shells. Place each oyster in a shell, then spoon 2 to 3 tablespoons of spinach mixture on top and broil or grill as above.

APPROXIMATE NUTRITIONAL INFORMATION PER SERVING

Total calories: 157
Total fat: 7 g
Saturated fat: 0 g
Dietary fiber: 2 g
Carbohydrates: 10 g
Protein: 15 g
Cholesterol: 73 mg
Sodium: 398 mg

Crab and Artichokes Dijon

8 servings

½ pound crabmeat

1 14½-ounce can water-packed artichoke hearts, drained

2 green onions, minced

2 tablespoons Dijon Vinaigrette (page 207)

Fresh parsley for garnish

8 slices crusty French bread, cut into halves

Combine crab, artichoke hearts, and green onion; chill. Just before serving, toss with Dijon Vinaigrette. Garnish with fresh parsley. Serve with crusty French bread.

APPROXIMATE NUTRITIONAL INFORMATION PER SERVING

Total calories: 101
Total fat: 1 g
Saturated fat: 0 g
Dietary fiber: 1 g
Carbohydrates: 14 g
Protein: 8 g
Cholesterol: 28 mg
Sodium: 336 mg

Spinach and Crab Cocotte

6 servings

6 cups trimmed fresh spinach (about 1 bunch)

¾ pound crabmeat

¼ teaspoon Dijon mustard

2 teaspoons light mayonnaise

3 to 4 drops Tabasco sauce

2 tablespoons grated reduced-fat cheddar cheese

6 cherry tomatoes for garnish

Tear spinach into bite-size pieces. Toss crabmeat with mustard and just enough mayonnaise to moisten; dot with Tabasco sauce. Line individual shells or ramekins with spinach; top with crab mixture. Sprinkle with cheese. Bake at 375°F. for 5 to 10 minutes, or just until cheese melts. Garnish with cherry tomatoes.

APPROXIMATE NUTRITIONAL INFORMATION PER SERVING

Total calories: 81
Total fat: 2 g
Saturated fat: 1 g
Dietary fiber: 0 g
Carbohydrates: 2 g
Protein: 13 g
Cholesterol: 58 mg
Sodium: 215 mg

Steamed Mussels with Wine and Garlic

6 servings

4 pounds fresh mussels

¾ cup dry white wine

3 garlic cloves

Scrub mussel shells with a wire brush. Remove and discard beards. Rinse mussels in cold water, discarding broken or open mussels. Place mussels in a steamer; add wine and garlic. Cover tightly; steam 6 to 8 minutes, or just until shells open. Drain. Serve hot or cold.

APPROXIMATE NUTRITIONAL INFORMATION PER SERVING

Total calories: 140
Total fat: 4 g
Saturated fat: 1 g
Dietary fiber: 0 g
Carbohydrates: 6 g
Protein: 19 g
Cholesterol: 45 mg
Sodium: 295 mg

Steamed Clams Bordelaise

4 servings

2 dozen clams

1 tablespoon extra-virgin olive oil

¼ cup dry white wine

1 small onion, chopped

2 garlic cloves, minced

1 celery stalk, chopped

Fresh Italian parsley

Fresh lemon wedges for garnish

Scrub clams and soak in salt water or cornmeal in water to remove sand. Rinse thoroughly. Place clams in a steamer. Add olive oil, wine, onion, garlic, and celery. Cover and bring to a boil. Reduce heat; simmer 10 minutes, or just until shells open. Drain. Arrange on a bed of fresh parsley. Garnish with lemon wedges.

APPROXIMATE NUTRITIONAL INFORMATION PER SERVING

Total calories: 46
Total fat: 1 g
Saturated fat: 0 g
Dietary fiber: 1 g
Carbohydrates: 4 g
Protein: 7 g
Cholesterol: 18 mg
Sodium: 32 mg

Sea Scallops with Tomatoes and Green Chilies

8 servings

1½ pounds fresh sea scallops

½ cup fresh lime juice

¼ cup chopped white onion

¼ cup chopped green chilies

1 large ripe tomato, chopped

¼ cup chopped fresh parsley

2 tablespoons extra-virgin olive oil

½ teaspoon salt

¼ teaspoon black pepper

6 drops Tabasco sauce

1 bunch fresh Italian parsley

1 lemon, cut into wedges, for garnish

Cut each scallop into thirds. Cover with lime juice and marinate in refrigerator 4 hours. Pour off juice.

Preheat a nonstick skillet. Add scallops and cook, turning frequently, 4 to 6 minutes, or just until scallops are tender. Remove from pan; drain all excess liquid. Chill scallops for several hours. Combine onion, green chilies, and tomato. Chill several hours.

Just before serving, combine scallops with tomato mixture; add chopped parsley. Toss with olive oil, salt, pepper, and Tabasco. Arrange on a bed of parsley in individual shells or ramekins. Garnish with lemon wedges.

Note: To adjust this recipe, plan on 3 scallops per person. This sea scallop dish makes a great appetizer or first course and may also be served as a salad.

APPROXIMATE NUTRITIONAL INFORMATION PER SERVING

Total calories: 109
Total fat: 4 g
Saturated fat: 1 g
Dietary fiber: 0 g
Carbohydrates: 7 g
Protein: 12 g
Cholesterol: 23 mg
Sodium: 247 mg

Layered Shrimp Dip

10 servings

1 8-ounce package reduced-fat cream cheese

⅓ cup cocktail sauce

½ pound small cooked shrimp or crabmeat

6 carrots, peeled and cut diagonally into thirds

6 celery stalks, cut diagonally into thirds

1 7-ounce package heart-healthy tortilla chips*

Spread cream cheese in center of a 10-inch serving tray, keeping the edges neat and uniform. Use the back of a serving spoon to smooth out the surface. Pour the cocktail sauce over the cream cheese and spread it evenly. Sprinkle shrimp or crabmeat over top. Chill until ready to serve. Ring with celery and carrot sticks and/or tortilla chips to scoop up the dip.

*Make sure the tortilla chips are made with a heart-healthy oil, such as sunflower, corn, soybean, or canola. Keep in mind about 13 tortilla chips have about 130 calories and 120 milligrams of sodium.

APPROXIMATE NUTRITIONAL INFORMATION PER SERVING

Total calories: 90
Total fat: 4 g
Saturated fat: 2 g
Dietary fiber: 2 g
Carbohydrates: 9 g
Protein: 8 g
Cholesterol: 40 mg
Sodium: 390 mg

Melon and Prosciutto

12 servings

1 3-pound cantaloupe

¼ pound thinly sliced prosciutto

1 bunch fresh Italian parsley

¼ pound seedless green grapes

¼ pound seedless red grapes

Cut cantaloupe into 12 thin wedges and remove rind. Wrap each wedge with a slice of prosciutto. Arrange on a parsley-lined tray; tuck grapes in center and among cantaloupe wedges.

APPROXIMATE NUTRITIONAL INFORMATION PER SERVING

Total calories: 67
Total fat: 2 g
Saturated fat: 0 g
Dietary fiber: trace
Carbohydrates: 11 g
Protein: 3 g
Cholesterol: 7 mg
Sodium: 252 mg

Sandwiches

French Veggie

1 sandwich

2 slices whole grain bread

1 teaspoon mayonnaise

¼ teaspoon Dijon mustard

2 slices ripe tomato

¼ zucchini, thinly sliced

leaf lettuce

Spread bread with mayonnaise and mustard. Layer with tomatoes, zucchini, and lettuce. Top with second slice of bread.

Variation: Add 1 ounce thinly sliced part-skim mozzarella. It adds 60 calories and 4 grams of fat per slice.

APPROXIMATE NUTRITIONAL INFORMATION PER SANDWICH

Total calories: 290
Total fat: 10 g
Saturated fat: 0 g
Dietary fiber: 0 g
Carbohydrates: 47 g
Protein: 11 g
Cholesterol: 0 mg
Sodium: 450 mg

Lettuce and Tomato on Whole-Grain

1 open-faced sandwich

1 slice toasted whole-grain bread

¼ teaspoon Dijon Vinaigrette (page 207)

Bibb lettuce

sliced ripe tomatoes

black pepper

Spread toast with Dijon Vinaigrette. Layer with lettuce and tomatoes. Season generously with black pepper.

APPROXIMATE NUTRITIONAL INFORMATION PER SANDWICH

Total calories: 92
Total fat: 2 g
Saturated fat: 0 g
Dietary fiber: 3 g
Carbohydrates: 17 g
Protein: 3 g
Cholesterol: 0 mg
Sodium: 197 mg

Veggie Sandwich with Cream Cheese

1 sandwich

2 slices whole-grain bread

1½ tablespoons reduced fat cream cheese

4 cucumber slices

2 lettuce leaves

2 tomato slices

1 white onion slice

Spread 1 slice of bread with cream cheese. Layer with remaining ingredients. Top with remaining slice of bread. Serve.

APPROXIMATE NUTRITIONAL INFORMATION PER SANDWICH

Total calories: 240
Total fat: 6 g
Saturated fat: 2 g
Dietary fiber: 5 g
Carbohydrates: 37 g
Protein: 10 g
Cholesterol: 10 mg
Sodium: 380 mg

Tuna, Red Onion, and Tomato

6 open-faced sandwiches

1 6-ounce can water-packed tuna

1 tablespoon fresh lemon juice

3 tablespoons light mayonnaise*

6 slices pumpernickel rye

1 red onion, thinly sliced

1 large ripe tomato, thinly sliced

Bibb lettuce

Thoroughly drain tuna. Using a fork, mix tuna with lemon juice, then mayonnaise. Spread mixture over bread. Top with onion, tomato, and lettuce.

*To further reduce the fat content of this recipe, use less mayonnaise.

APPROXIMATE NUTRITIONAL INFORMATION PER SERVING

Total calories: 150
Total fat: 4 g
Saturated fat: trace
Dietary fiber: 2 g
Carbohydrates: 19 g
Protein: 10 g
Cholesterol: 20 mg
Sodium: 390 mg

Tuna Salad Sandwich

3 sandwiches

1 tablespoon fresh lemon juice

1 6-ounce can water-packed tuna, drained

3 tablespoons minced onion

2 tablespoons minced celery

2 tablespoons finely chopped water chestnuts

3 tablespoons light mayonnaise

Dash of prepared mustard

6 slices whole-wheat or rye bread

6 ripe tomato slices

6 large lettuce leaves

Sprinkle lemon juice over tuna; toss with onion, celery, and water chestnuts. Moisten with mayonnaise and mustard. Spread 3 slices of bread with filling; top each with tomato and lettuce and second slice of bread. Cut sandwich in half and serve.

APPROXIMATE NUTRITIONAL INFORMATION PER SANDWICH

Total calories: 310
Total fat: 8 g
Saturated fat: 1 g
Dietary fiber: 5 g
Carbohydrates: 37 g
Protein: 22 g
Cholesterol: 35 mg
Sodium: 620 mg

Monte Cristo

3 sandwiches

1 6-ounce can water-packed tuna, drained

1 tablespoon lemon juice

3 tablespoons light mayonnaise

6 slices whole-wheat bread

2 eggs, beaten

Moisten tuna with lemon and mayonnaise. Dip 1 slice of bread into beaten egg; place on a preheated nonstick griddle. Spread with tuna. Dip second slice of bread into beaten egg; place over tuna. Brown sandwiches on both sides, turning only once. Cut sandwich in half and serve.

Variation: Add sliced tomato or white onion.

APPROXIMATE NUTRITIONAL INFORMATION PER SANDWICH

Total calories: 330
Total fat: 10 g
Saturated fat: 1.5 g
Dietary fiber: 4 g
Carbohydrates: 34 g
Protein: 25 g
Cholesterol: 145 mg
Sodium: 660 mg

Hot Tuna Sandwich

4 servings

1 6-ounce can water-packed tuna, drained

2 tablespoons finely chopped green pepper

2 tablespoons finely chopped celery

2 tablespoons finely chopped onion

2 tablespoons light mayonnaise

2 English muffins, halved and toasted

4 reduced fat cheddar cheese slices

Combine tuna, green pepper, celery, and onion; moisten with mayonnaise. Spread on muffin halves. Place under a preheated broiler for 2 to 3 minutes. Top with cheese; broil 2 to 3 minutes, or until cheese melts.

APPROXIMATE NUTRITIONAL INFORMATION PER SANDWICH

Total calories: 190
Total fat: 5 g
Saturated fat: 1 g
Dietary fiber: 0 g
Carbohydrates: 15 g
Protein: 19 g
Cholesterol: 30 mg
Sodium: 510 mg

Crabmeat and Tomato

1 sandwich

¼ cup crabmeat

2 teaspoons mayonnaise mixed with ¼ teaspoon fresh lemon juice

2 thick slices crusty French bread

2 ripe tomato slices

red leaf lettuce

Mix crabmeat with mayonnaise. Spread on bread. Top with tomato slices, lettuce, and second slice of bread.

APPROXIMATE NUTRITIONAL INFORMATION PER SANDWICH

Total calories: 465
Total fat: 12 g
Saturated fat: 2 g
Dietary fiber: 5 g
Carbohydrates: 70 g
Protein: 12 g
Cholesterol: 39 mg
Sodium: 765 mg

Hot Crab and Cheese Sandwich

4 open-face sandwiches

½ **teaspoon fresh lemon juice**

½ **pound crabmeat**

2 tablespoons minced white onion

2 tablespoons light mayonnaise

2 English muffins, halved and toasted

4 tomato slices

4 nonfat cheddar cheese slices

Squeeze lemon juice over crab; toss with onion. Moisten with mayonnaise. Spread over toasted muffin halves. Place under a preheated broiler for 2 to 3 minutes, or until hot. Top each muffin with tomato and cheese. Broil 3 to 5 minutes or until cheese melts.

APPROXIMATE NUTRITIONAL INFORMATION PER SANDWICH

Total calories: 200
Total fat: 6 g
Saturated fat: 1 g
Dietary fiber: 0 g
Carbohydrates: 16 g
Protein: 21 g
Cholesterol: 50 mg
Sodium: 530 mg

Lobster Sandwich

3 sandwiches

6 ounces cooked lobster meat

1 teaspoon lemon juice

2 celery stalks, minced

2 tablespoons light mayonnaise

6 slices rye or sourdough bread

6 tomato slices

6 lettuce leaves

Sprinkle lobster with lemon juice; toss with celery. Moisten with mayonnaise. Top 3 slices of rye or sourdough bread with lobster mixture, tomatoes, lettuce, and another slice of bread. Cut sandwich in half and serve.

APPROXIMATE NUTRITIONAL INFORMATION PER SANDWICH

Total calories: 272
Total fat: 6 g
Saturated fat: 1 g
Dietary fiber: 5 g
Carbohydrates: 36 g
Protein: 18 g
Cholesterol: 41 mg
Sodium: 658 mg

Lox and Bagels

4 servings

2 fresh bagels

3 tablespoons reduced-fat cream cheese

4 thin slices of white onion

¼ pound thinly sliced lox or smoked salmon

1 tomato, thinly sliced (optional)

Cut bagels in half. Spread each half with cream cheese. Top with onion and lox. Garnish with sliced tomatoes, if desired.

APPROXIMATE NUTRITIONAL INFORMATION PER SERVING

Total calories: 210
Total fat: 3.5 g
Saturated fat: 1.5 g
Dietary fiber: 1 g
Carbohydrates: 22 g
Protein: 10 g
Cholesterol: 15 mg
Sodium: 446 mg

Shrimp Baguette Sandwiches

6 servings

1 12-inch French baguette

1 tablespoon mayonnaise

6 tomato slices

12 English cucumber slices

1 cup shredded lettuce

½ pound cooked shrimpmeat

Cut a baguette in half lengthwise. Spread mayonnaise over each half. Layer bottom half with remaining ingredients. Top with remaining baguette half. Cut diagonally into 6 servings.

Serving Suggestions: Serve with Asparagus, Tomato and Pasta Salad (page 176) or Marinated Peppers and Onions (page 165) and Lemon Chiffon Pie (page 406).

APPROXIMATE NUTRITIONAL INFORMATION PER SERVING

Total calories: 257
Total fat: 5 g
Saturated fat: 1 g
Dietary fiber: 2 g
Carbohydrates: 37 g
Protein: 15 g
Cholesterol: 75 mg
Sodium: 486 mg

Chicken and Shrimp Club Sandwich

1 sandwich

3 slices whole-wheat toast

6 lettuce leaves

1 ounce cooked chicken breast, sliced

1½ teaspoons light mayonnaise

3 tomato slices

1 ounce small cooked shrimp

⅕ avocado, thinly sliced (optional)

Top first slice of toast with lettuce, chicken, and mayonnaise. Top with second slice of toast; add tomato slices, avocado, and shrimp; top with third slice of toast. Slice diagonally into quarters.

APPROXIMATE NUTRITIONAL INFORMATION PER SANDWICH

Total calories: 369
Total fat: 12 g
Saturated fat: 3 g
Dietary fiber: 8 g
Carbohydrates: 46 g
Protein: 23 g
Cholesterol: 77 mg
Sodium: 590 mg

Breast of Chicken Sandwich

1 sandwich

2 slices whole-wheat or multi-grain bread

2 teaspoons light mayonnaise

2 ounces poached chicken breast (page 295)

2 Bibb lettuce leaves

2 tomato slices

Spread 1 slice of bread with mayonnaise; top with remaining ingredients and other bread slice. Cut sandwich in half or diagonally into quarters and serve.

Variation: Substitute turkey for chicken.

APPROXIMATE NUTRITIONAL INFORMATION PER SANDWICH

Total calories: 268
Total fat: 8 g
Saturated fat: 2 g
Dietary fiber: 4 g
Carbohydrates: 29 g
Protein: 22 g
Cholesterol: 44 mg
Sodium: 412 mg

Chicken Salad Sandwich

Makes 3 sandwiches

1 cup chopped cooked chicken

½ cup finely chopped celery

¼ cup finely chopped water chestnuts

2 tablespoons light mayonnaise

6 slices whole-wheat or pumpernickel bread

6 large lettuce leaves

6 ripe tomato slices

Combine chicken, celery, water chestnuts, and mayonnaise. Chill. Just before serving, spread 3 slices of the bread with filling; top with lettuce, tomato, and an additional slice of bread. Cut sandwich in half and serve.

APPROXIMATE NUTRITIONAL INFORMATION PER SANDWICH

Total calories: 226
Total fat: 5 g
Saturated fat: 1 g
Dietary fiber: 4 g
Carbohydrates: 32 g
Protein: 15 g
Cholesterol: 23 mg
Sodium: 381 mg

Poached Chicken on Dill Rye

1 sandwich

½ poached chicken breast (see page 295)

2 slices dill rye bread

1 teaspoon mayonnaise

Bibb lettuce

Tear chicken into strings. Spread bread with mayonnaise. Layer with chicken. Top with lettuce and second slice of bread.

Serving Suggestion: Good on a picnic with pasta salad or Tuscan Bean Salad (page 179) and fresh fruit..

APPROXIMATE NUTRITIONAL INFORMATION PER SANDWICH

Total calories: 308
Total fat: 7 g
Saturated fat: 1 g
Dietary fiber: 3 g
Carbohydrates: 28 g
Protein: 30 g
Cholesterol: 67 mg
Sodium: 441 mg

Asian Chicken Sandwiches

12 silver-dollar-size sandwiches

1 tablespoon Chinese Five Spice*

1 teaspoon salt

1 teaspoon granulated sugar

½ teaspoon black pepper

1 pound skinned and boned chicken breasts

2 teaspoons olive oil

1 head Bibb lettuce

4 green onions, thinly sliced

Fresh cilantro (optional)

Black Bean Dip (page 91)

Chinese hot mustard

Hot Chili/Soy Sauce (below)

12 silver-dollar-size baked or steamed Chinese buns or soft dinner rolls, split in half

HOT CHILI/SOY SAUCE:

⅓ cup reduced-sodium soy sauce

1 teaspoon hot chili oil*

Combine Chinese Five Spice, salt, sugar, and pepper. Sprinkle over chicken to coat. Cover and chill overnight.

Thoroughly rinse chicken under cold running water to release salt and seasonings. Drain; pat dry with paper towels. Place chicken in an 8 x 8-inch ovenproof baking dish. Drizzle with olive oil. Bake at 350°F. 20–30 minutes or until done. Slice crosswise into pieces ¼-inch thick.

Line a platter with lettuce and arrange chicken on it. Garnish with green onions and cilantro. Surround with bowls of Black Bean Dip, Chinese hot mustard, and Hot Chili/Soy Sauce. Serve rolls in napkin-lined basket. Each person may then assemble his or her own sandwich.

Note: This recipe takes minutes to prepare the day ahead and less than 30 minutes to prepare before serving.

*Chinese Five Spice and hot chili oil are available in many supermarkets and Asian groceries. Five Spice usually consists of equal parts cinnamon, cloves, fennel, star anise and szechuan peppercorns. It is available in Asian markets and most supermarkets.

Serving Suggestion: Serve with asparagus and sliced oranges with fresh pineapple and papaya.

Add 23 calories per tablespoon of Black Bean Dip. Add 14 calories per tablespoon of Hot Chili/Soy Sauce. Add 18 calories per tablespoon of Chinese hot mustard.

APPROXIMATE NUTRITIONAL INFORMATION PER SANDWICH

Total calories: 159
Total fat: 4 g
Saturated fat: trace
Dietary fiber: 1 g
Carbohydrates: 15 g
Protein: 14 g
Cholesterol: 32 mg
Sodium: 350 mg

Roast Turkey in Pita

10 servings

1 pita (pocket bread)

½ teaspoon mayonnaise

2 ounces roast turkey breast (see page 310)

Bibb lettuce

2 ripe tomato slices

1 thin slice red onion

Spread pita pocket with mayonnaise. Stuff with turkey, lettuce, tomato, and onion.

Serving Suggestion: Good with White Bean Salad (page 178).

APPROXIMATE NUTRITIONAL INFORMATION PER SANDWICH

Total calories: 278
Total fat: 3 g
Saturated fat: 1 g
Dietary fiber: 2 g
Carbohydrates: 37 g
Protein: 23 g
Cholesterol: 50 mg
Sodium: 372 mg

Turkey, Tomato, and Cucumber

2 open-faced sandwiches

2 slices whole wheat or pumpernickel rye bread

½ teaspoon mayonnaise mixed with ⅛ teaspoon fresh lemon juice

2 ounces turkey breast, roasted (see page 310) or poached in broth

1 ripe tomato, thinly sliced

½ cucumber, thinly sliced

black pepper

Spread bread with mayonnaise. Layer each slice with turkey, tomato, and cucumber. Sprinkle with black pepper.

Serving Suggestion: Serve with fresh seasonal fruit.

APPROXIMATE NUTRITIONAL INFORMATION PER OPEN-FACED SANDWICH

Total calories: 147
Total fat: 2 g
Saturated fat: 0 g
Dietary fiber: 3 g
Carbohydrates: 19 g
Protein: 12 g
Cholesterol: 25 mg
Sodium: 217 mg

Cajun Turkey Sandwiches

4 sandwiches

½ **pound Roasted Cajun Turkey Breast**

4 French rolls

1 tablespoon mayonnaise

1 teaspoon Dijon mustard

2 cups shredded leaf lettuce

¾ **small onion, thinly sliced**

1 tomato, thinly sliced

Cut the turkey into thin slices. Spread rolls with mayonnaise and mustard. Fill with turkey, lettuce, onion, and tomato.

Serving Suggestion: Serve with Wild and White Rice Salad (page 177).

,

APPROXIMATE NUTRITIONAL INFORMATION PER SANDWICH

Total calories: 267
Total fat: 5 g
Saturated fat: 0 g
Dietary fiber: 1 g
Carbohydrates: 34 g
Protein: 21 g
Cholesterol: 44 mg
Sodium: 400 mg

Grilled Turkey Sandwiches

6 sandwiches

2 tablespoons fresh lemon juice

1 tablespoon olive oil

¼ **teaspoon black pepper**

1 pound very thin turkey breast fillets

6 very fresh sesame hamburger buns

1 large ripe tomato, sliced

6 thin slices white onion

1 small head Bibb lettuce

Dijon mustard or Lemon Mayonnaise, below (optional)

LEMON MAYONNAISE

¼ **cup mayonnaise**

1½ **teaspoons fresh lemon juice**

1 teaspoon grated lemon zest

In a bowl, combine 2 tablespoons lemon juice, olive oil and pepper; pour over turkey. Marinate 15–20 minutes at room temperature, turning occasionally to coat.

Prepare the grill for direct grilling over medium-high heat. Grill turkey 8–10 minutes on each side or until meat is white in center. Just before removing from grill, arrange buns over top of turkey for about 1 minute to warm. Slice turkey crosswise into pieces ¼ inch thick.

To assemble, pile turkey, tomato, onion, and lettuce on bottom half of bun. Spread top half with Dijon mustard and/or Lemon Mayonnaise, if desired.

Serving Suggestions: Serve with Marinated Potato Salad (page 170), Vegetable and Black Bean Antipasto (page 87), and fresh fruit. For heartier fare, include Fresh Lemonade (page 48) and homemade raisin oatmeal cookies.

Add 18 calories per tablespoon of Dijon mustard. Add 90 calories per tablespoon of Lemon Mayonnaise.

APPROXIMATE NUTRITIONAL INFORMATION PER SANDWICH WITHOUT DIJON MUSTARD OR LEMON MAYONNAISE

Total calories: 249
Total fat: 5 g
Saturated fat: 2 g
Dietary fiber: 0 g
Carbohydrates: 23 g
Protein: 27 g
Cholesterol: 63 mg
Sodium: 283 mg

Turkey Meat Loaf Sandwich

1 sandwich

2 slices crusty French bread or whole-wheat bread

1 teaspoon Dijon mustard

2 slices Turkey Meat Loaf (page 312)

2 teaspoons spicy tomato sauce (see Turkey Meat Loaf)

2 slices tomato

2 slices white onion

2 lettuce leaves

Spread bread with mustard. Top 1 slice with meat loaf. Spread meat loaf with spicy tomato sauce. Top with tomato and onion, then lettuce and other slice of bread.

Serving Suggestion: Serve with Two-Salsa Pasta Salad (page 174) and fresh fruit.

APPROXIMATE NUTRITIONAL INFORMATION PER SANDWICH

Total calories: 357
Total fat: 5 g
Saturated fat: 1 g
Dietary fiber: 5 g
Carbohydrates: 54 g
Protein: 24 g
Cholesterol: 62 mg
Sodium: 425 mg

Barbecued Beef Sandwich

1 sandwich

2 ounces cooked eye-of-round beef roast, thinly sliced

2 tablespoons barbecue sauce

1 French roll

Place beef in a saucepan; cover with sauce. Warm over low heat. Serve on French roll.

Note: Read the label before selecting a barbecue sauce.

APPROXIMATE NUTRITIONAL INFORMATION PER SANDWICH

Total calories: 308
Total fat: 6 g
Saturated fat: 1 g
Dietary fiber: 2 g
Carbohydrates: 40 g
Protein: 22 g
Cholesterol: 40 mg
Sodium: 408 mg

French Dip Sandwich

1 sandwich

1 teaspoon horseradish

1 French roll

2 ounces cooked eye-of-round beef roast, thinly sliced

⅓ cup reduced-fat beef broth, preferably homemade (page 151)

Spread horseradish lightly over French roll; top with beef. Heat broth to boiling; ladle into a shallow bowl. Serve the sandwich with the dipping sauce.

APPROXIMATE NUTRITIONAL INFORMATION PER SANDWICH

Total calories: 277
Total fat: 6 g
Saturated fat: 1 g
Dietary fiber: 2 g
Carbohydrates: 31 g
Protein: 24 g
Cholesterol: 40 mg
Sodium: 441 mg

Grilled Hamburgers

4 servings

1 pound extra-lean ground round (85%)

4 French rolls or hamburger buns, warmed

4 tomato slices

8 lettuce leaves

4 white onions

Press ground round into patties. Prepare the grill for direct grilling over high heat. Grill 6-8 minutes, turning when juices begin to form on top of meat. Place patties on warm French rolls or buns with tomato slices, lettuce, and onion. Serve immediately.

Variation: Top with 1 slice of cheese.

APPROXIMATE NUTRITIONAL INFORMATION PER SERVING

Total calories: 343
Total fat: 15 g
Saturated fat: 5 g
Dietary fiber: 1 g
Carbohydrates: 25 g
Protein: 26 g
Cholesterol: 71 mg
Sodium: 310 mg

Beef with Mushrooms and Tomatoes

2 open-faced sandwiches

2 slices pumpernickel rye bread

Dijon mustard

**2 ounces roast beef
(lean only), thinly sliced**

3 fresh mushrooms, sliced

1 ripe tomato, sliced

Spread bread with mustard. Layer each bread slice with beef, mushrooms, and tomato.

Note: Rump roast is the leanest cut of beef.

**APPROXIMATE
NUTRITIONAL
INFORMATION
PER OPEN-FACED
SANDWICH**

Total calories: 163
Total fat: 6 g
Saturated fat: 2 g
Dietary fiber: 3 g
Carbohydrates: 18 g
Protein: 11 g
Cholesterol: 22 mg
Sodium: 245 mg

Roast Veal with Red Onion

1 opened-faced sandwich

**1 slice black bread or
pumpernickel rye**

**½ teaspoon mayonnaise mixed
with a dab of fresh lemon juice**

**2 ounces roast veal
(lean only), thinly sliced**

2 slices red onion

red leaf lettuce

Spread bread with mayonnaise. Layer with roast veal. Top with red onion and leaf lettuce.

**APPROXIMATE
NUTRITIONAL
INFORMATION
PER SANDWICH**

Total calories: 197
Total fat: 6 g
Saturated fat: 2 g
Dietary fiber: 2 g
Carbohydrates: 16 g
Protein: 18 g
Cholesterol: 61 mg
Sodium: 252 mg

Soups, Stews & Chili

A NOTE ON BASIC SOUP STOCKS AND BROTHS

Soup is a great comfort food. By its nature, soup has to be eaten slowly, giving the family time to talk. Remember, too, that leftover soups make perfect after-school snacks.

A good soup depends on its base— good stock or broth. There are many acceptable versions on the market but homemade offers the maximum flavor and quality. It also allows you to control the fat and sodium content because you prepare it yourself. If you don't want to use homemade (or don't have the time), substitute a good grade of commercial stock or broth.

Watch out for sodium. There can be quite a difference between the amount used in homemade and in commercial varieties. Sodium levels can range from 400 to over 800 milligrams in one cup of commercial beef stock or chicken stock. The stock and broth recipes included here provide you with lower sodium options.

Pastina in Brodo

8 cups

2 quarts chicken broth (page 143)

1 cup egg pastina, alphabets, ancini pepe, orzo, or other tiny pasta shapes

¼ cup chopped fresh parsley

In a stock pot, heat stock just to boiling (do not boil). Stir in pastina. Reduce heat; simmer 6–7 minutes. Ladle into soup bowls. Sprinkle with parsley.

Serving Suggestions: Good choice for light lunch or first dinner course.

Variation: You can also substitute one dozen chicken or spinach tortellini for the pastina.

APPROXIMATE NUTRITIONAL INFORMATION PER CUP

Total calories: 67
Total fat: 1 g
Saturated fat: 0 g
Dietary fiber: 0 g
Carbohydrates: 8 g
Protein: 2 g
Cholesterol: 2 mg
Sodium: 227 mg

Curly Noodle Soup

4 servings

6 cups chicken broth, preferably homemade (page 143)

2 cups water

1 6-ounce package soba noodles

1¼ cups thinly sliced crimini mushrooms (optional)

1¼ cups snow peas, halved lengthwise (optional)

1 tablespoon reduced-sodium soy sauce

Asian noodles, also called buckwheat or soba noodles, are curly Japanese-style noodles made with wheat flour. They're available in Asian markets and in the Asian section of most supermarkets.

In a medium saucepan, bring 1 can of the chicken broth and the 2 cups of water to a boil. Add soba noodles and cook 5 to 6 minutes, or until noodles are tender. Drain and rinse.

In a 4-quart stockpot, heat the remaining 2 cups of broth just to boiling. Add mushrooms and snow peas, if desired, and cook 1 to 2 minutes. Add cooked noodles and soy sauce. Serve at once.

Note: To save time, use canned broth instead of homemade; however, in this recipe you can tell the difference. And remember, using canned broth will substantially increase the sodium.

APPROXIMATE NUTRITIONAL INFORMATION PER SERVING

Total calories: 299
Total fat: 4 g
Saturated fat: 1 g
Dietary fiber: 2 g
Carbohydrates: 52 g
Protein: 12 g
Cholesterol: 0 mg
Sodium: 377 mg using homemade chicken broth; 788 mg using canned chicken broth

Hearty Tortellini Soup

2 1/2 quarts (10 cups)

10 cups chicken broth (page 143) or commercial broth

1 chicken breast, skinned, boned, and diced

2 carrots, diced

1 8-ounce can mushroom pieces, drained

1½ dozen cooked spinach tortellini

¼ cup fresh Italian parsley, chopped

In a stock pot, combine stock, chicken breast, carrots, and mushrooms. Bring just to boiling (do not boil). Reduce heat; simmer 10-15 minutes. Add cooked tortellini; heat to serving temperature. Remove from heat. Ladle into bowls. Sprinkle with parsley.

Serving Suggestion: This soup makes a delightful main meal with a simple tossed salad and crusty French rolls.

APPROXIMATE NUTRITIONAL INFORMATION PER CUP

Total calories: 121
Total fat: 3 g
Saturated fat: 1 g
Dietary fiber: 1 g
Carbohydrates: 11 g
Protein: 9 g
Cholesterol: 16 mg
Sodium: 424 mg

Gazpacho

Approximately 3 quarts

1 fresh ripe tomato

1 green pepper

3 celery stalks

1 cucumber

1 small onion

3 tablespoons chopped fresh parsley

4 green onions

2 garlic cloves

¼ cup red wine vinegar

2 tablespoons extra-virgin olive oil

¾ teaspoon Kosher salt

6 cups canned plum tomatoes, chopped

¼ teaspoon horseradish

In a blender, combine all ingredients except horseradish; purée. Chill at least 3 hours. Just before serving, stir in horseradish.

Variation: Top each cup with 1 tablespoon small cooked shrimp and 1 teaspoon nonfat sour cream.

APPROXIMATE NUTRITIONAL INFORMATION PER CUP

Total calories: 60
Total Fat: 3 g
Saturated Fat: 0 g
Dietary Fiber: 2 g
Carbohydrates: 9 g
Protein: 2 g
Cholesterol: 4 mg
Sodium: 233 mg

IF USING SHRIMP AND NONFAT SOUR CREAM

Total calories: 69
aAll other values remain the same.

Spinach Soup Au Gratin

8 cups

1 large bunch fresh spinach

3 cups chicken broth (page 143) or commercial broth

2 slices crusty French bread

1 ounce part-skim mozzarella cheese, sliced

¼ teaspoon nutmeg

Wash and trim spinach; shake off excess moisture. In a saucepan, cook spinach, covered, just until leaves begin to wilt. (It is not necessary to add additional cooking liquid as the moisture on the leaves is sufficient.) Heat broth just to boiling. Reduce heat; simmer 5 minutes. Drain and discard any excess liquid. Set spinach aside. Toast bread, turning once, in a 350°F. oven 5 minutes, or until crisp; cut each slice into quarters. Layer toast with cheese and return to oven until cheese melts. Stir nutmeg into soup. Add cooked spinach. Ladle soup into bowls. Top with toasted cheese bread.

APPROXIMATE NUTRITIONAL INFORMATION PER CUP

Total calories: 62
Total Fat: 2 g
Saturated Fat: 1 g
Dietary Fiber: 2 g
Carbohydrates: 10 g
Protein: 4 g
Cholesterol: 3 mg
Sodium: 253 mg

Cream of Artichoke Soup

Approximately 3 quarts

1 medium onion, chopped

3 celery ribs, chopped

2 leeks with green tops, chopped

1 new potato with skin, quartered

6 cups chicken broth, preferably homemade (page 143)

1 14½ -ounce can water-packed artichoke hearts, drained and quartered

1½ cups broccoli florets, cooked until just crisp-tender

Freshly ground black pepper

Cook onion, celery, leeks, and potato in chicken broth until all vegetables are tender, pour into a blender and purée. Return to stockpot; simmer 30 minutes. Add artichoke hearts; simmer 10 minutes; add broccoli. Heat to serving temperature. Pass ground pepper.

Variation: Use ³/₄ pound cooked fresh artichoke hearts in place of the canned.

Serving Suggestion: Serve with Clams Italian Style (page 253), crusty French bread, and fresh fruit.

APPROXIMATE NUTRITIONAL INFORMATION PER CUP

Total calories: 65
Total Fat: 1 g
Saturated Fat: 0 g
Dietary Fiber: 1 g
Carbohydrates: 11 g
Protein: 4 g
Cholesterol: 1 mg
Sodium: 181 mg

Basic Bean Soup Stock

3 quarts

2 tablespoons dried parsley

1 tablespoon thyme

1 tablespoon marjoram

2 dried bay leaves

2 tablespoons celery seed

1 very meaty ham hock, about 2½ to 3 pounds

3 quarts water

1 tablespoon Kosher salt

A Note on Beans: In most cases, we use canned beans in our recipes. Home-cooked dried beans are preferable, but canned beans shorten cooking time.

Use this Basic Bean Soup Stock with the many prepackaged multi-bean soup mixes on the market. Your family will love how much better they taste using this as a base rather than water or the canned broths recommended on the boxes. To stretch your food dollars, cook a lean ham for a Sunday dinner. Make lunch-box sandwiches with the leftover ham. Use the bone for this delicious stock.

Measure parsley, thyme, marjoram, bay leaves ,and celery seed into a square of cheesecloth; tie cloth securely at the top with a string. In a stockpot, combine seasoning pouch with ham hock, water, and salt. Bring slowly to a boil, removing scum and fat that floats to the top. Cover and simmer 2½ to 3 hours. Do not boil or fat will be reabsorbed into the broth, making it cloudy. Refrigerate overnight. Skim and discard fat that floats to the top. Cut ham off bone, reserving only very lean meat. Dice meat and return to stockpot. Discard ham bones and ham fat. Use stock at once, or store in refrigerator or freezer for later use.

APPROXIMATE NUTRITIONAL INFORMATION PER CUP

Total calories: 33
Total Fat: 0 g
Saturated Fat: 0 g
Dietary Fiber: trace
Carbohydrates: trace
Protein: 3 g
Cholesterol: 5 mg
Sodium: 206 mg

French Market Soup

8 quarts (32 cups)

1 12-ounce package multi-bean soup mix

3 quarts Basic Bean Stock (page 126)

1 28-ounce can plum tomatoes, diced

2 medium yellow onions, chopped

6 stalks celery, chopped

2 cloves garlic, minced

1½ chicken breasts, skinned, boned, and diced

¼ pound extra-lean Italian sausage (as lean as you can find)

This recipe makes good use of commercial multi-bean soup packages. Because the homemade Basic Bean Stock is made with a ham hock, our kids used to call this "ham hock" soup. It's one of our family's favorite soups.

Thoroughly sort and wash bean soup mix and place in a large bowl. Cover with water. Soak overnight. Drain.

In a stockpot, heat Basic Bean Soup Stock just to boiling (do not boil). Add bean soup mix, tomatoes, onions, celery, and garlic; reduce heat; cover and simmer 3 hours, or until beans are tender. Uncover, add chicken and cook 30 minutes, or until chicken is cooked.

Meanwhile, slit open, remove, and discard casing on Italian sausage. Preheat a nonstick skillet over medium-high heat; add sausage and brown 6 to 8 minutes, or until cooked, breaking the sausage apart as it browns. Drain on paper towels; pat with additional paper toweling to remove all excess fat. Add to stockpot, when chicken is nearly cooked.

Serving Suggestion: Good with homemade bread and fresh seasonal fruit.

APPROXIMATE NUTRITIONAL INFORMATION PER CUP

Total calories: 74
Total Fat: 2 g
Saturated Fat: 1 g
Dietary Fiber: 4 g
Carbohydrates: 9 g
Protein: 5 g
Cholesterol: 8 mg
Sodium: 430 mg

Minestrone

3 1/2 quarts (14 cups)

4 cups chicken broth, preferably homemade (page 143)

1 medium onion, chopped

3 stalks celery, chopped

2 cloves garlic, chopped

1 leek, chopped, roots and green stems removed

1 28-ounce can plum tomatoes, diced

1 teaspoon basil

½ teaspoon oregano

¼ teaspoon black pepper

3 cups Chinese (Napa) cabbage, shredded

1 medium zucchini, thinly sliced

2 carrots, grated

1 8-ounce can garbanzo beans. drained and rinsed

1 15-ounce can red kidney beans, drained and rinsed

3 cups cooked elbow macaroni

In a stock pot, heat stock just to boiling (do not boil); add onion, celery, garlic, and leek. Reduce heat to simmer; cook 1 hour. Add tomatoes, basil, oregano, and pepper; simmer 30 minutes. Return stock just to boiling (do not boil). Add cabbage, zucchini, and carrots; reduce heat and simmer 20 minutes. Add remaining ingredients and heat.

Note: This soup tastes even better the second day.

APPROXIMATE NUTRITIONAL INFORMATION PER CUP

Total calories: 144
Total Fat: 1 g
Saturated Fat: 0 g
Dietary Fiber: 5 g
Carbohydrates: 27 g
Protein: 6 g
Cholesterol: 1 mg
Sodium: 336 mg

Black Bean Soup

10 cups

4 cups chicken broth (page 143) or commercial broth*

6 cloves garlic

1 medium onion, chopped

1 cup chopped celery

1 teaspoon ground coriander

¼ teaspoon crushed red pepper

¼ teaspoon Kosher salt

3 15-ounce cans black beans, drained and rinsed**

In a medium stockpot, simmer chicken broth, garlic, onion, celery, and seasonings 1 hour. In a blender or food processor, purée 1 can of the black beans; add to stockpot. Stir in remaining 2 cans of beans and heat through.

*Canned broth is higher in sodium.

**Rinsing will reduce sodium in canned beans by 40 percent.

Variation: Add 1 cup cooked elbow macaroni or shell-shaped pasta.

APPROXIMATE NUTRITIONAL INFORMATION PER CUP

Total calories: 125
Total Fat: 1 g
Saturated Fat: trace
Dietary Fiber: 4 g
Carbohydrates: 20 g
Protein: 9 g
Cholesterol: trace
Sodium: 302 mg

Hearty Black Bean Soup

4 1/2 quarts

2 quarts beef broth, preferably homemade (page 151)

1 quart of chicken broth, preferably homemade (page 143)

1 28-ounce can plum tomatoes, diced

1 large white onion, diced

3 stalks celery, diced

4 cloves garlic, peeled

1½ cups dry black beans

½ cup dry black-eyed peas

½ cup dry barley

2 teaspoons Kosher salt

(Optional) ½ cup lean (as you can find) Italian sausage

Black beans and black-eyed peas require soaking. Rinse and sort beans and peas. Place in large bowl and add 6 cups of water. Allow to stand overnight. Drain off soaking water and rinse beans and peas. Set aside.

Soak ½ cup barley in 1 cup of water. Allow to stand overnight. Set aside.

In a stock pot, bring beef broth and chicken broth to a boil. Add tomatoes, onion, celery, and garlic. Add soaked and drained black beans and black-eyed peas. Add barley with soaking liquid. Bring soup just to boiling but do not allow to boil. Reduce heat. Simmer on medium heat 2-3 hours or until beans are tender. Stir in salt.

(Optional) In a nonstick skillet, sauté the Italian sausage. Remove to plate and pat dry to remove excess fat. Add to soup.

Note: This soup is delicious, has fiber and is low in calories but is high in sodium. On days when you enjoy this soup, make sure your other meals are low in sodium. Also, you can cut the sodium by using our Basic Bean Soup Stock (page 126) in place of the beef stock and chicken broth called for in this recipe.

APPROXIMATE NUTRITIONAL INFORMATION PER CUP

Total calories: 90
Total Fat: 0 g
Saturated Fat: 0 g
Dietary Fiber: 5 g
Carbohydrates: 16 g
Protein: 7 g
Cholesterol: 0 mg
Sodium: 595 mg

Lentil Soup

14 cups

8 cups Bean Soup Stock (page 126)

1 6-ounce can tomato paste

2 medium carrots, diced

1 large potato, diced

1 large onion, chopped

3 cloves garlic, minced

¼ teaspoon powdered thyme

1 cup lentils

¾ teaspoon Kosher salt or to taste

In a medium stockpot, bring stock, tomato paste, carrots, potato, onion, garlic, and thyme just to boiling. Add lentils and reduce heat. Cover and simmer 1½ –2 hours or until lentils are cooked. Season with salt.

Variation: Add ½ cup alphabet pasta during last 15 minutes of cooking.

Serving Suggestion: Especially good for lunch on a cold winter day. Serve with Winter Vegetable Salad (page 169). For a fun dessert, try Hot Cross Buns (page 77).

APPROXIMATE NUTRITIONAL INFORMATION PER CUP

Total calories: 55
Total Fat: trace
Saturated Fat: trace
Dietary Fiber: 2 g
Carbohydrates: 10 g
Protein: 3 g
Cholesterol: 3 mg
Sodium: 569 mg

Three-Bean Soup

Approximately 3 quarts

1 28-ounce can plum tomatoes, diced

1 tablespoon chili powder

⅛ teaspoon ground cumin

⅛ teaspoon cayenne

½ teaspoon paprika

½ teaspoon Kosher salt

⅛ teaspoon black pepper

2 15-ounce cans cannellini beans, drained and rinsed

1 15-ounce can red pinto beans, drained and rinsed

2 15-ounce cans black beans, drained and rinsed

In a stockpot, combine tomatoes, chili powder, cumin, cayenne, paprika, salt, and pepper. Heat just to boiling, but do not allow to boil. Reduce heat and simmer 30 minutes. Add beans. Heat to serving temperature.

APPROXIMATE NUTRITIONAL INFORMATION PER CUP

Total calories: 171
Total Fat: 3 g
Saturated Fat: 0 g
Dietary Fiber: 9 g
Carbohydrates: 30 g
Protein: 9 g
Cholesterol: 0 mg
Sodium: 408 mg

Three-Bean Chili

8 servings

1 pound leanest ground beef

1 medium onion, chopped

2 garlic cloves, minced

1½ teaspoons Lawry's Chili Seasoning (optional)

1 28-ounce can diced plum tomatoes, with liquid

⅛ teaspoon ground cumin (¼ teaspoon for spicy)

½ teaspoon cayenne for a spicier flavor

1 tablespoon chili powder

¾ teaspoon Kosher salt

2 15-ounce cans red kidney beans, drained and rinsed

1 15-ounce can black beans, drained and rinsed

1 15-ounce can cannellini beans, drained and rinsed

Full of B vitamins as well as minerals, beans are one of the best sources of dietary fiber. Beans are especially good for you because they are a vegetable source of protein without the hidden fat. If you want a vegetarian meal, simply omit the ground beef.

In a nonstick skillet, brown ground beef with onion and garlic; drain excess fat and pat with paper toweling to remove any additional fat. Sprinkle meat with Lawry's Chili Seasoning, if desired.

In a stockpot pour the liquid from the can of tomatoes. Crush the tomatoes by hand or in a food processor fitted with a steel blade. Pulse 6-8 times. Pour tomatoes into an 8-quart saucepan and add seasonings. Heat just to boiling; reduce heat to simmer. Add ground beef and beans; simmer 10 minutes.

APPROXIMATE NUTRITIONAL INFORMATION PER CUP

Total calories: 255
Total Fat: 7 g
Saturated Fat: 2 g
Dietary Fiber: 11 g
Carbohydrates: 30 g
Protein: 22 g
Cholesterol: 35 mg
Sodium: 613 mg

Pasta and Bean Soup

12 cups

1 28-ounce can Italian plum tomatoes, diced

1 cup Bloody Mary Mix

1 cup beef broth (page 151) or canned broth

1 tablespoon freshly squeezed lemon juice

5 cloves garlic

½ cup chopped white onion

½ teaspoon ground cumin

½ teaspoon Tabasco sauce

½ teaspoon crushed basil

2 15-ounce cans cannelini beans, drained and rinsed, or 3 cups cooked white cannelini beans

1 cup chopped green pepper

2 cups cooked elbow macaroni

In a small stockpot, combine tomatoes, Bloody Mary Mix, beef stock, lemon juice, garlic, onion, cumin, Tabasco, and basil. Heat just to boiling, then reduce heat and simmer 25 minutes. Stir in beans and green pepper, and simmer 10 minutes. Add macaroni and heat through.

APPROXIMATE NUTRITIONAL INFORMATION PER CUP

Total calories: 98
Total Fat: 1 g
Saturated Fat: trace
Dietary Fiber: 1 g
Carbohydrates: 18 g
Protein: 5 g
Cholesterol: trace
Sodium: 496 mg

Tomato and Bean Soup

2 1/2 quarts (5 main-dish servings)

3 15-ounce cans cannellini beans

1 28-ounce can Italian plum tomatoes, diced

2 cups chicken broth preferably homemade (page 143)

1 fresh rosemary sprig

2 teaspoons olive oil

1 large carrot, diced

1 clove garlic, minced

1 medium onion, chopped

¼ pound extra-lean ham, diced

½ teaspoon Kosher salt

¼ teaspoon black pepper

¼ teaspoon Tabasco sauce

¼ cup freshly grated Parmesan cheese

The beans in this soup are packed with the kind of fiber that protects against clogged arteries. By combining them with a tomato soup, you will help your body absorb more of the nutrients. Simply omit the ham for an equally delicious, meatless soup.

Place cannellini beans in a colander; rinse with cold water and drain thoroughly. In a 6½ quart stockpot, combine tomatoes, chicken broth, and rosemary; heat just to boiling. Reduce heat and let simmer.

In a nonstick skillet, heat olive oil; add diced carrots and sauté 3–4 minutes. Add garlic and onions, and continue sautéing until the carrot is tender and the onion is soft. Add ham and sauté 2 to 3 minutes longer. Add to tomato mixture and heat to serving temperature. Season with salt, pepper, and Tabasco sauce. Serve in individual soup bowls. An option is to sprinkle with Parmesan cheese.

This recipe is high in sodium. Be sure to limit your sodium in other meals to keep your sodium intake for the day in balance.

APPROXIMATE NUTRITIONAL INFORMATION PER SERVING

Total calories: 325
Total Fat: 5 g
Saturated Fat: 2 g
Dietary Fiber: 13 g
Carbohydrates: 48 g
Protein: 20 g
Cholesterol: 18 mg
Sodium: 976 mg

Lentil-and-Barley Soup

9 cups

¾ cup dry pearl barley

4 cups hot water

6 cups Beef Stock, preferably homemade (page 150)

½ cup dry green (DuPuy) lentils

1 medium white onion, chopped

2 stalks celery, chopped

½ pound fresh mushrooms, sliced

1 16-ounce can tomatoes, diced

1 teaspoon salt

¼ teaspoon black pepper

½ pound extra-lean ground round or ground veal, browned and drained

Soak barley in 4 cups hot water for 1 hour. In a stock pot, heat stock just to boiling (do not boil). Add barley with soaking liquid to stock. Add lentils, onion, and celery; bring back just to boiling. Reduce heat; simmer 2–2½ hours, or until barley is tender and lentils are cooked. Stir in mushrooms, tomatoes, salt, pepper, and ground round or veal; simmer 10–15 minutes.

Serving Suggestion: Serve with low-sodium accompaniments such as warm tortillas and fresh seasonal fruit.

APPROXIMATE NUTRITIONAL INFORMATION PER CUP

Total calories: 148
Total Fat: 5 g
Saturated Fat: 2 g
Dietary Fiber: 5 g
Carbohydrates: 13 g
Protein: 11 g
Cholesterol: 19 mg
Sodium: 139 mg

Barley Mushroom Soup

12 cups

1 cup pearl barley

3 cups water

8 cups beef broth (page 151) or commercial broth*

1 tablespoon olive oil

2 cloves garlic, minced

1 onion, coarsely chopped

3 stalks celery

½ pound extra-lean ground round

½ pound fresh mushrooms

1 teaspoon Worcestershire sauce

⅛ teaspoon powdered thyme

⅛ teaspoon marjoram

½ teaspoon Kosher salt or to taste

¼ teaspoon black pepper

Soak barley in 3 cups water overnight. In a medium stockpot, bring beef broth to a boil; add barley with soaking liquid and cook, covered, about 45 minutes or until barley is tender. Meanwhile, heat olive oil in a nonstick skillet; add garlic and onions, and sauté 5–6 minutes. Add celery and sauté 3–4 minutes. Add ground round and sauté 5–6 minutes. Add mushrooms and sauté 4–5 minutes. When barley is tender, season with Worcestershire sauce, thyme, marjoram, salt, and pepper. Stir in beef-onion mixture.

*Canned broth is higher in sodium.

Note: This is a hearty, great-tasting soup that can be ready in under an hour after soaking the barley overnight.

APPROXIMATE NUTRITIONAL INFORMATION PER CUP

Total calories: 112
Total Fat: 1 g
Saturated Fat: 0 g
Dietary Fiber: 3 g
Carbohydrates: 15 g
Protein: 7 g
Cholesterol: 11 mg
Sodium: 460 mg

Swiss Barley Soup

4 quarts

1½ cups dry pearl barley

2 cups water

4 quarts chicken or turkey broth (page 143)

1 large yellow onion, chopped

½ cup dry yellow split peas

¼ cup dry egg pastina

1 tablespoon Kosher salt

¼ teaspoon black pepper

Soak barley in 2 cups water overnight. In a stock pot, heat stock just to boiling (do not boil). Add barley with soaking liquid and onion. Bring back just to boiling. Reduce heat to medium high heat and simmer, uncovered, 1½ hours. Add split peas and pastina; simmer 1–1½ hours, or until barley and split peas are tender. Stir in salt and pepper.

Ronzoni Acini Di Pepe may be used in place of egg pastina.

APPROXIMATE NUTRITIONAL INFORMATION PER CUP

Total calories: 49
Total Fat: 1 g
Saturated Fat: 0 g
Dietary Fiber: 2 g
Carbohydrates: 8 g
Protein: 2 g
Cholesterol: 1 mg
Sodium: 276 mg

Two-Mushroom Soup

4 servings

3 cups chicken broth (page 143) or commercial broth*

1 6-ounce can straw mushrooms, drained

1 8-ounce can button mushrooms, drained

In a saucepan, heat chicken broth just to boiling. Stir in mushrooms. Simmer 5 minutes. Ladle into bowls.

*Canned broth is higher in sodium.

Serving Suggestion: An easy-to-prepare first course. Good with chicken and fish.

Using fresh mushrooms decreases the sodium by more than 45 percent.

APPROXIMATE NUTRITIONAL INFORMATION PER SERVING

Total calories: 48
Total Fat: 1 g
Saturated Fat: 0 g
Dietary Fiber: 1 g
Carbohydrates: 4 g
Protein: 5 g
Cholesterol: 0 mg
Sodium: 486 mg

Straw Mushroom Soup with Green Onion

4 servings

3 cups chicken broth (page 143) or commercial broth*

1 6-ounce can straw mushrooms, drained

1 green onion, thinly sliced

In a saucepan, heat chicken broth just to boiling; stir in mushrooms. Simmer 5 minutes. Ladle into bowls. Sprinkle with green onions.

*Canned broth is higher in sodium.

Note: This soup has few calories and is an especially quick-to-prepare first course. Good with chicken and fish.

Using fresh mushrooms decreases the sodium by more than 45 percent.

APPROXIMATE NUTRITIONAL INFORMATION PER SERVING

Total calories: 38
Total Fat: 1 g
Saturated Fat: 0 g
Dietary Fiber: 0 g
Carbohydrates: 2 g
Protein: 4 g
Cholesterol: 0 mg
Sodium: 486 mg

Fresh Mushroom Soup with Mozzarella Cheese

Approximately 2 1/2 quarts

1 onion, chopped

1 carrot, quartered

1 cup chopped celery

6 cups beef broth, preferably homemade (page 151)

¾ cup fresh mushrooms, thinly sliced

1 tablespoon olive oil

½ teaspoon Kosher salt

¼ teaspoon pepper

¼ cup sherry (optional)

¾ cup grated reduced-fat mozzarella cheese

3 tablespoons chopped Italian parsley

Boil onion, carrot, and celery in beef broth until vegetables are tender; purée in a blender or food processor. Return to stockpot and simmer. Sauté mushrooms in olive oil until tender. Add mushrooms, salt, pepper, and sherry to simmering broth. Heat to serving temperature. Ladle into soup bowls. Sprinkle with cheese and parsley.

Variation: Place a slice of toasted French bread in each bowl; ladle soup over bread.

APPROXIMATE NUTRITIONAL INFORMATION PER CUP

Total calories: 85
Total Fat: 3 g
Saturated Fat: 1 g
Dietary Fiber: 1 g
Carbohydrates: 5 g
Protein: 6 g
Cholesterol: 6 mg
Sodium: 299 mg

Clam and Black Bean Chowder

14 cups

1 tablespoon olive oil

1 cup chopped onion

1 cup chopped celery

1 28-ounce can Italian plum tomatoes

1 6-ounce can V-8 juice

3 6½-ounce cans chopped clams with liquid

1½ pounds new potatoes, cubed and steamed or microwaved until crisp-tender

½ teaspoon Worcestershire sauce

1 15-ounce can black beans, drained and rinsed

¼ teaspoon Kosher salt (optional)

¼ teaspoon black pepper

In a nonstick pan, heat olive oil; add onion and celery, and sauté 8–10 minutes or until tender. Purée tomatoes in a blender or food processor. Combine all ingredients in a medium stockpot. Simmer 20 minutes. Serve.

Note: This is a great last-minute lunch or light supper, easy to prepare and using ingredients that are often on hand.

Variation: Omit the beans for a delicious, quick-to-fix clam chowder.

Serving Suggestion: Particularly good with Seafood Salad (page 209), Italian Pizza Bread with Garlic and Rosemary (page 78) and fresh fruit.

APPROXIMATE NUTRITIONAL INFORMATION PER CUP

Total calories: 111
Total Fat: 1 g
Saturated Fat: 0 g
Dietary Fiber: 2 g
Carbohydrates: 19 g
Protein: 6 g
Cholesterol: 24 mg
Sodium: 304 mg

Manhattan Clam Chowder

Approximately 3 quarts

1 28-ounce can plum tomatoes, chopped

1 large onion, chopped

3 celery stalks, thinly sliced

1 minced fresh thyme sprig or 1 teaspoon dried

1 tablespoon chopped fresh Italian parsley

½ teaspoon Kosher salt

2 peppercorns

⅛ teaspoon ground pepper

⅛ teaspoon Tabasco sauce

1 bay leaf

3 medium new potatoes, pared and diced

2 carrots, thinly sliced

3 6½-ounce cans chopped clams with their liquid

Combine tomatoes, onion, celery, thyme, parsley, salt, peppercorns, ground pepper, Tabasco sauce, and bay leaf in a stockpot; bring to a boil, reduce heat, and simmer 20 minutes. Bring to a second boil; add potatoes and carrots; reduce heat and simmer 45 minutes, or until vegetables are just tender. Add clams with their liquid; simmer 15 minutes. Remove bay leaf.

Note: Two pounds fresh clams, steamed, plus 1½ cups of their liquid may be used in place of canned clams.

APPROXIMATE NUTRITIONAL INFORMATION PER CUP

Total calories: 115
Total Fat: 1 g
Saturated Fat: 0 g
Dietary Fiber: 2 g
Carbohydrates: 15 g
Protein: 12 g
Cholesterol: 27 mg
Sodium: 246 mg

Northwest Seafood Chowder

8 servings

1 10-ounce can tomato purée

1 8-ounce bottle clam juice

¾ cup dry white wine

4 cups chicken broth (page 143) or commercial broth*

2 medium carrots, diced

1 large bay leaf

½ teaspoon crushed red pepper

½ teaspoon basil

½ teaspoon ground coriander

16 clams in their shells

1 tablespoon olive oil

2 medium onions, chopped

4 cloves garlic, chopped

1 large green pepper, seeded and chopped

1 lemon, thinly sliced

½ pound medium prawns, shelled and deveined

½ pound small bay scallops

½ pound halibut, cut into 1-inch cubes

½ pound sea bass, cut into 1-inch cubes

½ pound cavatelli or other shell-shaped pasta, cooked al dente

¼ cup chopped fresh parsley

In a medium stockpot, combine tomato purée, clam juice, wine, chicken stock, carrots, bay leaf, red pepper, basil, and coriander. Simmer, uncovered, 10 minutes. Add clams, cover and simmer 10–15 minutes.

Meanwhile, in a wok or heavy skillet, heat olive oil and sauté onions and garlic 3–4 minutes or until onions are crisp-tender; add green pepper and sauté 2–3 minutes. Add vegetables to stockpot.

When clams first begin to open, add lemon slices, prawns, scallops, halibut, and sea bass. Cover and simmer until prawns turn pink, clams are fully opened, and fish are cooked. Add pasta. Ladle into bowls. Garnish with parsley.

*Canned broth is higher in sodium.

Variation: Substitute 4 steamed and diced new potatoes for pasta.

Serving Suggestion: A good main meal soup. Serve with Italian Eggplant Dip (page 95) with crudités and Italian Breadsticks (page 57).

APPROXIMATE NUTRITIONAL INFORMATION PER SERVING

Total calories: 335
Total Fat: 5 g
Saturated Fat: 1 g
Dietary Fiber: 3 g
Carbohydrates: 34 g
Protein: 34 g
Cholesterol: 99 mg
Sodium: 652 mg

Fisherman's Soup

3 quarts (12 cups)

½ pound clams

½ pound mussels

8 cups chicken broth (page 143)

½ chicken breast, skinned, boned and cut into 1-inch cubes

¼ pound orange roughy or other whitefish, cut into 1-inch cubes

1 ¼ teaspoons arrowroot dissolved in ¼ cup water

¼ pound scallops, quartered and poached

3 cups cooked Saffron Rice (page 349)

¼ red pepper, diced

¼ green pepper, diced

Clean and soak clams and mussels in salt water to remove sand. In a covered vegetable steamer basket over boiling water, steam clams and mussels until shells open. Remove half of the clams and half of the mussels from their shells; leave the other half in their shells for garnish. Set aside.

In a stock pot, heat stock to boiling; add chicken. Reduce heat; cook 15 minutes. Add orange roughy; cook 2 minutes. Gradually add arrowroot, stirring constantly, until stock thickens slightly. Add scallops, rice, shelled clams, and mussels. Heat. Ladle into soup bowls. Garnish with unshelled clams and mussels.

Top with peppers.

APPROXIMATE NUTRITIONAL INFORMATION PER CUP

Total calories: 140
Total Fat: 2 g
Saturated Fat: 0 g
Dietary Fiber: 0 g
Carbohydrates: 15 g
Protein: 12 g
Cholesterol: 26 mg
Sodium: 273 mg

Seafood Stew

8 servings

1 2-pound can plum tomatoes, diced

1 tablespoon fresh basil or
½ teaspoon dried

1 tablespoon olive oil

1 yellow onion, chopped

1 large fennel bulb, chopped

6 cloves garlic, peeled

½ cup dry white wine

½ teaspoon saffron threads, crushed

1 pound mussels, soaked and cleaned

1 pound clams, soaked and cleaned

½ pound scallops

½ pound black cod fillets, cut into 2-inch squares

½ pound squid tubes, cleaned and cut into rings

2 tablespoons chopped Italian parsley

In a medium stock pot, combine tomatoes and basil. Simmer 30 minutes. In a nonstick skillet, heat olive oil. Sauté onion, fennel and garlic 5–10 minutes. Add to stock pot. Add wine. Simmer 20 minutes. Raise heat and bring just to a boil (do not boil). Add crushed saffron threads. Add mussels and clams. Reduce heat to medium. When mussels and clams begin to open, add scallops, cod and squid. Cook 5 minutes, or until most shells have opened and fish is cooked. Ladle into bowls. Sprinkle with parsley.

Serving Suggestion: Serve with Shallot-basil Bread (page 67) for dipping.

APPROXIMATE NUTRITIONAL INFORMATION PER SERVING

Total calories: 214
Total Fat: 3 g
Saturated Fat: 0 g
Dietary Fiber: 2 g
Carbohydrates: 14 g
Protein: 30 g
Cholesterol: 121 mg
Sodium: 449 mg

Seafood Gazpacho

8 cups

1 28-ounce can Italian plum tomatoes, diced

1 cup Mr. & Mrs. T Bloody Mary Mix

½ cup peeled and chopped English cucumber

⅓ cup chopped green pepper

½ cup chopped sweet onion

1 cup beef broth (page 151) or commercial broth*

1 tablespoon freshly squeezed lemon juice

1 tablespoon extra-virgin olive oil

1 tablespoon minced garlic (about 5 whole cloves)

½ teaspoon ground cumin

½ teaspoon Tabasco sauce

½ teaspoon Kosher salt

½ teaspoon crushed basil

½ pound cooked shrimpmeat

In a large glass bowl, combine all the ingredients except shrimp. Chill at least 2 hours. Just before serving, add shrimp.

*Canned broth is higher in sodium.

Serving Suggestion: Serve with Cracked Dungeness Crab (page 250) or smoked or grilled salmon.

APPROXIMATE NUTRITIONAL INFORMATION PER CUP

Total calories: 81
Total Fat: 2 g
Saturated Fat: trace
Dietary Fiber: 1 g
Carbohydrates: 8 g
Protein: 8 g
Cholesterol: 55 mg
Sodium: 567 mg

Seviche Soup

6 servings

½ **pound scallops, chopped**

½ **cup fresh lime juice**

1½ **cups Bloody Mary Mix**

1 **tablespoon olive oil**

2 **cups chicken broth (page 143)**

⅓ **cup chopped white onion**

3 **tablespoons chopped green chilies**

¼ **teaspoon Kosher salt**

1 **tablespoon chopped fresh Italian parsley**

1 **slice fresh lime, cut into 6 wedges**

Cover scallops with lime juice. Marinate in the refrigerator for 4 hours; pour off lime juice.

Heat olive oil in a nonstick skillet; add scallops. Cook, turning frequently, for 4 to 6 minutes, or just until scallops are tender. Remove from pan; drain any excess liquid. Chill scallops several hours.

Combine Bloody Mary mix, chicken broth, onion, green chilies, olive oil, and salt. Chill several hours.

Just before serving, add scallops to Bloody Mary mixture. Ladle into soup bowls. Sprinkle with parsley.

Garnish with fresh lime.

Serving Suggestion: Great first course on a hot summer day.

APPROXIMATE NUTRITIONAL INFORMATION PER SERVING

Total calories: 88
Total Fat: 3 g
Saturated Fat: trace
Dietary Fiber: 0 g
Carbohydrates: 6 g
Protein: 9 g
Cholesterol: 14 mg
Sodium: 543 mg

Cioppino

8 servings

1 pound mussels

1 pound clams

1 cup dry white wine

2 cups chicken broth, preferably homemade (page 143)

1 8-ounce can tomato sauce

3 tablespoons tomato paste

3 tablespoons olive oil

1 onion, chopped

1 leek with green tops, chopped

2 garlic cloves

3 fresh ripe tomatoes, chopped

1 14½-ounce can plum tomatoes, diced

2 fresh basil sprigs, or ½ teaspoon dried

1 bay leaf

Dash each of fennel, thyme, and cayenne

2 drops Tabasco sauce

¾ teaspoon Kosher salt

1 green or yellow pepper, chopped

¼ pound red snapper, cut into 3-inch cubes

¼ pound cod, cut into 3-inch cubes

¼ pound scallops

¼ pound cooked crab legs

4 cups cooked seashell-shaped pasta

Scrub mussel shells with a wire brush. Remove and discard beards. Rinse mussels in cold water; discard broken or open mussels.

Scrub clams. Place in a large bowl and cover with cold water. Sprinkle with cornmeal, and let stand 30 minutes. Drain and rinse; discard cornmeal.

Arrange clams and mussels on a rack in a covered steamer filled with 2 cups hot water. Steam 6 to 8 minutes, or just until shells open. Set aside.

Bring wine, chicken broth, tomato sauce, tomato paste, and 1 tablespoon olive oil to a boil. Add onion, leek, and garlic; simmer 20 minutes. Add fresh and canned tomatoes and remaining seasonings; heat just to boiling. Add green or yellow pepper.

Meanwhile, preheat a nonstick skillet with remaining 2 tablespoons olive oil; add red snapper, cod, and scallops. Cook, turning frequently, 4 to 6 minutes, or just until seafood is tender. Drain any liquid. Just before serving, add clams, mussels, sautéed seafood, crab legs, and pasta to sauce.

Serving Suggestion: Serve with crusty French bread.

APPROXIMATE NUTRITIONAL INFORMATION PER CUP

Total calories: 304
Total Fat: 8 g
Saturated Fat: 1 g
Dietary Fiber: 2 g
Carbohydrates: 33 g
Protein: 22 g
Cholesterol: 36 mg
Sodium: 597 mg

Bouillabaisse

10 servings

2 pounds clams

2 pounds mussels

2 cups dry white wine

4 cups chicken broth, preferably homemade (page 143)

¼ cup olive oil

1 onion, chopped

1 leek with green tops, chopped

4 garlic cloves

4 large ripe tomatoes, chopped

1 28-ounce can plum tomatoes, diced

2 fresh basil sprigs

3 drops Tabasco sauce

½ teaspoon Kosher salt

1 bay leaf

Dash each of cayenne, thyme, and fennel

2 green or yellow peppers, chopped

¾ pound red snapper, cut into 3-inch cubes

¾ pound cod, cut into 3-inch cubes

¼ pound scallops

¾ pound crab legs

6 red potatoes, steamed in their jackets until just tender and sliced

Scrub clams. Place in a large bowl and cover with cold water. Sprinkle with cornmeal and let stand 30 minutes. Drain and rinse; discard cornmeal.

Scrub mussel shells with a wire brush. Remove and discard beards. Rinse mussels in cold water; discard broken or open mussels.

Bring wine, chicken broth, and olive oil to a boil in a large stockpot. Add onion, leek, and garlic; simmer 20 minutes. Add fresh and canned tomatoes, basil, Tabasco sauce, and seasonings; heat just to boiling, but do not allow to boil. Add clams and mussels. Cover. Steam just until shells begin to open; add green peppers and remaining seafood. Cook 5 minutes. Add potatoes; simmer 2 to 3 minutes, or until clams and mussels have opened and seafood is cooked. Do not overcook seafood.

APPROXIMATE NUTRITIONAL INFORMATION PER SERVING

Total calories: 359
Total Fat: 9 g
Saturated Fat: 1 g
Dietary Fiber: 3 g
Carbohydrates: 30 g
Protein: 33 g
Cholesterol: 70 mg
Sodium: 526 mg

Tomato Shrimp Soup

4 servings

4 cups chicken broth (page 143) or commercial broth

2 medium tomatoes, coarsely chopped

1 cup English cucumber, peeled, seeded and cut into ¼-inch strips

½ cup firm tofu, cut into ¼-inch cubes

½ cup cooked shrimp meat

In a small stockpot, bring chicken broth just to boiling. Add tomatoes and simmer 2 minutes. Add cucumber, tofu, and shrimp, and simmer 1 minute.

Serving Suggestion: Excellent for a light first course.

APPROXIMATE NUTRITIONAL INFORMATION PER SERVING

Total calories: 128
Total Fat: 5 g
Saturated Fat: 1 g
Dietary Fiber: 1 g
Carbohydrates: 6 g
Protein: 16 g
Cholesterol: 56 mg
Sodium: 623 mg

Shrimp and Cannellini Bean Soup

Approximately 3 quarts

1 28-ounce can plum tomatoes, diced

1 tablespoon extra-virgin olive oil

4 garlic cloves, minced

2 15-ounce cans cannellini beans, drained and rinsed

3 cups cooked elbow macaroni

½ teaspoon Kosher salt

¼ teaspoon black pepper

⅔ pound small cooked shrimp

2 tablespoons finely chopped flat-leaf Italian parsley

2 to 3 fresh basil leaves for garnish (optional)

In a 3-quart saucepan, combine tomatoes, olive oil, and garlic. Heat just to boiling, but do not allow to boil. Reduce heat; simmer 30 minutes. Add cannellini beans, macaroni, salt, pepper, and shrimp. Heat 2 to 3 minutes, just to serving temperature. Garnish with Italian parsley and fresh basil.

Variation: Delete the shrimp.

APPROXIMATE NUTRITIONAL INFORMATION PER SERVING

Total calories: 163
Total Fat: 3 g
Saturated Fat: 0 g
Dietary Fiber: 5 g
Carbohydrates: 25 g
Protein: 12 g
Cholesterol: 43 mg
Sodium: 279 mg

Shrimp, Chicken, and Rice Gumbo

12 cups

2 cups beef broth (page 151) or commercial broth

1 14-ounce can Italian plum tomatoes, diced

1 teaspoon granulated sugar

½ teaspoon powdered thyme

½ teaspoon chili powder

¼ teaspoon black pepper

½ teaspoon crushed red pepper

¼ teaspoon filé powder

1 tablespoon extra-virgin olive oil

4 large cloves garlic, chopped

1 small white onion, coarsely chopped

½ cup coarsely chopped celery

1 small green pepper, coarsely chopped

⅔ pound medium prawns, cooked, shelled, and deveined

2 chicken breasts, skinned, boned, poached and cut into cubes

3 cups cooked basmati rice

In a medium stockpot, combine beef broth, plum tomatoes, sugar, thyme, chili powder, black pepper, crushed red pepper, and filé powder. Simmer 10 minutes.

In a nonstick skillet, heat olive oil. Add garlic, onion, and celery, and sauté 4–5 minutes or until onion becomes crisp-tender. Add green pepper and cook 2–3 minutes. Add to stockpot and simmer 10 minutes. Add prawns, chicken, and rice.

Serving Suggestion: Excellent as a main course. Serve with crisp vegetables and Hummus (page 93), Cajun Flatbread (page 60) and assorted seasonal fruits.

APPROXIMATE NUTRITIONAL INFORMATION PER CUP

Total calories: 162
Total Fat: 2 g
Saturated Fat: trace
Dietary Fiber: 10 g
Carbohydrates: 13 g
Protein: 16 g
Cholesterol: 72 mg
Sodium: 269 mg

Homemade Chicken Broth

4 quarts

1 3-to 4-pound chicken, cut up, plus 2 additional whole chicken breasts

1 large onion, peeled and quartered

2 carrots, peeled

2 garlic cloves, peeled

1 tablespoon chopped fresh basil leaves or ½ teaspoon dried

1 tablespoon Kosher salt

½ teaspoon black pepper

5 quarts cold water

Homemade chicken broth is worth the effort. Not only is the taste delicious, but the whole house smells wonderul while the broth is simmering on the stove.
It freezes well and is nice to have on hand. Plus the amount of sodium you cut by not using canned broth is truly amazing. For a quick-to-fix vegetable-based meal, just add beans, rice or leftover pasta, along with any vegetables in your refrigerator. Serve with oyster crackers or crusty French bread and seasonal fruit.

APPROXIMATE NUTRITIONAL INFORMATION PER CUP

Total calories: 27
Total Fat: 1 g
Saturated Fat: 0 g
Dietary Fiber: 0 g
Carbohydrates: 0 g
Protein: 4 g
Cholesterol: 2 mg
Sodium: 250 mg

Wash chicken parts and put all except the 2 additional chicken breasts into an 8-quart stockpot. Add onion, carrots, garlic, basil, salt, pepper, and enough water to cover (add additional water if necessary so that the chicken parts are totally covered by 1 to 2 inches of water).

Heat gradually to boiling point; add whole chicken breasts. Reduce heat to simmer and cook 20 to 30 minutes, or until the additional chicken breast meat is tender. Remove chicken breasts. Cool slightly. Reserve breast meat in refrigerator for later use in sandwiches, salads, or other dishes.

Simmer remaining chicken 2 to 2½ hours, or until chicken is tender and pulls away from the bone. Strain. Remove meat from bones (save meat for later use unless it's way too greasy). Refrigerate broth overnight; fat will float to the top. Skim and discard the fat.

Return broth to stockpot. Simmer, uncovered, 1 hour, or until broth is reduced by about one-fourth. Test seasonings. Sparingly add salt, if needed. Use broth at once, or store in refrigerator or freezer for later use.

Chicken Noodle Soup

Approximately 5 quarts

12 cups chicken broth, preferably homemade (page 143)

1½ cups diced cooked chicken

4 cups cooked egg pastina or alphabet pasta

Heat broth to boiling; add chicken and pastina. Heat and serve.

Note: Ronzoni brand ancini pepe pasta is a good alternative to egg pastina or alphabets.

Variations: Add cooked carrots, celery, or other vegetables. For Chicken with Rice Soup, substitute rice for pasta.

APPROXIMATE NUTRITIONAL INFORMATION PER CUP

Total calories: 78
Total Fat: 2 g
Saturated Fat: 0 g
Dietary Fiber: 0 g
Carbohydrates: 8 g
Protein: 7 g
Cholesterol: 21 mg
Sodium: 152 mg

Chicken and Pastina Soup

2 1/2 quarts (6 servings)

1 6-ounce package egg pastina

2 quarts chicken broth, preferably homemade (page 143)

1 cup finely chopped carrots

½ cup finely chopped fresh parsley

1 7-ounce can mushroom stems and pieces, drained (optional)

1 pound peas in the pod, shelled (optional)

This is one of our family's favorite recipes. When our children were sick, I often made it without the mushrooms and peas. I think simply the good smells alone helped them to feel better.

Cook pastina in boiling water according to package directions. Rinse and drain.

In a 3-quart saucepan, heat chicken broth. Add pastina and carrots; simmer 5 minutes. Add parsley, mushrooms, and peas; simmer 3 to 5 minutes longer.

Note: To save time, use canned broth instead of homemade; however, in this recipe you can tell the difference.

APPROXIMATE NUTRITIONAL INFORMATION PER CUP

Total calories: 173
Total Fat: 3 g
Saturated Fat: 1 g
Dietary Fiber: 2 g
Carbohydrates: 25 g
Protein: 12 g
Cholesterol: 40 mg
Sodium: 333 mg using homemade broth

Chicken Soup with Lemon

3 1-cup servings

3 cups chicken broth, preferably homemade (page 143)

2 tablespoons fresh lemon juice

Heat broth to boiling; add lemon juice. Serve.

Note: Nice as a first course with a seafood entrée.

APPROXIMATE NUTRITIONAL INFORMATION PER CUP

Total calories: 30
Total Fat: 1 g
Saturated Fat: 0 g
Dietary Fiber: 0 g
Carbohydrates: 1 g
Protein: 4 g
Cholesterol: 2 mg
Sodium: 275 mg

Chicken Soup with Tomato and Green Onion

4 1-cup servings

4 cups chicken broth, preferably homemade (page 143)

4 tomato slices

4 green onions with tops, thinly sliced

Heat chicken broth to boiling. Ladle into soup bowls. To each bowl, add 1 tomato slice and green onion. Serve at once.

APPROXIMATE NUTRITIONAL INFORMATION PER CUP

Total calories: 38
Total Fat: 1 g
Saturated Fat: 0 g
Dietary Fiber: 0 g
Carbohydrates: trace
Protein: 2 g
Cholesterol: 4 mg
Sodium: 280 mg

Chicken Soup with Soba Noodles

Approximately 4 quarts

12 cups chicken broth, preferably homemade (page 143)

1 6-ounce package soba (buckwheat) noodles

Heat broth to boiling; add uncooked noodles and bring to a second boil.

Cook 2 to 3 minutes, or until noodles are tender. Do not overcook.

Note: Chinese buckwheat (soba) noodles are found in Asian markets or in the Asian section of the supermarket; they look like "ramen" noodles.

APPROXIMATE NUTRITIONAL INFORMATION PER CUP

Total calories: 46
Total Fat: 1 g
Saturated Fat: 0 g
Dietary Fiber: 0 g
Carbohydrates: 5 g
Protein: 4 g
Cholesterol: 2 mg
Sodium: 235 mg

Chicken Soup with Chinese Vegetables

Approximately 4 quarts

12 cups chicken broth, preferably homemade (page 143)

½ pound fresh mushrooms, sliced

12 cups fresh spinach, washed and torn into bite-size pieces (2 bunches)

2 to 3 drops hot sauce

Heat chicken broth to boiling. Add mushrooms, then spinach; cook 2 minutes. Add hot sauce. Serve at once.

APPROXIMATE NUTRITIONAL INFORMATION PER CUP

Total calories: 33
Total Fat: 1 g
Saturated Fat: 0 g
Dietary Fiber: 2 g
Carbohydrates: 2 g
Protein: 4 g
Cholesterol: 2 mg
Sodium: 230 mg

Wonton Soup

Approximately 3 quarts

¾ pound extra-lean boneless pork chops, ground

¾ teaspoon Kosher salt

¼ teaspoon black pepper

6 shiitake mushrooms, chopped

10 green onions, chopped

2 dozen wonton wrappers, thawed

12 cups chicken broth, preferably homemade (page 143)

1 tablespoon reduced-sodium soy sauce

Sprinkle ground pork with salt and pepper. Mix with mushrooms and green onions. Place mixture by teaspoonful into center of wonton wrappers; squeeze edges of wrapper together to seal.

Drop wontons into 3½ quarts boiling water; bring to a second boil. Boil 2 minutes; add 2 cups cold water. Bring to a third boil; boil 2 to 3 minutes. Drain. Bring chicken broth just to boiling. Stir in soy sauce. Add wontons. Serve.

Note: Wontons may be cooked ahead and refrigerated. To reheat, drop into boiling broth. If fresh shiitake mushrooms are not available, the dried can be purchased in Asian markets or in the Asian section of most supermarkets. To reconstitute dried mushrooms, soak them in enough water to cover for 30 minutes, or until soft; remove and squeeze out the excess water. Remove and discard stems. Reserve soaking liquid; add to chicken broth.

APPROXIMATE NUTRITIONAL INFORMATION PER CUP

Total calories: 138
Total Fat: 7 g
Saturated Fat: 2 g
Dietary Fiber: 0 g
Carbohydrates: 6 g
Protein: 12 g
Cholesterol: 30 mg
Sodium: 359 mg

Egg Drop Soup

Approximately 5 1-cup servings

4 cups chicken broth, preferably homemade (page 143)

1 egg, beaten

6 to 8 cherry tomatoes, thinly sliced

4 green onions with tops, thinly sliced

Heat chicken broth to boiling. Pour egg through a wire strainer into hot broth. Ladle broth into soup bowls; add 1 to 2 sliced cherry tomatoes and sliced green onion to each bowl. Serve at once.

APPROXIMATE NUTRITIONAL INFORMATION PER SERVING

Total calories: 46
Total Fat: 2 g
Saturated Fat: 0 g
Dietary Fiber: trace
Carbohydrates: 0
Protein: 5 g
Cholesterol: 44 mg
Sodium: 237 mg

Chicken and Beef Stock

7 1/2 quarts

1½ pounds beef chuck, cut into 2-inch pieces*

2½ pounds chicken breasts and ribs

2 pounds beef soupbones

7 quarts cold water

3 cloves garlic

3 leeks, roots and green stems removed

1 large yellow onion, quartered

3 stalks celery with leaves

3 carrots, peeled

3 ripe tomatoes, quartered

2 bay leaves

¼ cup chopped fresh parsley

1 teaspoon thyme

1 tablespoon Kosher salt

3 black peppercorns

4 white peppercorns

In a stockpot, combine beef, chicken parts, soupbones, and water; bring slowly to a boil, removing scum and fat as they float to the top.

Add remaining ingredients and simmer 3½ hours. (Do not boil, or fat will be reabsorbed into the stock and will make it cloudy.) Strain stock. Refrigerate overnight. Skim fat from surface and discard.

Return stock to stockpot. Simmer, uncovered, 3 hours or until stock is reduced by one-third. Test seasoning; sparingly add additional salt, if needed. Use stock at once, or store in freezer or up to 2 weeks in refrigerator. (It's a good idea to freeze some stock in ice-cube trays to use for stir-frying or sautéing vegetables.)

*Remove meaty chicken parts and beef chuck from stock as soon as they are cooked (about 45–90 minutes). Reserve for stews, soups, salads, and sandwiches. Return any bones, scraps, and skins to stockpot for remainder of cooking.

APPROXIMATE NUTRITIONAL INFORMATION PER CUP

Total calories: 370
Total Fat: 1 g
Saturated Fat: 0 g
Dietary Fiber: 0 g
Carbohydrates: 0 g
Protein: 5 g
Cholesterol: 2 mg
Sodium: 275 mg

The Best Turkey Soup

4 quarts

1 recipe Basic Turkey Stock (below)

3 carrots, peeled and diced

2 celery stalks, diced

1 large onion, finely chopped

2 garlic cloves, minced

4 cups cooked elbow macaroni

½ pound fresh mushrooms, sliced (optional)

½ cup chopped fresh parsley

Basic Turkey Stock

1 turkey carcass with meaty bones

5 quarts water or enough to cover turkey parts by about 2 inches

3 garlic cloves, peeled

1 large yellow onion, quartered

3 carrots, peeled

3 celery stalks with leaves

3 tablespoons fresh basil leaves or 1 teaspoon dried

1 tablespoon Kosher salt

Stretch your food dollars. Cook a turkey not just on Thanksgiving but now and then on a weekend. The leftovers make great lunch-box sandwiches, and the carcass makes the best turkey soup.

Place turkey carcass in a stockpot (pull carcass apart so it will fit); add enough water to cover. Bring slowly to a boil, removing scum and fat that floats to the top. Add remaining ingredients and simmer 3½ hours. Do not boil or fat will be reabsorbed into the stock, making it cloudy. Strain stock; discard bones and vegetables, as they will be very greasy. Refrigerate overnight. Skim and discard fat that floats to the top.

Return stock to stockpot. Simmer, uncovered, 1 hour or until stock is reduced by one-third. Test seasoning. Sparingly add more salt, if needed. Use stock at once, or store in refrigerator or freezer for later use.

Bring reduced basic stock just to boiling; add carrots, celery, onion and garlic. Cover; reduce heat and simmer until vegetables are tender, about 30 minutes. Add macaroni and mushrooms; heat to serving temperature, about 2 to 3 minutes. Sprinkle with parsley.

APPROXIMATE NUTRITIONAL INFORMATION PER CUP

Total calories: 95
Total Fat: 2 g
Saturated Fat: 1 g
Dietary Fiber: 1 g
Carbohydrates: 13 g
Protein: 4 g
Cholesterol: 0 mg
Sodium: 262 mg

Chicken Chili

10 servings

1 tablespoon olive oil

½ cup Serrano chilies, chopped

2/3 cup sweet onion, chopped

1 cup yellow pepper, chopped

1 cup red pepper, chopped

2/3 cup celery

3 cloves garlic, minced

1 28-ounce can plum tomatoes with liquid

3 cups (8 ounces) cubed uncooked chicken breast

1 tablespoon chili powder

1/8 teaspoon ground cumin

½ teaspoon cayenne pepper

½ teaspoon Kosher salt

¼ teaspoon black pepper

2 15-ounce cans red kidney beans, drained and rinsed

2¼ cups fresh corn (5 ears)

Optional toppings:

Chopped onions

Grated Cheddar cheese

Sliced olives

Heat the olive oil in a nonstick skillet over medium heat. Add the Serrano chilies and the onion and sauté 8-10 minutes, until the onions are translucent. Add the peppers and celery, cook 2-3 minutes. Add garlic and cook for one minute.

Meanwhile, put the liquid from the tomatoes into an 8-quart stockpot. Squeeze the plum tomatoes by hand and add to stockpot. Heat just to boiling, but do not boil. Add chicken and seasonings and simmer uncovered for 20 minutes. Transfer onion mixture to stockpot. Stir in red beans and corn. Simmer 10 minutes. Serve into bowls. Pass toppings.

APPROXIMATE NUTRITIONAL INFORMATION PER SERVING

Total calories: 210
Total Fat: 4 g
Saturated Fat: 0 g
Dietary Fiber: 7 g
Carbohydrates: 35 g
Protein: 14 g
Cholesterol: 15 mg
Sodium: 368 mg

Beef Stock

7 1/2 quarts

4 pounds beef chuck, cut into 2-inch cubes*

4 pounds beef marrow bones

7 quarts cold water

3 cloves garlic

3 leeks, roots and green stems removed

1 large yellow onion, quartered

3 stalks celery with leaves

3 carrots, peeled

3 ripe tomatoes, quartered

2 bay leaves

¼ cup chopped fresh parsley

1 teaspoon thyme

1 tablespoon Kosher salt

3 black peppercorns

4 white peppercorns

In a stockpot, combine beef chuck, marrow bones and water; bring slowly to a boil, removing scum and fat as they float to the top.

Add remaining ingredients and simmer 3½ hours. Strain stock. Refrigerate overnight. Skim fat from surface and discard.

Return stock to stockpot. Simmer, uncovered, 3 hours or until stock is reduced by one-third. Test seasoning. Sparingly add salt, if needed.

Use stock at once, or store in freezer or up to 2 weeks in refrigerator. (You may want to freeze some stock in ice-cube trays to use for stir-frying or sautéing vegetables.)

*Remove choice pieces of meat from stock as soon as they are cooked (about 1½ hours). Serve for dinner with steamed red potatoes and Stir-Fried Snow Peas (page 381).

APPROXIMATE NUTRITIONAL INFORMATION PER CUP

Total calories: 37
Total Fat: 1 g
Saturated Fat: 0 g
Dietary Fiber: 0 mg
Carbohydrates: 0 g
Protein: 5 g
Cholesterol: 2 mg
Sodium: 262 mg

Beef Broth

Approximately 2 quarts

**6 pounds beef bones or
2–3 pounds beef shank
or short ribs**

9 cups water

3 stalks celery with leaves, diced

2 carrots, diced

1 onion, chopped

1 tomato, quartered

2 bay leaves

2 cloves garlic

¼ teaspoon thyme

¼ teaspoon marjoram

8 black peppercorns

1 tablespoon Kosher salt

Place meat, bones, and water in a stockpot. Simmer, uncovered, 3 hours (do not boil).

Strain. Remove any meat or marrow from bones. Add marrow to broth; reserve meat for soup. Chill broth overnight; skim fat from the surface and discard. Bring broth to boiling; add remaining ingredients and simmer, uncovered, 2 hours. Strain. Test seasonings. Sparingly add additional salt as needed. Reheat broth, or store in freezer or up to 2 weeks in refrigerator.

**APPROXIMATE
NUTRITIONAL
INFORMATION
PER CUP**

Total calories: 37
Total Fat: 1 g
Saturated Fat: 0 g
Dietary Fiber: 0 g
Carbohydrates: 0 g
Protein: 5 g
Cholesterol: 2 mg
Sodium: 480 mg

Beef Broth with Mushrooms

Approximately 3 1-cup servings

**1 leek with green tops, finely
chopped**

**3 cups reduced-fat beef broth,
preferably homemade (page 151)**

**½ cup thinly sliced fresh
mushrooms**

**½ teaspoon fresh tarragon or
thyme or ¼ teaspoon dried**

**¼ cup finely chopped
fresh parsley**

Sauté leek in a small amount of the broth; add mushrooms and stir over high heat for 1 minute. Add remaining broth and tarragon or thyme. Bring to a boil; cover, reduce heat, and simmer 20 minutes. Just before serving, sprinkle with parsley.

**APPROXIMATE
NUTRITIONAL
INFORMATION
PER CUP**

Total calories: 57
Total Fat: 1 g
Saturated Fat: 0 g
Dietary Fiber: 0 g
Carbohydrates: 4 g
Protein: 6 g
Cholesterol: 2 mg
Sodium: 281 mg

Veal Stock

3 1/2 quarts

1 pound veal chuck, cut into 2-inch pieces*

3 pounds veal bones

2 carrots, peeled

1 large yellow onion, quartered

3 quarts cold water

2 stalks celery with leaves

2 cloves garlic, peeled

1 bay leaf

2 teaspoons peppercorns

½ teaspoon thyme

1 tablespoon Kosher salt

2 tablespoons tomato paste

½ cup white wine

In a shallow baking dish, combine veal chuck, veal bones, carrots, and onion; bake at 350°F. 15–20 minutes. Remove to stock pot; add water. Bring slowly to a boil, removing scum (and fat) as it floats to the top. Add remaining ingredients and simmer 3 hours. (Do not boil or fat will be reabsorbed into the broth, making it cloudy.) Strain stock. Refrigerate overnight. Skim and discard fat that floats to the top.

Return broth to stock pot. Simmer, uncovered, 1 hour, or until broth is reduced by one-third. Test seasoning. Sparingly add salt, if needed. Use broth at once, or store in refrigerator or freezer for later use.

*Remove choice pieces of meat from stock as soon as they are cooked (about 1–1½ hours). Serve for dinner with fresh asparagus and a heavy-type pasta, such as penne, with Marinara Sauce (page 214).

APPROXIMATE NUTRITIONAL INFORMATION PER CUP

Total calories: 27
Total Fat: 0 g
Saturated Fat: 0 g
Dietary Fiber: 0 g
Carbohydrates: 0 g
Protein: 3 g
Cholesterol: 3 mg
Sodium: 230 mg

Beef and Bean Soup

6 main-dish servings

½ **pound leanest ground beef**

1 **onion, chopped**

1 **28-ounce can plum tomatoes, with liquid, diced**

1½ **cups chicken broth, preferably homemade (page 143)**

1 **packet (1 ounce) Lawry's Taco Seasoning**

1 **15-ounce can black beans, drained and rinsed**

1 **15-ounce can red kidney beans, drained and rinsed**

1 **4-ounce can diced green chilies (optional)**

2 **cups fresh or frozen corn**

1 **cup black olives, pitted and sliced (optional)**

The beef, beans, and corn will be very filling in this hearty soup. Filling equals satisfaction.

In a nonstick skillet, sauté ground beef and onion. Drain on paper towels; pat with additional paper toweling to remove excess fat.

Set aside.

In a 2-quart saucepan, combine remaining ingredients and heat through. Add ground beef and heat soup to serving temperature.

APPROXIMATE NUTRITIONAL INFORMATION PER SERVING

Total calories: 313
Total Fat: 7 g
Saturated Fat: 2 g
Dietary Fiber: 10 g
Carbohydrates: 45 g
Protein: 19 g
Cholesterol: 32 mg
Sodium: 507 mg

Salads

Lettuce, Onion, and Tomato Salad

4 servings

3 cups red leaf lettuce, torn into bite-size pieces

3 cups green leaf lettuce torn into bite-size pieces

1 tomato, cut into wedges

Dijon Vinaigrette (page 207)

4 red onion rings

In a bowl, toss red and green leaf lettuce and tomato with desired amount of dressing. Arrange on chilled salad plates. Garnish with red onion rings.

Add 28 calories per tablespoon of dressing.

APPROXIMATE NUTRITIONAL INFORMATION PER SERVING WITHOUT DRESSING

Total calories: 23
Total Fat: trace
Saturated Fat: trace
Dietary Fiber: 2 g
Carbohydrates: 5 g
Protein: 1 g
Cholesterol: 0 mg
Sodium: 12 mg

Lettuce and Bermuda Onion Salad

4 servings

1 head red leaf lettuce, torn into bite-size pieces

¼ Bermuda onion, cut into rings

Creamy Garlic Dressing (page 208)

In a salad bowl, toss the lettuce and onion with desired amount of vinaigrette. Arrange on chilled salad plates.

APPROXIMATE NUTRITIONAL INFORMATION PER SERVING WITHOUT DRESSING

Total calories: 8
Total Fat: trace
Saturated Fat: trace
Dietary Fiber: trace
Carbohydrates: 1 g
Protein: trace
Cholesterol: 0 mg
Sodium: 2 mg

Caesar Salad

6 servings

2 large heads romaine lettuce, torn into bite-size pieces

Juice of ½ lemon

⅓ cup extra-virgin olive oil, preferably Garlic Olive Oil (page 210)

2½ tablespoons red wine vinegar

2 cloves garlic

1 pasturized egg*

½ teaspoon salt

¼ teaspoon black pepper

½ teaspoon Worcestershire sauce

6 anchovy fillets, finely chopped (optional)

¾ cup unseasoned croutons

⅓ cup freshly grated Parmesan cheese

Arrange romaine in a large salad bowl. Drizzle with lemon juice. Add olive oil, vinegar, coddled egg, salt, pepper, and Worcestershire sauce; toss. Add anchovies and croutons; toss again. Sprinkle with Parmesan and toss lightly again.

Note: As with most Caesar salad recipes, this one is not low in fat. I have included it because it is one of my favorite "serve to company" menus.

As a first course, I serve Gazpacho (page 122). I accompany the salad with marinated grilled prawns, fresh cracked crab, and sourdough French bread.

By accompanying the salad with these other low-fat foods, and selecting low-fat foods for breakfast and lunch, it's possible to control your fat budget for the day.

*Raw eggs have been identified as a source of samonella. The American Egg Board recommends using only pasturized eggs to eliminate the risk. Pasturized eggs are available in many supermarkets.

APPROXIMATE NUTRITIONAL INFORMATION PER SERVING

Total calories: 174
Total Fat: 15 g
Saturated Fat: 3 g
Dietary Fiber: 1 g
Carbohydrates: 6 g
Protein: 6 g
Cholesterol: 39 mg
Sodium: 430 mg

Shrimp Caesar Salad

6 servings

Caesar Salad (see preceding recipe)

1½ cups small cooked shrimp

Prepare recipe for Caesar Salad as directed. Divide salad among individual salad plates. Top with shrimp.

Variation: Substitute crabmeat or chicken breast for shrimp.

APPROXIMATE NUTRITIONAL INFORMATION PER SERVING

Total calories: 213
Total Fat: 15 g
Saturated Fat: 3 g
Dietary Fiber: 1 g
Carbohydrates: 6 g
Protein: 13 g
Cholesterol: 95 mg
Sodium: 514 mg

Romaine Salad

4 servings

½ **English cucumber, peeled and thinly sliced**

½ **red onion, cut into 1-inch cubes**

2 medium tomatoes, cut into 1-inch cubes

Italian Vinaigrette (page 204)

1 small head romaine lettuce, torn into bite-size pieces

In a salad bowl, toss cucumber, onion, and tomatoes with desired amount of dressing. Chill 2 hours. Just before serving, add romaine and toss.

Add 90 calories per tablespoon of Italian Vinaigrette.

APPROXIMATE NUTRITIONAL INFORMATION PER SERVING WITHOUT DRESSING

Total calories: 30
Total Fat: trace
Saturated Fat: trace
Dietary Fiber: 2 g
Carbohydrates: 6 g
Protein: 2 g
Cholesterol: 0 mg
Sodium: 10 mg

Spinach Salad

4 servings

2 bunches fresh spinach

1 bunch radishes, sliced

8 fresh mushrooms, sliced

Mustard-and-Lemon Vinaigrette (page 206) or Oil-free Lemon Vinaigrette (page 205)

Wash and trim spinach. Chill. Tear into bite-size pieces. Put in a bowl and toss with radishes and mushrooms. Pour dressing into cruet; pass with salad.

Add 108 calories per tablespoon of Mustard and Lemon Vinaigrette.

Add 2 calories per tablespoon of Oil-Free Lemon Vinaigrette.

APPROXIMATE NUTRITIONAL INFORMATION PER SERVING

WITHOUT DRESSING

Calories: 49
Total fat: 1 g
Saturated fat: 0 g
Dietary fiber: 5 g
Carbohydrate: 8 g
Protein: 6 g
Cholesterol: 0 mg
Sodium: 138 mg

Warm Spinach Salad

6 servings

2 tablespoons reduced-sodium soy sauce

¼ cup sake

1 teaspoon sesame oil

1 teaspoon granulated sugar

1 bunch fresh spinach leaves, torn into bite-size pieces

¼ pound fresh mushrooms, sliced

1½ tablespoons toasted sesame seeds

In a small saucepan, combine soy sauce, sake, sesame oil and sugar. Simmer 5 minutes.

Put spinach and mushrooms into a salad bowl. Toss with warm dressing. Sprinkle with sesame seeds. Serve at once.

Serving Suggestion: Especially good with grilled seafoods.

APPROXIMATE NUTRITIONAL INFORMATION PER SERVING WITHOUT DRESSING

Total calories: 47
Total Fat: 2 g
Saturated Fat: 0 g
Dietary Fiber: 3 g
Carbohydrates: 5 g
Protein: 3 g
Cholesterol: 0 mg
Sodium: 167 mg

Spinach and Onion Salad

6 servings

3 cloves garlic

6 tablespoons fresh lemon juice

¼ cup extra-virgin olive oil

¾ teaspoon salt or to taste

1 bunch fresh spinach leaves, torn into bite-size pieces

½ white onion, thinly sliced into rings

In a small bowl, combine garlic, lemon juice, olive oil, and salt. In a salad bowl, toss spinach and onion with desired amount of dressing.

Most of the fat is in the dressing. Remember to use a moderate amount.

Add 46 calories, 4 grams of fat, and 145 mg of sodium per tablespoon of dressing.

APPROXIMATE NUTRITIONAL INFORMATION PER SERVING WITHOUT DRESSING

Total calories: 20
Total Fat: trace
Saturated Fat: trace
Dietary Fiber: 2 g
Carbohydrates: 3 g
Protein: 2 g
Cholesterol: 0 mg
Sodium: 66 mg

Cucumber and Onion Salad

6 servings

1 English cucumber, thinly sliced

1 white onion, thinly sliced into rings

⅓ cup rice vinegar

1½ tablespoons granulated sugar

½ teaspoon Kosher salt

⅛ teaspoon black pepper

In a 2-quart glass bowl, toss cucumber and onion. In a jar with cover, combine vinegar, sugar, salt, and pepper. Pour over cucumber and onion. Chill 2 hours. Drain.

Note: Quality rice vinegar is the key to this simple salad. Our favorite brand is O Yuzu Rice Vinegar.

APPROXIMATE NUTRITIONAL INFORMATION PER SERVING

Total calories: 26
Total Fat: trace
Saturated Fat: trace
Dietary Fiber: trace
Carbohydrates: 6 g
Protein: trace
Cholesterol: 0 mg
Sodium: 146 mg

English Cucumber Salad

4 servings

1 English cucumber, unpeeled

2 teaspoons Kosher salt (to be rinsed off)

2 tablespoons rice vinegar

Cut cucumber crosswise into 1/8 -inch flat slices. Arrange in a bowl and sprinkle with salt. Let stand 10 minutes. Arrange in a colander and rinse thoroughly. Drain and pat dry. Chill. Drizzle with rice vinegar.

Note: Quality rice vinegar is the key to this simple salad. Our favorite brand is O Yuzu Rice Vinegar.

APPROXIMATE NUTRITIONAL INFORMATION PER SERVING

Total calories: 13
Total Fat: 0 g
Saturated Fat: 0 g
Dietary Fiber: 1 g
Carbohydrates: 3 g
Protein: 1 g
Cholesterol: 0 mg
Sodium: 384 mg

Santa Fe Salad

4 servings

Dressing

3 tablespoons extra-virgin olive oil

1 tablespoon cider vinegar

1 garlic clove, minced

¼ teaspoon Kosher salt

⅛ teaspoon black pepper

dash bottled hot sauce

2 cups torn mixed greens

3 cups fresh baby spinach leaves

1 chopped ripe tomato

This dressing keeps a long time so you may want to double or even triple the recipe. Use a good grade of olive oil. The flavor is so intense, you'll find you need only a small amount of dressing to add flavor to your salads. A sliced, ripe avocado is a nice addition to the salad— with the fat coming from the healthy monounsaturated type.

In a screw-top jar, combine olive oil, vinegar, garlic, salt, pepper, and hot suace. Cover and shake well.

In a medium salad bowl, combine mixed greens, spinach leaves and tomato. Pour dressing over. Toss lightly with dressing to coat.

APPROXIMATE NUTRITIONAL INFORMATION PER SERVING

Total calories: 104
Total Fat: 10 g
Saturated Fat: 1 g
Dietary Fiber: 2 g
Carbohydrates: 3 g
Protein: 2 g
Cholesterol: 0 mg
Sodium: 144 mg

Fresh Basil and Tomato Salad

4 servings

1 bunch fresh basil

4 ripe tomatoes, quartered

black pepper to taste

pinch Kosher salt

4 teaspoons extra-virgin olive oil

Wash and trim basil. Spread over chilled salad plates. Arrange tomatoes over basil. Drizzle teaspoon of olive oil over each salad. Sprinkle with black pepper and Kosher salt.

Variation: Squeeze lemon or lime juice over tomatoes and basil for a wonderful flavor.

Note: Heirloom tomatoes are our favorites. The flavor is superior.

APPROXIMATE NUTRITIONAL INFORMATION PER SERVING

Total calories: 73
Total Fat: 46 g
Saturated Fat: 0 g
Dietary Fiber: 1 g
Carbohydrates: 6 g
Protein: 1 g
Cholesterol: 0 mg
Sodium: 11 mg

Tomatoes with Fresh Mozzarella and Basil

6 servings

1 large bunch fresh basil leaves

4 large ripe tomatoes, preferably heirloom, sliced into ¼-inch slices

½ pound fresh buffalo mozzarella cheese, cut into ¼-inch slices

1 tablespoon extra-virgin olive oil

Kosher salt and coarse black pepper to taste

This quick salad is especially good in the summer when tomatoes and basil are at their peak.

Wash and trim basil. Spread basil leaves on an oval platter. Arrange alternating slices of tomatoes and mozzarella over the basil. Drizzle with olive oil. Season with salt and pepper.

APPROXIMATE NUTRITIONAL INFORMATION PER SERVING

Total calories: 139
Total Fat: 9 g
Saturated Fat: 4 g
Dietary Fiber: 2 g
Carbohydrates: 6 g
Protein: 27 g
Cholesterol: 13 mg
Sodium: 212 mg

Zucchini and Tomato Salad with Dijon Vinaigrette

6 servings

2 small zucchini, peeled and sliced lengthwise into julienne strips

12 cherry tomatoes, halved

¼ cup Dijon Vinaigrette (page 207)

1 head Bibb lettuce

Toss zucchini with vinaigrette. Line a salad bowl with lettuce leaves; fill with zucchini. Dot with tomatoes.

APPROXIMATE NUTRITIONAL INFORMATION PER CUP

Total calories: 130
Total Fat: 2 g
Saturated Fat: 0 g
Dietary Fiber: 1 g
Carbohydrates: 3 g
Protein: 1 g
Cholesterol: 0 mg
Sodium: 50 mg

Green Chili and Tomato Salad

Approximately 9 1/2-cup servings

2 ripe tomatoes, chopped

1 4-ounce can chopped green chilies

4 green onions, chopped

1 bunch leaf lettuce, torn into bite-size pieces

¼ pound sliced fresh mushrooms, steamed 2 to 3 minutes, chilled

¼ cup Italian Vinaigrette (page 204)

Combine tomatoes, green chilies, and onions. Chill for 3 hours. Just before serving, toss tomatoes, chilies, onions, and lettuce with mushrooms. Drizzle with dressing. Toss.

Serving Suggestion: Great salad with Three-Bean Chili (page 127). Garnish with tortilla chips made with a heart-healthy oil such as sunflower, safflower, soy, or corn. .

APPROXIMATE NUTRITIONAL INFORMATION PER SERVING

Total calories: 60
Total Fat: 5 g
Saturated Fat: trace
Dietary Fiber: 1 g
Carbohydrates: 4 g
Protein: 1 g
Cholesterol: 0 mg
Sodium: 60 mg

Pepper, Onion and Tomato Salad

4 servings

4 cups leaf lettuce torn into bite-size pieces

2 ripe tomatoes, quartered

½ red pepper, cut into strips

½ green, yellow, or orange pepper, cut into strips

Italian Vinaigrette (page 204)

¼ red onion, cut into rings

In a bowl, toss lettuce, tomatoes, and peppers with desired amount of vinaigrette. Arrange on chilled salad plates. Garnish with red onion rings.

Add 90 calories per tablespoon of Italian Vinagrette.

APPROXIMATE NUTRITIONAL INFORMATION PER SERVING WITHOUT DRESSING

Total calories: 30
Total Fat: trace
Saturated Fat: trace
Dietary Fiber: 2 g
Carbohydrates: 6 g
Protein: 1 g
Cholesterol: 0 mg
Sodium: 12 mg

Corn and Tomato Salad

6 servings

2 cups fresh (5 cobs) corn kernels

1 white onion, chopped

1½ cups chopped ripe tomatoes, preferably heirloom

1 tablespoon rice wine vinegar

2 tablespoons fresh lime juice

2 tablespoons extra-virgin olive oil

½ teaspoon Kosher salt

¼ teaspoon black pepper

¼ cup chopped fresh cilantro

12 whole fresh cilantro leaves for garnish

In a medium bowl, combine corn, onion, and tomatoes. Chill at least 2 hours. In a covered jar, combine rice wine vinegar, lime juice, olive oil, salt, and pepper; pour over corn. Add chopped cilantro. Garnish with remaining cilantro, and serve at once.

For spicier version, I add one 4-ounce can mild or hot diced jalapeños. Great with tortilla chips. And really great with tacos.

APPROXIMATE NUTRITIONAL INFORMATION PER SERVING

Total calories: 120
Total Fat: 5 g
Saturated Fat: 1 g
Dietary Fiber: 2 g
Carbohydrates: 18 g
Protein: 2 g
Cholesterol: 0 mg
Sodium: 242 mg

Green Beans, Tomatoes, Artichokes, and Mushroom Salad

10 cups

1 pound fresh green beans, cooked

1 14½ -ounce can water-packed artichoke hearts

1 8-ounce can sliced water chestnuts

½ pound fresh mushrooms, steamed 2 to 3 minutes, sliced

½ cup Italian Vinaigrette (page 204)

15 cherry tomatoes, chilled

Drain beans, artichokes, water chestnuts, and mushrooms. Chill. Just before serving, moisten with dressing; toss with chilled tomatoes.

Add 90 calories per tablespoon of Italian Vinagrette.

APPROXIMATE NUTRITIONAL INFORMATION PER CUP

Total calories: 64
Total Fat: 3 g
Saturated Fat: 0 g
Dietary Fiber: 2 g
Carbohydrates: 9 g
Protein: 2 g
Cholesterol: 0 mg
Sodium: 110 mg

Marinated Peppers and Onions

4 servings

1 medium yellow or green pepper

1 medium red pepper

½ medium white onion

½ medium red onion

1 large tomato

1½ tablespoons extra-virgin olive oil

1½ tablespoons fresh lemon juice

1½ tablespoons fresh lime juice

½ teaspoon Kosher salt

¾ teaspoon black pepper

½ teaspoon Tabasco or Sriracha sauce

Cut peppers in half, remove seeds, and cut crosswise into ¼-inch rings. Cut onions into ¼-inch rings. Coarsely chop tomato. In a covered jar, combine olive oil, lemon juice, lime juice, salt, pepper, and hot sauce. Pour over vegetables and toss. Chill 2–3 hours.

APPROXIMATE NUTRITIONAL INFORMATION PER SERVING WITH DRESSING

Total calories: 70
Total Fat: 5 g
Saturated Fat: trace
Dietary Fiber: 1 g
Carbohydrates: 6 g
Protein: 1 g
Cholesterol: 0 mg
Sodium: 223 mg

Vegetable Antipasto Salad

8 servings

1 clove garlic, minced

¼ cup fresh lemon juice

1 tablespoon olive oil

½ teaspoon salt

¼ teaspoon black pepper

4 small carrots, peeled and thinly sliced on the diagonal

1 small zucchini, peeled and sliced on the diagonal into matchstick strips

¼ pound broccoli florets

6 tiny red potatoes, quartered

¼ pound fresh green beans

½ red onion, cut into rings

6 plum tomatoes, quartered

In a covered jar, combine garlic, lemon juice, olive oil, salt, and pepper. Set aside. In a steamer over boiling water, steam vegetables, one type at a time, just until crisp-tender; carrots, zucchini and broccoli about 2 minutes each; potatoes and green beans about 6–10 minutes each. As each vegetable is cooked, remove to a 13 x 9 x 2-inch glass casserole dish. Tuck onion rings and tomatoes among vegetables as garnish. Chill at least 3 hours. Just before serving, toss with dressing.

APPROXIMATE NUTRITIONAL INFORMATION PER SERVING WITH DRESSING

Total calories: 112
Total Fat: 2 g
Saturated Fat: trace
Dietary Fiber: 4 g
Carbohydrates: 22 g
Protein: 3 g
Cholesterol: 0 mg
Sodium: 157 mg

Farmer's Market Salad

1 serving

2 leaves red leaf lettuce

2 leaves green leaf lettuce

1 broccoli floret, steamed or microwaved 1–2 minutes or until crisp-tender

1 cauliflower floret, steamed or microwaved 2 minutes or until crisp-tender

1 large carrot, grated

1 medium ripe tomato, diced

2 very thin raw turnip slices

3 very thin red onion rings

⅓ cup homemade Tomato and Chili Salsa (p. 216) or commercial tomato salsa

Layer lettuce leaves on a chilled dinner plate. Arrange the remaining vegetables on the lettuce. Accompany with tomato salsa.

Variation: Add ½ cup 1% or 2% cottage cheese, ½ cup couscous or ½ cup saffron-flavored rice. (To make saffron rice, stir in ¼ teaspoon powdered saffron to cooked rice.)

Serving Suggestion: Excellent for lunch accompanied with a whole-wheat roll or a slice of hearty bread.

The sodium will fluctuate depending on the brand of salsa. Homemade tomato and chili salsa has 28 mg of sodium per ⅓ cup. Some commercial brands may have as much as 400 mg.

APPROXIMATE NUTRITIONAL INFORMATION PER SERVING WITH SALSA

Total calories: 145
Total Fat: 1 g
Saturated Fat: trace
Dietary Fiber: 9 g
Carbohydrates: 32 g
Protein: 6 g
Cholesterol: 0 mg
Sodium: 100 mg

Layered Salad

10 side-dish servings

1 small head iceberg lettuce, finely chopped

½ cup green onion, thinly sliced

1 cup celery, thinly sliced

1 8-ounce can sliced water chestnuts, drained

2 cups fresh baby peas

1 cup light mayonnaise

¼ teaspoon Kosher salt

¼ teaspoon black pepper

2 tablespoons grated reduced-fat cheddar cheese

1 tomato, thinly sliced

3 slices crisp-broiled Canadian bacon, finely chopped

Using a shallow glass bowl, layer lettuce, green onion, celery, water chestnuts, and peas. Cover and chill. Just before serving, spread with mayonnaise. Season with salt and pepper. Sprinkle with cheese and spread tomato and Canadian bacon over top. Do not toss; serve layered.

Note: Homemade mayonnaise takes only a few minutes to make and is delicious on this salad.

APPROXIMATE NUTRITIONAL INFORMATION PER SERVING

Total calories: 150
Total Fat: 9 g
Saturated Fat: 2 g
Dietary Fiber: 2 g
Carbohydrates: 12 g
Protein: 5 g
Cholesterol: 5 mg
Sodium: 370 mg

Farm Salad

6 servings

½ **head Bibb lettuce**

½ **head Boston lettuce**

½ **head red leaf lettuce**

1 English cucumber unpeeled and cut into julienne strips

Szechuan Vinaigrette or Oil-Free Szechuan Vinaigrette (page 205).

Wash lettuces and tear into bite-size pieces. Combine in a bowl. Garnish with cucumber. Pour dressing into cruet; pass with salad.

This is a wonderful treat in midsummer with fresh garden lettuce at its best.

Add 75 calories per tablespoon of Szechuan Vinaigrette.

Add 5 calories per tablespoon of Oil-Free Szechuan Vinaigrette.

APPROXIMATE NUTRITIONAL INFORMATION PER SERVING

Total calories: 14
Total Fat: trace
Saturated Fat: 0 g
Dietary Fiber: 1 g
Carbohydrates: 3 g
Protein: 1 g
Cholesterol: 0 mg
Sodium: 3 mg

Build-Your-Own Salad

6 servings

BUTTERMILK DRESSING:

½ **cup nonfat sour cream**

½ **cup nonfat cottage cheese**

1 cup low-fat (1%) buttermilk

1 0.4-ounce package Hidden Valley Ranch Original Ranch Salad Dressing Mix (Buttermilk Recipe) or Uncle Dan's Original Southern Salad Dressing Mix

SALAD:

6 cups mixed greens (make at least 2 cups of them spinach)

1 cup broccoli florets

1 cup cauliflower florets

4 large carrots, cut into julienne strips

1 bunch chopped green onions

1 large cucumber, peeled and diced

1 large ripe tomato, coarsely chopped

When kids make their own salads, they often eat more vegetables than they do when someone serves them. They'll love this home salad bar.

Combine sour cream, cottage cheese, buttermilk and salad dressing mix. Chill. Makes 2 cups.

Arrange mixed greens in a medium salad bowl. In separate bowls, arrange the broccoli, cauliflower, carrots, green onions, cucumber, tomatoes, and ¾ cup of the Buttermilk Dressing. Each person can then build his or her own salad. Reserve remaining dressing for later use.

Add 8 calories for each additional tablespoon of dressing.

APPROXIMATE NUTRITIONAL INFORMATION PER SERVING

Total calories: 128
Total Fat: 1 g
Saturated Fat: 0 g
Dietary Fiber: 7 g
Carbohydrates: 26 g
Protein: 8 g
Cholesterol: 2 mg
Sodium: 182 mg
Calcium: 135 mg

Tijuana Salad

4 servings

1 head iceberg lettuce, shredded

10 fresh mushrooms, sliced and steamed 1–2 minutes

¼ cup chopped white onion

¼ cup grated reduced-fat Cheddar cheese

2 tablespoons sunflower seeds

2 ripe tomatoes, quartered

tomato salsa

Arrange lettuce on chilled salad plates. Top with mushrooms and onions. Sprinkle with cheese. Garnish with sunflower seeds. Ring with tomatoes. Pass with salsa.

Serving Suggestion: Good for lunch or light supper.

APPROXIMATE NUTRITIONAL INFORMATION PER SERVING

Total calories: 262
Total Fat: 4 g
Saturated Fat: 1 g
Dietary Fiber: 4 g
Carbohydrates: 10 g
Protein: 6 g
Cholesterol: 4 mg
Sodium: 88 mg

Add 4 calories per tablespoon of salsa

Ensenada Salad

4 servings

½ cucumber, peeled

3 cups red leaf lettuce torn into bite-size pieces

1½ cups Bibb lettuce

1½ cups fresh spinach leaves

2 medium tomatoes, diced

Jalapeño Vinaigrette (page 208)

Cut cucumber in half lengthwise, then slice crosswise into ¼-inch pieces. In a salad bowl, toss lettuces, spinach, cucumber, and tomatoes. Drizzle with Jalapeño Vinaigrette to taste.

APPROXIMATE NUTRITIONAL INFORMATION PER SERVING WITHOUT DRESSING

Total calories: 27
Total Fat: trace
Saturated Fat: trace
Dietary Fiber: 2 g
Carbohydrates: 5 g
Protein: 2 g
Cholesterol: 0 mg
Sodium: 40 mg

Chinese Tossed Salad

6 servings

1 2-inch piece ginger root, peeled

2 whole chicken breasts, skinned, boned and halved

4 cups chicken broth (page 143)

1 6½ -ounce package Maifun rice sticks*

10 black forest (Shiitake) mushrooms,* cut into strings**

1 English cucumber, thinly sliced

3–4 green onions, cut into strings

Szechuan Vinaigrette or Oil-free Szechuan Vinaigrette (page 205)

Grate ginger root; squeeze pulp to make juice. Pour ginger juice over chicken breasts. Let stand 30 minutes. In a medium saucepan, bring stock to a boil. Add chicken and cook over medium heat 20 minutes, or until chicken is done. Remove chicken from broth (reserve broth). As soon as chicken is hot, tear into strings.

Bring broth to a second boil. Add rice sticks and mushrooms, and cook 5–7 minutes, or until rice sticks are tender. Drain any excess moisture (the rice sticks will soak up most of the broth in cooking).

Toss rice sticks with chicken, mushrooms, and cucumber. Top with green onions. Pour dressing into cruet; pass with salad.

*Rice sticks and Shiitake mushrooms are available in Asian markets, if not in your supermarket.

**If fresh black forest mushrooms are not available, use dried Shiitake mushrooms. Reconstitute by soaking them in water 30 minutes, or until soft (save the soaking water for soup).

Variations: Substitute buckwheat (soba) noodles for Maifun rice sticks. Substitute 1 cup snow peas, steamed 1–2 minutes, for green onions.

APPROXIMATE NUTRITIONAL INFORMATION PER SERVING

Total calories: 369
Total Fat: 11 g
Saturated Fat: 1 g
Dietary Fiber: 7 g
Carbohydrates: 44 g
Protein: 26 g
Cholesterol: 34 mg
Sodium: 471 mg

Winter Vegetable Salad

4 servings

3 cups romaine lettuce torn into bite-size pieces

1½ cups Bibb lettuce torn into bite-size pieces

1½ cups iceberg lettuce torn into bite-size pieces

6 mushrooms sliced

2 medium tomatoes, cut into wedges

½ red onion, thinly sliced into rings

Creamy Garlic Dressing (page 208)

Layer lettuce onto chilled salad plates. Arrange mushrooms, tomatoes, and onion rings over top. Drizzle with dressing.

APPROXIMATE NUTRITIONAL INFORMATION PER SERVING WITHOUT DRESSING

Total calories: 30
Total Fat: trace
Saturated Fat: trace
Dietary Fiber: 2 g
Carbohydrates: 6 g
Protein: 2 g
Cholesterol: 0 mg
Sodium: 13 mg

Marinated Potato Salad

8 servings

¾ **pound tiny new red potatoes, cooked until barely tender**

¼ **cup extra-virgin olive oil**

¾ **cup cider vinegar**

¾ **teaspoon Kosher salt**

¼ **teaspoon black pepper**

3 ripe plum tomatoes, quartered

1 14-ounce can water-packed artichoke hearts, quartered

½ **medium red onion, cut into rings**

½ **red pepper, cut into thin strips**

1 5-ounce can whole baby corn, drained

Into a salad bowl, cut potatoes in quarters. In a jar with cover, combine olive oil, vinegar, salt, and pepper; pour over warm potatoes. Chill 2 hours. Add remaining ingredients. Toss to coat the salad with dressing. Chill 2 more hours.

APPROXIMATE NUTRITIONAL INFORMATION PER SERVING WITH DRESSING

Total calories: 167
Total Fat: 7 g
Saturated Fat: 1 g
Dietary Fiber: 2 g
Carbohydrates: 26 g
Protein: 4 g
Cholesterol: 0 mg
Sodium: 283 mg

Old-Fashioned Potato Salad

10 cups; dressing makes 1 cup

1 **pasturized egg***

1 **teaspoon red wine vinegar**

2 **teaspoons fresh lemon juice**

1 **teaspoon Dijon mustard**

3 **cloves garlic**

½ **teaspoon Kosher salt**

1 **cup extra-virgin olive oil**

2¾ **pounds new potatoes, cooked**

3 **hard-boiled eggs**

2 **stalks celery, finely chopped**

½ **cup finely chopped white onion**

1 **huge dill pickle, finely chopped**

salt and black pepper to taste

15 **ripe black or Kalamata olives, pitted and halved**

paprika

1 **tomato, cut into wedges**

In a blender or food processor, combine egg, vinegar, lemon juice, mustard, garlic, and salt. With machine running, gradually add olive oil, 1 tablespoon at a time. Chill at least 4 hours.

Into a large salad bowl, cut cooled, cooked potatoes in 1-inch cubes and all egg whites in 1-inch chunks. Crumble yolks over potatoes. Add celery, onion and pickle. Chill.

Just before serving, toss the potato-egg mixture with desired amount of dressing. Season to taste with salt and pepper. Sprinkle with olives, then with paprika. Garnish with tomato wedges.

Serving Suggestion: Good for a summer party or buffet. Serve with grilled meats, poultry, or seafood. Accompany with other salads such as Three-Bean Salad (page 201), Two-Salsa Pasta Salad (page 193), Wild and White Rice Salad (page 196), and a tray of assorted seasonal fruits.

New potatoes work great in this salad because they retain their shape after being cooked and cut. New potatoes taste best when used within 3 days of purchase

Add 125 calories per tablespoon of dressing.

*Raw eggs have been identified as a source of samonella. The American Egg Board recommends using only pasturized eggs to eliminate the risk. Pasturized eggs are available in many supermarkets..

APPROXIMATE NUTRITIONAL INFORMATION PER 1/2 CUP OF SALAD WITHOUT DRESSING

Total calories: 85
Total Fat: 1 g
Saturated Fat: 0 g
Dietary Fiber: 2 g
Carbohydrates: 17 g
Protein: 3 g
Cholesterol: 21 mg
Sodium: 111 mg

Classic Pasta Salad

5 quarts

DRESSING:

9 tablespoons extra-virgin olive oil

3 tablespoons red wine vinegar

¾ teaspoon Kosher salt

¼ teaspoon pepper

PASTA SALAD:

1 pound pennette (little penne), small shells, or rotini

1 6½-ounce jar marinated artichoke hearts* (with marinade)

1 15-ounce can water-packed artichoke hearts, drained and quartered

1 cup finely chopped red pepper (1 medium pepper)

1 cup finely chopped green or yellow pepper (1 medium pepper)

1 15-ounce can whole spears baby corn on the cob, drained

1 7-ounce can mushroom stems and pieces, drained

4 cups tiny broccoli florets

4 cups cherry tomatoes, halved

½ cup Kalamata or black olives, halved, for garnish

1 cup fresh basil leaves for garnish

This classic pasta salad is an example of a recipe that offers red, yellow, green, and dark green leafy vegetables all in one dish.

Cook pasta according to package directions; rinse, drain, and transfer to large salad bowl. While pasta is still warm, add marinated artichoke hearts with their marinade. Toss until pasta is well coated. Let cool to room temperature. Layer remaining vegetables over pasta. Chill.

Measure olive oil, vinegar, salt, and pepper into a small bowl; mix with wire whisk or fork until well blended.

Just before serving, toss with dressing. Garnish with olives and fresh basil leaves.

*The most heart-healthy brands of marinated artichoke hearts available are those in which the oil is a non-hydrogenated soybean, sunflower, or olive oil.

Variation: Add 2 cups diced poached chicken or ¾ pound diced, smoked turkey breast. An excellent main-meal salad.

APPROXIMATE NUTRITIONAL INFORMATION PER CUP

Total calories: 164
Total Fat: 7 g
Saturated Fat: 1 g
Dietary Fiber: 2 g
Carbohydrates: 21 g
Protein: 5 g
Cholesterol: 0 mg
Sodium: 205 mg

void preground, packaged varieties of Parmesan cheese, which are expensive and almost flavorless. Buy a small wedge of fresh Parmesan and grate as needed, or buy freshly grated in the amount you need.

Pasta, Basil, and Tomato Salad

2 quarts (8 cups)

1 pound package rotini, cooked al dente

2 cups fresh basil

2 cups diced ripe tomatoes, preferably heirloom

¼ pound buffalo mozzarella cheese, cubed

Italian Vinaigrette (page 204)

black pepper

In a salad bowl, combine rotini, basil, tomatoes, and cheese. Pour dressing into cruet; pass with salads. Accompany with black pepper.

Serving Suggestion: Serve hot or cold.

Add 90 calories per tablespoon of Italian Vinaigrette.

APPROXIMATE NUTRITIONAL INFORMATION PER 1/2 CUP

WITHOUT DRESSING

Total calories: 123
Total Fat: 2 g
Saturated Fat: 2 g
Dietary Fiber: 2 g
Carbohydrates: 22 g
Protein: 6 g
Cholesterol: 4 mg
Sodium: 42 mg

Cold Noodle Salad

6 servings

3 cups chicken broth (page 143) or commercial broth

1 6-ounce package buckwheat (soba) noodles*

¾ pound snow peas

6 carrots, thinly sliced on the diagonal

1 head Chinese (Napa) cabbage, shredded

1 6½-ounce can whole water chestnuts

Szechuan Vinaigrette or Oil-free Szechuan Vinaigrette (page 205)

APPROXIMATE NUTRITIONAL INFORMATION PER 1/2 CUP SERVING

WITHOUT DRESSING

Total calories: 319
Total Fat: 1 g
Saturated Fat: 0 g
Dietary Fiber: 6 g
Carbohydrates: 45 g
Protein: 10 g
Cholesterol: 1 mg
Sodium: 555 mg

In bottom of a double boiler, bring stock to a boil. Add noodles; cook 5–6 minutes, or until noodles are tender. Remove noodles from broth to a colander, using salad tongs so that the broth remains in the double boiler. Rinse noodles; set aside. Bring broth back to boiling. Snap ends from snow peas.

In a covered vegetable steamer basket over boiling broth, steam snow peas and carrots 1–2 minutes, or just until color begins to deepen; plunge into ice water. Drain snow peas and carrots, and chill with noodles. Arrange shredded cabbage over salad plates. Top with noodles. Mound snow peas, carrots, and water chestnuts in sections over noodles. Serve with dressing.

*Soba noodles are available in Asian markets, if not in your supermarket.

Add 75 calories per tablespoon of Szechuan Vinaigrette. Add 5 calories per tablespoon of Oil-Free Szechuan Vinaigrette.

Two-Salsa Pasta Salad

20 cups (approximately 8 servings as a main course)

1 pound fresh tomatillos, husks removed

I cup water, just enough to cover

3 fresh jalapeño peppers

3 cloves garlic

1 cup chopped white onion

¼ cup chopped fresh cilantro

1 tablespoon olive oil

¼ teaspoon Kosher salt

¼ cup fresh lime juice

1 pound fusilli or other curly pasta, cooked al dente

1 cup chopped red onion

1 medium ripe tomato, diced

½ red pepper, diced

½ yellow, green, or red pepper, diced

½ cup chopped fresh cilantro for garnish

6–8 very thin red onion rings for garnish

½ cup homemade or commercial tomato salsa (optional)

In a medium saucepan, boil tomatillos in just enough water to cover 7–10 minutes or just until barely tender. Drain. In a blender or food processor, combine tomatillos, jalapeño peppers, garlic, white onion, and ¼ cup cilantro. Purée 5–10 seconds or just to chunky stage. Pour into medium stockpot. Add olive oil and cook 5 minutes, stirring constantly. Remove from heat. Cool. Stir in salt and lime juice. Chill 8 hours — overnight is even better.

Arrange pasta in a shallow serving bowl. Toss with tomatillo sauce, red onion, diced tomato, and peppers. Garnish with cilantro or parsley and onion rings. Serve with salsas.

Serving Suggestion: An excellent addition to any salad buffet. A wonderful side dish with tacos, taco salad, or any Mexican meal.

APPROXIMATE NUTRITIONAL INFORMATION PER CUP WITHOUT SALSA

Total calories: 119
Total Fat: 1 g
Saturated Fat: 0 g
Dietary Fiber: 2 g
Carbohydrates: 23 g
Protein: 4 g
Cholesterol: 0 mg
Sodium: 15 mg

Add 20 calories per 1/4 cup of tomato salsa. Sodium will vary depending on the brand of salsa selected.

Pasta and Bean Salad

8 cups

2 15-ounce cans cannellini beans, drained and rinsed

1 15-ounce can black beans, drained and rinsed

2 large tomatoes, coarsely chopped

1 red onion, coarsely chopped

2 cups cavatelli or other shell-shaped pasta cooked al dente

2 tablespoons extra-virgin olive oil

2 tablespoons white wine vinegar

¾ teaspoon Kosher salt

¼ teaspoon black pepper

3 cloves garlic, minced

½ cup fresh basil (optional)

In a salad bowl, combine beans, tomatoes, onion, and pasta. In a covered jar, combine olive oil, vinegar, salt, pepper, and garlic; pour over pasta and beans, and toss. Chill at least 3 hours. Just before serving, garnish with basil, if desired.

Serving Suggestion: Good with grilled chicken. Great with sandwiches.

APPROXIMATE NUTRITIONAL INFORMATION PER 1/2 CUP WITH DRESSING

Total calories: 84
Total Fat: 2 g
Saturated Fat: trace
Dietary Fiber: 1 g
Carbohydrates: 13 g
Protein: 4 g
Cholesterol: 0 mg
Sodium: 241 mg

Asparagus, Tomato, and Pasta Salad

16 cups

¼ cup extra-virgin olive oil

1 tablespoon freshly squeezed lemon juice

¼ teaspoon Kosher salt

¼ teaspoon black pepper

2 cloves garlic, minced

1 pound elbow macaroni, cooked al dente

2 medium tomatoes, preferably heirloom, coarsely chopped

1 small English cucumber, peeled, halved lengthwise, seeded, and cut crosswise into ¼-inch strips

1 small red onion, chopped

1 8-ounce can mushroom stems and pieces, drained

1 bunch fresh asparagus, steamed 2–3 minutes and cut diagonally into 1½-inch pieces

In a jar with cover, combine olive oil, lemon juice, salt, pepper, and garlic. In a large salad bowl, toss pasta with dressing. Add remaining ingredients and toss again. Serve hot or cold.

Serving Suggestion: A good side dish with hamburgers, chicken burgers, or grilled poultry or seafood.

APPROXIMATE NUTRITIONAL INFORMATION PER CUP WITH DRESSING

Total calories: 142
Total Fat: 4 g
Saturated Fat: trace
Dietary Fiber: 2 g
Carbohydrates: 24 g
Protein: 5 g
Cholesterol: 0 mg
Sodium: 36 mg

Wild and White Rice Salad

12 cups

7 cups White and Wild Rice (p. 346)

beef broth

1 red onion, coarsely chopped

1 8-ounce can mushroom stems and pieces, drained

½ green pepper, coarsely chopped

½ red pepper, coarsely chopped

Salt and black pepper to taste

DRESSING:

¾ cup extra-virgin olive oil

¼ cup cider vinegar

¾ teaspoon Kosher salt

¼ teaspoon black pepper

Steam wild rice according to package directions, substituting beef broth for ½ of the water called, which enhances the flavor. Cook 65-75 minutes or until the liquid is absorbed, the rice is tender, and texture is fluffy. In a separate pan, steam white rice (see Long Grain White Rice p. 347.) Allow 20–30 minutes' cooking time.

In a large salad bowl, combine cooked wild and white rice. Add onion, mushrooms, and green and red peppers.

In a jar with cover, combine dressing ingredients. Pour ½ cup of dressing over salad and toss. (Reserve remaining dressing for later use.) Season to taste with salt and pepper.

*Brown rice in place of white rice yields 3 times as much fiber.

APPROXIMATE NUTRITIONAL INFORMATION PER 1/2 CUP WITH DRESSING

Total calories: 100
Total Fat: 3 g
Saturated Fat: 1 g
Dietary Fiber: trace
Carbohydrates: 15 g
Protein: 1 g
Cholesterol: trace
Sodium: 98 mg

Georgetown Rice Salad

10 cups

3 cups Long Grain White Rice* (p. 347)

¼ cup extra-virgin olive oil

2 tablespoons rice vinegar

1 teaspoon dry mustard

¾ teaspoon Kosher salt or to taste

½ teaspoon black pepper

1 yellow or red pepper, diced

1 green pepper, diced

3 large ripe tomatoes, diced

Prepare Long Grain White Rice according to directions on page 347. Cool cooked rice and spoon into a low salad bowl.

In a jar with cover, combine olive oil, vinegar, mustard, salt and pepper. Pour over rice and toss. Sprinkle diced peppers and tomatoes over rice. Toss again. Chill.

*Brown rice in place of white rice yields 3 times as much fiber.

Serving Suggestion: Especially good with chicken and fish or as a side dish with sandwiches.

APPROXIMATE NUTRITIONAL INFORMATION PER CUP

Total calories: 71
Total Fat: 3 g
Saturated Fat: 0 g
Dietary Fiber: 1 g
Carbohydrates: 9 g
Protein: 1 g
Cholesterol: 0 mg
Sodium: 95 mg

White Bean Salad

3 1/2 quarts (14 cups)

1 pound small dry white beans

2 stalks celery

2 teaspoons Kosher salt

1 red onion, diced

2 ripe tomatoes, diced

2 stalks celery, diced

Olive Oil-and-Lemon Vinaigrette (page 204)

½ cup fresh parsley, chopped

black pepper to taste

1 bunch fresh spinach, washed and trimmed

1 lemon, sliced into rounds

Wash beans and put into a stock pot. Add 2 quarts water; cover and bring to a boil. Remove from heat and let soak 1 hour. Drain. Return beans to stock pot with 2 quarts fresh water; bring to a boil. Add 2 stalks celery and salt; reduce heat to medium. Cook 35–40 minutes, or until beans are tender. Drain. Discard celery stalks. Rinse beans with cold water and chill. Just before serving, toss beans with onion, tomato, diced celery, and just enough vinaigrette to moisten. Sprinkle with parsley and season generously with black pepper. Line a shallow salad bowl with spinach greens. Spoon beans into center. Ring beans with lemon rounds.

Variation: Steam fresh asparagus tips and fresh mushrooms 1–2 minutes. Chill. Toss with beans; add sliced cucumbers and toss again.

Serving Suggestion: Especially good with barbecued chicken.

Add 61 calories per tablespoon of dressing.

APPROXIMATE NUTRITIONAL INFORMATION PER 1/2 CUP WITHOUT DRESSING

Total calories: 123
Total Fat: 1 g
Saturated Fat: 0 g
Dietary Fiber: 8 g
Carbohydrates: 23 g
Protein: 8 g
Cholesterol: 0 mg
Sodium: 340 mg

Tuscan Bean Salad

8 servings

DRESSING:

2 garlic cloves, minced

3 tablespoons fresh lemon juice

¼ cup extra-virgin olive oil

½ teaspoon Kosher salt

¼ teaspoon black pepper

SALAD:

3 15-ounce cans cannellini beans, rinsed

1½ cups coarsely chopped red onion

2 large ripe tomatoes, coarsely chopped

½ cup chopped celery

¾ cup coarsely chopped fresh flat-leaf parsley

This salad is a good way to get kids to eat more beans.

Combine garlic, lemon juice, olive oil, salt, and pepper in a covered jar and shake until well blended. Arrange cannellini beans in a shallow salad bowl and toss with 2 tablespoons of the dressing. Chill beans and remaining dressing. Just before serving, toss beans with onion, tomatoes, celery, parsley, and remainder of dressing.

Variation: Sort and wash one 16-ounce package of small white beans and put them into a stockpot with 2 quarts of water; cover and bring to a boil. Remove from heat and let soak for 1 hour. Drain.

Bring beans and 6 cups water to a boil in a stockpot. Add 1 teaspoon salt, 1 quartered onion, 2 bay leaves, and 1 teaspoon powdered coriander. Boil gently, uncovered, until beans are tender, 35 to 40 minutes (add water to keep beans covered). Drain. Remove onion and bay leaves. Rinse beans with cold water; drain again. Proceed with recipe as above.

APPROXIMATE NUTRITIONAL INFORMATION PER SERVING

Total calories: 245
Total Fat: 8 g
Saturated Fat: 1 g
Dietary Fiber: 9 g
Carbohydrates: 34 g
Protein: 12 g
Cholesterol: 0 mg
Sodium: 142 mg

Black Beans with Vegetables and Shrimp

4 servings

1½ cups Chili Salsa (page 216), or commercial salsa

1 cup Black Bean Dip (page 91)

⅔ pound medium prawns, cooked, shelled, and deveined

1 English cucumber, thinly sliced

8 stalks celery, sliced diagonally into thirds

8 carrots, sliced diagonally into thirds

fresh parsley for garnish

1 lime, cut into wedges

1 1-inch-square piece tomato for garnish

Into the center of a medium dish, spread ½ cup of the salsa. Mound bean dip over salsa. Arrange prawns, cucumber, celery, and carrots around dip. Tuck in parsley and lime wedges for garnish. Top bean dip with small piece of tomato and touch of parsley. Pour remaining cup of salsa into bowl and pass with vegetables.

Variation: Add tortilla chips. Be sure they are made with a heart-healthy oil such as safflower or corn oil.

Serving Suggestion: An excellent accompaniment to a soup meal. Also good as an appetizer.

APPROXIMATE NUTRITIONAL INFORMATION PER SERVING

Total calories: 183
Total Fat: 2 g
Saturated Fat: 0 g
Dietary Fiber: 7 g
Carbohydrates: 28 g
Protein: 17 g
Cholesterol: 98 mg
Sodium: 595 mg

Three-Bean Salad

6 cups

3 tablespoons extra-virgin olive oil

5 cloves garlic

2 tablespoons fresh lemon juice

1¼ teaspoons ground cumin

½ teaspoon oregano

2 teaspoons hot chili oil

½ teaspoon Kosher salt or to taste

¼ teaspoon black pepper

1 15-ounce can red kidney beans, drained and rinsed

1 15-ounce can cannellini beans, drained and rinsed

1 15-ounce can black beans, drained and rinsed

1 small white onion, coarsely chopped

In a covered jar, combine olive oil, garlic, lemon juice, cumin, oregano, hot chili oil, salt, and pepper. Chill at least 3 hours.

In a salad bowl, combine beans. Chill. Just before serving, add onion and toss with dressing.

Serving Suggestion: Especially good with grilled chicken and red meats.

APPROXIMATE NUTRITIONAL INFORMATION PER 1/2 CUP WITH DRESSING

Total calories: 149
Total Fat: 5 g
Saturated Fat: 1 g
Dietary Fiber: 6 g
Carbohydrates: 21 g
Protein: 7 g
Cholesterol: 0 mg
Sodium: 333 mg

Corn and Black Bean Salad

8 servings

2 15-ounce cans black beans, drained and rinsed

2 cups cooked corn kernels (from 5 cobs)*

2 tablespoons finely chopped jalapeño pepper (optional)

1 cup finely chopped red bell pepper (1 medium pepper)

½ cup finely chopped red onion

1 cup coarsely chopped ripe tomato (1 large tomato), preferably heirloom

¼ cup extra-virgin olive oil

3 tablespoons fresh lime juice

½ teaspoon ground cumin

⅛ teaspoon cayenne pepper

¾ teaspoon Kosher salt

¼ cup finely chopped fresh cilantro for garnish (optional)

This salad is high in complex carbohydrates, which provide fuel for our everyday energy needs.

Combine all ingredients except cilantro in a medium salad bowl. Toss. Serve at once, or cover and chill in refrigerator. Just before serving, garnish with the cilantro, if desired.

*This salad is a good way to use leftover corn.

APPROXIMATE NUTRITIONAL INFORMATION PER SERVING

Total calories: 194
Total Fat: 8 g
Saturated Fat: 1 g
Dietary Fiber: 7 g
Carbohydrates: 26 g
Protein: 8 g
Cholesterol: 0 mg
Sodium: 517 mg

Mixed Greens Salad with Crab Legs

4 servings

1 cup torn red leaf lettuce

1 cup torn fresh spinach

1 cup torn romaine lettuce

¼ cup Olive Oil and Lemon Vinaigrette (page 204)

½ cup heart-healthy croutons

4 crab legs for garnish

Toss greens with vinaigrette. Top with croutons. Garnish with crab legs.

APPROXIMATE NUTRITIONAL INFORMATION PER SERVING

Total calories: 89
Total Fat: 4 g
Saturated Fat: 1 g
Dietary Fiber: 1 g
Carbohydrates: 8 g
Protein: 5 g
Cholesterol: 14 mg
Sodium: 167 mg

English Cucumber and Crabmeat Salad

40 slices

1 English cucumber, sliced

2 tablespoons non-fat sour cream

1 tablespoon mayonnaise

2 tablespoons tomato salsa

¼ pound crabmeat

1 bunch watercress, for garnish

Arrange cucumber slices on a serving tray. Blend sour cream and mayonnaise, and put a small dollop in center of each cucumber slice. Top with a dab of salsa and a small piece of crabmeat. Garnish with watercress.

Serving Suggestion: Also good as an hors d'oeuvre.

APPROXIMATE NUTRITIONAL INFORMATION PER CUCUMBER SLICE

Total calories: 7
Total Fat: 0 g
Saturated Fat: 0 g
Dietary Fiber: 0 g
Carbohydrates: 0 g
Protein: 0 g
Cholesterol: 2 mg
Sodium: 35 mg

Crab Louis

4 servings

1 head lettuce

½ pound crabmeat

¼ cup sliced water chestnuts

2 celery stalks, thinly sliced

3 green onions with tops, thinly sliced

½ green pepper, chopped

½ cup Seafood Salad Dressing (page 189)

2 tomatoes, cut into wedges

1 bunch asparagus spears, steamed 2 to 4 minutes

Lemon Wedges

Line chilled salad bowls with outside leaves of lettuce; shred remaining lettuce. Toss shredded lettuce, crabmeat, water chestnuts, celery, green onion, and green pepper with dressing to moisten; spoon into lettuce-lined bowls. Arrange tomatoes, asparagus, and lemon wedges around the salad. Accompany with Seafood Salad Dressing.

Variation: Substitute shrimp for crabmeat. The fat content will be the same.

Add 92 calories per tablespoon of dressing.

APPROXIMATE NUTRITIONAL INFORMATION PER SERVING

Total calories: 162
Total Fat: 5 g
Saturated Fat: 1 g
Dietary Fiber: 3 g
Carbohydrates: 18 g
Protein: 16 g
Cholesterol: 57 mg
Sodium: 212 mg

Crab-and-Shrimp Sushi Salad

5 servings

SPINACH

5 cups fresh spinach leaves torn into bite-size pieces

RICE

1½ cups uncooked short-grain rice (sushi rice)

1¾ cups water, plus 2 tablespoons

⅓ cup seasoned rice vinegar

CARROTS

2 large carrots, peeled

⅓ cup rice vinegar

½ teaspoon hot chili oil

SNOW PEAS

¼ pound snow peas

½ teaspoon sesame oil

CUCUMBER

1 English cucumber, peeled

3 tablespoons rice vinegar

MUSHROOMS

1 7-ounce package dried forest mushrooms (Shiitake)

2 cups warm water

¼ teaspoon granulated sugar

2 teaspoons sake

2 tablespoons reduced-sodium soy sauce

SEAFOOD

⅓ pound cooked shrimpmeat

⅓ pound cooked crabmeat

DRESSING

⅓ cup rice vinegar

3 tablespoons granulated sugar

¼ teaspoon salt

½ teaspoon hot chili oil

2 teaspoons sesame oil

In a 3-quart saucepan, rinse rice with water until water runs clear; drain. Add water to rice and bring to a boil. Reduce heat, cover, and simmer 20–25 minutes or until water is absorbed. Remove from heat; stir in vinegar. Let stand at room temperature until ready to serve.

Cut carrots into matchstick pieces 3 inches long. In a 2-quart saucepan, bring vinegar to a boil. Add carrots and cook, stirring often, just until crisp-tender, about 60 seconds. Drain. Drizzle with hot chili oil. Set aside. In a covered pan over boiling water, steam snow peas 1–2 minutes or just until crisp-tender. Drizzle with sesame oil. Set aside.

Cut cucumber into matchstick pieces 3 inches long. Toss with vinegar. Set aside.

Soak mushrooms in 2 cups warm water 20 minutes or until soft. Cut off and discard hard stems. Pour mushrooms with their soaking liquid into a 2-quart saucepan; add sugar, sake, and soy sauce. Bring to a boil. Cook, stirring often, until most of liquid is absorbed. Remove from pan and cut into matchstick pieces. Set aside.

Combine dressing ingredients in a jar with cover.

To Assemble: Line 5 individual salad bowls with spinach leaves. Top spinach with rice. Arrange carrots, snow peas, cucumbers, and mushrooms around rice. Top with seafood. Accompany with dressing.

Serving Suggestion: Serve with a watermelon basket of seasonal fruits or a heartier dessert such as Berry Cobbler (see page 396).

Sushi Salad is high in sodium. Serve it with low-sodium accompaniments such as those suggested. Choosing low-sodium foods for other meals will keep the total sodium for the day under control.

APPROXIMATE NUTRITIONAL INFORMATION PER SERVING

Total calories: 530
Total Fat: 5 g
Saturated Fat: 1 g
Dietary Fiber: 9 g
Carbohydrates: 101 g
Protein: 22 g
Cholesterol: 70 mg
Sodium: 1,100 mg

Shrimp and Spinach Salad

6 servings

½ cup cooked shrimpmeat

**1 English cucumber,
very thinly sliced**

¼ cup rice vinegar

**1 teaspoon reduced-sodium
soy sauce**

1 tablespoon granulated sugar

½ teaspoon Kosher salt

**10 fresh spinach leaves, stems
removed, steamed, and chilled**

In a salad bowl, combine the shrimp and cucumber. In a jar with cover, combine vinegar, soy sauce, sugar, and salt, and pour over shrimp and cucumber. Chill 1 hour.

Just before serving, mix in spinach. Spoon into small bowls or custard cups. Serve with chopsticks.

Serving Sugestion: A good light appetizer or first course to complement an Asian meal.

APPROXIMATE NUTRITIONAL INFORMATION PER SERVING WITH DRESSING

Total calories: 38
Total Fat: trave
Saturated Fat: trace
Dietary Fiber: trace
Carbohydrates: 4 g
Protein: 5 g
Cholesterol: 37 mg
Sodium: 236 mg

Shrimp and Soba Noodle Salad

8 servings

¼ cup rice wine vinegar

1 tablespoon soy sauce

1 tablespoon extra-virgin olive oil

1 tablespoon sesame oil

2 teaspoons brown sugar

½ teaspoon hot chili oil

**2 cups chicken broth, preferably
homemade (page 143)**

2 cups water

**1 6-ounce package soba
(buckwheat) noodles**

**4 cups chopped Chinese cabbage
or Napa cabbage**

**1 recipe Stir-Fried Broccoli
and Cauliflower with Red Peppers
(page 397)**

½ pound small cooked shrimp

Combine rice wine vinegar, soy sauce, olive oil, sesame oil, brown sugar, and hot chili oil. Set aside.

In 2-quart saucepan, bring chicken broth and water to a boil. Add soba noodles. Stir lightly. Boil 5 to 8 minutes, or until noodles are just tender. Drain and rinse.

Layer chopped cabbage in bottom of a serving bowl. Top with soba noodles and pan-steamed broccoli and cauliflower.

Drizzle with dressing. Arrange the shrimp over top. Serve at once.

APPROXIMATE NUTRITIONAL INFORMATION PER SERVING

Total calories: 167
Total Fat: 5 g
Saturated Fat: 1 g
Dietary Fiber: 2 g
Carbohydrates: 21 g
Protein: 11 g
Cholesterol: 44 mg
Sodium: 531 mg

Asian Shrimp Salad

5 servings

4 cups chicken broth (page 143) or canned broth*

1 6-ounce package buckwheat (soba) noodles

3 cups fresh spinach leaves

3 cups Bibb lettuce

⅔ pound medium prawns, cooked, shelled, and deveined

½ pound snow peas, steamed 2 to 3 minutes or until crisp-tender

½ pound fresh asparagus, steamed 3–4 minutes or until barely tender

3 carrots, sliced diagonally into 4 or 5 pieces and steamed 3–4 minutes or until crisp-tender

½ English cucumber, peeled and thinly sliced

1 small bunch radishes, trimmed and thinly sliced

½ cup canned water chestnuts, drained

Wasabi Vinaigrette (page 208)

In a medium saucepan, bring chicken broth to a boil. Add noodles and boil 5–7 minutes or until noodles are tender. Drain.

Arrange spinach and lettuce leaves over chilled salad plates. Mound noodles to one side of each plate. Arrange prawns next to noodles. Surround with snow peas, asparagus, carrots, and cucumber. Garnish with radishes and water chestnuts. Serve hot or cold with Wasabi Vinaigrette.

*Canned broth is higher in sodium.

Serving Suggestion: Great as a main meal salad. Serve with warm tortillas and Fresh Pineapple with Papaya Purée (page 423).

APPROXIMATE NUTRITIONAL INFORMATION PER SERVING

Total calories: 319
Total Fat: 3 g
Saturated Fat: 1 g
Dietary Fiber: 5 g
Carbohydrates: 47 g
Protein: 26 g
Cholesterol: 118 mg
Sodium: 413 mg

Cold Scallop and Noodle Salad

6 servings

1 tablespoon olive oil

1 pound scallops

½ cup thinly sliced celery

1 8-ounce can sliced water chestnuts

4 green onions, cut into strings

1 6-ounce package buckwheat (Soba) noodles,* cooked and drained

6 cups Napa cabbage

¼ cup reduced-sodium soy sauce

2 tablespoons rice vinegar

Heat olive oil in a nonstick skillet. Ad scallops and sauté 2–3 minutes, or until cooked. Chill scallops, celery, water chestnuts, onions, noodles, and lettuce. Just before serving, arrange cabbage over chilled salad plates. Top with noodles, then with scallops, celery, water chestnuts, and green onions. Combine soy sauce and vinegar; drizzle over salads.

*Soba noodles are available in Asian markets, if not in your supermarket.

Serving Suggestion: Dishes made with soy sauce, even reduced-sodium soy sauce, are high in sodium. Keep this in mind and serve with low-sodium accompaniments.

APPROXIMATE NUTRITIONAL INFORMATION PER SERVING

Total calories: 266
Total Fat: 3 g
Saturated Fat: 0 g
Dietary Fiber: 3 g
Carbohydrates: 36 g
Protein: 18 g
Cholesterol: 40 mg
Sodium: 406 mg

Bibb Lettuce, Tomato, and Scallop Salad with Tomato Salsa

8 servings

3 heads Bibb lettuce

1 recipe Sea Scallops with Tomatoes and Green Chilies (page 100)

1½ cups fresh Tomato Salsa, preferably homemade (page 214)

Divide Bibb lettuce among 8 salad plates. Spread with scallop mixture. Top with salsa.

APPROXIMATE NUTRITIONAL INFORMATION PER CUP

Total calories: 129
Total Fat: 4 g
Saturated Fat: 1 g
Dietary Fiber: 1 g
Carbohydrates: 11 g
Protein: 14 g
Cholesterol: 23 mg
Sodium: 274 mg

Mussel and Tomato Salad

4 servings

1½ pounds mussels, in their shells

2 heads Bibb lettuce

¼ cup diced ripe tomatoes

Dijon Vinaigrette (page 207)

Wash and clean mussels. Steam just until shells open. Chill. Arrange lettuce leaves over chilled salad plates. Garnish with mussels and tomatoes. Pour dressing into cruet; pass with salad.

Add 24 calories per tablespoon of Dijon Vinaigrette.

APPROXIMATE NUTRITIONAL INFORMATION PER SERVING

WITHOUT DRESSING

Total calories: 159
Total Fat: 4 g
Saturated Fat: 1 g
Dietary Fiber: 1 g
Carbohydrates: 9 g
Protein: 21 g
Cholesterol: 48 mg
Sodium: 492 mg

Calamari Salad

8 cups salad; dressing makes 2/3 cup

1 pound squid tubes

½ teaspoon extra-virgin olive oil

1 large tomato, diced

1¾ cups coarsely chopped red onion

⅔ cup chopped green onion

1 cup coarsely chopped celery

DRESSING:

3 tablespoons extra-virgin olive oil

3 tablespoons fresh lemon juice

3 tablespoons fresh lime juice

¾ teaspoon Kosher salt

1 teaspoon black pepper

1 teaspoon Tabasco sauce

Clean squid tubes and cut into ½-inch rings. Toss with ½ teaspoon olive oil. In a nonstick skillet, sauté squid 3–4 minutes or until color changes and squid are cooked. Plunge into ice water. Drain and pat dry.

In a shallow bowl, combine squid, tomato, red and green onions and celery; set aside.

In a jar with cover, combine all the dressing ingredients. Pour desired amount of dressing over squid and vegetables. Chill 2–3 hours, tossing 2–3 times.

Add 33 calories per tablespoon of dressing.

APPROXIMATE NUTRITIONAL INFORMATION PER CUP WITHOUT DRESSING

Total calories: 55
Total Fat: trace
Saturated Fat: trace
Dietary Fiber: 2 g
Carbohydrates: 10 g
Protein: 3 g
Cholesterol: 3 mg
Sodium: 591 mg

Salade Niçoise

6 servings

1 bunch leaf lettuce, torn into bite-size pieces

1 6⅛ -ounce can water-packed tuna, drained

3 red potatoes, quartered and steamed

¾ pound fresh green beans, cooked al dente

6 water-packed artichoke hearts, quartered

3 large carrots, sliced on the diagonal and steamed

½ green pepper, cut into thin strips

½ red pepper, cut into thin strips

1 jalapeño or serrano pepper, cut into thin strips (optional)

½ white onion, halved, thinly sliced, and separated

6 ripe plum tomatoes, quartered

12 Greek olives

⅓ cup Niçoise Dressing (page 209)

Arrange lettuce over a tray or shallow salad bowl. Mound tuna in center. Arrange potatoes, green beans, artichoke hearts, carrots, and peppers around tuna. Add onion slices, tomatoes, and olives. Chill. Just before serving, drizzle with dressing.

APPROXIMATE NUTRITIONAL INFORMATION PER SERVING WITH DRESSING

Total calories: 320
Total Fat: 11 g
Saturated Fat: 1.5 g
Dietary Fiber: 11 g
Carbohydrates: 45 g
Protein: 12 g
Cholesterol: 15 mg
Sodium: 480 mg

Seafood Salad

6 servings; dressing makes 3/4 cup

DRESSING:

⅔ cup mayonnaise

5 cloves garlic, finely minced

2 tablespoons lemon juice, plus 1 teaspoon

1 teaspoon black pepper

¼ teaspoon Tabasco sauce

¾ teaspoon salt

2 teaspoons fresh dill (optional)

2 tablespoons grated white onion

SALAD:

6 cups baby spinach

6 cups shredded lettuce

¼ cup finely chopped green onion

1 cup chopped celery

½ pound cooked crabmeat

¾ pound cooked shrimpmeat

2 medium tomatoes, cut into wedges

APPROXIMATE NUTRITIONAL INFORMATION PER SERVING

WITHOUT DRESSING

Total calories: 114
Total Fat: 1 g
Saturated Fat: trace
Dietary Fiber: 2 g
Carbohydrates: 5 g
Protein: 20 g
Cholesterol: 113 mg
Sodium: 269 mg

Add 92 calories per additional tablespoon of dressing.

ONE TABLESPOON OF DRESSING

Total calories: 92
Total Fat: 10 g
Saturated Fat: 2 g
Dietary Fiber: 0 g
Carbohydrates: 1 g
Protein: trace
Cholesterol: 7 mg
Sodium: 204 mg

In a jar with cover, combine dressing ingredients. Chill at least 1 hour.

Toss spinach, lettuce, onion, and celery with ¼ cup of the dressing. Add crab and shrimp. Toss. Garnish with tomato wedges. Divide salad among chilled salad plates. Pass the remaining dressing.

Excellent as a main meal salad.

Seafood Primavera

6 servings; dressing makes 2 cups

DRESSING:

1 whole pasturized egg*

1 pasturized egg yolk*

1 tablespoon Dijon mustard

2 tablespoons freshly squeezed lemon juice

2 tablespoons red wine vinegar

½ teaspoon Kosher salt

½ cup whole leaf fresh basil

1 cup extra-virgin olive oil

SALAD:

½ pound snow peas

1 pound ziti or elbow macaroni, cooked al dente

6 green onions, thinly sliced

1 red pepper, diced

1 green pepper, diced

3 stalks celery, diced

½ pound cooked shrimpmeat

½ pound cooked crabmeat

2 medium tomatoes, diced

1 cup fresh basil

In a blender, combine all dressing ingredients except olive oil. Process 2 minutes. With machine running, gradually add olive oil 1 tablespoon at a time. Chill.

Microwave or steam snow peas 2–3 minutes until crisp-tender.

In a large salad bowl, toss pasta, snow peas, onion, peppers, and celery. Sprinkle with shrimp, crab, and tomatoes. Garnish with the 1 cup basil. Chill. Serve with dressing on the side.

Serving Suggestion: Excellent as a main meal salad.

*Raw eggs have been identified as a source of salmonella. The American Egg Board recommends using only pasturized eggs to eliminate the risk. Pasturized eggs are available in many markets. supermarkets.

APPROXIMATE NUTRITIONAL INFORMATION PER SERVING

WITHOUT DRESSING

Total calories: 283
Total Fat: 1 g
Saturated Fat: trace
Dietary Fiber: 5 g
Carbohydrates: 43 g
Protein: 23 g
Cholesterol: 94 mg
Sodium: 524 mg

ONE TABLESPOON OF DRESSING

Total calories: 65
Total Fat: 7 g
Saturated Fat: 1 g
Dietary Fiber: 0 g
Carbohydrates: trace
Protein: trace
Cholesterol: 13 g
Sodium: 50 mg

Paella Salad

6 servings

½ **pound clams, steamed
(see page 250)**

½ **pound mussels, steamed
(see page 250)**

½ **pound scallops, poached
(see page 244)**

**3 cups cooked Saffron Rice
(page 349)**

1 red pepper, diced

1 green or yellow pepper, diced

2 ripe tomatoes, quartered

**1 head romaine lettuce, torn into
bite-size pieces**

1 bunch baby spinach

2 fresh lemons, quartered

Chill seafood, rice, and vegetables. Line a large serving platter with romaine and baby spinach. Mound rice in center. Arrange clams, mussels, and scallops around rice. Garnish with red and green peppers. Ring with tomtoes and lemons.

**APPROXIMATE
NUTRITIONAL
INFORMATION
PER SERVING**

Total calories: 229
Total Fat: 3 g
Saturated Fat: 0 g
Dietary Fiber: 5 g
Carbohydrates: 18 g
Protein: 8 g
Cholesterol: 4 mg
Sodium: 436 mg

Chicken, Shrimp, and Pasta Salad

5 1/2 quarts (approximately 8 servings as a main course)

¼ **head cauliflower, florets only**

**2 carrots, peeled and thinly sliced
on the diagonal**

½ **pound snow peas**

1 leek, thinly sliced

1 head Bibb lettuce

**1 pound cavatelli or other shell-
shaped pasta, cooked al dente**

**1 chicken breast, skinned, boned,
poached, and cut into strips
½-inch wide**

**8 medium prawns, cooked,
shelled, and deveined**

**1 7-ounce can water-packed
artichoke hearts, drained**

Aïoli Sauce (page 212)

Separately blanch cauliflower, carrots, snow peas and leek 1–2 minutes or just until crisp-tender.

Arrange lettuce over dinner plates. Mound pasta, chicken, prawns and vegetables over lettuce. Serve with Aïoli Vinaigrette.

Serving Suggestion: Serve with Cheese Popovers (page 84) and fresh fruit. Or omit the popovers and fruit, and serve a dessert such as Berry Cobbler (page 396).

**APPROXIMATE
NUTRITIONAL
INFORMATION
PER CUP WITHOUT
DRESSING**

Total calories: 124
Total Fat: trace
Saturated Fat: trace
Dietary Fiber: 2 g
Carbohydrates: 22 g
Protein: 7 g
Cholesterol: 16 mg
Sodium: 34 mg

Tomato, Spinach, and Chicken Salad

4 servings

1 large ripe tomato, diced

**½ pound fresh spinach,
torn into 2-inch pieces**

**½ pound skinless chicken breast,
cooked and cut into 2-inch cubes**

2 fresh lemons, quartered

Freshly ground pepper

Chill diced tomato, spinach, and chicken.
Layer spinach on 4 individual salad plates.
Cover with diced tomato. Top with chicken.
Squeeze lemon juice over top. Sprinkle
with pepper.

Serving Suggestion: Serve as a first course
with Minestrone (page 125) or Three-Bean
Soup (page 127).

**APPROXIMATE
NUTRITIONAL
INFORMATION
PER SERVING**

Total calories: 97
Total Fat: 2 g
Saturated Fat: 0 g
Dietary Fiber: 2 g
Carbohydrates: 10 g
Protein: 15 g
Cholesterol: 33 mg
Sodium: 77 mg

Country Chicken Salad

6 servings

**2 whole chicken breasts, skinned
and boned**

1 tablespoon peanut oil

**1 small head cauliflower,
florets only**

**3 stalks celery, cut on the diagonal
into 1½-inch pieces**

12 fresh mushrooms, sliced

**1 6½ -ounce can whole water
chestnuts, drained**

**½ red pepper, cut into
julienne strips**

**1 head Chinese (Napa)
cabbage, shredded**

¼ cup reduced-sodium soy sauce

2 tablespoons rice vinegar

Cut chicken into julienne strips and sauté
in a nonstick skillet 10–15 minutes, or
until cooked; chill. Heat oil in a wok. Add
cauliflower; stir-fry 4 minutes. Add celery;
stir-fry 2 minutes. Add mushrooms, water
chestnuts, and red and green pepper; stir-fry
3–4 minutes, or until all vegetables are
crisp-tender. Chill. Before serving, toss
vegetables with chicken and cabbage. Combine
soy sauce and vinegar; pour over vegetables.

Serving Suggestion: To compensate for
the sodium in the soy sauce, serve with
low-sodium accompaniments.

**APPROXIMATE
NUTRITIONAL
INFORMATION
PER SERVING**

Total calories: 154
Total Fat: 4 g
Saturated Fat: 1 g
Dietary Fiber: 51 g
Carbohydrates: 14 g
Protein: 19 g
Cholesterol: 33 mg
Sodium: 518 mg

Pasta with Chicken Salad

4 1/2 quarts (18 cups)

1 1-pound package rotini, cooked al dente

Italian Vinaigrette (page 204)

2 cups chicken broth (page 143)

2 whole chicken breasts, skinned and boned

½ bunch broccoli, florets only

½ head cauliflower, florets only

12 fresh mushrooms, thinly sliced

1 red pepper, diced

1 green pepper, diced

1 15-ounce can artichoke hearts, quartered

1 15-ounce can whole baby corn spears

12 cherry tomatoes

Salt and black pepper to taste

In a bowl, while rotini are still warm, toss with just enough vinaigrette to moisten. Chill.

Bring stock to a boil; add chicken and cook over medium heat 20 minutes, or until chicken is done. Drain chicken. Cool. Cut into 1-inch cubes. Chill. Reserve broth for another use. In a covered vegetable steamer basket over boiling water, steam broccoli and cauliflower 1–2 minutes, or until crisp-tender. Chill.

Just before serving, combine the pasta, chicken, and vegetables. Toss with additional Italian Vinaigrette; season with salt and pepper.

Variation: Just before serving, sprinkle with ⅓ cup freshly grated Parmesan cheese.

APPROXIMATE NUTRITIONAL INFORMATION PER CUP WITHOUT DRESSING

Total calories: 137
Total Fat: 1 g
Saturated Fat: 0 g
Dietary Fiber: 2 g
Carbohydrates: 29 g
Protein: 11 g
Cholesterol: 0 mg
Sodium: 140 mg

Add 90 calories per tablespoon of Italian Vinaigrette.

Hot Chicken Salad

6 servings

NOODLES:

3 cups chicken broth (page 143) or commeccial broth

3 cups water

1 tablespoon reduced-sodium soy sauce

1 6-ounce package buckwheat (soba) noodles

CHICKEN:

¾ pound chicken breast, skinned and boned

1 cup chicken broth (page 143) or canned broth

1 tablespoon peeled, coarsely chopped fresh gingerroot

3 green onions, coarsely chopped

VEGETABLES:

5 cups shredded Napa cabbage

1 English cucumber, peeled, cut into thirds, and julienned

DRESSING:

¼ cup reduced-sodium soy sauce

1 tablespoon rice vinegar

2 tablespoons hot chili oil

2 tablespoons sesame oil

1 tablespoon water

2½ teaspoons granulated sugar

3 tablespoons finely chopped green onion

½ tablespoon minced garlic (about 5 cloves)

3 tablespoons finely chopped green onion, white part only (about 6–8 onions)

1 tablespoon ginger juice*

In a medium stockpot, bring chicken broth and water to a boil; add noodles. Boil 4–5 minutes or until noodles are tender. Drain. Toss with soy sauce.

In a medium saucepan, combine all chicken ingredients, and heat to boiling. Reduce heat, cover, and simmer 20 minutes or until done. Cool in stock 10 minutes. Drain. Cool slightly. Tear chicken into julienne strips.

Combine all dressing ingredients in a jar with cover.

To Assemble: Line 6 salad bowls with lettuce. Top lettuce with noodles, chicken, and cucumber. Drizzle with dressing.

*To make ginger juice, grate a chunk of fresh ginger, then squeeze the pulp to yield desired amount of juice.

Serving Suggestion: Excellent as a main meal salad. Serve with Italian Bread (page 55) and Lemon Custard (page 410).

Most of the sodium is in the dressing. Remember to use a moderate amount.

APPROXIMATE NUTRITIONAL INFORMATION PER SERVING

WITHOUT DRESSING	PER TABLESPOON OF DRESSING
Total calories: 254	Total calories: 33
Total Fat: 4 g	Total Fat: 3 g
Saturated Fat: 1 g	Saturated Fat: 1 g
Dietary Fiber: 2 g	Dietary Fiber: trace
Carbohydrates: 31 g	Carbohydrates: 1 g
Protein: 23 g	Protein: trace
Cholesterol: 41 mg	Cholesterol: 0 mg
Sodium: 327 mg	Sodium: 134 mg

Chicken Taco Salad

8 servings

1 28-ounce can plum tomatoes, with liquid

2 garlic cloves, peeled

¾ teaspoon Kosher salt

¾ teaspoon dry mustard

1¼ teaspoons chili powder

½ teaspoon Lawry's Chili Seasoning (optional)

⅛ teaspoon ground cumin (¼ teaspoon for spicy)

⅛ teaspoon cayenne pepper (¼ teaspoon for spicy)

2 skinned and boned chicken breasts (1 pound chicken)

1 tablespoon sake

2 tablespoons potato starch (available in the Asian section of the supermarket)

1 tablespoon olive oil

3 15-ounce cans red kidney beans, drained and rinsed

8–12 cups shredded lettuce

2 large ripe tomatoes, coarsely chopped

1 medium white onion, coarsely chopped

1 cup grated reduced-fat cheddar cheese

½ cup nonfat sour cream

1 cup commercially prepared tomato salsa

8 6-inch warm flour tortillas

This taco salad is juicier and tastier than the fast-food version. Your kids will want to eat it with a spoon.

Put canned tomatoes and garlic into the work bowl of a food processor and process until smooth. Transfer to a 3-quart saucepan and add seasonings. Heat just to boiling (do not allow to boil). Reduce heat and let simmer 8 to 10 minutes.

Cut chicken into ½-inch strips. Toss with sake. Sprinkle with potato starch. Heat olive oil in a nonstick skillet over medium-high heat. Add chicken strips and stir-fry 8 to 10 minutes, or until done. Set aside.

Add kidney beans to tomato mixture. Heat to serving temperature.

Meanwhile, line shallow soup bowls with shredded lettuce (this shredded lettuce replaces the fried tortilla shell used in fast-food taco salads). Spoon bean mixture over lettuce. Top with chicken, then with chopped tomatoes, onion, and each type of cheese. Accompany with sour cream and salsa. Serve with warm tortillas.

Variation: For Shrimp Taco Salad, omit chicken, sake, potato starch, and olive oil. Just before serving, add ½ pound cooked baby shrimp to bean-and-tomato mixture. Garnish salad with sliced avocado, if desired.

This recipe is high in sodium. Be sure to choose lower-sodium foods at your other meals to keep sodium intake for the day in balance.

APPROXIMATE NUTRITIONAL INFORMATION PER SERVING

Total calories: 389
Total Fat: 9 g
Saturated Fat: 2 g
Dietary Fiber: 11 g
Carbohydrates: 47 g
Protein: 29 g
Cholesterol: 43 mg
Sodium: 710 mg

Chicken and Rice Salad

6 servings

1¾ cups water

1 cup long grain basmati rice

⅛ teaspoon saffron threads

2½ tablespoons extra-virgin olive oil

1½ tablespoons tarragon-flavored white wine vinegar

½ teaspoon Kosher salt

1 cup cooked and cubed chicken

½ medium green pepper, cubed

½ medium red pepper, cubed

1 small ripe tomato, cubed

1 6-ounce jar marinated artichoke hearts, drained and cubed

4 large green onions (some with tops), chopped

1 2-ounce jar sliced pimientos, drained

In a medium saucepan, bring water and rice to a boil; stir in saffron. Cover, reduce heat, and simmer 15 minutes or until rice is tender and water is absorbed. Remove from heat and let stand covered 10 minutes longer. Combine olive oil, vinegar, and salt; pour over rice. Toss until well coated. Cool to room temperature. Add chicken, peppers, tomato, and artichoke hearts. Refrigerate 3–4 hours or until thoroughly chilled. Garnish with green onions and pimientos.

Serving Suggestion: For dessert, serve seasonal fruits or Berry Cobbler (page 396).

APPROXIMATE NUTRITIONAL INFORMATION PER SERVING

Total calories: 320
Total Fat: 14 g
Saturated Fat: 1 g
Dietary Fiber: 1 g
Carbohydrates: 24 g
Protein: 26 g
Cholesterol: 64 mg
Sodium: 208 mg

Pasta Salad with Turkey, Peppers, Olives, and Tomatoes

8 servings

1 pound fusilli or rotini, cooked al dente

1 pound smoked turkey breast, diced

1 pound fresh broccoli florets, cooked al dente

1 6-ounce jar roasted peppers, drained and diced

1 14½ ounce can water-packed artichoke hearts, drained and quartered

1 15-ounce can whole baby corn spears, drained

1 cup pitted black olives

8 plum tomatoes, quartered

6 tablespoons extra-virgin olive oil

2 tablespoons cider vinegar

½ teaspoon Kosher salt

¼ teaspoon pepper

½ cup freshly grated Parmesan cheese

6 sprigs fresh basil leaves for garnish

In a large salad bowl, toss pasta, turkey, brocoli, roasted red peppers, artichoke hearts, and baby corn. Chill. In a separate bowl, chill olives and tomatoes.

Just before serving, combine olive oil, vinegar, salt, and pepper. Pour over pasta and vegetables. Toss. Add olives and tomatoes. Toss again. Sprinkle with Parmesan cheese. Garnish with fresh basil leaves.

APPROXIMATE NUTRITIONAL INFORMATION PER SERVING

Total calories: 498
Total Fat: 15 g
Saturated Fat: 3 g
Dietary Fiber: 3 g
Carbohydrates: 1 g
Protein: 31 g
Cholesterol: 51 mg
Sodium: 621 mg

Rice, Smoked Turkey, and Sun-Dried Tomato Salad

8 servings

2 cups chicken broth, preferably homemade (page 143)

2 cups water

1 cup wild rice

10 fresh mushrooms, sliced

1 cup long-grain brown basmati rice (p. 344)

¼ cup extra-virgin olive oil

2 tablespoons red wine vinegar

½ teaspoon Kosher salt

¼ teaspoon pepper

4 plum tomatoes, diced

10 sun-dried tomatoes, diced

1 English cucumber, peeled and diced

1 bunch green onions, diced

½ pound smoked turkey breast, diced

Fresh spinach leaves

In a 2-quart saucepan, bring chicken broth, water, and wild rice to a boil. Reduce heat. Cover and simmer 65-95 minutes, or until rice is tender and broth is nearly absorbed. Add mushrooms. Cover; simmer 4 to 5 minutes longer, or until mushrooms are cooked and moisture is absorbed.

Meanwhile, cook basmati rice according to recipe on page 344.

In a small covered jar, combine olive oil, vinegar, salt, and pepper.

In a large salad bowl, combine wild rice, basmati rice, plum tomatoes, sun-dried tomatoes, cucumber, green onion, and turkey. Just before serving, toss with dressing. Serve on spinach-lined salad plates.

Serving Suggestion: Perfect main meal salad. For dessert, serve Lemon Ice cream (page 414) and skewered fresh seasonal fruit.

APPROXIMATE NUTRITIONAL INFORMATION PER SERVING

Total calories: 248
Total Fat: 6 g
Saturated Fat: trace
Dietary Fiber: 3 g
Carbohydrates: 39 g
Protein: 16 g
Cholesterol: 12 mg
Sodium: 353 mg

Super Taco Salad

8 servings

1 28-ounce can plum tomatoes

¾ teaspoon Kosher salt

¾ teaspoon dry mustard

1¼ teaspoons chili powder

¼ teaspoon ground cumin

¼ teaspoon cayenne

1 small garlic clove, minced

2½ cups cubed cooked, skinless chicken breast

1 15-ounce can red kidney beans, drained and rinsed

2 15-ounce cans black beans, drained and rinsed

¾ head lettuce, chopped

1 medium onion, chopped

½ cup grated reduced-fat cheddar or mozzarella cheese

48 heart-healthy tortilla chips made with a heart-healthy oil such as sunflower, corn, soybean or canola

1 cup Tomato Salsa, preferably homemade (page 214)

½ cup nonfat sour cream

APPROXIMATE NUTRITIONAL INFORMATION PER SERVING

USING CHICKEN	USING EXTRA-LEAN GROUND ROUND
Total calories: 315	Total calories: 355
Total Fat: 6 g	Total Fat: 12 g
Saturated Fat: 1 g	Saturated Fat: 4 g
Dietary Fiber: 9 g	Dietary Fiber: 9 g
Carbohydrates: 39 g	Carbohydrates: 39 g
Protein: 30 g	Protein: 28 g
Cholesterol: 52 mg	Cholesterol: 53 mg
Sodium: 542 mg	Sodium: 542 mg

Purée tomatoes in a blender or food processor; pour into a medium saucepan. Add salt, dry mustard, chili powder, cumin, cayenne, and garlic; heat just to boiling. Reduce heat and simmer 5 minutes; add chicken, kidney beans, and black beans. Heat.

Just before serving, spoon mixture into individual bowls. Top with lettuce, onion, cheese; add tortilla chips, salsa, and sour cream.

Variation: Substitute 1 pound extra-lean ground round for chicken.

Beef, Noodle, and Mushroom Salad

6 servings

⅓ cup rice vinegar

½ bunch white radishes, cut into julienne strips

4 cups beef stock (page 151) or canned broth

1 6-ounce package buckwheat (soba) noodles

1 tablespoon olive oil

8 cloves garlic, slivered

¾ pounds lean beef sirloin, cut into stir-fry strips

1 7-ounce package dried forest mushrooms (Shiitake), reconstituted in water to soften and then cut into julienne strips

½ English cucumber, peeled, seeded and cut into julienne strips

6 green onions, sliced on the diagonal into thirds

SAUCE:

¼ cup reduced-sodium soy sauce

2 tablespoons oyster sauce

2 tablespoons rice vinegar

1 tablespoon extra virgin olive oil

¼ teaspoon crushed red pepper

APPROXIMATE NUTRITIONAL INFORMATION PER SERVING

WITHOUT DRESSING	PER TABLESPOON OF SAUCE
Total calories: 326	Total calories: 20
Total Fat: 9 g	Total Fat: 1 g
Saturated Fat: 2 g	Saturated Fat: 0 g
Dietary Fiber: 2 g	Dietary Fiber: 0 g
Carbohydrates: 35 g	Carbohydrates: trace
Protein: 23 g	Protein: trace
Cholesterol: 45 mg	Cholesterol: trace
Sodium: 221 mg	Sodium: 333 mg

Most of the fat and sodium are in the sauce. Remember to use a moderate amount.

Pour vinegar over radishes and marinate 30 minutes at room temperature. Rinse and pat dry.

Meanwhile, in a medium saucepan, bring beef stock to a boil; add noodles and cook 5–6 minutes or until noodles are tender. In a small saucepan, combine all the sauce ingredients and simmer 5 minutes.

In a nonstick skillet, heat olive oil, add garlic and stir-fry 1–2 minutes; add beef and julienned mushrooms, and stir-fry 2–3 minutes.

To serve, arrange noodles in a copper skillet or large platter. Spoon beef and mushrooms over top. Garnish with radishes, cucumber, and green onions. Pass the sauce.

Serving Suggestion: Excellent as a main meal salad. Serve with Frozen Yogurt Parfait with Fruit Sauces (page 416).

Summer Fruit Salad

2 servings

3 leaves red or green leaf lettuce

½ cup Greek non-fat vanilla or peach yogurt

3 large ripe strawberries, thinly sliced

3 slices fresh peach

1 slice fresh pineapple, cut into chunks

1 small wedge cantaloupe, cubed

1 small wedge honeydew melon, cubed

1 small wedge watermelon, cubed

Layer the lettuce on a chilled dinner plate. Spoon yogurt into individual custard cup or soufflé bowl; place on center or side of plate. Surround with fresh fruits.

Note: This is a great salad when you're watching calories. It looks like a lot of food, takes a long time to eat, and is a special treat in spring and early summer when fruits are just becoming available in the markets.

Serving Suggestion: Serve with Applesauce Oatmeal Muffins (page 76).

APPROXIMATE NUTRITIONAL INFORMATION PER SERVING

Total calories: 74
Total Fat: trace
Saturated Fat: 0 g
Dietary Fiber: 2 g
Carbohydrates: 14 g
Protein: 4 g
Cholesterol: 1 mg
Sodium: 51 mg

Mixed Fruit Salad

4 servings

Lettuce leaves

2 cups Greek non-fat vanilla or fruit-flavored yogurt

½ cup 2-inch-cubed watermelon

½ cup 2-inch-cubed cantaloupe

½ cup 2-inch-cubed honeydew

½ cup 2-inch-cubed fresh pineapple

½ cup 3-inch-cubed fresh papaya

1 cup raspberries, strawberries, or blueberries

Fresh mint for garnish

Arrange lettuce on 4 chilled salad plates. Spoon yogurt into 1-cup-size soufflé dishes, and center each dish in a salad plate. Surround with fruit. Garnish with mint.

Note: Perfect lunch or light supper after a night or two of overeating.

APPROXIMATE NUTRITIONAL INFORMATION PER SERVING

Total calories: 116
Total Fat: 1 g
Saturated Fat: 0 g
Dietary Fiber: 4 g
Carbohydrates: 25 g
Protein: 5 g
Cholesterol: 1 mg
Sodium: 56 mg

Watermelon Basket Salad

Approximately 10 quarts

1 10- to 12-pound watermelon

1 2-pound honeydew

1 3-pound cantaloupe

2 pounds grapes

4 cups strawberries

4 cups raspberries

4 cups blueberries

Fresh mint for garnish

Pick a roly-poly watermelon, which will be carved into a basket. Cut off the top third of the watermelon by cutting lengthwise from each end toward the center. Leave a center portion $2^{1}/_{2}$ inches wide for the handle. Using a serrated knife, make big scallops around the rim of the watermelon.

With a melon baller, form balls from watermelon, honeydew, and cantaloupe. Toss with grapes and berries. Scrape inside of watermelon with a spoon to remove excess melon. Fill with fruit. Garnish with fresh mint.

Note: At the end of the meal, rinse watermelon basket; pat dry and freeze for later use.

APPROXIMATE NUTRITIONAL INFORMATION PER CUP

Total calories: 68
Total Fat: trace
Saturated Fat: 0 g
Dietary Fiber: 4 g
Carbohydrates: 17 g
Protein: 1 g
Cholesterol: 0 mg
Sodium: 7 mg

Dressings, Sauces & Spreads

A NOTE ON OILS

Of the monounsaturated oils, olive and canola oils are the most highly recommended. Olive oil ranges from mild-flavored to rich-flavored. Use a lighter variety for cooking and a stronger one for salads. The finest quality, labeled "extra-virgin" or "virgin," has a more intense flavor, so the amount of oil can be reduced. Remember, light olive oil has the same calories as regular olive oil. Canola oil is the lowest in saturated fat, has a light taste, and is particularly good in recipes calling for butter, margarine, or lard. Of the polyunsaturated oils, safflower oil is the least saturated of all, followed in order by soybean, sunflower, corn, cottonseed, and sesame.

Italian Vinaigrette

1 cup

¼ **cup cider vinegar**

¾ **cup extra-virgin olive oil**

¾–1 **teaspoon Kosher salt**

¼ **teaspoon black pepper**

Combine ingredients in a covered jar and shake well.

Oil-based dressings are high in calories and fat. Use them judiciously.

APPROXIMATE NUTRITIONAL INFORMATION PER TABLESPOON

Total calories: 90
Total Fat: 11 g
Saturated Fat: 1.5 g
Dietary Fiber: 0 g
Carbohydrates: 0 g
Protein: 0 g
Cholesterol: 0 mg
Sodium: 90 mg

Olive Oil-and-Lemon Vinaigrette

1/2 cup

¼ **cup fresh lemon juice**

¼ **cup extra-virgin olive oil**

½ **teaspoon Kosher salt**

¼ **teaspoon black pepper**

Combine ingredients in a covered jar and shake well.

APPROXIMATE NUTRITIONAL INFORMATION PER TABLESPOON

Total calories: 62
Total Fat: 7 g
Saturated Fat: 0 g
Dietary Fiber: 0 g
Carbohydrates: 1 g
Protein: 0 g
Cholesterol: 0 mg
Sodium: 120 mg

Oil-Free Lemon Vinaigrette

1/3 cup

⅓ cup fresh lemon juice

½ teaspoon Kosher salt

¼ teaspoon black pepper

Combine ingredients in a covered jar and shake well.

APPROXIMATE NUTRITIONAL INFORMATION PER TABLESPOON

Total calories: 4
Total Fat: 0
Saturated Fat: 0 g
Dietary Fiber: 0 g
Carbohydrates: 0 g
Protein: 1 g
Cholesterol: 0 mg
Sodium: 195 mg

Szechuan Vinaigrette

2/3 cup

1 tablespoon rice vinegar

1 tablespoon fresh lemon juice

1 tablespoon sesame oil

½ teaspoon Kosher salt

⅛ teaspoon black pepper

⅓ cup extra-virgin olive oil

3–4 drops hot chili oil*

Combine vinegar, lemon juice, sesame oil, salt, and pepper in a blender or food processor. With machine running, gradually add olive oil, 1 tablespoon at a time. Add chili oil.

*Hot chili oil is available in Asian markets, if not in your supermarket.

Oil-based dressings are high in calories and fat. Use them judiciously.

APPROXIMATE NUTRITIONAL INFORMATION PER TABLESPOON

Total calories: 70
Total Fat: 8 g
Saturated Fat: 1 g
Dietary Fiber: 0 g
Carbohydrates: 0 g
Protein: 0 g
Cholesterol: 0 mg
Sodium: 90 mg

Oil-Free Szechuan Vinaigrette

1/2 cup

¼ cup reduced-sodium soy sauce

2 tablespoons rice vinegar

Combine ingredients in a covered jar and shake well.

Dressings made with soy sauce, even reduced-sodium soy sauce, are high in sodium. Be judicious in their use.

APPROXIMATE NUTRITIONAL INFORMATION PER TABLESPOON

Total calories: 6
Total Fat: 0 g
Saturated Fat: 0 g
Dietary Fiber: 0 g
Carbohydrates: 1 g
Protein: 0 g
Cholesterol: 0 mg
Sodium: 575 mg

Champagne Vinaigrette

2 cups

1 tablespoon Dijon mustard

⅓ cup champagne vinegar

¾ teaspoon Kosher salt

¼ teaspoon pepper

1 teaspoon fresh lemon juice

1½ cups extra-virgin olive oil

APPROXIMATE NUTRITIONAL INFORMATION PER TABLESPOON

Total calories: 90
Total Fat: 11 g
Saturated Fat: 1.5 g
Dietary Fiber: 0 g
Carbohydrates: 0 g
Protein: 0 g
Cholesterol: 0 mg
Sodium: 55 mg

Combine mustard, vinegar, salt, pepper and lemon juice in a blender or food processor. With machine running, gradually add oil 1 tablespoon at a time. Chill.

Mustard-and-Lemon Vinaigrette

3/4 cup

2 cloves garlic, peeled

2 tablespoons fresh lemon juice

½ teaspoon Dijon mustard

¾ teaspoon Kosher salt

⅔ cups extra virgin olive oil

APPROXIMATE NUTRITIONAL INFORMATION PER TABLESPOON

Total calories: 110
Total Fat: 12 g
Saturated Fat: 1 g
Dietary Fiber: 0 g
Carbohydrates: 0 g
Protein: 0 g
Cholesterol: 0 mg
Sodium: 125 mg

Combine garlic, lemon juice, mustard, and salt in a blender or food processor. With machine running, gradually add oil, 1 tablespoon at a time.

Serving Suggestion: Especially good on Spinach Salad (page 158).

Oil-based dressings are high in calories and fat. Use them judiciously.

Garlic Vinaigrette

3/4 cup

3 cloves garlic, peeled

1 tablespoon white wine vinegar

1 tablespoon red wine vinegar

2 tablespoons Dijon mustard

¼ teaspoon Kosher salt

¼ teaspoon black pepper

½ cup extra-virgin olive oil

Combine garlic, lemon juice, mustard, and salt in a blender or food processor. With machine running, gradually add oils, 1 tablespoon at a time.

Serving Suggestion: Especially good on Spinach Salad (page 158).

APPROXIMATE NUTRITIONAL INFORMATION PER TABLESPOON

Total calories: 80
Total Fat: 9 g
Saturated Fat: 1.5 g
Dietary Fiber: 0 g
Carbohydrates: 0 g
Protein: 0 g
Cholesterol: 1 mg
Sodium: 100 mg

Mustard-and-Garlic Vinaigrette

1 cup

¼ cup cider vinegar

2 cloves garlic, peeled

1 tablespoon Dijon mustard

¼ teaspoon black pepper

½ teaspoon Kosher salt

¾ cup extra-virgin olive oil

Combine all ingredients in a covered jar. Shake.

APPROXIMATE NUTRITIONAL INFORMATION PER TABLESPOON

Total calories: 92
Total Fat: 10 g
Saturated Fat: 1 g
Dietary Fiber: 0 g
Carbohydrates: 0 g
Protein: 0 g
Cholesterol: 35 mg
Sodium: 82 mg

Dijon Vinaigrette

1 1/4 cups

¼ cup Dijon mustard

3 tablespoons red wine vinegar

1 tablespoon white wine vinegar

¼ teaspoon Kosher salt

2 cloves garlic, peeled

1 tablespoon chopped fresh basil or ½ teaspoon dried

⅛ teaspoon black pepper

2 drops hot sauce

1 tablespoon grated onion

½ cup extra-virgin olive oil

Combine mustard and vinegars in a blender. Add salt, garlic, basil, pepper, hot sauce, and onion; whirl. With machine running, add olive oil, 1 tablespoon at a time.

APPROXIMATE NUTRITIONAL INFORMATION PER TABLESPOON

Total calories: 28
Total Fat: 3 g
Saturated Fat: 0 g
Dietary Fiber: 0 g
Carbohydrates: 1 g
Protein: 0 g
Cholesterol: 0 mg
Sodium: 63 mg

Jalapeno Vinaigrette

1 cup

2 tablespoons freshly squeezed lime juice

2½ tablespoons sherry vinegar

½ teaspoon Dijon mustard

1 teaspoon Kosher salt

½ teaspoon black pepper

½ fresh jalapeño pepper, seeded

⅓ cup extra-virgin olive oil

APPROXIMATE NUTRITIONAL INFORMATION PER TABLESPOON

Total calories: 41
Total Fat: 4 g
Saturated Fat: 1 g
Dietary Fiber: trace
Carbohydrates: trace
Protein: trace
Cholesterol: 0 mg
Sodium: 125 mg

In a blender or food processor, combine all ingredients except the olive oil and whirl 1–2 minutes. With machine running, add olive oil 1 tablespoon at a time. Chill.

Serving Suggestion: Serve with Ensenada Salad (page 168) for an especially good accompaniment to a Mexican-style meal.

Wasabi Vinaigrette

scant 1/2 cup

3 tablespoons rice vinegar

1 tablespoon extra-virgin olive oil

3 tablespoons reduced-sodium soy sauce

1 teaspoon wasabi (prepared Japanese horseradish)

APPROXIMATE NUTRITIONAL INFORMATION PER CUP

Total calories: 21
Total Fat: 2 g
Saturated Fat: trace
Dietary Fiber: 0 g
Carbohydrates: trace
Protein: 0 g
Cholesterol: trace
Sodium: 229 mg

In a small bowl, combine vinegar, olive oil, and soy sauce. Stir in wasabi.

Note: Wasabi comes in a tube and is available in Asian markets or in the Asian section of most supermarkets.

Creamy Garlic Dressing

2 1/4 cups

1 16-ounce container low-fat (2%) cottage cheese

2 tablespoons mayonnaise

½ teaspoon Kosher salt

¼ teaspoon black pepper

3 cloves garlic, finely minced (about 1½ –2 teaspoons)

1½ tablespoons finely minced onion

2 tablespoons finely minced green onion

1 teaspoon minced fresh Italian parsley

In a medium bowl, combine all ingredients. Chill.

Serving Suggestion: An excellent salad dressing, especially for Winter Vegetable Salad (page 169), and a great dip with carrot and celery sticks. Also good on baked potatoes.

For lower fat, reduce the mayonnaise to 1 tablespoon. To lower sodium, reduce the salt to ¼ teaspoon. The dip will still taste very good.

APPROXIMATE NUTRITIONAL INFORMATION PER CUP

Total calories: 18
Total Fat: 1 g
Saturated Fat: 0 g
Dietary Fiber: trace
Carbohydrates: 1 g
Protein: 2 g
Cholesterol: 2 mg
Sodium: 79 mg

Lemon and Hot Mustard Dressing

1/4 cup

¼ cup fresh lemon juice

¼ teaspoon Chinese hot mustard

¼ teaspoon freshly ground pepper

Combine all ingredients in a covered jar; shake well. Use at once.

Serving suggestions: Great on fresh spinach greens.

APPROXIMATE NUTRITIONAL INFORMATION PER TABLESPOON

Total calories: 5
Total Fat: trace
Saturated Fat: 0 g
Dietary Fiber: 0 g
Carbohydrates: 2 g
Protein: 0 g
Cholesterol: 0 mg
Sodium: 0 mg

Niçoise Dressing

3/4 cup

½ cup extra-virgin olive oil

2 tablespoons tarragon-flavored vinegar

2 tablespoons fresh lemon juice

2 garlic cloves, chopped

1½ teaspoons dry mustard

¾ teaspoon Kosher salt

½ teaspoon black pepper

Combine all ingredients in a covered jar. Shake well.

APPROXIMATE NUTRITIONAL INFORMATION PER TABLESPOON

Total calories: 83
Total Fat: 9 g
Saturated Fat: 1 g
Dietary Fiber: 0 g
Carbohydrates: 1 g
Protein: 0 g
Cholesterol: 0 mg
Sodium: 86 mg

Low-Fat Niçoise Dressing

1/3 cup

¼ cup fresh lemon juice

1 tablespoon Garlic Olive Oil (page 210)

½ teaspoon Kosher salt

¼ teaspoon pepper

Combine all ingredients in a covered jar. Shake well.

APPROXIMATE NUTRITIONAL INFORMATION PER TABLESPOON

Total calories: 26
Total Fat: 3 g
Saturated Fat: 0 g
Dietary Fiber: 9 g
Carbohydrates: 30 g
Protein: 9 g
Cholesterol: 0 mg
Sodium: 162 mg

Hot Mustard and Sesame Seeds

8 servings

½ cup hot Chinese mustard

¼ cup toasted sesame seeds

Mound hot mustard in center of a salad-size plate. Ring with sesame seeds.

Note: Hot Chinese mustard and toasted sesame seeds are available in Asian markets and in Asian sections of many supermarkets.

Serving Suggestion: Use with Roast Chicken Asian Style (page 308) and Spring Rolls (page 89).

APPROXIMATE NUTRITIONAL INFORMATION PER SERVING OF 1-TABLESPOON MUSTARD AND 1/2 TABLESPOON SESAME SEEDS

Total calories: 38
Total Fat: 3 g
Saturated Fat: 0 g
Dietary Fiber: trace
Carbohydrates: 2 g
Protein: 1 g
Cholesterol: 0 mg
Sodium: 190 mg

Garlic Olive Oil

1 1/2 cups

1½ cups extra-virgin olive oil

1 head garlic, separated into cloves and peeled

Pour olive oil into a pint-size jar; add garlic. Cover tightly and let mellow 2 to 3 days; remove garlic. Store in a dark place. Keeps 3 to 4 weeks.

Note: Garlic Olive Oil is very flavorful. A little goes a long way, making it possible to use a lot less oil and still have great taste. It works well in salad dressings, in marinades for grilled vegetables, and over toasted bread such as bruschetta, focaccia, and garlic bread.

APPROXIMATE NUTRITIONAL INFORMATION PER TABLESPOON

Total calories: 121
Total Fat: 14 g
Saturated Fat: 2 g
Dietary Fiber: 2 g
Carbohydrates: 0 g
Protein: 0 g
Cholesterol: 0 mg
Sodium: 0 mg

Hot Chili Marinade

3/4 cup

2 Anaheim chilies

1 teaspoon extra-virgin olive oil

6 cloves garlic

⅓ cup pineapple juice

2 tablespoons distilled white vinegar

½ teaspoon Kosher salt

⅛ teaspoon black pepper

¼ cup Hot Chili Sauce (page 215)

Cut chilies in half lengthwise and remove seeds and stems. In a nonstick skillet, sauté chilies in olive oil 3–4 minutes or until tender. In a blender or food processor, purée the chilies, garlic, pineapple juice, vinegar, salt, and pepper. Stir in Hot Chili Sauce.

Note: Anaheim chilies, also called Texas, California, New Mexico, Colorado, guajillo, long red or long green chilies, are usually available in Spanish and Mexican markets and in most supermarkets. Although the flavor will be slightly different, any other fresh hot chilies may be substituted.

Serving Suggestion: Try Hot Chili marinade on grilled steaks, barbecued turkey and chicken, lamb and pork roast. An excellent recipe is Hot-and-Spicy Southwest Turkey (page 296).

Remember, used as a marinade or barbecue sauce, you will be consuming a lot less than 1/4 cup, so fat and sodium are less than shown in nutritional analysis.

APPROXIMATE NUTRITIONAL INFORMATION PER ¼ CUP

Total calories: 56
Total Fat: 2 g
Saturated Fat: trace
Dietary Fiber: trace
Carbohydrates: 10 g
Protein: 1 g
Cholesterol: trace
Sodium: 422 mg

Homemade Mayonnaise

1 1/2 cups

1 pasturized egg*

1 teaspoon red wine vinegar

2 teaspoons fresh lemon juice

1 teaspoon Dijon mustard

½ teaspoon Kosher salt

1½ cups extra-virgin olive oil

Combine egg, vinegar, lemon juice, mustard, salt, and ¼ cup olive oil in a blender; whirl. With machine running, add remaining 1¼ cup oil, 1 tablespoon at a time. Refrigerate. Keeps several weeks.

Variation: To make herbed mayonnaise, add 1 teaspoon chopped fresh basil, dill, tarragon, or parsley, or ½ teaspoon dried, just before serving.

*Raw eggs have been identified as a source of salmonella. The American Egg Board recommends using only pasturized eggs to eliminate the risk. Pasturized eggs are available in many supermarkets.

APPROXIMATE NUTRITIONAL INFORMATION PER TABLESPOON

Total calories: 124
Total Fat: 14 g
Saturated Fat: 1 g
Dietary Fiber: 0 g
Carbohydrates: trace
Protein: trace
Cholesterol: 9 mg
Sodium: 41 mg

Aioli Sauce

1 1/2 cups

2 tablespoons raspberry champagne vinegar

3 tablespoons non-fat milk

5 cloves garlic, peeled

2 pasturized egg yolks*

½ teaspoon Kosher salt

¼ teaspoon white pepper

1 cup extra-virgin olive oil

2 tablespoons fresh lemon juice

2 tablespoons non-fat sour cream

Combine vinegar, milk, garlic, egg yolks, salt, and pepper in a blender or food processor. Process 3–4 minutes, or until mixture begins to thicken. With machine running, add olive oil in a steady stream, 1 tablespoon at a time. When oil is absorbed, add lemon juice and sour cream.

Serving Suggestion: Serve as a dip with crudités or as a sauce on potatoes, vegetables, and seafood.

This is a creative adaptation of the classic Provencale sauce that historically uses an uncooked egg and yolk. However, salmonella has been traced to raw egg in dishes. If you are unsure of the quality of your eggs, avoid recipes that use them raw. A reasonable substitute can be made with commercial mayonnaise flavored with garlic and lemon juice.

*Raw eggs have been identified as a source of salmonella. The American Egg Board recommends using only pasturized eggs to eliminate the risk. Pasturized eggs are available in many supermarkets.

APPROXIMATE NUTRITIONAL INFORMATION PER TABLESPOON

Total calories: 89
Total Fat: 1 g
Saturated Fat: 1 g
Dietary Fiber: 0 g
Carbohydrates: 1 g
Protein: 1 g
Cholesterol: 17 mg
Sodium: 30 mg

Mustard Sauce

1/2 cup

⅓ cup Dijon mustard

1 teaspoon rice vinegar

2 teaspoons sesame oil

Combine mustard, vinegar, and sesame oil in a bowl or covered jar. Stir until smooth.

Serving Suggestion: Good on warm vegetables, especially broccoli, cauliflower, and fresh green beans.

APPROXIMATE NUTRITIONAL INFORMATION PER TABLESPOON

Total calories: 20
Total Fat: 2 g
Saturated Fat: 0 g
Dietary Fiber: 0 g
Carbohydrates: 2 g
Protein: 0 g
Cholesterol: 0 mg
Sodium: 240 mg

Horseradish Sauce

1/2 cup

⅓ cup non-fat sour cream

2 tablespoons prepared horseradish

Combine sour cream with horseradish. Stir until smooth.

Variation: For an even hotter flavor, use prepared horseradish that is labeled "hot" or "extra-hot."

Serving Suggestion: Good as a dip with crudités and grilled vegetables and as a sauce with red meats.

APPROXIMATE NUTRITIONAL INFORMATION PER TABLESPOON

Total calories: 12
Total Fat: 0 g
Saturated Fat: 0 g
Dietary Fiber: 0 g
Carbohydrates: 2 g
Protein: 1 g
Cholesterol: 1 mg
Sodium: 11 mg

Barbecue Sauce

2 cups

1 15-ounce can tomato sauce

½ cup cider vinegar

¾ teaspoons Tabasco

¾ teaspoon Dijon mustard

3 cloves garlic, squeezed

2 tablespoons brown sugar

In a medium stock pot, combine ingredients. Bring to a boil over high heat, stirring frequently. Reduce heat and simmer, uncovered, 1½ hours.

Note: Sauce will keep 4–5 weeks in the refrigerator and may be frozen. The flavor is superior to that of commercial barbecue sauce.

Serving Suggestions: Excellent on chicken, salmon, scallops, and oysters—especially oysters on the half shell.

APPROXIMATE NUTRITIONAL INFORMATION PER TABLESPOON

Total calories: 7
Total Fat: 1 g
Saturated Fat: 0 g
Dietary Fiber: 0 g
Carbohydrates: 2 g
Protein: 0 g
Cholesterol: 0 mg
Sodium: 61 mg

Pesto

2 2/3 cups

5 cups fresh basil

8 cloves garlic

1 teaspoon Kosher salt

½ cup pine nuts

¾ cup extra-virgin olive oil

Combine basil, garlic, salt, and pine nuts in a blender or food processor and purée. With machine running, add olive oil 1 tablespoon at a time. Blend until smooth and oil is absorbed.

Note: Never double the pesto recipe as the oil will not absorb properly. To make several consecutive batches (25 half-pints), you'll need the following quantities of ingredients: 11 bunches fresh basil, 10 whole bulbs fresh garlic, 1²/₃ pounds pine nuts, 3½ quarts olive oil, and salt per batch as in above recipe. Fill half-pint jars ¾ full with pesto. Spoon 1 tablespoon olive oil over pesto to seal. Screw lids tightly onto jars. Store jars in freezer.

Serving Suggestions: Pesto is delicious on pasta, chicken, seafood, vegetables and potatoes.

Oil-based dressings are high in calories and fat. Use them judiciously.

APPROXIMATE NUTRITIONAL INFORMATION PER TABLESPOON

Total calories: 50
Total Fat: 5 g
Saturated Fat: .5 g
Dietary Fiber: 0 g
Carbohydrates: 1 g
Protein: 1 g
Cholesterol: 0 mg
Sodium: 45 mg

Marinara Sauce

4 1/4 cups

1 28-ounce can plum tomatoes, diced

2 tablespoons tomato paste

½ teaspoon oregano

½ teaspoon dried basil or ¼ cup fresh

½ teaspoon black pepper

1 tablespoon olive oil

¼ teaspoon cider vinegar

In a medium saucepan, combine tomatoes, tomato paste, oregano, basil, and black pepper. Simmer 20 minutes (do not allow to boil). Stir in olive oil and vinegar. Simmer 10 minutes.

Serving Suggestions: For a quick last-minute meal, serve over pasta. Accompany with a green salad and Grilled Garlic Bread (page 55).

This is also an excellent sauce to use on pizza or on grilled or baked eggplant.

APPROXIMATE NUTRITIONAL INFORMATION PER ¼ CUP

Total calories: 20
Total Fat: 1 g
Saturated Fat: 0 g
Dietary Fiber: 1 g
Carbohydrates: 2 g
Protein: 1 g
Cholesterol: 0 mg
Sodium: 110 mg

Tomato Salsa

4 cups

1 28-ounce can plum tomatoes, diced

2½ teaspoons pure ground mild chili powder*

¼ teaspoon ground cumin

¼ teaspoon Kosher salt

¼ teaspoon black pepper

¼ teaspoon cayenne pepper

½ teaspoon extra-virgin olive oil

2 tablespoons diced green chilies, regular or hot

Combine ingredients in a covered jar. For best flavor, chill at least 2 hours.

*Take the time to search for a Spanish or Mexican market or a supermarket that carries pure ground chili powder. Pure ground chili powder is made by grinding dried chilies; its flavor is far superior to commercial chili powder, which is most often 40% salt and 20% additives.

For a thicker salsa add 1 tablespoon tomato paste.

APPROXIMATE NUTRITIONAL INFORMATION PER TABLESPOON

Total calories: 4
Total Fat: 0 g
Saturated Fat: 0 g
Dietary Fiber: 0 g
Carbohydrates: 1 g
Protein: 0 g
Cholesterol: 0 mg
Sodium: 45 mg

Fresh Salsa Cruda

3 cups

1 ½ cups chopped ripe tomatoes, preferably heirloom

3 tablespoons chopped green onion

½ cup chopped red onion

2 finely chopped, fresh jalapeño peppers

2 garlic cloves, minced

1 tablespoon fresh lemon juice

½ teaspoon Kosher salt

½ teaspoon black pepper

Combine all ingredients in a glass bowl. Chill.

Serving Suggestion: Great on Tijuana Salad (page 168) and on grilled chicken.

If you like spicy add hot diced green chilies to taste.

APPROXIMATE NUTRITIONAL INFORMATION PER TABLESPOON

Total calories: 3
Total Fat: trace
Saturated Fat: 0 g
Dietary Fiber: trace
Carbohydrates: 1 g
Protein: 0 g
Cholesterol: 0 mg
Sodium: 20 mg

Hot Chili Sauce

2 cups

½ cup chicken broth (page 143) or commercial broth*

½ cup distilled white vinegar

3 dried negro chilies, stemmed and seeded

5 cloves garlic

1 medium onion

1 medium ripe tomato

1 teaspoon Kosher salt

In a saucepan, combine chicken broth, vinegar, and chilies, and bring to a boil. Remove from heat and let chilies soak 5–10 minutes or until soft.

In a blender or food processor, combine broth-vinegar mixture, softened chilies, garlic, onion, tomato, and salt. Blend until puréed.

*Canned broth is higher in sodium.

Note: Negro chilies, also called ancho, poblano, pasilla, and mulatto, are available in many supermarkets and Spanish or Mexican markets. Although the flavor will be slightly different, any hot dried chilies may be substituted.

Serving Suggestion: Use as a barbecue sauce with pork, beef, chicken, and shrimp.

APPROXIMATE NUTRITIONAL INFORMATION PER ¼ CUP

Total calories: 36
Total Fat: trace
Saturated Fat: 0 g
Dietary Fiber: trace
Carbohydrates: 7 g
Protein: trace
Cholesterol: trace
Sodium: 356 mg

Chili Salsa

1 quart

1-2 teaspoons finely diced Thai chilies

3 tablespoons distilled white vinegar

2 cloves garlic

⅛ teaspoon ground cumin

⅛ teaspoon oregano

½ teaspoon Kosher salt

1 28-ounce can Italian plum tomatoes, diced

In a blender or food processor, combine prepared chilies, vinegar, garlic, cumin, oregano, salt, and tomatoes, and purée.

Pour into quart jar. Refrigerate what you will use within two weeks; freeze remaining salsa.

Note: Arbol chilies also called chimayo may be used in place of the Thai chilies. Both pack a firey punch.

Serving Suggestion: This salsa is great. It's especially good with Hot-and-Spicy Southwest Turkey (page 296).

APPROXIMATE NUTRITIONAL INFORMATION PER ½ CUP

Total calories: 30
Total Fat: trace
Saturated Fat: trace
Dietary Fiber: trace
Carbohydrates: 6 g
Protein: 1 g
Cholesterol: 0 mg
Sodium: 305 mg

A NOTE ON STORE-BOUGHT CANNED TOMATO PRODUCTS

Italian plum tomatoes are the best substitute for fresh tomatoes. It is important to buy the best quality available. Progresso Plum Tomatoes and S&W Pear Tomatoes are especially good, as are many of the imported brands such as Di Napoli and San Marzano. The better the grade, the more flavorful the sauce. For recipes in this book that call for diced plum tomatoes, buy the whole plum tomatoes and simply dice them yourself or buy San Marzano diced tomatoes.

Store-bought tomato sauce, tomato purée, and tomato paste should also be of the highest grade available. Progresso and Contadina brands are among the best. Freeze any leftover paste by the tablespoonful on a sheet of waxed paper; once frozen, remove to a plastic freezer bag and store in the freezer for later use.

Fresh Tomato and Chili Salsa

1 pint

1½ cups diced ripe tomatoes, preferably heirloom

¼ cup diced serrano or other mild fresh chilies

8 green onions, diced

3 cloves garlic, minced

½ cup diced white onion

1 tablespoon lemon juice

¼ teaspoon black pepper

¼ cup finely chopped cilantro

In a medium bowl, combine all ingredients. Use at once or chill. Store in refrigerator up to 3 days.

Serving Suggestion: Excellent as a dip, sauce, salsa, or salad dressing.

APPROXIMATE NUTRITIONAL INFORMATION PER ¼ CUP

Total calories: 20
Total Fat: trace
Saturated Fat: trace
Dietary Fiber: trace
Carbohydrates: 4 g
Protein: trace
Cholesterol: 0 mg
Sodium: 5 mg

Soy Sauce and Rice Vinegar Sauce

Approximately 1/3 cup

¼ cup reduced-sodium soy sauce

2 tablespoons rice vinegar

½ teaspoon hot chili oil

Combine all ingredients. Mix well.

APPROXIMATE NUTRITIONAL INFORMATION PER TABLESPOON

Total calories: 21
Total Fat: trace
Saturated Fat: 0 g
Dietary Fiber: 0 g
Carbohydrates: 3 g
Protein: 1 g
Cholesterol: 0 mg
Sodium: 585 mg

Old-Fashioned Gravy

2 1/2 cups

1 cup chicken broth, preferably homemade (page 143)

1 cup beef broth (page 153)

3 tablespoons de-fatted meat juices and drippings (optional)

¼ cup all-purpose flour

½ cup cold water

¼ teaspoon Kosher salt

⅛ teaspoon black pepper

Bring broths and de-fatted meat drippings to a boil. Shake flour and water in a covered jar to form a smooth paste; gradually add to boiling broth. Reduce heat; simmer 5 to 10 minutes, stirring constantly, until thick. Season.

Note: To de-fat meat juices and drippings, pour the juices and drippings into a bowl; add a few ice cubes. Chill in the freezer for 10 to 15 minutes, or until the fat congeals at the top and around ice cubes. Discard ice cubes and congealed fat.

It is not necessary to use meat juices and drippings to make a satisfactory gravy with the above recipe.

Variation: For a really great gravy that works with poultry mix ½ cup + 2 tablespoons nonfat milk with one can Healthy Request Cream of Chicken Soup.

APPROXIMATE NUTRITIONAL INFORMATION PER ¼ CUP

Total calories: 17
Total Fat: trace
Saturated Fat: 0 g
Dietary Fiber: 0 g
Carbohydrates: 2 g
Protein: 1 g
Cholesterol: 0 mg
Sodium: 134 mg

Fat-Free Gravy

2 cups (8 servings)

1 cup chicken broth, preferably homemade (page 143)

1 cup beef broth

¼ cup all-purpose flour

½ cup very cold water

¼ teaspoon Kosher salt

⅛ teaspoon black pepper

The combination of the chicken broth and the beef broth gives this gravy a richer flavor than it would have using only chicken broth or only beef broth. It's a quick gravy that can be made in a saucepan.

Pour broths into the skillet used for Southern Fried Chicken recipe, or into a nonstick skillet and bring to a boil. In a screw-top jar, combine flour and water and shake to form a smooth paste; gradually add to boiling broth. Reduce heat to medium and cook, stirring constantly, 3 to 5 minutes, or until gravy has thickened and the remaining brown bits in the skillet are loosened. Season with salt and pepper.

APPROXIMATE NUTRITIONAL INFORMATION PER SERVING

Total calories: 46
Total Fat: 1 g
Saturated Fat: 0 g
Dietary Fiber: 0 g
Carbohydrates: 8 g
Protein: 2 g
Cholesterol: 1 mg
Sodium: 294 mg

Apple Butter

1 1/2 pints

4 large Granny Smith apples, peeled, cored, and quartered

½ cup apple juice

3 tablespoons brown sugar

1½ teaspoons cinnamon

¼ teaspoon allspice

⅛ teaspoon ground cloves

In a stock pot, combine apples and juice. Cover and cook over low heat 45–60 minutes, or until apples are soft and sauce-like. Stir in sugar, cinnamon, allspice, and cloves; cook, uncovered, 5–10 minutes, stirring often. Store in covered jar in refrigerator.

Serving Suggestion: Serve warm over whole-wheat toast, English muffins, or popovers.

APPROXIMATE NUTRITIONAL INFORMATION PER TABLESPOON

Total calories: 11
Total Fat: 0 g
Saturated Fat: 0 g
Dietary Fiber: 0 g
Carbohydrates: 3 g
Protein: 0 g
Cholesterol: 0 mg
Sodium: 0 mg

Strawberry Preserves

1/2 pint

2 tablespoons water

3 cups strawberries, sliced

1 tablespoon granulated sugar

2 teaspoons cornstarch combined with 1 tablespoon water

⅛ -¼ teaspoon almond extract

¼ teaspoon fresh lemon juice

In a saucepan over low heat, bring berries and water to a boil, stirring frequently. Add sugar and reduce heat; simmer 25–30 minutes. Gradually add cornstarch mixture; simmer 10 minutes. Stir in almond extract and lemon juice; simmer 10–15 minutes. Cool. Preserves may be frozen.

APPROXIMATE NUTRITIONAL INFORMATION PER TABLESPOON

Total calories: 13
Total Fat: trace
Saturated Fat: 0 g
Dietary Fiber: 1 g
Carbohydrates: 3 g
Protein: trace
Cholesterol: 0 mg
Sodium: trace

Cranberry Relish

2 quarts

1 pound (4 cups) fresh cranberries

2 oranges, unpeeled and cut into eighths

2 red delicious apples, unpeeled and cut into eighths

⅓ cup sugar, or to taste

Wash cranberries; discard any that are soft or blemished. Put cranberries, oranges, and apples through the medium blade of a grinder or chop in a food processor. Drain off excess juice; reserve. Add sugar; stir. Pour about half of the reserved juice into the relish (relish should be very moist, but not runny). Chill 24 hours. Keeps 2 to 3 weeks.

APPROXIMATE NUTRITIONAL INFORMATION PER ¼ CUP

Total calories: 58
Total Fat: 1 g
Saturated Fat: 0 g
Dietary Fiber: 1 g
Carbohydrates: 11 g
Protein: 0 g
Cholesterol: 0 mg
Sodium: 1 mg

Pasta

Mostaccioli with Tomatoes

Approximately 4 quarts

¼ cup extra-virgin olive oil

2 tablespoons balsamic vinegar

3 cloves garlic

2 ounces fresh basil

1 teaspoon Kosher salt

¼ teaspoon black pepper

1 pound mostaccioli or other tube-shaped pasta, cooked al dente

1½ pounds ripe tomatoes, preferably heirloom, cut into 1-inch cubes

1 cup Calamata olives, pitted and halved

In a blender or food processor, combine olive oil, vinegar and garlic. Add ½ of the basil and whirl 1 minute. Add salt and pepper. Pour over mostaccioli while pasta is still warm. Add tomatoes and olives; toss. Garnish with remaining whole basil leaves.

Serving Suggestion: Especially good with salmon.

Calamata olives are high in fat as well as sodium. If you choose to omit them, the calories change to 159; the sodium to 138 mg.

APPROXIMATE NUTRITIONAL INFORMATION PER CUP

Total calories: 167
Total Fat: 5 g
Saturated Fat: 1 g
Dietary Fiber: 2 g
Carbohydrates: 27 g
Protein: 5 g
Cholesterol: 0 mg
Sodium: 281 mg

Pasta with Fresh Tomatoes, Basil, and Mozzarella

8 servings

1 pound fresh, ripe tomatoes

4 cups fresh basil

1 tablespoon olive oil

½ teaspoon Kosher salt

¼ teaspoon black pepper

1 pound ziti or tube-shaped pasta, cooked al dente

1½ cups grated part-skim mozzarella cheese

Plunge tomatoes into boiling water for 1–2 minutes to soften skins, then into ice water; peel and coarsely chop. Coarsely chop 3 cups of the basil leaves; reserve remaining whole leaves for garnish.

In a nonstick skillet, heat olive oil and add tomatoes. Bring to a boil. Reduce heat to simmer and add chopped basil, salt, and pepper. While pasta is still warm, toss with sauce and mozzarella. Turn pasta over and over to mix ingredients and melt cheese. Garnish with remaining 1 cup basil.

Serving Suggestion: An excellent main meal pasta. Serve with Italian Pizza Bread with Rosemary and Garlic (page 66) and fresh fruit.

APPROXIMATE NUTRITIONAL INFORMATION PER SERVING

Total calories: 365
Total Fat: 10 g
Saturated Fat: 3 g
Dietary Fiber: 3 g
Carbohydrates: 51 g
Protein: 19 g
Cholesterol: 24 mg
Sodium: 311 mg

Tortellini and Tomatoes

4 1-cup servings

1 10-ounce package spinach tortellini

1 cup Pesto (page 213)

2 cups ripe cherry tomatoes

½ cup freshly grated Parmesan cheese

Cook the tortellini in boiling water according to the instructions. Drain and while still hot, toss with pesto or vinaigrette. Wash the tomatoes; pat dry and remove stems. Toss tomatoes with pasta and pesto or vinaigrette and Parmesan cheese.

Variation: Cut ¾ pound part-skim mozzarella cheese into 1-inch cubes. Toss with tortellini, tomatoes, and pesto while tortellini are still hot.

Serving Suggestion: The calories from fat are high in this dish. Keep this in mind and serve with low-fat accompaniments such as watermelon, cantaloupe or whatever fresh fruit is in season and crusty French bread. This is a sensational hors d'oeuvre. To serve, alternate tortellini and tomatoes on long skewers and arrange in a low pasta bowl or on individual bread-and-butter plates with cocktail forks.

APPROXIMATE NUTRITIONAL INFORMATION PER CUP WITH DRESSING

Total calories: 250
Total Fat: 19 g
Saturated Fat: 5 g
Dietary Fiber: 1 g
Carbohydrates: 14 g
Protein: 7 g
Cholesterol: 30 mg
Sodium: 520 mg

Pesto is made with heart-healthy olive oil, but is still high in fat. Be sure to budget for that by eating lowfat foods at other meals throughout the day A less spectacular but low-calorie alternative is to use Marinara Sauce (page 225) at about 7 calories per tablespoon.

Penne with Sun-Dried Tomatoes

8 servings

4 large ripe tomatoes, coarsely chopped, preferably heirloom

10 oil-packed sun-dried tomatoes, drained and coarsely chopped

6 large garlic cloves, chopped

¼ cup extra-virgin olive oil

½ teaspoon Kosher salt

¼ teaspoon pepper

1½ cups fresh basil leaves

1 pound penne

Crushed red pepper (optional)

Combine ripe tomatoes, sun-dried tomatoes, garlic, olive oil, salt, and pepper. Let stand at room temperature for 1 hour. Coarsely chop 1 cup of the basil leaves; reserve the remaining leaves for garnish.

Cook pasta; drain. While pasta is still hot, toss with tomato mixture. Add chopped basil and toss again. Just before serving, garnish with remaining basil leaves. Accompany with crushed red pepper, if desired.

Serving Suggestion: Great as a main course with crusty French bread or as an accompaniment to an entrée of grilled salmon or swordfish.

APPROXIMATE NUTRITIONAL INFORMATION PER SERVING

Total calories: 299
Total Fat: 10 g
Saturated Fat: 1 g
Dietary Fiber: 3 g
Carbohydrates: 46 g
Protein: 10 g
Cholesterol: 0 mg
Sodium: 172 mg

Penne Puttanesca

8 servings

1 tablespoon olive oil

1 cup chopped white onion

5 cloves garlic, minced

1 28-ounce can Italian plum tomatoes, coarsely chopped

½ teaspoon crushed red pepper

½ teaspoon Kosher salt

1 cup Calamata olives, pitted and chopped

1 2-ounce can anchovy fillets, drained and finely chopped, optional

3 tablespoons drained capers

1 pound penne or other tube-shaped pasta, cooked al dente

⅓ cup Parmesan cheese

In a nonstick skillet, heat olive oil. Add onions and garlic, and sauté 6–8 minutes. Pour into a small stockpot. Add tomatoes, crushed red pepper, and salt. Heat just to boiling; reduce heat and simmer 10 minutes. Add olives, anchovies, and capers. Serve over pasta. Sprinkle with Parmesan.

Serving Suggestion: Serve with tossed green salad, crusty French bread and seasonal fruits.

Note: Penne Puttanesca is high in sodium. Be sure to serve it with low-sodium accompaniments.

APPROXIMATE NUTRITIONAL INFORMATION PER SERVING

Total calories: 290
Total Fat: 6 g
Saturated Fat: 1.5 g
Dietary Fiber: 2 g
Carbohydrates: 51 g
Protein: 10 g
Cholesterol: 5 mg
Sodium: 560 mg

Add 20 calories and 260 mg soldium per serving with anchovies.

Spaghetti with Meatless Sauce

16 servings

1 28-ounce can plum tomatoes

1 28-ounce can tomato purée

1 12-ounce can tomato paste

1 8-ounce can tomato sauce

3 cups water

1 ½ teaspoons Kosher salt

2 tablespoons chopped fresh basil leaves or 1 ½ teaspoons dried

1 ½ tablespoons minced fresh oregano leaves or ¾ teaspoon dried

2 pounds spaghetti or corkscrew-shaped pasta

fresh basil sprigs for garnish

crushed red pepper (optional)

In a food processor, purée tomatoes until smooth; transfer to a stockpot. Add canned tomato purée, tomato paste, tomato sauce, water, salt, basil, and oregano. Stir thoroughly to combine ingredients. Heat sauce just to boiling (do not allow to boil). Reduce to a simmer.

One half-hour before serving, cook pasta according to package directions. Drain and transfer to a pasta bowl. Pour one cup of sauce over the top—just enough for color. Garnish with sprigs of fresh basil. Serve into individual bowls. Let each person add desired amount of sauce. Accompany with crushed red pepper, if desired.

Serving Suggestion: Serve in individual bowls. Let each person add desired amount of sauce.

APPROXIMATE NUTRITIONAL INFORMATION PER SERVING (1 CUP PASTA AND ¼ CUP SAUCE)

Total calories: 250
Total Fat: 3 g
Saturated Fat: 0 g
Dietary Fiber: 2 g
Carbohydrates: 52 g
Protein: 11 g
Cholesterol: 0 mg
Sodium: 360 mg

Pasta with Marinara Sauce

15 servings

1 2-pound can plum tomatoes, diced

2 tablespoons tomato paste

½ teaspoon oregano

½ teaspoon dried basil

½ teaspoons Kosher salt

½ teaspoon black pepper

1 tablespoon olive oil

¼ teaspoon cider vinegar

1 1-pound package spaghetti, rigatoni, rotini, or penne pasta, cooked al dente

In a medium saucepan, combine tomatoes, tomato paste, oregano, basil, salt, and black pepper. Simmer 20 minutes (do not allow to boil). Stir in olive oil and vinegar. Simmer 10 minutes. Serve over pasta.

Variation: Add one 8-ounce can drained mushroom stems and pieces and one 15-ounce can drained artichoke hearts.

Serving Suggestion: This is perfect for a quick-to-fix, last-minute meal.

APPROXIMATE NUTRITIONAL INFORMATION PER SERVING (½ CUP PASTA AND ⅓ CUP SAUCE)

Total calories: 134
Total Fat: 1 g
Saturated Fat: 0 g
Dietary Fiber: 1 g
Carbohydrates: 26 g
Protein: 5 g
Cholesterol: 0 mg
Sodium: 168 mg

Macaroni and Cheese

12 servings

1 pound large elbow macaroni

¼ cup all-purpose flour

2½ cups nonfat milk

1 tablespoon butter

¼ teaspoon paprika

1 teaspoon dry mustard

½ teaspoon hot sauce

2 teaspoons Worcestershire sauce

1 teaspoon salt

¼ teaspoon pepper

1 pound reduced-fat cheddar cheese, shredded

1 large ripe tomato, sliced

3 tablespoons freshly grated Parmesan cheese

Cook macaroni according to package directions. Drain and set aside.

In a screw-top jar, combine flour with ½ cup of the nonfat milk to form a smooth paste. Set aside.

In a saucepan over medium heat, melt margarine; add the remaining nonfat milk, paprika, mustard, hot sauce, Worcestershire sauce, salt, and pepper, stirring constantly. When milk is hot, gradually stir in reserved flour mixture.

Cook, stirring constantly, until slightly thickened and bubbly. Add cheddar cheese; stir until melted. Stir macaroni into cheese sauce. Transfer to a 2-quart casserole. Arrange tomato slices over top, pushing edges of each slice into the macaroni. Bake, uncovered, at 350° F. for 45 minutes. Sprinkle with Parmesan the last five minutes of cooking.

APPROXIMATE NUTRITIONAL INFORMATION PER SERVING

Total calories: 294
Total Fat: 9 g
Saturated Fat: 4 g
Dietary Fiber: 2 g
Carbohydrates: 33 g
Protein: 20 g
Cholesterol: 29 mg
Sodium: 541 mg

Pasta e Fagioli

2 servings

½-pound of small shell-shaped pasta, cooked al dente

1 recipe of Three-Bean Chili, (p. 127), warmed

Divide pasta into bowls. Ladle chili over top.

APPROXIMATE NUTRITIONAL INFORMATION PER CUP

Total calories: 249
Total Fat: 10 g
Saturated Fat: 4 g
Dietary Fiber: 5 g
Carbohydrates: 22 g
Protein: 10 g
Cholesterol: 39 mg
Sodium: 746 mg

Pasta Primavera

6 side-dish servings

SAUCE

1¼ cups fresh basil leaves

2 large garlic cloves, peeled

¼ teaspoon salt

2 tablespoons pine nuts

¼ cup extra-virgin olive oil

½ pound rotini

1 6½-ounce jar marinated artichoke hearts, drained

2 cups broccolini florets

2 cups cauliflower, florets only

¾ cups thinly sliced baby carrots

1½ cups diced plum tomatoes, preferably heirloom

¼ cup kalamata olives, optional

This recipe is a great way to get your children to eat and to actually love cruciferous vegetables, such as cauliflower and broccoli.

Combine basil, garlic, salt, and pine nuts in a food processor and process until fairly smooth, 2 to 3 minutes. With machine running, add olive oil one tablespoon at a time. Process until the oil is incorporated and mixture is smooth, 2 to 3 minutes longer.

In a large pot of boiling water, cook pasta according to package directions. Drain. While pasta is still hot, toss it with artichokes,. Add broccolini, cauliflower, and carrots. Add pesto and toss. Add tomatoes and toss again. If desired, sprinkle with olives.

APPROXIMATE NUTRITIONAL INFORMATION PER SERVING

Total calories: 284
Total Fat: 10 g
Saturated Fat: 1 g
Dietary Fiber: 6 g
Carbohydrates: 39 g
Protein: 10 g
Cholesterol: 0 mg
Sodium: 372 mg

Orzo With Stir-Fried Vegetables

8 servings

1½ tablespoons olive oil

1 bunch fresh asparagus

2 cups fresh broccolini

2 cups fresh cauliflower florets

1½ cups snow peas

1 pound orzo, cooked al dente

1 English cucumber, peeled, halved, and sliced

¼ cup Soy Wasabi Sauce (page 244)

Heat olive oil in a nonstick skillet. Add asparagus, broccolini, cauliflower, and snow peas. Stir fry 3-4 minutes until crisp-tender. Arrange orzo in a serving dish. Ring with steamed vegetables. Serve with Soy Wasabi Sauce.

APPROXIMATE NUTRITIONAL INFORMATION PER SERVING WITHOUT SAUCE

Calories: 258
Total fat: 2 g
Saturated fat: 0 g
Dietary fiber: 3 g
Carbohydrates: 49 g
Protein: 11 g
Cholesterol: 0 mg
Sodium: 157 mg

Pasta with Pesto and Tomatoes

8 servings

1 pound rotelli, cooked al dente

1 cup Pesto (page 213)

3 large fresh ripe tomatoes, diced, preferably heirloom

¼ cup freshly grated Parmesan cheese

Arrange rotelli in a large bowl. Toss with pesto. Add tomatoes and toss again. Transfer to pasta bowls. Sprinkle with Parmesan cheese.

Variation: Rub 1 whole boneless, skinless chicken breast with ½ teaspoon olive oil. Grill over medium-high for 6 to 7 minutes on each side, or until chicken is cooked. Dice. Add to Pasta with Pesto and Tomatoes; toss and sprinkle with Parmesan.

APPROXIMATE NUTRITIONAL INFORMATION PER SERVING

Total calories: 330
Total Fat: 9 g
Saturated Fat: 2 g
Dietary Fiber: 3 g
Carbohydrates: 47 g
Protein: 10 g
Cholesterol: 2 mg
Sodium: 135 mg

Fettuccine with Vegetables and Pesto

8 servings

½ bunch fresh broccoli, florets only

⅓ head cauliflower, florets only

1 1-pound package fettuccine, cooked al dente

1 cup Pesto (page 213)

1 15-ounce can artichoke hearts, quartered

8–10 fresh mushrooms, sliced

10 cherry tomatoes, halved

⅓ cup freshly grated Parmesan cheese

black pepper to taste

In a covered vegetable steamer basket over boiling water, steam broccoli and cauliflower 2–3 minutes.

In a bowl, toss fettuccine with pesto. Add artichoke hearts, mushrooms, tomatoes, broccoli, and cauliflower. Toss. Sprinkle with Parmesan and toss again. Season with black pepper.

Serving Suggestion: Good hot or cold as an accompaniment or as an entrée.

APPROXIMATE NUTRITIONAL INFORMATION PER SERVING

Total calories: 260
Total Fat: 2 g
Saturated Fat: 1 g
Dietary Fiber: 4 g
Carbohydrates: 48 g
Protein: 12 g
Cholesterol: 3 mg
Sodium: 213 mg

Pasta with Eggplant

15 servings

1 large eggplant

1 tablespoons olive oil

8–10 fresh mushrooms, sliced

4 cups warm Marinara Sauce (page 214)

1 pound heavy-type pasta (such as penne or rigatoni), cooked al dente

dash Kosher salt (optional)

black pepper to taste

1 teaspoon crushed red pepper (optional)

Slice unpeeled eggplant lengthwise into strips, French-fry style. In a nonstick skillet over medium heat, heat olive oil. Add eggplant and sauté 15 minutes. Add | mushrooms and sauté 10 minutes, or until eggplant is done. Pour sauce over pasta. Toss with eggplant and mushrooms. Season. Sprinkle with crushed red pepper, if desired.

Variation: Omit crushed red pepper. Toss with ½ cup freshly grated Parmesan cheese.

Serving Suggestion: This is a good side dish with roast lamb or chicken.

APPROXIMATE NUTRITIONAL INFORMATION PER ½ CUP

Total calories: 150
Total Fat: 3 g
Saturated Fat: 0 g
Dietary Fiber: 2 g
Carbohydrates: 28 g
Protein: 5 g
Cholesterol: 0 mg
Sodium: 94 mg

Rigatoni with Eggplant, Mushrooms, and Tomatoes

8 servings

1 medium eggplant, peeled and diced (about 4 cups)

1 tablespoon salt (to be rinsed off)

1 tablespoon olive oil

2 cups sliced fresh mushrooms (about 20)

⅓ cup diced sun-dried tomatoes

1 28-ounce can plum tomatoes, diced

½ teaspoon Kosher salt

½ teaspoon pepper

½ teaspoon dried oregano

3 tablespoons chopped fresh basil or ¾ teaspoon dried

1 pound rigatoni, cooked al dente

In a colander, toss eggplant with 1 tablespoon salt and allow to drain for 30 to 60 minutes. Rinse eggplant with water and drain well; pat dry.

In a medium nonstick skillet, heat olive oil. Add eggplant and sauté over medium-high heat 3 to 4 minutes; add mushrooms and sauté 2 to 3 minutes longer. Set aside.

In a medium saucepan, combine sun-dried tomatoes, plus tomatoes, salt, pepper, oregano, and basil; simmer 8 to 10 minutes. Add eggplant and mushrooms; simmer 5 minutes. Serve over rigatoni.

APPROXIMATE NUTRITIONAL INFORMATION PER SERVING

Total calories: 259
Total Fat: 2 g
Saturated Fat: 0 g
Dietary Fiber: 4 g
Carbohydrates: 52 g
Protein: 9 g
Cholesterol: 0 mg
Sodium: 605 mg

Noodle Casserole with Tuna

8 servings

1 pound elbow macaroni

2 10¾-ounce cans Healthy Request Campbell's Cream of Chicken Soup*

1 cup nonfat milk

1 6-ounce can water-packed tuna

1 8-ounce can sliced water chestnuts, drained

2 tablespoons freshly grated Parmesan cheese

Serve this dish with broccoli so your kids can dip the vegetables into the sauce. It will help teach them to like all vegetables, even broccoli.

Cook macaroni according to package directions. Drain and set aside.

Meanwhile, in a saucepan, heat Cream of Chicken Soup; gradually stir in nonfat milk and cook, stirring, until mixture is smooth and bubbly. Gently stir in tuna, water chestnuts, and the cooked macaroni. Transfer to a 2-quart casserole. Bake at 375°F. for 15 minutes; sprinkle with Parmesan. Bake 5 minutes longer. Serve at once.

*Simply using reduced-fat cream of chicken soup yields fat and calorie savings that make this old favorite fit into today's eating plan.

APPROXIMATE NUTRITIONAL INFORMATION PER SERVING

Total calories: 288
Total Fat: 3 g
Saturated Fat: 0 g
Dietary Fiber: 0 g
Carbohydrates: 46 g
Protein: 16 g
Cholesterol: 15 mg
Sodium: 253 mg

Scallop-and-Pesto Fettucini

8 servings

3 tablespoons dry white wine

1 pound fresh scallops

1 pound fettuccine, cooked al dente

1 cup Pesto (page 213)

2 ripe tomatoes, diced

½ cup freshly grated Parmesan cheese

In a nonstick skillet, heat wine. Add scallops. Cover and poach 5–6 minutes, or until scallops are tender. Drain. Turn fettuccine into a shallow pasta bowl. Toss with pesto. Add scallops, tomatoes and cheese. Toss.

Serving Suggestion: Serve with crudités, hearts of romaine with fresh lemon juice, crusty French bread, and fresh fruit.

APPROXIMATE NUTRITIONAL INFORMATION PER SERVING

Total calories: 299
Total Fat: 3 g
Saturated Fat: 1 g
Dietary Fiber: 2 g
Carbohydrates: 45 g
Protein: 20 g
Cholesterol: 24 mg
Sodium: 360 mg

Linguine with Clam Sauce

8 servings

- **1 pound linguine**
- **1 28-ounce can plum tomatoes, with liquid, diced**
- **1½ tablespoons extra-virgin olive oil**
- **4 large garlic cloves, finely minced**
- **1 cup dry white wine**
- **¾ teaspoon Kosher salt**
- **½ teaspoon pepper**
- **2 6½ -ounce cans chopped clams with liquid**
- **2 pounds shell clams (steamers)**
- **¼ cup chopped fresh parsley**
- **crushed red pepper (optional)**

Tired of the same old spaghetti sauce? Here's a quick, tasty variation on a red sauce. This recipe is delicious even without fresh clams.

Cook linguine according to package directions. Drain and set aside.

Meanwhile, in a 1½-quart saucepan, combine tomatoes, olive oil, garlic, wine, salt, pepper, and chopped clams. Simmer, uncovered, for 15 to 20 minutes.

Wash steamers thoroughly, discarding any clams with broken or open shells. Place in steamer with ½ cup hot water; cover tightly and steam 5 to 10 minutes, or until clams open. Discard any shells that do not open. Divide linguine into individual pasta bowls; ladle sauce over pasta. Top with steamed clams in their shells. Sprinkle with fresh parsley. Accompany with crushed red pepper, if desired.

APPROXIMATE NUTRITIONAL INFORMATION PER SERVING

Total calories: 304
Total Fat: 4 g
Saturated Fat: 0 g
Dietary Fiber: 3 g
Carbohydrates: 45 g
Protein: 14 g
Cholesterol: 12 mg
Sodium: 513 mg

Linguine with Clams and Artichoke Hearts

8 servings

1 2-pound can plum tomatoes, diced

1 tablespoon tomato paste

½ teaspoon oregano

½ teaspoon dried basil or ¼ cup fresh

½ teaspoon black pepper

1 tablespoon extra-virgin olive oil

¼ teaspoon cider vinegar

¾ pound fresh mushrooms, thinly sliced

2 15-ounce cans artichoke hearts, drained

3 pounds clams, soaked, cleaned, and steamed (see page 250)*

1 1-pound package linguine, cooked al dente

¼ cup finely chopped fresh parsley

In a stock pot, combine tomatoes, tomato paste, oregano, basil, black pepper, olive oil, and vinegar. Heat just to boiling (do not boil). Reduce heat and simmer, uncovered, 30 minutes. Add mushrooms and simmer 10 minutes. Add artichoke hearts and clams. Heat. Divide pasta into bowls. Ladle sauce over pasta. Sprinkle with parsley.

*For a quick-to-fix meal, substitute three 6½-ounce cans chopped clams for the fresh clams. Remember that using canned clams instead of fresh will increase the sodium substantially.

APPROXIMATE NUTRITIONAL INFORMATION PER SERVING

Total calories: 394
Total Fat: 5 g
Saturated Fat: 1 g
Dietary Fiber: 3 g
Carbohydrates: 55 g
Protein: 32 g
Cholesterol: 58 mg
Sodium: 474 mg

Seafood Linguine with Pesto

8 servings

1 pound linguine

¼ cup dry white wine, vermouth or broth

½ pound orange roughy, halibut, red snapper, or other whitefish, cut into 2-inch pieces

½ pound scallops, poached (see page 244)

1 cup Pesto (page 213)

½ pound clams in shells, steamed (see page 250)

½ pound mussels in shells, steamed (see page 250)

⅓ cup freshly grated Parmesan cheese

Cook linguine; set aside. In a nonstick skillet, heat wine, vermouth, or broth. Add whitefish and scallops. Cover and poach 4–6 minutes, or until done.

Toss linguine with pesto. Arrange in a shallow paella-type dish. Garnish with seafood and sprinkle with Parmesan cheese.

APPROXIMATE NUTRITIONAL INFORMATION PER SERVING

Total calories: 332
Total Fat: 4 g
Saturated Fat: 1 g
Dietary Fiber: 1 g
Carbohydrates: 45 g
Protein: 26 g
Cholesterol: 39 mg
Sodium: 224 mg

Penne with Prawns, Olives, and Tomatoes

10 servings

2 teaspoons Garlic Olive Oil (page 210), or 2 teaspoons olive oil plus 2 minced garlic cloves

1 pound large prawns, shelled and deveined

¼ cup extra-virgin olive oil

2 tablespoons balsamic vinegar

3 large garlic cloves

1 teaspoon Kosher salt

½ teaspoon pepper

3 cups fresh basil leaves

1 pound penne or other tube-shaped pasta, cooked al dente

1½ pounds ripe tomatoes, cut into 1-inch cubes

1 cup kalamata olives, pitted and halved

In a nonstick skillet over medium-high heat, heat Garlic Olive Oil; add prawns and cook 5 to 6 minutes, or until prawns are cooked. Remove from heat.

In a blender or food processor, combine olive oil, vinegar, garlic, salt, pepper, and 2 cups of the basil; whirl 1 minute. Pour over penne while pasta is still warm. Add tomatoes and olives, toss. Add prawns; toss again. Garnish with remaining basil leaves.

Serving Suggestion: Serve with French bread and fresh fruit.

APPROXIMATE NUTRITIONAL INFORMATION PER SERVING

Total calories: 311
Total Fat: 12 g
Saturated Fat: 1 g
Dietary Fiber: 1 g
Carbohydrates: 39 g
Protein: 13 g
Cholesterol: 52 mg
Sodium: 234 mg

Linguine with Calamari

8 servings

1½ pounds squid, cleaned

1 cup white wine

2 garlic cloves

1 pound linguine, cooked al dente

¼ cup extra-virgin olive oil

Juice of 1 lemon

½ teaspoon Kosher salt

¼ teaspoon pepper

3 ripe tomatoes, preferably heirloom, coarsely chopped

2 tablespoons chopped fresh Italian parsley

APPROXIMATE NUTRITIONAL INFORMATION PER SERVING

Total calories: 371
Total Fat: 10 g
Saturated Fat: 1 g
Dietary Fiber: 2 g
Carbohydrates: 43 g
Protein: 22 g
Cholesterol: 198 mg
Sodium: 151 mg

WITH RED CALAMARI SAUCE

Total calories: 377
Total Fat: 9 g
Saturated Fat: 1 g
Dietary Fiber: 3 g
Carbohydrates: 47 g
Protein: 23 g
Cholesterol: 198 mg
Sodium: 388 mg

Heat wine and garlic in a wok or heavy skillet. Sauté squid for 3 to 5 minutes, or just until color changes and squid become tender; do not overcook or squid will become rubbery. Drain off liquid.

Arrange squid over pasta; sprinkle with olive oil, lemon juice, salt, pepper, tomatoes, and parsley. Toss until squid and linguine are well coated.

Note: If you are not familiar with the proper method to clean squid, ask the personnel at your fish market to show you.

Variation: To make a red calamari sauce, decrease the olive oil to 3 tablespoons and add 1 28-ounce can plum tomatoes, diced, and an additional ¼ teaspoon salt.

Bow Tie Pasta with Chicken

8 servings

1 pound farfalle (bow tie pasta)

1½ pounds skinned and boned chicken breasts, cut into 1-inch cubes

1½ tablespoons extra-virgin olive oil

2 large garlic cloves, minced

¼ cup finely chopped onion

1 28-ounce can crushed, peeled tomatoes in heavy purée

½ cup water

¼ cup chopped fresh Italian flatleaf parsley plus additional whole leaves of Italian parsley for garnish

¾ teaspoon Kosher salt

¼ teaspoon pepper

This dish is a quick variation on Penne with Meat Sauce (page 237).

Cook farfalle according to package directions. Drain and set aside.

In a nonstick skillet over medium-high heat, brown chicken breasts. Remove from pan; set aside. In the same skillet, heat the olive oil. Add garlic and onion, and sauté 4 to 5 minutes. Transfer to a large saucepan. Add tomatoes, water, and chopped Italian parsley; cook over medium heat 5 to 10 minutes. Add the chicken. Partially cover and allow the sauce to simmer gently for 20 minutes, stirring occasionally. Season with salt and pepper. Serve over pasta. Garnish with remaining whole Italian parsley leaves.

APPROXIMATE NUTRITIONAL INFORMATION PER SERVING

Total calories: 365
Total Fat: 6 g
Saturated Fat: 1 g
Dietary Fiber: 4 g
Carbohydrates: 48 g
Protein: 29 g
Cholesterol: 55 mg
Sodium: 365 mg

Soba Noodles with Chicken and Vegetables

8 servings

1 tablespoon sesame oil

1 whole chicken breast, skinned, boned, and diced

1 tablespoon minced fresh ginger

5 garlic cloves, minced

1 cup broccoli florets

1 cup snow peas

1 bunch green onions, chopped

⅓ cup reduced-sodium soy sauce

⅓ cup sake

1 tablespoon olive oil

2 tablespoons rice wine vinegar

¾ drops hot chili oil

1 6-ounce package soba noodles, cooked

Heat sesame oil in a nonstick skillet or wok. Add chicken and stir-fry 2 to 3 minutes. Add ginger, garlic, broccoli, snow peas, and green onion, and stir-fry 2 to 3 minutes longer. Meanwhile, combine soy sauce, sake, olive oil, rice vinegar, and hot chili oil. Pour over chicken and vegetables; cook 30 seconds longer. Remove wok from heat. Add noodles. Toss.

APPROXIMATE NUTRITIONAL INFORMATION PER SERVING

Total calories: 336
Total Fat: 5 g
Saturated Fat: 1 g
Dietary Fiber: 4 g
Carbohydrates: 52 g
Protein: 17 g
Cholesterol: 18 mg
Sodium: 572 mg

Macaroni with Chicken and Beans

Approximately 12 cups

1 28-ounce can plum tomatoes, diced

½ teaspoon Kosher salt

1½ teaspoons dry mustard

1½ teaspoons chili powder

2 small garlic cloves, minced

1 pound chicken breast, skinned, boned, cooked, and diced

2 15-ounce cans red kidney beans, drained and rinsed

2 cups cooked elbow macaroni

APPROXIMATE NUTRITIONAL INFORMATION PER CUP
Total calories: 171
Total Fat: 2 g
Saturated Fat: 0 g
Dietary Fiber: 5 g
Carbohydrates: 18 g
Protein: 20 g
Cholesterol: 38 mg
Sodium: 221 mg

USING GROUND ROUND
Total calories: 221
Total Fat: 8 g
Saturated Fat: 4 g
Dietary Fiber: 5 g
Carbohydrates: 18 g
Protein: 19 g
Cholesterol: 49 mg
Sodium: 217 mg

Combine tomatoes, salt, dry mustard, chili powder, and garlic; simmer uncovered for 20 minutes. Add chicken cook 20 minutes longer. Add kidney beans; heat just to boiling. Just before serving, stir in macaroni. Heat to serving temperature.

Variation: Ground round can be used in place of chicken.

Pasta Bolognese

12 servings

1 pound extra-lean ground round

3 tablespoons chopped onion

2 tablespoons chopped carrot

2 tablespoons chopped celery

1 cup dry white wine

½ cup nonfat milk

⅛ teaspoon nutmeg

1 28-ounce can plum tomatoes, diced

1 1-pound package spaghetti, rotini, rotelle, or penne, cooked al dente

In a nonstick skillet, sauté ground round, onion, carrot, and celery. When meat is nearly cooked, add wine. Cook over medium heat, stirring frequently, until the wine has evaporated. Reduce heat slightly; add milk and nutmeg. Cook, stirring frequently, until the milk has evaporated. Add tomatoes. Reduce heat and simmer 2 hours, stirring occasionally. Serve pasta into bowls. Ladle sauce over pasta.

Serving Suggestion: Serve with green salad tossed with Italian Vinaigrette (page 224), Grilled Garlic Bread (page 67) and fresh seasonal fruit.

APPROXIMATE NUTRITIONAL INFORMATION PER ¾ CUP
Total calories: 261
Total Fat: 7 g
Saturated Fat: 3 g
Dietary Fiber: 2 g
Carbohydrates: 32 g
Protein: 13 g
Cholesterol: 26 mg
Sodium: 142 mg

Penne with Meat Sauce

8 servings

1 pound penne

1 28-ounce can plum tomatoes, with liquid, diced

1 15-ounce can tomato sauce

¼ cup dry white wine

1½ teaspoons extra-virgin olive oil

2 garlic cloves, minced

½ pound ground veal (lean as you can find)

½ cup fresh basil leaves, chopped

salt and pepper to taste

Cook penne according to package directions. Drain and set aside.

Meanwhile, in a 4-quart saucepan, heat tomatoes, tomato sauce, and wine; allow to simmer.

In a nonstick skillet, heat olive oil; add garlic and ground veal, and sauté until veal is cooked. Add veal to tomato sauce. Season with fresh basil, salt, and pepper.

Divide penne into individual bowls; top with sauce.

APPROXIMATE NUTRITIONAL INFORMATION PER SERVING

Total calories: 288
Total Fat: 4 g
Saturated Fat: 1 g
Dietary Fiber: 4 g
Carbohydrates: 49 g
Protein: 4 g
Cholesterol: 22 mg
Sodium: 460 mg

Little Ear Pasta with Sausage

8 servings

1 pound orecchiette (little ear) pasta or medium shell-shaped pasta

¾ pound extra-lean sweet Italian sausage (lean as you can find)

4 medium garlic cloves, minced

1 28-ounce can plum tomatoes, with liquid, diced

2 tablespoons tomato paste

1½ teaspoons minced fresh oregano or ½ teaspoon dried

2 tablespoons chopped fresh basil leaves or ½ teaspoon dried

½ teaspoon Kosher salt

¼ teaspoon pepper

⅛ – ¼ teaspoon crushed red pepper (optional)

fresh basil leaves for garnish

This recipe provides a good way to enjoy the taste of sausage without all the calories and fat you would get from an entrée-size portion.

Cook pasta according to package directions. Drain and set aside.

Slit open, remove, and discard the casing on the Italian sausage. In a preheated nonstick skillet over medium heat, brown the sausage 6 to 8 minutes, or until cooked, breaking it apart as it browns. Drain on paper towels; pat dry with additional toweling to remove all excess fat. Set aside.

Meanwhile, in a medium saucepan, combine garlic, tomatoes, tomato paste, oregano, basil, salt, pepper, and crushed red pepper. Simmer 10 to 15 minutes; stir sausage into sauce. Serve over pasta. Garnish with fresh basil leaves.

APPROXIMATE NUTRITIONAL INFORMATION PER SERVING

Total calories: 346
Total Fat: 9 g
Saturated Fat: 1 g
Dietary Fiber: 3 g
Carbohydrates: 45 g
Protein: 17 g
Cholesterol: 33 mg
Sodium: 604 mg

Spaghetti with Meatballs

16 servings

1 28-ounce can plum tomatoes

1 28-ounce can tomato purée

1 12-ounce can tomato paste

1 8-ounce can tomato sauce

3 cups water

1½ teaspoons Kosher salt

2 tablespoons chopped fresh basil leaves or 1½ teaspoons dried

1½ tablespoons minced fresh oregano leaves or ¾ teaspoon dried

½ pound boneless pork chops

MEATBALLS

1 pound ground beef (lean as you can find)

1 cup dried breadcrumbs

5 cloves garlic, minced

1 egg

¼ cup nonfat milk

½ cup chopped fresh parsley

salt and pepper to taste

2 pounds spaghetti or corkscrew-shaped pasta

fresh basil sprigs for garnish

crushed red pepper (optional)

In a food processor, purée tomatoes until smooth; transfer to a stockpot. Add canned tomato purée, tomato paste, tomato sauce, water, salt, basil, and oregano. Stir thoroughly to combine ingredients. Heat sauce just to boiling (do not allow to boil). Reduce to a simmer.

Trim all visible fat from pork chops. In a nonstick skillet, brown chops 3 to 4 minutes on each side. Remove from skillet and drain on paper towels; pat dry with additional paper toweling to remove all excess fat. Add chops to sauce.

Meanwhile, put ground beef in a medium bowl. Add bread crumbs, garlic, egg, nonfat milk, parsley, salt and pepper. Knead until mixture is smooth and ingredients are combined, adding nonfat milk if needed for moisture. Form 20 firm golf ball-size meatballs and add to the sauce. Continue to simmer sauce for 2 to 2½ hours.

One half-hour before serving, cook pasta according to package directions. Drain and transfer to a pasta bowl. Pour one cup of sauce over the top just enough for color. Garnish with sprigs of fresh basil. Serve with meatballs and additional sauce. Accompany with crushed red pepper, if desired.

Variation: Italian Sausage Sauce: In a nonstick skillet over medium-high heat, sauté 6 extra-lean (lean as you can find) Italian sausages 8 to 10 minutes or microwave the sausages on full power in a covered dish 8 to 10 minutes, turning once. Drain and pat with paper towels to remove excess fat. Cut each sausage crosswise into thirds. Add to spaghetti sauce along with the meatballs. Simmer as directed above. Add 97 calories and 7 grams of fat per ⅓ sausage.

APPROXIMATE NUTRITIONAL INFORMATION PER SERVING (1 CUP PASTA, ¾ CUP SAUCE AND 1 MEATBALL)

Total calories: 365
Total Fat: 8 g
Saturated Fat: 2 g
Dietary Fiber: 5 g
Carbohydrates: 55 g
Protein: 20 g
Cholesterol: 40 mg
Sodium: 435 mg

Add 62 calories and 3 grams of fat for each additional meatball.

Pasta Stuffed with Basil and Tomato

8 servings

SAUCE

1 28-ounce can plum tomatoes

1 carrot, chopped

1 small white onion, chopped

4 large cloves garlic

½ teaspoon salt

¼ teaspoon black pepper

1 cup fresh basil leaves

FILLING

1 15-ounce container part-skim ricotta cheese

2 cups freshly grated Parmesan cheese

1 cup fresh basil leaves

2 eggs

½ teaspoon salt

¼ teaspoon black pepper

1 12-ounce package jumbo pasta shells, cooked very al dente

¼ cup grated part-skim mozzarella cheese

To Make the Sauce: Combine tomatoes, carrot, onion and garlic in a blender or food processor. Pour into saucepan. Add salt and pepper; simmer sauce 30 minutes. Add basil leaves and simmer 10 minutes longer.

To Make Filling: In a blender or food processor, combine ricotta, Parmesan, basil, eggs, salt, and pepper. Stuff mixture into cooked jumbo pasta shells.

Arrange shells in a single layer in a 9 x 13 x 2-inch ovenproof dish. Cover with sauce. (Be sure each shell is completely covered with sauce, or pasta will dry out.) Sprinkle with mozzarella. Bake, uncovered, at 425°F. 20–25 minutes or until sauce is bubbly.

Serving Suggestion: Serve with Pepper, Onion and Tomato Salad (page 163) with Italian Vinaigrette (page 204) and chilled melon.

APPROXIMATE NUTRITIONAL INFORMATION PER SHELL

Total calories: 109
Total Fat: 4 g
Saturated Fat: 1 g
Dietary Fiber: 1 g
Carbohydrates: 11 g
Protein: 7 g
Cholesterol: 25 mg
Sodium: 270 mg

Meatless Lasagna

12 servings

Prepare recipe for Lasagne (page 241) omitting the sausage. It's equally delicious.

APPROXIMATE NUTRITIONAL INFORMATION PER SERVING

Total calories: 321
Total Fat: 9 g
Saturated Fat: 1 g
Dietary Fiber: 3 g
Carbohydrates: 40 g
Protein: 23 g
Cholesterol: 20 mg
Sodium: 906 mg

Classic Lasagna

12 servings

- 1 12-ounce package lasagna noodles
- 1 pound extra-lean Italian sausage (lean as you can find)
- 2 garlic cloves, minced
- 1 small onion, chopped
- 3 16-ounce cans plum tomatoes, with liquid
- 2 tablespoons extra-virgin olive oil
- 3 8-ounce cans tomato sauce
- ½ teaspoon dried oregano
- 1 teaspoon dried basil
- 1 teaspoon Kosher salt
- ¼ teaspoon pepper
- 2 bunches fresh spinach leaves
- 2 cups nonfat ricotta cheese
- 1 pound part-skim mozzarella cheese, grated

Save your fat calories for another day by making your own lasagna. Compare this homemade version with a store-bought type and you'll see that not only does it taste better but you save 5 to 10 grams of fat per serving.

Cook the lasagna noodles according to package directions. Drain and set aside.

Meanwhile, slit open, remove, and discard the casing on the Italian sausage. In a preheated nonstick skillet over medium heat, brown sausage with garlic and onion until sausage is done and onion is tender. Drain on paper towels; pat dry with additional paper toweling to remove all excess fat. Set aside.

In a food processor, purée tomatoes; add olive oil, tomato sauce, oregano, basil, salt, and pepper. Process 2 to 3 minutes, or until smooth. Set aside. Wash spinach; shake dry and remove any tough stems. Steam in a covered skillet 2 to 3 minutes, or until wilted. Squeeze dry; chop. Combine spinach, sausage, and ricotta.

Combine reduced-fat mozzarella with fat-free mozzarella.

Cover bottom of a 13 x 9 x 2-inch pan with some tomato sauce. Add a layer of lasagna noodles. Spread with meat mixture. Add a layer of mozzarella. Cover with a little more sauce. Repeat layers two or three more times. Pour remaining sauce over final layer. Top with additional cheese. Bake, covered, at 350°F. for 60 minutes. (For a smaller group, use two 8-inch square pans and freeze one.)

APPROXIMATE NUTRITIONAL INFORMATION PER SERVING

Total calories: 385
Total Fat: 15 g
Saturated Fat: 6 g
Dietary Fiber: 6 g
Carbohydrates: 39 g
Protein: 32 g
Cholesterol: 55 mg
Sodium: 722 mg

Seafood

Pan-Seared Scallops

4 servings

1 tablespoon olive oil

1 pound scallops

SOY WASABI SAUCE

(makes 1 cup)

¾ cup reduced-sodium soy sauce

1 tablespoon prepared wasabi (in tube)

1 tablespoon finely chopped shallots

2 cloves minced garlic

Heat olive oil in nonstick skillet; add scallops. Cook 6-10 minutes, turning frequently, or just until scallops are tender.

SOY WASABI SAUCE

Blend soy sauce, wasabi, shallots, and garlic in a small bowl. Spoon over scallops. Makes 1 cup.

APPROXIMATE NUTRITIONAL INFORMATION PER SERVING FOR SCALLOPS

Calories: 130
Total fat: 4 g
Saturated fat: 0 g
Dietary fiber: 0 g
Carbohydrates: 3 g
Protein: 1 g
Cholesterol: 37 mg
Sodium: 289 mg

Poached Scallops

4 servings

3 tablespoons dry white wine, vermouth, or fresh lemon juice

1 pound scallops

In a nonstick skillet, heat wine, vermouth or lemon juice. Add scallops. Cover and poach 4–6 minutes, or just until scallops are tender. (Do not overcook.)

APPROXIMATE NUTRITIONAL INFORMATION PER SERVING

Total calories: 107
Total fat: 1 g
Saturated fat: 0 g
Dietary fiber: 0 g
Carbohydrates: 3 g
Protein: 19 g
Cholesterol: 37 mg
Sodium: 183 mg

Scallops with Tomatoes and Artichokes

4 servings

1 tablespoon olive oil

1 pound scallops

1 sweet onion

1 green pepper

1 red pepper

12 cherry tomatoes

12 fresh mushrooms

1 15-ounce can artichoke hearts, drained

Toss scallops and vegetables with oil. On skewers, alternate scallops with vegetables.

Prepare grill for direct grilling over medium-high heat. Cover grill with foil. Grill scallops 6-10 minutes, turning frequently, or until tender.

Serving Suggestions: Accompany with Saffron Rice (page 349).

Add 20 calories and 530 mg of sodium per tablespoon of Wasabi Sauce.

APPROXIMATE NUTRITIONAL INFORMATION PER SERVING

Total calories: 216
Total fat: 3 g
Saturated fat: trace
Dietary fiber: 4 g
Carbohydrates: 24 g
Protein: 25 g
Cholesterol: 38 mg
Sodium: 574 mg

Skewered Scallops with Tomatoes

4 servings

1 pound fresh scallops

2 tablespoons olive oil

juice of 2 limes (¼ cup)

3 cloves garlic, minced (1 tablespoon)

10 ripe cherry tomatoes

1 bunch fresh spinach

1 fresh lemon, cut into wedges

1 fresh lime, cut into wedges

Marinate scallops in lime juice, olive oil, and garlic for 3 hours. Toss tomatoes with a dab of olive oil. On skewers, alternate scallops, and tomatoes.

Prepare grill for direct grilling over medium-high heat. Cover grill with foil. Grill scallops 6-10 minutes, turning frequently, or until tender.

While seafood is grilling, wash and trim spinach; shake off excess moisture. Cook, covered, in a nonstick skillet 1–2 minutes, or just until leaves begin to wilt (no additional moisture is necessary because of the moisture in the spinach and on the leaves).

Arrange spinach on a heated serving plate. Layer brochettes over spinach. Garnish with lemon and lime wedges.

Serving Suggestion: Accompany with pasta salad.

APPROXIMATE NUTRITIONAL INFORMATION PER SERVING

Total calories: 165
Total Fat: 2 g
Saturated Fat: trace
Dietary Fiber: 5 g
Carbohydrates: 16 g
Protein: 23 g
Cholesterol: 37 mg
Sodium: 256 mg

Scallops and Prawns with Risotto

6 servings

1 recipe Risotto Milanese (page 349)

½ pound scallops, thawed if frozen, cut into halves if large

1 tablespoon olive oil

⅔ pound prawns, cooked, shelled, and deveined

Prepare Risotto Milanese according to instructions. While risotto is cooking, in a nonstick skillet, sauté scallops in olive oil 4 minutes then add shrimp and cook 2 more until scallops are tender and shrimp are heated. Mound risotto in center of serving platter; surround with scallops and prawns.

Serving Suggestion: Serve with fresh asparagus and seasonal fruit.

APPROXIMATE NUTRITIONAL INFORMATION PER SERVING

Total calories: 467
Total Fat: 7 g
Saturated Fat: trace
Dietary Fiber: 2 g
Carbohydrates: 72 g
Protein: 30 g
Cholesterol: 114 mg
Sodium: 497 mg

Grilled Scallops Dijon

Approximately 4 servings

1 tablespoon olive oil

2 tablespoons prepared Dijon mustard

2 tablespoons honey

¾ teaspoon curry powder

½ teaspoon lemon juice

1 pound sea scallops

2 fresh lemons, cut into wedges

1 bunch fresh parsley for garnish

APPROXIMATE NUTRITIONAL INFORMATION PER SERVING

Total calories: 140
Total Fat: 2 g
Saturated Fat: 0 g
Dietary Fiber: 0 g
Carbohydrates: 18 g
Protein: 17 g
Cholesterol: 30 mg
Sodium: 250 mg

Combine olive oil, mustard, honey, curry, and lemon juice; pour over scallops. Marinate 10 minutes. Remove scallops from marinade and shake off excess.

Prepare grill for direct grilling over medium-high heat. Cover grill with foil. Grill 6-10 minutes, turning and basting frequently, until tender. Serve with fresh lemon wedges. Garnish with parsley.

Variation: Skewer scallops, mushroom caps, cherry tomatoes, and red, yellow, and green peppers; brush with sauce. Grill.

Sautéed Shrimp

4 servings

1 tablespoon extra-virgin olive oil

3 large cloves finely minced garlic

1 pound large shrimp, peeled and deveined, tails left on

2 tablespoons finely chopped Italian flat-leaf parsley

Lightly sautéing the shrimp in a small amount of oil gives them flavor, not heaviness.

In a nonstick skillet, heat olive oil. Add garlic and cook over medium-high heat for 1minute. Add shrimp and cook 3 to 4 minutes. Turn; sprinkle with parsley and cook 3 minutes more, or until opaque. Serve with rice.

APPROXIMATE NUTRITIONAL INFORMATION PER SERVING

Total calories: 153
Total Fat: 5 g
Saturated Fat: 1 g
Dietary Fiber: 0 g
Carbohydrates: 2 g
Protein: 23 g
Cholesterol: 172 mg
Sodium: 169 mg

Stir-fried Scallops with Shrimp

4 servings

½ pound medium shrimp

1 tablespoon extra-virgin olive oil

2 garlic cloves, minced

½ pound sea scallops

1 bunch fresh Italian flat-leaf parsley

2 fresh lemons, cut into wedges

If you peel and devein the shrimp early in the day or buy precooked shrimp that are already peeled and deveined, this dish can be prepared and on the table in under 10 minutes.

Peel and devein shrimp, leaving tails on. In a nonstick skillet, heat olive oil over medium-high heat. Add garlic and scallops, and sauté 2 to 3 minutes on each side; add shrimp and cook 2 to 3 minutes longer, or until scallops and shrimp are cooked. Serve on a parsley-lined platter. Garnish with lemon wedges.

APPROXIMATE NUTRITIONAL INFORMATION PER SERVING

Total calories: 149
Total Fat: 5 g
Saturated Fat: 0
Dietary Fiber: 0 g
Carbohydrates: 4 g
Protein: 22 g
Cholesterol: 106 mg
Sodium: 182 mg

Grilled Sweet and Sour Shrimp Kabobs

4 servings

1 large red pepper

1 large yellow pepper

1 large green pepper

1 medium white onion

1 medium red onion

1 pound large shrimp

¼ cup extra-virgin olive oil

1½ teaspoons balsamic vinegar

2 tablespoons fresh lemon juice

4 garlic cloves, chopped

2 tablespoons chopped fresh basil leaves

12 cherry tomatoes

1 cup fresh or canned pineapple chunks, drained

The unique presentation of a grilled kabob varies the look and adds interest to your family mealtime.

Prepare grill for direct grilling at medium-high heat.

Wash peppers and remove seeds; cut into 2-inch chunks. Peel onions; cut into 2-inch cubes. Shell and devein shrimp; pat dry.

In a shallow bowl, combine olive oil, vinegar, lemon juice, garlic, and basil. Add peppers, onions, and shrimp; marinate 20 to 30 minutes, turning each two or three times to coat with sauce. Thread shrimp, vegetables, tomatoes and pineapple onto metal skewers. Grill 8 to 10 minutes, turning frequently, until shrimp turn pink and are cooked.

APPROXIMATE NUTRITIONAL INFORMATION PER SERVING

Total calories: 231
Total Fat: 8 g
Saturated Fat: 1 g
Dietary Fiber: 3 g
Carbohydrates: 16 g
Protein: 25 g
Cholesterol: 172 mg
Sodium: 180 mg

Grilled Lobster Tails

4 servings

4 6-ounce lobster tails

1 tablespoon extra-virgin olive oil

1 tablespoon dry white wine

2 fresh lemons, cut into wedges

1 bunch fresh parsley for garnish

Split lobster tail lengthwise halfway through the body; spread tail open. Remove whole meat from tails. Bend shells backward until cracked in several places. Replace meat in shells. Insert skewers lengthwise between shell and meat to prevent curling. Baste with olive oil.

Prepare grill for direct grilling at medium-high heat. Grill for 5 to 10 minutes on shell side; turn and cook 5 minutes longer on flesh side. Baste with wine the last 2 minutes. Serve with lemon wedges. Garnish with parsley.

Variation: To broil, place on broiler rack 3 inches from heat; broil 6 to 8 minutes on shell side. Turn; broil 5 to 10 minutes on flesh side. Baste with wine the last 2 minutes.

To bake, bake uncovered at 475°F. for 16 minutes, baste.

Note: If using frozen lobster tails, thaw before cooking.

APPROXIMATE NUTRITIONAL INFORMATION PER SERVING

Total calories: 117
Total fat: 4 g
Saturated fat: 0 g
Dietary fiber: 0 g
Carbohydrates: 7 g
Protein: 15 g
Cholesterol: 73 mg
Sodium: 439 mg

Cracked Dungeness Crab

4 servings

1 ripe tomato, finely chopped

3 tablespoons olive oil

½ cup fresh lemon juice

¼ teaspoon Kosher salt or to taste

½ teaspoon black pepper

1 bunch fresh parsley

2 pounds Dungeness crab, cooked, cracked and cleaned

1 lemon, cut into wedges

½ cup cocktail sauce (optional)

In a sauce dish, combine tomato, olive oil, lemon juice, salt and pepper. Line a platter with parsley and arrange crab on it. Garnish with lemon wedges. Pass sauce, if desired.

Serving Suggestion: Serve with Seafood Gazpacho (page 137), Caesar Salad (page 157), Angel Food Cake with Fresh Strawberries (page 398) with Chocolate, Orange or Vanilla Glaze (page 399). For more elaborate fare, in addition to the above, include Mussels and Clams with Tomato and Basil (page 253), and Cheese-and-Herb Flatbread (page 59).

Add 26 calories and 99 mg of sodium per tablespoon of cocktail sauce.

APPROXIMATE NUTRITIONAL INFORMATION

PER 1/4 POUND-SERVING WITHOUT SAUCE

Total calories: 115
Total fat: 2 g
Saturated fat: 0 g
Dietary fiber: trace
Carbohydrates: 3 g
Protein: 22 g
Cholesterol: 60 mg
Sodium: 296 mg

Steamed Clams and Mussels

4 servings

2 pounds clams

2 pounds mussels

Thoroughly wash clams and mussels.* Cover with salt water (⅓ cup salt to 1 gallon of cold water). Let stand 30 minutes. Rinse. Repeat cleaning process 2 times.

Place clams and mussels on rack in stock pot with 2 cups hot water. Cover tightly and steam 5–10 minutes, or just until shells open.

*For mussels, use a stiff wire brush to remove the tough outer beard that clings to the shells.

APPROXIMATE NUTRITIONAL INFORMATION PER POUND OF CLAMS AND MUSSELS IN SHELLS

Total calories: 220
Total fat: 5 g
Saturated fat: 1 g
Dietary fiber: 0 g
Carbohydrates: 9 g
Protein: 31 g
Cholesterol: 75 mg
Sodium: 668 mg

Garlic Steamed Clams

4 servings

4 pounds clams

½ cup dry white wine

10 cloves garlic, peeled

4 fresh lemons, cut into wedges

Clean clams (previous page). In a stock pot, combine clams, wine and garlic. Cover and steam 5–10 minutes, or just until shells open.

Accompany with fresh lemons.

Serving Suggestion: Serve with Steamed Red Potatoes (page 374).

APPROXIMATE NUTRITIONAL INFORMATION PER SERVING

Total calories: 282
Total fat: 2 g
Saturated fat: 1 g
Dietary fiber: 0 g
Carbohydrates: 9 g
Protein: 48 g
Cholesterol: 129 mg
Sodium: 176 mg

Steamed Clams with Lemon Vinaigrette

4 servings

Prepare Garlic Steamed Clams (page 251). Just before serving, drizzle clams with 3 tablespoons Olive Oil-and-Lemon Vinaigrette (page 205).

APPROXIMATE NUTRITIONAL INFORMATION PER SERVING

Total calories: 344
Total fat: 9 g
Saturated fat: 1 g
Dietary fiber: 0 g
Carbohydrates:10 g
Protein: 48 g
Cholesterol: 129 mg
Sodium: 321 mg

Steamer Clams with Fresh Lemon

Approximately 4 servings

5 dozen steamer clams

3 gallons cold water for soaking solution

1 cup cornmeal for soaking solution

1 bunch fresh parsley for garnish

5 fresh lemons, cut into wedges

Scrub steamers. Place in a large bowl and cover with cold water. Sprinkle with cornmeal and let stand 30 minutes. Drain and rinse; discard cornmeal; discard any clams that are not tightly closed or that do not close when pressed.

Arrange clams on a rack in a steamer or Dutch oven; add 2 cups hot water. Cover tightly and steam over medium-high heat 5 to 10 minutes, or just until shells open. Discard any clams that do not open. Reserve nectar for chowder.

Arrange clams on a serving platter. Garnish with fresh parsley and lemon wedges.

Serving Suggestion: Serve with tossed green salad, toasted or grilled garlic bread, and baked potato with nonfat sour cream, chives, and green onion.

APPROXIMATE NUTRITIONAL INFORMATION PER SERVING

Total calories: 82
Total fat: 1 g
Saturated fat: 0 g
Dietary fiber: trace
Carbohydrates: 17 g
Protein: 11 g
Cholesterol: 23 mg
Sodium: 47 mg

Steamer Clams Italian Style

Approximately 4 servings

5 dozen steamer clams

3 gallons cold water for soaking solution

1 cup cornmeal for soaking solution

1 tablespoon olive oil

1 onion, chopped

1 garlic clove, minced

2 celery stalks, chopped

1 28-ounce can plum tomatoes, diced

¼ cup chopped fresh parsley

Freshly ground pepper

Scrub clams. Place in a large bowl and cover with cold water. Sprinkle with cornmeal and let stand 30 minutes. Drain and rinse; discard cornmeal; discard any clams that are not tightly closed or that do not close when pressed.

Arrange clams on a rack in a steamer or Dutch oven, add 2 cups hot water. Cover tightly and steam over medium-high heat 5 to 10 minutes, or just until shells open. Discard any clams that do not open. Reserve nectar for chowder.

Heat olive oil in a nonstick skillet; add onion, garlic, and celery, and sauté until tender. Add tomatoes.
Reduce heat and simmer 30 minutes.

To serve, arrange clams in their shells in soup bowls; cover with tomato mixture. Sprinkle with fresh parsley and ground pepper.

APPROXIMATE NUTRITIONAL INFORMATION PER SERVING

Total calories: 129
Total fat: 4 g
Saturated fat: 0 g
Dietary fiber: 3 g
Carbohydrates: 15 g
Protein: 11 g
Cholesterol: 23 mg
Sodium: 399 mg

Mussels and Clams with Tomato and Basil

4 servings

2 tablespoons fresh basil

2 tablespoons olive oil

¼ cup minced parsley

1 tablespoon minced garlic

½ cup white wine

½ teaspoon Kosher salt

¼ teaspoon black pepper

½ teaspoon crushed red pepper

4 large ripe tomatoes, diced

3 pounds mussels, washed, soaked and bearded

1 pound clams, soaked and cleaned

In a large steamer over boiling water, combine all the ingredients. Cover and steam 5–10 minutes, removing each clam and mussel as it opens.

Serving Suggestion: Serve with pasta nests, Caesar Salad (page 157), seasonal fruit, and Lemon Ice (page 414).

APPROXIMATE NUTRITIONAL INFORMATION PER SERVING

Total calories: 263
Total fat: 8 g
Saturated fat: 4 g
Dietary fiber: 2 g
Carbohydrates: 15 g
Protein: 29 g
Cholesterol: 67 mg
Sodium: 584 mg

Mussels and Clams in Wine and Garlic

4 servings

¼ cup white wine

2½ tablespoons olive oil

8 large cloves garlic

Juice of 1 lemon

½ teaspoon Kosher salt

¼ teaspoon black pepper

3 pounds clams, soaked and cleaned

1 pound fresh mussels, washed, soaked, and bearded

In large steamer over boiling water, combine all ingredients. Cover and steam 5–10 minutes, removing each clam and mussel as it opens.

APPROXIMATE NUTRITIONAL INFORMATION PER SERVING

Total calories: 207
Total fat: 5 g
Saturated fat: 2 g
Dietary fiber: trace
Carbohydrates: 9 g
Protein: 29 g
Cholesterol: 73 mg
Sodium: 420 mg

Mussels Italian Style

Approximately 4 servings

5 dozen mussels

1 leek including greens, chopped

1 medium onion, thinly sliced

1 large garlic clove, halved

1½ cups dry white wine

¾ cup water

½ teaspoon Kosher salt, or to taste

1 14½-ounce can plum tomatoes, diced

1 tablespoon extra-virgin olive oil

¼ cup chopped fresh parsley

Scrub mussel shells with a wire brush. Remove and discard beards. Rinse mussels in cold water; discard broken or open mussels.

Place mussels on a rack in a steamer or Dutch oven; add leek, onion, garlic, vermouth, water, and salt. Cover tightly and steam over medium-high heat for 6 to 8 minutes, or just until shells open. Remove to a serving dish and cover lightly to keep warm.

Boil cooking liquid for 2 to 3 minutes to reduce. Add tomatoes and olive oil. Heat to serving temperature. Pour sauce over mussels. Sprinkle with parsley.

Variation: Serve over linguine.

Serving Suggestion: Serve with tossed green salad and crusty French bread.

APPROXIMATE NUTRITIONAL INFORMATION PER SERVING

Total calories: 276
Total fat: 7 g
Saturated fat: 1 g
Dietary fiber: 2 g
Carbohydrates: 16 g
Protein: 23 g
Cholesterol: 51 mg
Sodium: 694 mg

Calamari Seviche

4 servings

1 pound squid bodies

1 tablespoon extra-virgin olive oil

2 large beefsteak tomatoes, cut into 3-inch cubes

3/4 medium red onion, coarsely chopped

2 tablespoons diced jalapeño peppers

3 cloves garlic, peeled

¼ cup rice vinegar

¼ cup fresh lime juice

Clean squid. Slice into $1/3$-inch rings. Toss with olive oil. In a nonstick skillet, sauté squid 3–4 minutes, or until color changes and squid are cooked. Plunge into ice water. Drain. Pat dry. Combine squid, tomatoes, onion, jalapeño peppers, and garlic. Toss with rice vinegar and fresh lime juice. Chill 2–3 hours.

Serving Suggestion: Good as an appetizer or served as a salad over red and green leaf lettuce.

APPROXIMATE NUTRITIONAL INFORMATION PER SERVING

Total calories: 240
Total fat: 8 g
Saturated fat: 2 g
Dietary fiber: 2 g
Carbohydrates: 13 g
Protein: 19 g
Cholesterol: 264 mg
Sodium: 61 mg

Calamari with Stir-fried Vegetables

4 servings

1 pound squid bodies, cleaned and cut into strips ¼ inch wide

2 tablespoons olive oil

1 tablespoon finely minced gingerroot

3 cloves garlic, slivered

1 medium white onion, thinly sliced

1 red pepper, seeded and thinly sliced

1 yellow or green pepper, seeded and thinly sliced

⅓ pound fresh mushrooms, thinly sliced

1 8-ounce can sliced water chestnuts, drained

3 stalks celery, thinly sliced

¼ cup bottled oyster sauce

1 tablespoon reduced-sodium soy sauce

½ teaspoon sesame oil

In a nonstick skillet, toss squid with 1 tablespoon of the olive oil and sauté over medium heat 2–3 minutes or until squid turns white. Remove from heat.

In a wok, heat remaining tablespoon olive oil. Add gingerroot, garlic, and onions, and stir-fry 3–4 minutes or until onions begin to soften. Add peppers, mushrooms, water chestnuts, and celery, and stir-fry 2–3 minutes or just until peppers are crisp-tender. Add squid. Combine oyster sauce, soy sauce, and sesame oil, and pour over vegetables and squid.

Note: Oyster sauce is available in most supermarkets and Asian groceries.

Serving Suggestion: Serve with Tomato Shrimp Soup (page 141), steamed rice and, for dessert, Fresh Pineapple with Papaya Purée (page 423).

This is not a low-sodium recipe, so be sure to choose lower-sodium foods at your other meals to balance out the day.

APPROXIMATE NUTRITIONAL INFORMATION PER SERVING

Total calories: 240
Total fat: 7 g
Saturated fat: 2 g
Dietary fiber: 2 g
Carbohydrates: 20 g
Protein: 21 g
Cholesterol: 264 mg
Sodium: 843 mg

Shellfish with Aioli Sauce

6 servings

2 pounds mussels

2 pounds clams

1½ cups dry white wine

¾ cup water

¾ teaspoon or less Kosher salt

1 leek, including greens, chopped

4 cloves garlic, peeled

1 tablespoon olive oil

1 pound scallops

1 whole crab, cracked and cleaned

1 bunch fresh Italian parsley

Aioli Sauce (page 212)

Wash and soak clams and mussels (page 250). Remove beards from mussels, if necessary. In a stock pot, combine wine, water, salt, leeks, and garlic. Bring to a boil. Add clams and mussels. Cover and steam 6–8 minutes, or until shells open. Remove seafood from liquid. Meanwhile, heat olive oil in a nonstick skillet over medium high heat. Add scallops and cook 4-6 minutes or until scallops are tender. Arrange mussels, clams, scallops and crab on a parsley-lined tray. Serve with Aioli Sauce on the side.

Serving Suggestions: This dish is good served hot or cold. It is suitable as an appetizer, light lunch, or main meal.

Add 70 calories per tablespoon of Aioli Sauce. For fewer carlories, serve with fresh lemon juice or tomato sauce.

APPROXIMATE NUTRITIONAL INFORMATION PER SERVING WITHOUT AIOLI SAUCE

Total calories: 270
Total fat: 4 g
Saturated fat: 1 g
Dietary fiber: 0 g
Carbohydrates: 9 g
Protein: 30 g
Cholesterol: 125 mg
Sodium: 416 mg

Mixed Seafood Grill

4 servings

½ pound fresh tuna fillets

½ pound fresh halibut fillets

½ pound fresh scallops

1 tablespoon olive oil

1 bulb fresh fennel, chopped

1 bunch fresh fennel greens

8 cherry or small plum tomatoes, skewered

1½ lemons, cut into wedges

1½ limes, cut into wedges

Rub tuna, halibut, and scallops with olive oil. Set aside.

Prepare grill for direct grilling over medium-high heat. Cover grill with foil. Grill halibut, scallops, and tomatoes 4-6 minutes on each side, or until they reach desired doneness. Be careful not to overcook.

Layer fennel greens on a serving platter (this looks sensational in a large copper skillet or on an oval fish platter). Arrange seafood and tomatoes over fennel. Garnish with lemons and limes.

Variation: If fresh fennel is not available, use fresh dill.

Serving Suggestion: Serve with Quinoa with Tomatoes and Parsley (page 351) and Stir-fried Broccoli and Cauliflower with Red Peppers (page 365).

APPROXIMATE NUTRITIONAL INFORMATION PER SERVING

Total calories: 294
Total fat: 9 g
Saturated fat: 2 g
Dietary fiber: 5 g
Carbohydrates: 17 g
Protein: 38 g
Cholesterol: 64 mg
Sodium: 232 mg

Asian-Style Seafood

4 servings

1 pound fillet of sole, cod, halibut, or other white fish

6 tablespoons sake

3 tablespoons ginger juice*

3 tablespoons lemon juice

Dash of salt

6 fresh shiitake mushrooms

1 to 2 fresh lemons, cut into wedges

Divide fish into 4 servings. Place each portion on a piece of aluminum foil; fold edges of foil upward to make a bowl. Cover each fillet with a generous amount of sake, ginger juice, lemon juice, and salt; top with 1 to 2 mushrooms. Pinch top edges of foil together to seal, leaving a small amount of space between top of fish and top of foil. Place in a 350°F. oven and steam for 20 minutes, or until done. Garnish with plenty of fresh lemon.

Note: Shiitake mushrooms can usually be found in most supermarkets and Asian markets. If fresh are unavailable, reconstitute dried shiitake mushrooms by soaking them in water for 30 minutes, or until soft.

*To make ginger juice, grate a 2 1/2-inch piece of peeled fresh ginger; squeeze the pulp to obtain ginger juice.

APPROXIMATE NUTRITIONAL INFORMATION PER SERVING

Total calories: 124
Total fat: 1 g
Saturated fat: 0 g
Dietary fiber: 0 g
Carbohydrates: 10 g
Protein: 18 g
Cholesterol: 0 mg
Sodium: 257 mg

Seafood with Vermouth and Orange Sauce

4 servings

1 pound fillet of halibut, red snapper, cod, sole, or other white fish

2 teaspoons olive oil

½ cup fresh orange juice

½ cup white wine

1 orange, thinly sliced for garnish

Watercress for garnish

Rub fish with olive oil. Heat orange juice and wine just to boiling; reduce heat and simmer 2 to 3 minutes. Pour over fish. Bake uncovered at 450° F. for 15 to 20 minutes, basting frequently. When fish is done, pour juices into a saucepan; boil 3 to 4 minutes to reduce. Spread a serving plate with orange slices; top with fish. Spoon ¼ of the sauce over fish. Garnish with watercress. Pass remaining sauce.

APPROXIMATE NUTRITIONAL INFORMATION PER SERVING

Total calories: 229
Total fat: 6 g
Saturated fat: 1 g
Dietary fiber: 0 g
Carbohydrates: 8 g
Protein: 31 g
Cholesterol: 47 mg
Sodium: 83 mg

Seafood with Wine and Tomato Sauce

4 servings

1 tablespoon olive oil

1 onion, chopped

2 to 3 celery stalks, chopped

2 carrots, diced

1 garlic clove, minced

1 cup white wine

1 8-ounce can tomato sauce

3 tablespoons chopped Italian parsley

1 pound fillet of halibut, red snapper, sole, cod, or other white fish

Dash Kosher salt

Dash freshly ground black pepper

Heat olive oil in a nonstick skillet. Add onion and saute 4-6 minutes. Add celery and carrots and saute 2-3 minutes. Add garlic, saute 1 minute. Add wine and tomato sauce. Simmer 15 minutes. Pour a quarter of the sauce into a baking dish; arrange fish on top. Cover with remaining sauce. Bake, covered, at 350° F. for 15 to 20 minutes. Sprinkle with parsley. Season with salt and pepper.

APPROXIMATE NUTRITIONAL INFORMATION PER SERVING

Total calories: 269
Total fat: 6 g
Saturated fat: 1 g
Dietary fiber: 2 g
Carbohydrates: 12 g
Protein: 32 g
Cholesterol: 47 mg
Sodium: 151 mg

Grilled Rainbow Trout

4 servings

1 pound fresh rainbow trout fillet

juice of 1/2 lemon

2 teaspoons olive oil

salt

black pepper

paprika

1 clove garlic, finely minced

1 teaspoon fresh thyme leaves

1 lemon, cut into wedges

1 lime, cut into wedges

Prepare grill for direct grilling over medium-high heat.

Arrange trout fillet on a sheet of foil. Drizzle with lemon and olive oil. Sprinkle with salt, pepper, paprika, garlic, and thyme.

Grill about 4-5 minutes per side or until fish flakes easily when pricked with a fork. Serve with plenty of fresh lemon and lime wedges.

Serving Suggestion: Serve with Georgetown Rice Salad (page 177), Grilled Corn in Husks (page 367), and Strawberry Sherbet with Strawberry Sauce (page 415).

APPROXIMATE NUTRITIONAL INFORMATION PER SERVING

Total calories: 206
Total fat: 7 g
Saturated fat: 1 g
Dietary fiber: trace
Carbohydrates: 6 g
Protein: 30 g
Cholesterol: 83 mg
Sodium: 107 mg

Crab-stuffed Trout

Approximately 2 servings

2 6-ounce trout fillets

2 teaspoons olive oil

1 small onion, thinly sliced

¼ pound crabmeat

¼ pound fresh mushrooms, sliced

Juice of ½ lemon

3 tablespoons white wine

2 fresh lemons

1 bunch fresh Italian parsley for garnish

Rub trout inside and out with olive oil. Arrange in a 9 x 13 x 2-inch baking dish; stuff cavity with onion, crab, and mushrooms.

Combine lemon juice and wine; pour over fish both inside and outside. Cover baking dish with aluminum foil.

Bake at 400° F. about 20 minutes, or until skin pulls easily away from fish. Baste frequently during cooking. Serve with plenty of fresh lemon; garnish with parsley.

Variation: Any other type of whole fish may be used in place of trout.

Serving Suggestion: For a refreshing dessert, try Lemon Gelato.

APPROXIMATE NUTRITIONAL INFORMATION PER SERVING

Total calories: 157
Total fat: 5 g
Saturated fat: 1 g
Dietary fiber: 2 g
Carbohydrates: 10 g
Protein: 19 g
Cholesterol: 45 mg
Sodium: 265 mg

Cajun-style Whitefish

4 servings

1 ½ cups fresh orange juice

2 tablespoons fresh lemon juice

3 tablespoons fresh lime juice

1 tablespoon rice vinegar

3 cloves garlic, peeled

2 tablespoons jalapeno peppers, diced

2 tablespoons chili powder

2 teaspoons Kosher salt

¼ teaspoon black pepper

1 pound halibut, black cod, red snapper, monkfish, sole or perch

In a bowl, combine orange juice, lemon juice, lime juice, rice vinegar, garlic, jalapeno peppers, chili powder, salt and black pepper. Let sauce stand at room temperature 3 hours.

Arrange each fillet on a sheet of aluminum foil. Bring edges of foil upwards to form a bowl. Spoon 2 tablespoons of sauce over each fillet. Pinch top edges of foil together to seal (leave a small amount of space for steam between top of fish and top of foil.)

Arrange foil packets in a baking dish. Steam at 450°F. 8-10 minutes, or until fish flakes easily when tested with a fork.

APPROXIMATE NUTRITIONAL INFORMATION PER SERVING WITH 2 TABLESPOONS OF SAUCE

Total calories: 140
Total fat: 3 g
Saturated fat: 0 g
Dietary fiber: 0 g
Carbohydrates: 17 g
Protein: 27 g
Cholesterol: 40 g
Sodium: 90 mg

Fillet of Sole with Cheese

4 servings

1 tablespoon olive oil

1 medium white onion, chopped

⅔ pound fresh mushrooms, sliced

1 cup grated part-skim mozzarella cheese

1 pound fillet of sole

Heat olive oil in a nonstick skillet, add onions and saute 3 minutes. Add mushrooms, saute 2 minutes. In a shallow baking dish, layer half the onions, then half the mushrooms, then half the cheese. Arrange the sole over the cheese. Top sole with remaining onions, then mushrooms, then cheese. Bake at 400°F. 15–20 minutes, or until cheese is just melted and fish flakes easily when tested with a fork. Do not overcook.

APPROXIMATE NUTRITIONAL INFORMATION PER SERVING

Total calories: 225
Total fat: 7 g
Saturated fat: 4 g
Dietary fiber: 1 g
Carbohydrates: 6 g
Protein: 33 g
Cholesterol: 72 mg
Sodium: 270 mg

Sole with Shrimp, Crab and Mushrooms

4 servings

1 cup chicken broth (page 143) or canned broth

½ cup dry vermouth or a dry white wine

¼ cup fresh lemon juice

¼ teaspoon Kosher salt

¼ teaspoon black pepper

1 pound sole fillets

1 tablespoon olive oil or canola oil

1 tablespoon finely chopped leek, white part only

¼ pound fresh mushrooms, sliced

1½ teaspoons arrowroot

3 tablespoons cold water

¼ pound cooked shrimpmeat

¼ pound cooked crabmeat

¼ cup freshly grated Parmesan cheese

In a skillet, combine chicken broth, wine and lemon juice, and bring to a boil. Add salt and pepper. Place sole in the liquid; cover and poach 4–5 minutes or until fish is barely cooked. Remove sole from stock and drain on paper towels. Transfer remaining stock to a saucepan and bring to a boil. Reduce heat and simmer, uncovered, 5 minutes to reduce to 1 cup.

In the same skillet, heat olive oil. Add leek and mushrooms, and sauté 3–4 minutes or until mushrooms are tender.

Bring fish stock back to boiling. Dissolve arrowroot in cold water and gradually add to fish stock. Cook and stir until stock begins to thicken. Add shrimpmeat, crabmeat, leek, mushrooms and half the cheese. Arrange sole in ovenproof baking dish. Pour sauce over sole. Sprinkle with remaining cheese. Broil 2–3 minutes or until cheese is melted.

Serving Suggestion: Serve with steamed tiny red potatoes, fresh asparagus, and Frosty Lemon Supreme (page 417).

APPROXIMATE NUTRITIONAL INFORMATION PER SERVING

Total calories: 281
Total fat: 8 g
Saturated fat: 1 g
Dietary fiber: trace
Carbohydrates: 4 g
Protein: 39 g
Cholesterol: 144 mg
Sodium: 543 mg

Clam-stuffed Sole

Approximately 4 servings

¼ cup chopped green onion

1 garlic clove, minced

1 tablespoon olive oil

1½ cups sliced fresh mushrooms

1 6½ -ounce can chopped clams, drained

2 tablespoons chopped parsley

1 teaspoon minced fresh oregano or ½ teaspoon dried

2 teaspoons minced fresh basil or ½ teaspoon dried

¼ teaspoon Kosher salt

⅛ teaspoon pepper

1 pound sole fillets

1 tablespoon lemon juice

Fresh parsley for garnish

Fresh lemon wedges for garnish

Sauté onion and garlic in olive oil until tender. Add mushrooms; cook 2 to 3 minutes. Stir in clams, parsley, oregano, basil, salt, and pepper.

Layer half the sole fillets in a baking dish and drizzle with lemon juice. Cover each with clam and mushroom filling. Stack remaining fillets over top. Bake covered at 350° F. for 25 minutes. Garnish with fresh parsley and lemon.

Note: Fresh clams may be used in place of canned. Any type of white fish may be used in place of sole.

APPROXIMATE NUTRITIONAL INFORMATION PER SERVING

Total calories: 172
Total fat: 5 g
Saturated fat: 0 g
Dietary fiber: 1 g
Carbohydrates: 7 g
Protein: 26 g
Cholesterol: 20 mg
Sodium: 133 mg

Grilled Black Cod

4 servings

1 pound black cod fillets

1 tablespoon olive oil

1 bunch fresh Italian parsley

2 fresh lemons cut into wedges

SPICY ITALIAN TOMATO SAUCE

1 tablespoon extra virgin olive oil

½ cup chopped onion

2 cloves minced garlic

1 15-ounce can whole plum tomatoes with liquid

½ cup white wine

½ teaspoon fresh oregano

¼ cup fresh basil

¼ teaspoon red pepper flakes

¼ teaspoon Kosher salt

Rub fish with olive oil. Prepare grill for direct grilling over medium-high heat. Cover grill with foil. Grill fish 5-6 minutes. Turn; grill 2-3 minutes or until fish flakes easily when tested with a fork. Serve on a bed of Italian parsley with lemon wedges.

Accompany with Spicy Italian Tomato Sauce. Combine ingredients for sauce in a medium saucepan. Simmer 20 minutes while grilling fish. Makes 4 cups.

APPROXIMATE NUTRITIONAL INFORMATION PER SERVING FOR FISH

Calories: 136
Total fat: 3 g
Saturated fat: 0 g
Dietary fiber: 3 g
Carbohydrates: 6 g
Protein: 21 g
Cholesterol: 42 mg
Sodium: 85 mg

APPROXIMATE NUTRITIONAL INFORMATION PER ¼ CUP SERVING FOR SAUCE

Calories: 45
Total fat: 2 g
Saturated fat: 0 g
Dietary fiber: 0 g
Carbohydrates: 4 g
Protein: 1 g
Cholesterol: 0 mg
Sodium: 150 mg

Szechuan-Style Sole

18 spring rolls

1 tablespoon ginger juice*

1 pound sole fillets, cubed

2 green onions with tops, finely chopped

1/8 teaspoon pepper

1/8 teaspoon salt

2 tablespoons olive oil

1 tablespoon sesame oil

1 tablespoon sake

1 tablespoon potato starch

1 egg white, beaten

1/2 teaspoon potato starch plus 1/2 cup water

18 spring roll (lumpia) wrappers, thawed, if frozen

SAUCE

2 cups chicken broth, preferably homemade (page 143)

1 1/2 tablespoons sesame oil

1 1/2 tablespoons sake

3 tablespoons all-purpose flour plus 1/2 cup cold water

3 to 4 green onions, sliced

2 to 3 drops hot chili oil

Squeeze ginger juice over fish; let stand 10 minutes. Add green onions, pepper, salt, olive oil, sesame oil, sake, and 1 tablespoon potato starch. Toss. Fold in beaten egg white.

Heat the 1/2 teaspoon potato starch and the 1/2 cup water to boiling to form a glue; cool to room temperature.

Lay spring roll wrappers flat; place 2 tablespoons of fish filling in center of each. Brush outside edges of each wrapper with starch mixture; fold edges over, envelope style, and seal outside seam. Preheat a nonstick skillet; brown spring rolls on one side over medium-high heat for 10 to 15 minutes. Turn; brown on other side.

Meanwhile, prepare sauce. Bring broth, sesame oil, and sake to a boil. Combine the flour and water; gradually add to broth, stirring until thickened. Stir in green onions and chili oil; pour over spring rolls. Serve at once.

*To make ginger juice, purée a 2 1/2-inch piece of peeled fresh ginger in a food processor; squeeze the pulp to obtain the ginger juice.

APPROXIMATE NUTRITIONAL INFORMATION PER ROLL WITH 2 TABLESPOONS SAUCE

Total calories: 295
Total fat: 5 g
Saturated fat: 0 g
Dietary fiber: 0 g
Carbohydrates: 61 g
Protein: 16 g
Cholesterol: 0 mg
Sodium: 76 mg

Blackened Halibut

4 servings

1 pound halibut fillets, sliced ½-inch thick

2 tablespoons olive oil

¹/ teaspoon Kosher salt

½ teaspoon black pepper

½ teaspoon cayenne pepper

2 teaspoons fresh thyme

2 teaspoons fresh oregano

1 teaspoon paprika

Italian parsley

2 lemons cut into wedges

Rub halibut with olive oil. Combine salt, peppers, thyme, oregano, and paprika. Sprinkle on fish.

Prepare the grill for direct grilling over medium-high heat. Cover grill with foil. Grill fish for 5-7 minutes. Turn and grill for 2-3 minutes or until done. Serve on bed of Italian parsley with lemon wedges.

APPROXIMATE NUTRITIONAL INFORMATION PER SERVING

Total calories: 210
Total fat: 10 g
Saturated fat: 1 g
Dietary fiber: 2 g
Carbohydrates: 6 g
Protein: 25 g
Cholesterol: 36 mg
Sodium: 304 mg

Grilled Halibut Steaks with Soy Wasabi Sauce

4 servings

1 pound halibut steaks

1 tablespoon olive oil

Soy Wasabi Sauce (page 244)

Rub halibut with olive oil. Prepare the grill for direct grilling over medium-high heat. Grill fish 5-7 minutes. Turn and grill for 2-3 minutes or until fish flakes easily when tested with a fork.

Serve with Soy Wasabi Sauce.

APPROXIMATE NUTRITIONAL INFORMATION PER SERVING WITHOUT DRESSING

Calories: 170
Total fat: 6 g
Saturated fat: 0 g
Dietary fiber: 0
Carbohydrates: 3 g
Protein: 24 g
Cholesterol: 36 mg
Sodium: 421 mg

A tablespoon of Soy Wasabi Sauce has 20 calories, 0 fat, and 530 mg. of sodium.

266 Healthy Heart Cookbook

Grilled Halibut on a Bed of Fennel

4 servings

1 pound of halibut, red snapper, cod, sole, or other white fish

1 tablespoon olive oil

Juice of 1 lemon

2-3 green onions, finely chopped

1 bunch fresh fennel

LEMON CAPER SAUCE

¾ cup mayonnaise

2 garlic cloves, crushed

⅓ cup finely chopped onion

2 tablespoons capers

¼ teaspoon Kosher salt

⅛ teaspoon black pepper

⅓ cup lemon juice

1 teaspoon Tabasco sauce

Rub fish with olive oil; cover with lemon juice. Sprinkle with green onion. Prepare the grill for direct grilling at medium-high heat. Cover grill with foil. Place ½ of fennel on the foil. Place fish on the foil and the remaining fennel on top of the fish. Grill 5-7 minutes. Turn and grill 2-3 minutes or until fish flakes easily when tested with a fork. Serve with Lemon Caper Sauce.

LEMON CAPER SAUCE
Combine all ingredients in a small bowl. Makes 1 ½ cups.

If light mayonnaise is used, one teaspoon of Soy Wasabi Sauce has 25 calories, 2 grams of fat, and 95 mg. of sodium.

APPROXIMATE NUTRITIONAL INFORMATION PER SERVING WITHOUT DRESSING

Calories: 165
Total fat: 6 g
Saturated fat: 1 g
Dietary fiber: 0 g
Carbohydrates: 1 g
Protein: 25 g
Cholesterol: 38 mg
Sodium: 66 mg

APPROXIMATE NUTRITIONAL INFORMATION PER 1 TABLESPOON SERVING OF SAUCE

Calories: 50
Total fat: 6 g
Saturated fat: 0 g
Dietary fiber: 0 g
Carbohydrates: 1 g
Protein: 0 g
Cholesterol: 5 mg
Sodium: 100 mg

Grilled Red Snapper

4 servings

1 pound red snapper fillet, or cod

1 tablespoon olive oil

2 tablespoons fresh rosemary

2 tablespoons fresh thyme

⅛ teaspoon Kosher salt

** teaspoon pepper**

2 fresh lemons, peeled and finely diced

¼ cup fresh parsley, chopped

ARUGULA SALAD

8 cups arugula

¼ cup Italian Vinaigrette (page 204)

¼ cup shaved Parmesan

Rub fish with olive oil. Sprinkle generously with rosemary, thyme, salt, and black pepper. Prepare grill for direct grilling over medium-high heat. Cover grill with foil. Grill fish for 3-5 minutes, turn and cook another 2-3 minutes, or until it flakes easily with a fork.

Accompany with aragula salad (2 bunches fresh aragula—about 8 cups—dressed with Italian Vinaigrette and sprinkled with shaved Parmesan cheese. 4 servings.)

APPROXIMATE NUTRITIONAL INFORMATION PER SERVING FOR FISH

Calories: 157
Total fat: 5 g
Saturated fat: 0 g
Dietary fiber: 3 g
Carbohydrates: 6 g
Protein: 24 g
Cholesterol: 42 mg
Sodium: 77 mg

APPROXIMATE NUTRITIONAL INFORMATION PER SERVING FOR SALAD

Calories: 120
Total fat: 12 g
Saturated fat: 2 g
Dietary fiber: 1 g
Carbohydrates: 2 g
Protein: 3 g
Cholesterol: 5 mg
Sodium: 180 mg

Sea Bass with Shrimp

4 servings

- **1 pound sea bass steaks or halibut**
- **1 tablespoon olive oil**
- **2 medium ripe tomatoes, diced**
- **1 8-ounce can mushroom stems and pieces, drained**
- **3 cloves garlic, thinly sliced**
- **½ pound cooked shrimpmeat**
- **¼ bunch fresh parsley**
- **1 lemon, cut into wedges**
- **2 medium tomatoes, cut into wedges**

In a shallow baking pan, arrange sea bass in a single layer. Rub with 1 teaspoon of the olive oil. Combine remaining olive oil, diced tomatoes, mushrooms, and garlic, and pour over sea bass.

Bake, uncovered, at 400°F. 10 minutes per inch of thickness of fish. Three to four minutes before fish is cooked, sprinkle shrimp over top. When sea bass turns white and flakes readily when touched with a fork, remove to a platter lined with parsley. Garnish with lemon and tomato wedges.

Serving Suggestions: Serve with steamed rice or red potatoes, fresh asparagus and, for dessert, Vanilla Angel Food Cake (page 398) with Orange Glaze (page 399).

APPROXIMATE NUTRITIONAL INFORMATION PER SERVING

Total calories: 207
Total fat: 6 g
Saturated fat: 1 g
Dietary fiber: 3 g
Carbohydrates: 10 g
Protein: 30 g
Cholesterol: 130 mg
Sodium: 183 mg

Halibut with Sun-Dried Tomato Crust

4 servings

8 marinated sun-dried tomatoes, drained

3 garlic cloves

1 tablespoon extra-virgin olive oil

6 fresh lemon slices

1 pound halibut fillets

1 tablespoon fresh lemon juice

8 kalamata olives, pitted and halved

Lemon wedges

Process sun-dried tomatoes, garlic, and olive oil in a food processor until tomatoes are finely chopped.

Prepare grill for direct grilling over medium-high heat. Cover grill with foil. Place lemon slices on foil. Place fish on lemon slices. Using a spatula, spread the sun-dried tomato mixture heavily over top of fish. Close grill lid. Cook fish 10 minutes per inch of thickness of fish, or until fish flakes easily when tested with fork. Sprinkle with kalamata olives the last 3 minutes of cooking time. Serve with fresh lemon wedges.

APPROXIMATE NUTRITIONAL INFORMATION PER SERVING

Total calories: 174
Total fat: 7 g
Saturated fat: 1 g
Dietary fiber: 0 g
Carbohydrates: 7 g
Protein: 21 g
Cholesterol: 91 mg
Sodium: 314 mg

Orange Roughy

4 servings

1 tablespoon olive oil

juice of 1 lemon

1 pound orange roughy fillets

2 fresh lemons, quartered

Pinch Kosher salt

Pinch fresh ground black pepper to taste

In a large skillet, heat lemon juice. Add orange roughy. Cover and poach 3–8 minutes, or until fish flakes easily when tested with a fork. Serve with fresh lemons salt, and black pepper.

Serving Suggestion: Accompany with Vermicelli-Stuffed Tomatoes (pages 386).

APPROXIMATE NUTRITIONAL INFORMATION PER SERVING

Total calories: 116
Total fat: 4 g
Saturated fat: trace
Dietary fiber: 1 g
Carbohydrates: 4 g
Protein: 0 g
Cholesterol: 23 mg
Sodium: 72 mg

Green Peppercorn Salmon

4 servings

1 tablespoon olive oil

2 tablespoons fresh lime juice

2 tablespoons green peppercorns

1 pound fresh salmon fillets

2 fresh limes, sliced into rounds

Combine olive oil, lime juice, and peppercorns. Place salmon in a dish and arrange lime slices over and under it. Cover with lime juice and peppercorn mixture and marinate 30 minutes.

Prepare grill for direct grilling over medium-high heat. Cover grill with foil. Place fish on grill. Grill 5-7 minutes. Turn and grill for 2-3 minutes or until salmon flakes easily when tested with a fork. Serve over sliced limes on a platter. Sprinkle with lemon juice and salt to tase.

APPROXIMATE NUTRITIONAL INFORMATION PER SERVING

Total calories: 204
Total fat: 10 g
Saturated fat: 2 g
Dietary fiber: 1 g
Carbohydrates: 5 g
Protein: 23 g
Cholesterol: 62 mg
Sodium: 51 mg

Teriyaki Salmon

4 servings

3 tablespoons reduced-sodium soy sauce

½ cup sake

1 teaspoon sugar

1 tablespoon extra-virgin olive oil

1 pound salmon fillets

2 bunches fresh spinach, washed

1 lemon, cut into wedges

In a bowl or covered jar, combine soy sauce, sake, sugar, and olive oil. Pour over salmon and marinate at room temperature 30 minutes, basting frequently. Drain off marinade.

Prepare grill for direct grilling over medium-high heat. Cover the grill with foil. Grill salmon skin side up, 5–6 minutes. Turn and cook 2–3 minutes, or until salmon flakes easily when tested with a fork. Place on a bed of spinach. Garnish with lemon.

Serving Suggestion: Serve with Mostaccioli with Tomatoes (page 222).

APPROXIMATE NUTRITIONAL INFORMATION PER SERVING

Total calories: 228
Total fat: 9 g
Saturated fat: 2 g
Dietary fiber: 1 g
Carbohydrates: 5 g
Protein: 28 g
Cholesterol: 46 mg
Sodium: 363 mg

Grilled Salmon with Fresh Fennel

4 servings

1 tablespoon olive oil

1 pound salmon fillets

½ pound fresh fennel greens

½ fresh lemon

½ fresh lime

black pepper to taste

Rub the salmon with olive oil. Prepare grill for direct grilling over medium-high heat. Cover grill with foil. Put fish on the grill. Grill salmon 10 minutes per inch of thickness, usually about 6-8 minutes. Turn. Grill 2-3 minutes, or until fish flakes when tested with a fork.

Line a heated serving platter with fennel. Arrange salmon over fennel. Squeeze lemon and lime juice over fish. Sprinkle with black pepper.

Variation: Substitute fresh dill for fennel. Substitute scallops for salmon.

APPROXIMATE NUTRITIONAL INFORMATION PER SERVING

Total calories: 157
Total fat: 14 g
Saturated fat: 3 g
Dietary fiber: 3 g
Carbohydrates: 8 g
Protein: 37 g
Cholesterol: 93 mg
Sodium: 120 mg

Salmon with Lemon Vinaigrette

4 servings

1 pound salmon steaks

1 tablespoon extra-virgin olive oil

1 bunch fresh spinach

½ lemon, cut into wedges

½ lime, cut into wedges

Olive Oil-and-Lemon Vinaigrette (page 205)

Rub salmon with olive oil. Prepare grill for direct grilling over medium-high heat. Cover grill with foil. Grill fish 5-6 minutes. Turn and grill 2-3 minutes, or until salmon flakes easily when tested with a fork.

Toss spinach with Olive Oil-and-Lemon Vinaigrette. Place salmon on the bed of spinach. Garnish with lemon and lime wedges.

APPROXIMATE NUTRITIONAL INFORMATION PER SERVING WITHOUT DRESSING

Calories: 186
Total fat: 7 g
Saturated fat: 2 g
Dietary fiber: trace
Carbohydrates: 2 g
Protein: 27 g
Cholesterol: 46 mg
Sodium: 115 mg

APPROXIMATE NUTRITIONAL INFORMATION PER TABLESPOON OF VINAIGRETTE

Calories: 62
Total fat: 7 g
Saturated fat: 1 g
Dietary fiber: 0 g
Carbohydrates: 1 g
Protein: 0 g
Cholesterol: 0 mg
Sodium: 145 mg

Mushroom-Stuffed Salmon

10 servings

2 tablespoons sake

1 tablespoon sesame oil

1 tablespoon olive oil

3 tablespoons reduced-sodium soy sauce

1 jalapeño pepper, seeded and coarsely chopped

1 tablespoon fresh ginger, peeled and chopped

6 cloves garlic

1 whole salmon, about 3 pounds

1 onion, sliced

½ pound shiitake mushrooms

Combine sake, sesame oil, olive oil, soy sauce, jalapeño pepper, ginger and garlic to make a marinade.

Arrange salmon on aluminum foil. Stuff inside cavity to bulging with onion and mushrooms. Fold foil around salmon to form a bowl. Pour marinade over fish. Wrap fish in two thickness of foil.

Prepare grill for direct grilling over medium-high heat. Cover grill with foil. Grill salmon with lid down 10 minutes per inch of thickness of fish, usually 25-35 minutes, or until fish is just cooked.

Serving Suggestions: Serve with Shrimp and Spinach Salad (page 184), Wild and White Rice (page 346), and Stir-Fried Snow Peas (page 381) and tangerines.

APPROXIMATE NUTRITIONAL INFORMATION PER SERVING

Total calories: 100
Total fat: 1 g
Saturated fat: 0 g
Dietary fiber: 0 g
Carbohydrates: 3 g
Protein: 1 g
Cholesterol: 37 mg
Sodium: 289 mg

Grilled Fresh Tuna

4 servings

1 pound tuna fillets

1 tablespoon olive oil

1 large clove garlic; halved

Arrange tuna in a shallow baking dish. Brush both sides with olive oil. Rub with cut garlic. Let stand 1 hour.

Prepare grill for direct grilling over medium-high heat. Cover grill with foil. Grill tuna 3-5 minutes per side, or until done.

APPROXIMATE NUTRITIONAL INFORMATION PER SERVING

Total calories: 195
Total fat: 9 g
Saturated fat: 2 g
Dietary fiber: 0 g
Carbohydrates: 0 g
Protein: 27 g
Cholesterol: 43 mg
Sodium: 44 mg

Halibut with Tomato-and-Basil Sauce

4 servings

2 tablespoons extra-virgin olive oil

2 cloves garlic

3 tomatoes, diced

¼ cup finely chopped fresh basil

½ teaspoon Kosher salt

¼ teaspoon black pepper

**1 pound fresh halibut filet
(about ½ inch thick)**

1 bunch arugula or red leaf lettuce

Freshly ground pepper to taste

1 lime cut into wedges

In a blender or food processor, combine 1 ½ tablespoons olive oil, garlic, tomatoes, basil, salt, and pepper, and purée until smooth. Pour into bowl. Add remaining tomatoes.

Prepare grill for direct grilling over medium-high heat. Grill 5-7 minutes. Turn and cook for 2-3 minutes or to desired doneness. Line individual plates with arugula leaves. Arrange halibut on top and line dish with lime wedges. Pass with sauce.

Serving Suggestions: Serve with Antipasto Vegetables (page 391).

APPROXIMATE NUTRITIONAL INFORMATION PER SERVING

Total calories: 198
Total fat: 7 g
Saturated fat: 3 g
Dietary fiber: 1 g
Carbohydrates: 3 g
Protein: 31 g
Cholesterol: 49 mg
Sodium: 78 mg

Grilled Swordfish

4 servings

1 pound fresh swordfish fillets

1 tablespoon olive oil

**1 fresh fennel bulb, cut into
½-inch cubes**

½ cup chopped fresh fennel greens

½ fresh lime, cut into wedges

½ fresh lemon, cut into wedges

Rub swordfish with olive oil. Prepare grill for direct grilling over medium-high heat. Grill the fish, turning once , about 4-5 minutes per side, until it is opaque throughout and flakes easily with a fork. Serve on a bed fresh fennel greens. Garnish with lemon and lime wedges.

APPROXIMATE NUTRITIONAL INFORMATION PER SERVING

Total calories: 208
Total fat: 8 g
Saturated fat: 1 g
Dietary fiber: 3 g
Carbohydrates: 9 g
Protein: 25 g
Cholesterol: 45 mg
Sodium: 159 mg

Grilled Swordfish Steaks

4 servings

MARINADE

1 tablespoon extra-virgin olive oil

¼ cup fresh lemon juice

2 garlic cloves, minced

1 tablespoon minced parsley

1½ tablespoons fresh rosemary sprigs

1 pound swordfish steaks (about 1 inch thick)

fresh rosemary and thyme sprigs for garnish (optional)

1 lime, cut into wedges

¼ cup pitted and chopped Kalamata olives (optional)

2 teaspoons capers (optional)

Each year, seafood ranks higher on the popularity poll of Americans. Introduce fresh fish to kids to start them on their way to acquiring another healthy habit.

Prepare grill for direct grilling over medium-high heat. In a small bowl, combine the marinade ingredients.

Arrange swordfish in an 8 x 8 x 2-inch casserole. Pour marinade over swordfish and marinate at room temperature for 15 to 20 minutes.

Remove swordfish from marinade and place on grill. Grill, turning once, until just cooked, about 9 to 10 minutes. Place swordfish on a bed of fresh herb sprigs, if desired. Garnish with lime. Sprinkle with olives and capers.

APPROXIMATE NUTRITIONAL INFORMATION PER SERVING

Total calories: 173
Total fat: 8 g
Saturated fat: 1 g
Dietary fiber: 0 g
Carbohydrates: 2 g
Protein: 22 g
Cholesterol: 57 mg
Sodium: 168 mg

Poultry

A NOTE ON POULTRY

The best choice for poultry is skinless white breast (white meat is leaner than dark). The skin should always be removed from poultry, since that's where there is fat. Three ounces of skinless chicken breast contains just 3 grams of fat; with skin, it contains twice that amount. Similarly, 3 ounces of skinless turkey breast has just 2.7 grams of fat; with skin, it has 8.7 grams of fat. Watch out for ground turkey and ground chicken-—both can be higher in fat than ground round.

Pan-Fried Chicken

4 servings

2 whole chicken breasts, skinned, boned and halved

2 teaspoons olive oil

Preheat a nonstick skillet over medium-high heat. Add chicken breasts rubbed with olive oil and brown 10 minutes on each side. Reduce heat. Cook 5–10 minutes, turning occasionally until chicken is done.

Variation: Rub chicken breasts with pinch powdered rosemary, Kosher salt, and black pepper before cooking.

Serving Suggestion: For an easy and delicious dinner, serve with Roast Potatoes with Rosemary (page 378) and Pan-steamed Asparagus (page 360).

APPROXIMATE NUTRITIONAL INFORMATION PER SERVING

Total calories: 154
Total fat: 8 g
Saturated fat: 1 g
Dietary fiber: 0 g
Carbohydrates: 0 g
Protein: 0 g
Cholesterol: 49 mg
Sodium: 55 mg

Chicken Piccata

4 servings

1 tablespoon olive oil

2 very thin whole chicken breasts, skinned, boned, and halved

juice of 2 lemons (½ cup)

¼ cup dry white wine

1 lemon, thinly sliced

pinch Kosher salt

pinch coarse ground black pepper

In a nonstick skillet, heat oil. Add chicken and sauté over medium-high heat 5-7 minutes. Turn and cook 7 minutes longer or until chicken is nearly done. Remove chicken to heated plates. Add lemon juice and wine to the pan and deglaze over high heat 2–3 minutes, stirring constantly. Pour over chicken. Top each piece of chicken with lemon slices. Sprinkle with Kosher salt and coarsely ground black pepper.

Serving Suggestions: Serve with orzo (a type of pasta), Snow Peas (page 380) and Grilled Herbed Tomatoes (page 383).

Variation: For Veal Piccata substitute veal for chicken.

APPROXIMATE NUTRITIONAL INFORMATION PER SERVING

Total calories: 194
Total fat: 11 g
Saturated fat: 3 g
Dietary fiber: 1 g
Carbohydrates: 4 g
Protein: 18 g
Cholesterol: 54 mg
Sodium: 56 mg

Chicken Primavera

4 servings

2 boneless chicken breasts, skinned and halved

¾ cup dry white wine

1 cup chicken broth (page 143) or commercial broth*

1 tablespoon tomato paste

1 tablespoon minced Italian parsley

½ teaspoon powdered thyme

1 large white onion, sliced (about 2 cups)

3 large cloves garlic, minced

1 tablespoon olive oil

2 green peppers, halved and sliced into half-rings

1 pint cherry tomatoes, halved

In a large nonstick skillet, brown chicken breasts 5–7 minutes on each side. In a saucepan, warm wine, chicken broth, tomato paste, parsley, and thyme; pour over browned chicken breasts. Reduce heat and simmer, uncovered, 20–30 minutes, basting with sauce and turning often.

In a medium nonstick skillet, sauté onion and garlic in olive oil 7–10 minutes or until onions are softened. Remove from heat; add green peppers and tomatoes. Just before serving, add to chicken, raise heat to high, and cook 2–3 minutes or until sauce is bubbly and peppers and onions are warmed.

*Canned broth is higher in sodium.

APPROXIMATE NUTRITIONAL INFORMATION PER SERVING

Total calories: 272
Total fat: 7 g
Saturated fat: 1 g
Dietary fiber: 3 g
Carbohydrates: 14 g
Protein: 30 g
Cholesterol: 73 mg
Sodium: 327 mg

Mushroom and Artichoke Chicken

4 servings

2 chicken breasts, skinned and boned

4 teaspoons olive oil

¼ teaspoon salt

¼ teaspoon black pepper

1 tablespoon fresh rosemary

⅛ teaspoon paprika

1 14-ounce can water-packed artichoke hearts, drained and cut into quarters

¼ pound fresh mushrooms, sliced

2 green onions, chopped

⅔ cup chicken broth (page 143) or commercial broth*

¼ cup dry white wine

2 tablespoons all-purpose flour

¼ cup cold water

Rub chicken with 2 teaspoons of the olive oil. Sprinkle with salt, pepper, rosemary, and paprika. Brown in a nonstick skillet 3-5 minutes on each side. Remove to oven proof baking dish. Add artichokes. Heat remaining 2 teaspoons of olive oil in the skillet. Add mushrooms and onions and saute 4-6 minutes. Spoon over chicken. Bring chicken broth and wine to boil in the skillet.

Combine flour with water. Add to broth mixture, stirring constantly 2–3 minutes. Pour sauce over chicken and artichokes. Cover with foil or lid. Bake at 375°F. 20 minutes or until heated.

*Canned broth is higher in sodium.

Serving Suggestion: Serve with brown rice, fresh asparagus, Lettuce and Bermuda Onion Salad (page 156), Creamy Garlic Dressing (page 208) and, for dessert, fresh berries or seasonal fruit.

APPROXIMATE NUTRITIONAL INFORMATION PER SERVING

Total calories: 231
Total fat: 6 g
Saturated fat: 1 g
Dietary fiber: 1 g
Carbohydrates: 10 g
Protein: 29 g
Cholesterol: 73 mg
Sodium: 355 mg

Garlic Chicken

4 servings

6 large cloves garlic, crushed

3 tablespoons extra-virgin olive oil

pinch powdered rosemary

2 chicken breasts, skinned and boned

1 tablespoon grated orange zest

In a small bowl combine garlic with olive oil. Add rosemary. Arrange chicken breasts in an 8 x 8-inch ovenproof baking dish. Sprinkle with orange zest. Pour marinade over all and marinate in the refrigerator 3–4 hours.

Prepare grill for direct grilling over medium-high heat. Grill chicken 6-8 minutes. Turn, grill another 6-8 minutes or until chicken is cooked.

Serving Suggestion: Serve with Eggplant Parmigiana (page 368), Country Italian Bread (page 55), and Amaretto Oranges with Strawberries (page 427).

APPROXIMATE NUTRITIONAL INFORMATION PER SERVING

Total calories: 194
Total fat: 8 g
Saturated fat: 2 g
Dietary fiber: 0 g
Carbohydrates: 2 g
Protein: 27 g
Cholesterol: 73 mg
Sodium: 65 mg

Lemon Chicken

4 3 ½-ounce servings

2 skinned and boned chicken breasts

2 tablespoons fresh lemon juice

2 tablespoons extra-virgin olive oil

1 lemon, cut into wedges

Pinch Kosher salt

Pinch freshly ground pepper

1 bunch fresh cilantro

Marinate chicken in lemon juice and olive oil several hours or overnight. Prepare grill for direct grilling over medium-high heat. Grill about 6-8 minutes on each side. Season with Kosher salt and freshly ground black pepper.

Serve with lemon wedges on a bed of cilantro.

Serving Suggestion: For a real low-fat dinner, serve with fresh raw spinach with a dressing of fresh lemon and ground pepper, sliced tomatoes with fresh basil, and long-grain rice.

APPROXIMATE NUTRITIONAL INFORMATION PER SERVING

Total calories: 150
Total fat: 3 g
Saturated fat: 1 g
Dietary fiber: 0 g
Carbohydrates: 0 g
Protein: 29 g
Cholesterol: 77 mg
Sodium: 63 mg

Soft Chicken Tacos

4 servings

4 cups chicken broth (page 143), preferably homemade

1½ chicken breasts, skinned and boned

4 10-inch flour tortillas

2 ripe tomatoes, diced

½ white onion, diced

½ head leaf lettuce, shredded

½ cup grated reduced fat Cheddar cheese

½ cup tomato salsa (optional)

¼ cup kalamata olives (optional)

¼ cup jalapno peppers (optional)

In a medium saucepan, bring stock to a boil. Add chicken. Reduce heat to medium-high and cook 20–25 minutes, or until chicken is tender. Cool. Tear into strings.

Warm tortillas. Lay each tortilla flat. Fill centers with chicken, tomatoes, onions, lettuce, and cheese. Drizzle with salsa. Fold sides of tortillas over center.

APPROXIMATE NUTRITIONAL INFORMATION PER SERVING

Total calories: 382
Total fat: 8 g
Saturated fat: 2 g
Dietary fiber: 4 g
Carbohydrates: 45 g
Protein: 27 g
Cholesterol: 42 mg
Sodium: 577 mg

Chicken Enchiladas

8 servings

2 whole chicken breasts, skinned and boned

3 stalks celery, cut into chunks

1 medium onion, cut into chunks

2 cloves garlic

1½ cups chicken broth (page 143) or commercial broth*

FILLING

½ medium green pepper, diced

½ medium white onion, diced

1 large tomato, diced

1 3½ -ounce can whole green chilies, diced

¼ cup chicken broth (page 143) or commercial broth*

¼ teaspoon Kosher salt

¼ teaspoon black pepper

8 flour or corn tortillas

2 ounces part-skim mozzarella cheese, thinly sliced

½ cup commercial or homemade enchilada sauce (page 313)

½ cup tomato salsa, preferably homemade

In a medium stockpot, combine chicken, celery, onion, garlic and chicken broth, and bring to a boil. Cover, reduce heat and simmer 30 minutes. Remove from heat. Remove celery, onion and garlic from stock and discard.
(They will be grease-laden.) Reserve remaining stock for later use. Tear chicken into strings.

To Prepare Filling: In a medium stockpot, combine green pepper, diced onion, tomato, green chilies, ¼ cup chicken broth, salt, and pepper. Cook over low heat 20 minutes or until vegetables are soft. Add chicken.

To Assemble: Place ¼ cup filling in each tortilla, along with a thin slice of mozzarella cheese and 1 teaspoon enchilada sauce. Rolland place seam side down in a lightly greased 9 x 13-inch ovenproof baking dish. Pour remaining enchilada sauce over top. Cover with foil. Bake at 350°F. 20–25 minutes or until hot. Accompany with tomato salsa.

*Commercial broth and salsa are higher in sodium than homemade.

Serving Suggestion: Serve with Refried Black Beans (page 343), steamed short-grain rice and fresh seasonal fruits.

APPROXIMATE NUTRITIONAL INFORMATION PER ENCHILADA

Total calories: 220
Total fat: 5 g
Saturated fat: 1 g
Dietary fiber: 1 g
Carbohydrates: 24 g
Protein: 19 g
Cholesterol: 41 mg
Sodium: 416 mg

Chicken Tostadas

6 servings

2 chicken breasts, skinned and boned

2 cups chicken broth (page 143) or commercial broth*

⅛ teaspoon ground cumin

¾ teaspoon chili powder

1 8-ounce can tomato sauce

¼ teaspoon salt

⅛ teaspoon black pepper

1 small onion, diced

1 large tomato, diced

3 cups shredded lettuce

½ cup shredded reduced fat Cheddar or part-skim mozzarella cheese

6 8-inch flour tortillas, warmed

1 cup Black Bean Dip (page 91)

In a 2-quart saucepan, bring chicken and chicken broth to boiling. Reduce heat and simmer 20 minutes or until chicken is done. Remove chicken from broth. Dice and sprinkle with ½ teaspoon of the cumin and ½ teaspoon of the chili powder.

In a small saucepan, combine tomato sauce, the remaining teaspoon of cumin, the remaining ¼ teaspoon chili powder, salt and pepper, and warm over low heat.

Arrange chicken, onion, tomato, lettuce and cheese on a serving platter. Place warm tortillas in a napkin-lined basket, and put tomato sauce and Black Bean Dip into serving bowls.

To Assemble: Have each person spread a tortilla with bean dip, sprinkle with chicken, add sauce and then lettuce, tomato, onion and cheese.

*Canned broth is higher in sodium.

Serving Suggestions: Serve with steamed rice, chilled watermelon and fresh berries.

APPROXIMATE NUTRITIONAL INFORMATION PER SERVING

Total calories: 313
Total fat: 7 g
Saturated fat: 3 g
Dietary fiber: 3 g
Carbohydrates: 34 g
Protein: 29 g
Cholesterol: 54 mg
Sodium: 745 mg

Mexican Chicken

4 servings

¼ cup orange juice

1 tablespoon lime juice

2 teaspoons cider vinegar

1 tablespoon olive oil

½ teaspoon oregano

½ teaspoon Kosher salt

¼ teaspoon black pepper

2 chicken breasts, skinned, boned, and quartered

Prepare marinade by combining orange juice, lime juice, vinegar, olive oil and seasonings. Pour over chicken and marinate in the refrigerator at least 2 hours. Drain, reserving marinade.

Prepare grill and cover the grill rack with foil.

Prepare grill for direct grilling over high heat. Grill chicken 6-8 minutes. Turn and grill 5-10 minutes, turning frequently, until chicken is cooked. Baste frequently with reserved marinade during cooking.

Serving Suggestion: Serve with Rice with Chilies (page 347), and fresh strawberries.

Variation: Prepare sauce as directed. Put chicken in an oven-proof baking dish. Cover with ⅔ of the sauce. Bake uncovered at 350°F. for 30 minutes or until chicken is cooked.

APPROXIMATE NUTRITIONAL INFORMATION PER SERVING

Total calories: 171
Total fat: 5 g
Saturated fat: 1 g
Dietary fiber: trace
Carbohydrates: 2 g
Protein: 27 g
Cholesterol: 73 mg
Sodium: 280 mg

Chicken Cortez

4 servings

1 6-ounce can pineapple juice

2 tablespoons lime juice

1 tablespoon distilled white vinegar

6 cloves garlic, minced

½ teaspoon Kosher salt

½ teaspoon oregano

¼ teaspoon chili powder

¼ teaspoon black pepper

1 tablespoon olive oil

2 chicken breasts, skinned, boned and halved

Prepare marinade by combining pineapple juice, lime juice, vinegar, garlic, salt, oregano, chili powder, pepper, and olive oil. Pour over chicken and marinate in the refrigerator 2 hours or as long as overnight. Drain off marinade and reserve.

Prepare grill for direct grilling over high heat. Grill chicken 6-8 minutes. Turn and grill 5-10 minutes, turning frequently until chicken is cooked.

Serving Suggestion: Serve with warm tortillas, Ensenada Salad (page 168) with Jalapeño Vinaigrette (page 208), and fresh strawberries.

APPROXIMATE NUTRITIONAL INFORMATION PER SERVING

Total calories: 207
Total fat: 7 g
Saturated fat: 1 g
Dietary fiber: trace
Carbohydrates: 9 g
Protein: 27 g
Cholesterol: 73 mg
Sodium: 150 mg

Chicken Black Bean Burritos

4 servings

4 8-inch flour tortillas

2 chicken breasts, prepared as for Mexican Chicken (page 284)

½ head lettuce, shredded

½ cup Black Bean Dip (page 91)

½ cup Chili Salsa (page 216) or commercial salsa

Warm tortillas.

Slice chicken breasts into thin strips. Arrange lettuce, chicken, and bean dip on serving platter. Accompany with salsa and warm tortillas.

To prepare burrito: Spoon bean dip along center of each tortilla. Divide chicken among tortillas and top with lettuce. Fold opposite sides of each tortilla over filling. Fold ends over folded sides.

Serving Suggestion: Serve with Rice with Chilies (page 347), Vegetable Antipasto of carrot, celery and sliced English cucumber sticks and seasonal fruits.

APPROXIMATE NUTRITIONAL INFORMATION PER SERVING

Total calories: 338
Total fat: 9 g
Saturated fat: 1 g
Dietary fiber: 3 g
Carbohydrates: 31 g
Protein: 33 g
Cholesterol: 73 mg
Sodium: 599 mg

Southern-Fried Chicken

4 servings

1 cup low-fat (1%) buttermilk

2 whole chicken breasts, skinned, boned, and halved

1 cup all-purpose flour

1½ teaspoons Kosher salt

½ teaspoon pepper

2 teaspoons paprika

1 tablespoon extra-virgin olive oil

Imagine not having to give up fried chicken! Follow the braising technique in this recipe to enjoy an old favorite.

Pour buttermilk into an 8 x 8 x 2-inch pan. Dip chicken in buttermilk, turning once to coat.

Combine flour, salt, pepper, and paprika in a paper bag. Add chicken and shake to coat.

In a nonstick skillet over medium-high heat, heat olive oil. Add chicken and cook 10 to 15 minutes, turning chicken frequently to brown evenly. Add 3 tablespoons water and cover. Reduce heat and cook 25 minutes longer. Uncover and cook 5 to 10 minutes more, or until chicken is tender. Remove to serving platter. Set the skillet aside so that the drippings and brown bits can be used for Old Fashioned Gravy (page 218).

APPROXIMATE NUTRITIONAL INFORMATION PER SERVING

Total calories: 314
Total fat: 7 g
Saturated fat: 2 g
Dietary fiber: 1 g
Carbohydrates: 28 g
Protein: 32 g
Cholesterol: 75 mg
Sodium: 241 mg

Chicken with Rice

6 servings

1 tablespoon olive oil

1 large onion, chopped

4 cloves garlic, minced

¼ cup all-purpose flour

1 teaspoon cayenne pepper

2 chicken breasts, skinned, boned, halved, and cut into quarters

1 16-ounce can diced Italian plum tomatoes, with liquid

2¾ cups chicken broth (page 143) or commercial broth*

⅛ teaspoon saffron threads crushed

½ teaspoon Kosher salt

1 cup uncooked long-grain rice

In a nonstick skillet, heat olive oil. Add onion and garlic, and sauté 6–8 minutes or until onion is just tender.

Combine flour and cayenne. Dredge chicken in flour mixture. Add to skillet and brown 2–3 minutes on each side. Add tomatoes, chicken broth, saffron, and salt, and bring to a boil. Stir in rice. Cover and simmer 30–45 minutes or until rice is tender and chicken is cooked. Stir in peas. Serve at once.

APPROXIMATE NUTRITIONAL INFORMATION PER SERVING

Total calories: 372
Total fat: 7 g
Saturated fat: 2 g
Dietary fiber: 3 g
Carbohydrates: 49 g
Protein: 26 g
Cholesterol: 49 mg
Sodium: 592 mg

Chicken Curry

8 servings

½ cup chopped onion

2 cups chicken broth, preferably homemade (page 143)

2 cups nonfat milk

½ cup all-purpose flour

½ teaspoon Kosher salt

1 tablespoon curry powder

¼ teaspoon ground ginger

1 tablespoon lemon juice

4 cups cubed cooked chicken breast

1 8-ounce can sliced water chestnuts

6 cups steamed rice

¼ cup raisins for garnish (optional)

⅔ cup pineapple chunks for garnish (optional)

Sauté onion in a small amount of chicken broth until tender; add remaining broth. Bring to a boil. Shake milk and flour in a covered jar to form a smooth paste; gradually add to boiling broth, stirring constantly until thick. Add seasonings. Pour lemon juice over chicken; add to broth. Stir in water chestnuts. Heat. Serve over steamed rice. If desired, garnish with raisins and pineapple..

APPROXIMATE NUTRITIONAL INFORMATION PER SERVING

Total calories: 413
Total fat: 4 g
Saturated fat: 1 g
Dietary fiber: 1 g
Carbohydrates: 62 g
Protein: 30 g
Cholesterol: 57 mg
Sodium: 262 mg

Saffron Chicken

4 servings

2 teaspoons olive oil

¼ teaspoon saffron threads crushed

½ teaspoon thyme

2 whole chicken breasts, skinned, boned, and halved

Rub chicken with olive oil. In a bowl, combine oil, saffron, and thyme.

Prepare grill for direct grilling over medium-high heat. Grill chicken 6-8 minutes. Turn. Cook another 6-8 minutes, or until chicken is tender.

Serving Suggestion: Serve with Pan-steamed Asparagus (page 360), and fresh pineapple and papaya.

APPROXIMATE NUTRITIONAL INFORMATION PER SERVING

Total calories: 114
Total fat: 3 g
Saturated fat: 1 g
Dietary fiber: 0 g
Carbohydrates: 0 g
Protein: 20 g
Cholesterol: 49 mg
Sodium: 55 mg

Szechuan Chicken

6 servings

2 tablespoons olive oil

1½ pounds chicken breast, skinned and boned

1 teaspoon hot chili oil

1 teaspoon reduced-sodium soy sauce

¼ teaspoon fresh green peppercorns, ground

Juice of ½ lemon

Pinch of Kosher salt

Pinch of black pepper

In a food processor combine lemon juice, olive oil, hot chili oil, soy sauce, and peppercorns. Process until peppercorns are crushed. Pour over chicken. Marinate several hours or overnight in the refrigerator.

Prepare grill for direct grilling over medium-high heat. Grill chicken 6-8 minutes. Turn and grill 6-8 minutes more or until chicken is done.

Variation: Serve over lettuce as a salad. Garnish with sliced English cucumber. For a dressing, try Szechuan Vinaigrette (page 205.)

Serving Suggestion: Serve with Chinese Vegetables Stir-fry (page 389) and fresh pineapple and papaya.

The leftover chicken makes great sandwiches.

APPROXIMATE NUTRITIONAL INFORMATION PER SERVING

Calories: 153 g
Total fat: 4 g
Saturated fat: 1 g
Dietary fiber: 0 g
Carbohydrates: 1 g
Protein: 26 g
Cholesterol: 66 mg
Sodium: 103 mg

Teriyaki Chicken

4 servings

2 chicken breasts skinned, boned and cut into 1¼-inch cubes

¼ cup reduced-sodium soy sauce

½ cup sake

1 teaspoon granulated sugar

2 teaspoons sesame oil

1 red onion, cut into cubes

**1 yellow, red, or green pepper, cut into
cubes**

¼ pound fresh mushroom buttons

8 cherry tomatoes

1 zucchini, peeled and cut into cubes

Arrange chicken in a shallow dish. In a small bowl, combine soy sauce, sake, sugar, and sesame oil. Pour marinade over chicken and marinate 30 minutes at room temperature. Drain marinade and reserve. On skewers, alternate chicken, onion, pepper, mushrooms, tomatoes, and zucchini.

Prepare grill for direct grilling over high heat. Grill skewers 8-12 minutes, turning and basting frequently, until chicken is done and vegetables are crisp-tender.

Serving Suggestion: Serve with Sticky Rice (page 345) and Fresh Lemon Ice (page 414).

APPROXIMATE NUTRITIONAL INFORMATION PER SERVING

Total calories: 242
Total fat: 7 g
Saturated fat: 1 g
Dietary fiber: 3 g
Carbohydrates: 11 g
Protein: 30 g
Cholesterol: 73 mg
Sodium: 371 mg

Chicken and Noodles

6 servings

1 tablespoon olive oil

1 whole chicken breast, skinned, boned and cut into julienne strips

½ onion, thinly sliced

2 cups chicken broth (page 143) or commercial broth

1 tablespoon reduced sodium soy sauce

2 tablespoons cornstarch dissolved in ¼ cup cold water

3 stalks celery, cut on the diagonal into 1-inch pieces

1 red pepper, cut into julienne strips

10 fresh mushrooms, sliced

1 8-ounce can water chestnuts

1 6-ounce package buckwheat (soba) noodles, cooked and drained

In a saucepan, combine chicken broth with soy sauce; bring to a boil. Gradually add cornstarch and water mixture, stirring constantly 2-3 minutes, or until sauce thickens. Reduce heat to simmer.

Heat olive oil in a nonstick skillet or wok. Add chicken, cook 3-4 minutes. Add onions, celery; stir-fry 2-3 minutes. Add red peppers and mushrooms, stir-fry 2-3 minutes. Add water chestnuts. Remove from heat. Pour sauce over. Remove to serving bowl. Add noodles and toss.

APPROXIMATE NUTRITIONAL INFORMATION PER SERVING

Calories: 236
Total fat: 3 g
Saturated fat: 1 g
Dietary fiber: 2 g
Carbohydrates: 39 g
Protein: 14 g
Cholesterol: 19 mg
Sodium: 534 mg

Thai Chicken

8 servings

MARINADE

½ cup olive oil

1 teaspoon sesame oil

3 tablespoons reduced-sodium soy sauce

⅓ cup rice vinegar

2 green onions, chopped

1 jalapeño pepper, chopped

4 large cloves garlic, minced

2 teaspoons freshly squeezed lime juice

2 teaspoons crushed red pepper

¼ teaspoon Tabasco sauce

¼ teaspoon black pepper

¼ teaspoon Kosher salt

2 chicken breasts skinned, boned and cut into strips

½ pound fresh spinach linguine, cooked al dente

½ pound fresh regular linguine, cooked al dente

¾ pound fresh asparagus, steamed 2–3 minutes or until crisp-tender and cut diagonally into thirds

½ cup fresh cilantro, chopped (optional)

APPROXIMATE NUTRITIONAL INFORMATION PER SERVING

INCLUDING THE 4 TABLESPOONS OF MARINADE CALLED FOR IN THE RECIPE	PER ADDITIONAL TABLESPOON OF MARINADE
Total calories: 415	Total calories: 67
Total fat: 8 g	Total fat: 7 g
Saturated fat: 2 g	Saturated fat: 1 g
Dietary fiber: 6 g	Dietary fiber: trace
Carbohydrates: 580 g	Carbohydrates: 1 g
Protein: 25 g	Protein: trace
Cholesterol: 73 mg	Cholesterol: 0 mg
Sodium: 87 mg	Sodium: 149 mg

In a small saucepan, combine marinade ingredients. Place the chicken breasts in a bowl with 3 tablespoons of the marinade and marinate 20–30 minutes at room temperature.
In a nonstick pan, sauté the chicken 7 to 10 minutes or until cooked. Warm remaining marinade.

Meanwhile, arrange pasta in a large, low serving bowl; toss with 1 tablespoon warmed marinade. Spread chicken over top of pasta. Top with asparagus. Garnish with cilantro. Accompany with remaining warmed marinade.

Variation: Sprinkle with ¼ cup peanuts.

Serving Suggestion: Serve with sliced fresh peaches and apricots.

Kung Pao Chicken

4 servings

½ cup chicken broth (page 143) or commercial broth

⅓ cup reduced-sodium soy sauce

½ cup sake

2 cloves garlic, minced

1 tablespoon hot chili oil

2 chicken breasts, skinned, boned and cut into strips ¼ inch thick

1 tablespoon olive oil

2 tablespoons potato starch

2 tablespoons cold water

½ pound sugar snap peas

1 8-ounce can whole water chestnuts, drained

6 green onions, cut diagonally into 1-inch pieces

In a 2-quart saucepan, combine chicken broth, soy sauce, sake, garlic and hot chili oil. In a small bowl, dissolve 1 tablespoon of potato starch in two tablespoons cold water. Bring sauce to a boil and gradually add potato starch mixture. Stir 2-3 minutes or until sauce thickens. Simmer.

Sprinkle chicken with remaining 1 tablespoon of potato starch. In a nonstick skillet, heat olive oil. Add chicken and sauté 6-8 minutes. Add sugar snap peas; cook 2-3 minutes. Add water chestnuts and green onions. Pour sauce over and toss.

Serving Suggestion: Serve with short-grain rice and oranges, papaya, pineapple and fortune cookies.

APPROXIMATE NUTRITIONAL INFORMATION PER SERVING

Calories: 300
Total fat: 10 g
Saturated fat: 1 g
Dietary fiber: 4 g
Carbohydrates: 21 g
Protein: 25 g
Cholesterol: 60 mg
Sodium: 429 mg

Stir-Fried Chicken

4 servings

1 pound chicken breasts, skinned and boned

1 tablespoon sake

2 tablespoons potato starch

1 tablespoon olive oil

Cut chicken breasts into cubes or strips. Toss with sake. Sprinkle with potato starch. In a nonstick skillet, heat olive oil over medium heat. Add chicken and stir-fry 8–10 minutes or until done.

APPROXIMATE NUTRITIONAL INFORMATION PER SERVING

Total calories: 226
Total fat: 7 g
Saturated fat: 2 g
Dietary fiber: trace
Carbohydrates: 3 g
Protein: 35 g
Cholesterol: 96 mg
Sodium: 83 mg

Ginger Chicken

4 3½-ounce servings

2 whole skinless, boneless chicken breasts

1 celery stalk with leaves, chopped

1 small onion, chopped

1 carrot, sliced

Piece of fresh ginger, peeled

Remove skin from chicken breasts; bone if desired. Place chicken in a small stockpot; add celery, onion, carrot, and a piece of fresh ginger. Add enough cold water to cover by 2 inches; bring to a boil. Cook 10 to 20 minutes, or until chicken is tender and no sign of pink remains; do not overcook.

Note: A great way to prepare chicken for salads or for dishes with soba noodles.

APPROXIMATE NUTRITIONAL INFORMATION PER SERVING

Total calories: 181
Total fat: 4 g
Saturated fat: 1 g
Dietary fiber: 1 g
Carbohydrates: 5 g
Protein: 29 g
Cholesterol: 77 mg
Sodium: 78 mg

Percentage of calories from fat: 16%

Stir-Fried Chicken with Vegetables

6 servings

2 whole chicken breasts, skinned, boned, and cut into julienne strips

1 tablespoon olive oil

2 small bunches broccolini florets

12 fresh mushrooms, sliced

1 6½-ounce can water chestnuts, drained

½ red pepper, cut into julienne strips

½ green pepper, cut into julienne strips

¼ cup reduced-sodium soy sauce

2 tablespoons rice vinegar

Heat olive oil in a nonstick skillet or wok. Add chicken and saute 10-15 minutes or until nearly done. Reduce heat.

Add cauliflower; stir-fry 4 minutes. Add celery; stir-fry 2 minutes. Add mushrooms, water chestnuts, and peppers; stir-fry 3–4 minutes, or until all vegetables are bright in color and crisp-tender.

Combine soy sauce and vinegar in a small bowl. Pass with chicken and vegetables.

APPROXIMATE NUTRITIONAL INFORMATION PER SERVING

Total calories: 167
Total fat: 8 g
Saturated fat: 2 g
Dietary fiber: 3 g
Carbohydrates: 10 g
Protein: 22 g
Cholesterol: 36 mg
Sodium: 424 mg

Chicken with Fresh Spinach

6 servings

3 whole chicken breasts, skinned and boned

1 tablespoon ginger juice*

1 tablespoon sake

½ fresh lemon

2 cups chicken broth, preferably homemade (page 143)

¼ cup all-purpose flour

½ cup water

2 tablespoons potato starch

1 tablespoon olive oil

6 cups fresh baby spinach leaves

Cut chicken into cubes. Sprinkle with ginger juice and sake. Let stand 10 minutes.

Bring broth to a boil in a medium saucepan. Shake flour and water in a covered jar to form a smooth paste; gradually add to boiling broth, stirring constantly until thick. Reduce heat and let simmer 5 to 10 minutes. Remove to serving bowl.

Sprinkle chicken with potato starch. Heat olive oil in a wok or heavy skillet. Add chicken and stir fry 8-10 minutes.

Layer spinach onto a serving platter, squeeze lemon over spinach. Top with chicken. Accompany with sauce.

*To make ginger juice, grate a 2½ -inch piece of peeled fresh ginger and squeeze the pulp to obtain the ginger juice.

APPROXIMATE NUTRITIONAL INFORMATION PER SERVING

Total calories: 165
Total fat: 3 g
Saturated fat: 1 g
Dietary fiber: 1 g
Carbohydrates: 6 g
Protein: 27 g
Cholesterol: 66 mg
Sodium: 351 mg

Poached Chicken

4 servings

4 cups chicken broth (page 143)

2 whole chicken breasts, skinned, boned, and halved

In a saucepan, bring stock to a boil; add chicken breasts and bring to a second boil. Reduce heat to medium; cook 20 minutes, or until chicken is done. Remove chicken and reserve stock for later use. If chicken is to be used for sandwiches, cool 10 minutes and tear into strings or slice diagonally across top.

Variation: Substitute turkey breasts for chicken breasts.

Serving Suggestion: Chicken poached in stock is excellent for sandwiches, salads, and stir-fries, as well as for an entrée.

APPROXIMATE NUTRITIONAL INFORMATION PER SERVING

Total calories: 121
Total fat: 2 g
Saturated fat: 0 g
Dietary fiber: 0 g
Carbohydrates: 0 g
Protein: 21 g
Cholesterol: 51 mg
Sodium: 330 mg

Hot and Spicy Southwest Turkey

9 servings

1 2-pound fresh turkey breast, bone in, skin on

1 cup Hot Chili Sauce (page 215)

½ cup Chili Salsa (page 216)

Roast turkey on a rack in a 350°F. oven for 15-20 minutes; baste with ½ cup Hot Chili Sauce. Cook 35-40 minutes more or until turkey is cooked, basting frequently
(meat thermometer should read 180°). In a small saucepan, combine remaining ½ cup Chili Sauce with Chili Salsa and heat. Pass the sauce with the turkey.

Note: The leftovers make great sandwiches.

Serving Suggestion: Serve with Rice with Chilies (page 347). Refried Black Beans (page 343), warm tortillas, and fresh strawberries or seasonal fruit.

APPROXIMATE NUTRITIONAL INFORMATION PER SERVING

Total calories: 140
Total fat: 1 g
Saturated fat: trace
Dietary fiber: trace
Carbohydrates: 4 g
Protein: 27 g
Cholesterol: 74 mg
Sodium: 264 mg

Chicken Spring Rolls

12 servings

2 cups chicken broth (page 143)

1 pound skinless, boneless chicken or turkey breast

1 package spring roll wrappers, thawed

1 head Bibb lettuce, shredded

6 green onions, cut lengthwise into strings

½ cup hot Chinese mustard

2 tablespoons toasted sesame seeds

¼ cup reduced-sodium soy sauce

2 tablespoons rice vinegar

In a large pot, bring broth and chicken to a boil. Reduce heat to medium. Cook 20 minutes, or until chicken is done. Remove chicken. Reserve stock for soup. Let chicken cool 10 minutes; tear into strings.

In a covered bamboo steamer basket or a vegetable steamer basket over boiling water, steam the wrappers 5–7 minutes, or until wrappers are hot. Remove from basket.

Lay wrappers flat. Mound some chicken, some lettuce, and some green onion in center of each wrapper. Fold bottom edge up, top edge down, and left and right sides over (work quickly so wrappers are still hot when served).

Mound Chinese mustard and sesame seeds in center of serving tray. Ring with Chicken Spring Rolls. In a small bowl, combine soy sauce and vinegar; pass with Spring Rolls.

Serving Suggestion: Serve with Sticky Rice (page 345) and fresh seasonal fruit. Also good as an appetizer.

APPROXIMATE NUTRITIONAL INFORMATION PER SERVING

Total calories: 200
Total fat: trace
Saturated fat: 0 g
Dietary fiber: 0 g
Carbohydrates: 20 g
Protein: 26 g
Cholesterol: 60 mg
Sodium: 270 mg

* The dipping sauces are very high in sodium, so use sparingly. (one tablespoon of light soy sauce has 575 mg of sodium.)

Chicken Fajitas

4 servings

MARINADE

¼ cup fresh lime juice

¼ cup reduced-sodium soy sauce

3 tablespoons olive oil

2 whole chicken breasts, skinned, boned and cut into thin strips

1 medium sweet onion, cut into thin wedges

1 medium green pepper, seeded and cut into thin strips

1 yellow pepper, seeded and cut into thin strips

1 medium red pepper, seeded and cut into thin strips

4 6-inch flour or corn tortillas, warmed

½ cup commercial or homemade tomato salsa (page 238)

Prepare marinade by combining lime juice, soy sauce, and 2 tablespoons olive oil. Pour marinade over chicken and marinate in the refrigerator 1–2 hours, turning once or twice.

Prepare grill for direct grilling over medium-high heat. Grill breasts for 5-7 minutes each side, or until well done.

Meanwhile, in a wok or heavy skillet, heat remaining 1 tablespoon of olive oil. Add onion and stir-fry 2–3 minutes. Add peppers and stir-fry 2–3 minutes. Toss with chicken and tomatoes, and serve immediately on a hot platter. Garnish with tomato salsa. Serve with warm tortillas.

Note: To warm tortillas in a microwave, place tortillas between 2 slightly dampened paper towels. Microwave on high 1–2 minutes or until warm; keep wrapped until ready to serve.

Serving Suggestion: Serve with steamed rice, Refried Black Beans (page 371), and fresh berries and melons.

Accompany with salsa. Homemade has just 45 mg of sodium per tablespoon. The same amount of commercial salsa has 135 mg.

APPROXIMATE NUTRITIONAL INFORMATION PER SERVING WITHOUT SALSA

Total calories: 252
Total fat: 7 g
Saturated fat: 2 g
Dietary fiber: 3 g
Carbohydrates: 29 g
Protein: 19 g
Cholesterol: 45 mg
Sodium: 617 mg

Grilled Chicken with Salsa

4 servings

1 tablespoon olive oil

Juice of 1 large lime (about ⅓ cup)

2 whole chicken breasts, skinned, boned, and halved

1 cup commercial or homemade tomato salsa

In a medium bowl, pour lime juice over chicken and marinate at room temperature 1 hour, turning to coat. Drain off marinade. Rub chicken with olive oil.

Prepare grill for direct grilling over medium-high heat. Grill chicken 6-8 minutes on each side or until done. Place chicken on serving plates and drizzle salsa over top.

Serving Suggestion: Serve with Romaine Salad (page 158) and Black Beans and Rice (page 343).

APPROXIMATE NUTRITIONAL INFORMATION PER SERVING

Total calories: 167
Total fat: 5 g
Saturated fat: trace
Dietary fiber: 0 g
Carbohydrates: 6 g
Protein: 27 g
Cholesterol: 73 mg
Sodium: 285 mg

Spicy Barbecued Chicken

4 servings; sauce makes 2 ½ cups (enough for 3 pounds of chicken)

1 pound chicken breasts, skinned and boned

1 tablespoon olive oil

1 bunch fresh cilantro

Pinch Kosher salt

Pinch black pepper

SAUCE

1 15-ounce can tomato sauce

2 teaspoons olive oil

1 tablespoon chili powder

1 teaspoon paprika

1 tablespoon Worcestershire sauce

1 teaspoon crushed red pepper

¼ teaspoon Kosher salt

2 tablespoons cider vinegar

½ teaspoon black pepper

2 cloves garlic, minced

¾ teaspoon prepared mustard

3 tablespoons onion, finely minced

Your family and guests will rave about this barbecue sauce. Double the chicken and use the leftovers for BBQ chicken sandwiches in pita pockets.

In a jar with a cover, combine all sauce ingredients. Refrigerate until ready to use. Sauce may be used at once, but the best flavors are achieved if it sits for a day or two.

Rub chicken with olive oil. Prepare grill for direct grilling over medium-high heat. Place chicken on the grill, baste with sauce, and cook 6-8 minutes. Turn, baste with sauce, and grill 6-8 minutes longer or until chicken is done. Baste generously with sauce during last few minutes of cooking. Season with pinch of salt and pepper to taste. Serve on bed of cilantro.

APPROXIMATE NUTRITIONAL INFORMATION PER SERVING WITH ⅔ CUP OF SAUCE

Calories: 210
Total fat: 5 g
Saturated fat: 1 g
Dietary fiber: trace
Carbohydrates: 4 g
Protein: 36 g
Cholesterol: 96 mg
Sodium: 341 mg

Grilled Herbed Chicken

4 servings

2 tablespoons extra-virgin olive oil

1 tablespoon fresh lemon juice

1 tablespoon minced fresh thyme

½ tablespoon minced fresh rosemary

¾ teaspoon Kosher salt

½ teaspoon pepper

2 whole skinned and boned chicken breasts

Pinch Kosher salt

Pinch black pepper

Cooking with fresh herbs makes such a difference! Try this recipe on your family and enjoy the compliments.

In an 8 x 8 x 2-inch casserole, combine olive oil, lemon juice, thyme, rosemary, salt, and pepper. Add chicken breasts and turn chicken over in the marinade so both sides are coated. Marinate 10 minutes.

Prepare grill for direct grilling over medium-high heat. Grill chicken breasts about 6-8 minutes on each side, or until chicken is cooked. When chicken is done, it will feel firm to the touch but not hard. Season with pinch of salt and pepper to taste.

APPROXIMATE NUTRITIONAL INFORMATION PER SERVING

Total calories: 184
Total fat: 8 g
Saturated fat: 1 g
Dietary fiber: 0 g
Carbohydrates: 1 g
Protein: 27 g
Cholesterol: 73 mg
Sodium: 252 mg

Grilled Chicken with Fresh Lime

6 servings

3 skinless, boneless chicken breasts

¼ cup fresh lime juice

¼ cup fresh lemon juice

2 tablespoons olive oil

3 cloves minced garlic

Pinch Kosher salt

Pinch freshly ground black pepper

Combine lime juice, lemon juice, olive oil, and garlic. Pour over chicken. Marinate several hours or overnight in the refrigerator.

Prepare grill for direct grilling over medium-high heat. Grill chicken about 6-8 minutes. Turn. Grill another 6-8 minutes. Baste with marinade frequently. Season with pinch of salt and pinch of pepper to taste.

APPROXIMATE NUTRITIONAL INFORMATION PER SERVING

Total calories: 161
Total fat: 5 g
Saturated fat: 2 g
Dietary fiber: 0 g
Carbohydrates: 2 g
Protein: 27 g
Cholesterol: 73 mg
Sodium: 63 mg

Grilled Chicken Italian Style

6 servings

1 cup Italian Vinaigrette (page 204)

2 tablespoons Dijon mustard

¼ cup dry white wine

3 6-ounce whole skinless, boneless chicken breasts

½ pound fresh mushrooms

2 red, green, or yellow sweet peppers, seeded and quartered

2 onions, quartered

2 tomatoes, halved

pinch Kosher salt

pinch fresh ground black pepper

Combine vinaigrette, mustard and wine. Arrange chicken in a bowl; arrange vegetables in a separate bowl. Pour half the marinade over the chicken and half over the vegetables. Marinate each 2 hours or overnight in the refrigerator. Remove chicken and vegetables from marinade. Pat dry with paper towels to remove most of the marinade.

Prepare grill for direct grilling over medium-high heat. Grill chicken for 6-8 minutes. Alternate mushrooms, onions, and tomatoes on 6-inch skewers and place on grill. Turn chicken and cook another 6-8 minutes. Rotate vegetable skewers. Baste chicken and vegetables frequently with marinade during cooking. Cook until chicken is tender and vegetables are hot. Season with pinch of Kosher salt and pinch of black pepper.

APPROXIMATE NUTRITIONAL INFORMATION PER SERVING

Calories: 140
Total fat: 2 g
Saturated fat: 0 g
Dietary fiber: 2 g
Carbohydrates: 10 g
Protein: 17 g
Cholesterol: 45 mg
Sodium: 210 mg

Chicken Skewers

6 servings

3 whole chicken breasts, skinned and boned

2 tablespoons olive oil

¼ cup fresh lemon juice

1 teaspoon honey

Dash of tarragon

Dash of oregano

12 cherry tomatoes

12 fresh mushrooms

2 onions, cut into 2-inch cubes

2 red, yellow, or green peppers, seeded and quartered

½ fresh pineapple, cut into chunks

Cut chicken into 2-inch cubes. Combine olive oil, lemon juice, honey, tarragon, and oregano. Pour marinade over chicken and vegetables. Marinate 20 to 30 minutes.

Alternate chicken, vegetables, and fruit on skewers. Prepare grill for direct grilling over medium-high heat. Grill skewers, turning and basting frequently, for 15-20 minutes, or until chicken is done to desired doneness.

APPROXIMATE NUTRITIONAL INFORMATION PER SERVING

Total calories: 213
Total fat: 5 g
Saturated fat: 1 g
Dietary fiber: 2 g
Carbohydrates: 15 g
Protein: 28 g
Cholesterol: 73 mg
Sodium: 69 mg

Grilled Chicken Burgers

4 servings

2 tablespoons fresh lemon juice

2 tablespoons olive oil

Pinch Kosher salt

Pinch freshly ground pepper

2 whole boneless, skinless chicken breasts

4 very fresh sesame hamburger buns

1 large ripe tomato, sliced

4 thin slices white onion

4 Bibb lettuce leaves

2 tablespoons Dijon mustard and/ or lemon mayonnaise (below)

LEMON MAYONNAISE

2 tablespoons regular mayonnaise

¾ teaspoon fresh lemon juice

½ teaspoon grated lemon zest

In a bowl, combine lemon juice, olive oil, and pepper. Pour over chicken. Marinate 15 to 20 minutes at room temperature, turning occasionally to coat.

Grill chicken for 8 to 10 minutes on each side. Just before removing chicken from grill, arrange buns over top of chicken to warm.

To Assemble: Place chicken, tomato, onion, and lettuce on bottom half of bun. Spread top half with Dijon mustard and/or combined lemon mayonnaise ingredients.

Two teaspoons of lemon mayonnaise adds 60 calories and 6 grams of fat. Two teaspoons of light mayonnaise adds 23 calories and 1 gram of fat.

APPROXIMATE NUTRITIONAL INFORMATION PER SERVING USING MUSTARD

Total calories: 310
Total fat: 8 g
Saturated fat: 2 g
Dietary fiber: 1 g
Carbohydrates: 26 g
Protein: 31 g
Cholesterol: 73 mg
Sodium: 407 mg

Easy Chicken

4 servings

1 15-ounce can chicken broth or 2 cups homemade (page 143)

2 cups water

1 pound chicken breasts, skinned and boned, or chicken tenderloins

This chicken is excellent for sandwiches and salads, as well as for an entrée dish. Double the recipe and serve part as a dinner entrée one night and the rest for lunch-box sandwiches the following day.

In a 1½ -quart saucepan, bring chicken broth and water to a boil. Add chicken and bring to a second boil. Reduce heat to medium and cook 20 minutes, or until chicken is done. Remove chicken and reserve stock for later use.

If chicken is to be used for sandwiches, cool 10 minutes and tear into strings or slice diagonally across top.

Variation: For Asian Garlic Chicken, combine 3 tablespoons rice wine vinegar, 1 tablespoon extra-virgin olive oil, 1 tablespoon reduced-sodium soy sauce, and 2 finely minced garlic cloves in a small bowl. Pass with prepared Easy Chicken. Serve with Sticky Rice (page 345) and Stir-Fried Vegetables (page 389).

APPROXIMATE NUTRITIONAL INFORMATION PER SERVING OF EASY CHICKEN

Total calories: 157
Total fat: 4 g
Saturated fat: 1 g
Dietary fiber: 0 g
Carbohydrates: 0 g
Protein: 28 g
Cholesterol: 73 mg
Sodium: 178 mg

APPROXIMATE NUTRITIONAL INFORMATION PER SERVING OF ASIAN GARLIC CHICKEN

Total calories: 192
Total fat: 8 g
Saturated fat: 2 g
Dietary fiber: 0 g
Carbohydrates: 0 g
Protein: 28 g
Cholesterol: 73 mg
Sodium: 328 mg

Quick Microwave Chicken

4 3-ounce servings

2 whole chicken breasts, skinned, boned, and halved.

Place chicken in a glass pie plate, placing larger pieces to the outside of dish. Cover with microwave-safe, chlorine free premium plastic wrap; prick a hole in the plastic for steam to escape. Cook at full power for 8 minutes; turn. Rearrange pieces in dish; cook 6 minutes longer, or until done.

APPROXIMATE NUTRITIONAL INFORMATION PER SERVING

Total calories: 142
Total fat: 3 g
Saturated fat: 1 g
Dietary fiber: 0 g
Carbohydrates: 0 g
Protein: 27 g
Cholesterol: 73 mg
Sodium: 63 mg

Extra-Crispy Oven-Fried Chicken

4 3-ounce servings

2 whole chicken breasts, halved

½ cup nonfat milk

1 egg lightly beaten

½ cup Grape-Nuts flakes

Remove skin from chicken, bone if desired. Dip chicken in egg, then milk, then in Grape-Nuts flakes. Bake in a nonstick pan at 400°F. for 20 minutes. Reduce heat to 350° F. Cover loosely with foil. Bake 20 to 25 minutes longer or until chicken is cooked. Do not turn chicken during baking.

APPROXIMATE NUTRITIONAL INFORMATION PER SERVING

Total calories: 203
Total fat: 3 g
Saturated fat: 1 g
Dietary fiber: 0 g
Carbohydrates: 13 g
Protein: 29 g
Cholesterol: 83 mg
Sodium: 177 mg

Chicken Parmesan

4 servings

1 cup oyster crackers or saltines

¼ cup freshly grated Parmesan cheese

2 tablespoons finely chopped Italian parsley

1 tablespoon fresh thyme leaves or ½ teaspoon ground thyme

1 tablespoon fresh basil leaves or ½ teaspoon dried basil

½ teaspoon dried oregano

½ teaspoon paprika

½ teaspoon Kosher salt

½ teaspoon black pepper

2 whole skinned and boned chicken breasts, halved

1 tablespoon olive oil

½ cup low-fat (1%) buttermilk

Try this homemade version of Shake-and-Bake Chicken. You'll love the taste.

Put the oyster crackers in a gallon or jumbo-size zip-lock plastic bag and crush them with your hands or a rolling pin. Add Parmesan cheese and seasonings. Shake the bag to combine the ingredients.

Brush chicken with olive oil, dip in buttermilk, and place in the plastic bag; shake bag until chicken pieces are evenly coated with seasonings. Put chicken in a nonstick pan and bake at 400°F. for 20 minutes. Reduce heat to 350°F. and bake 10 minutes longer, or until chicken is tender.

APPROXIMATE NUTRITIONAL INFORMATION PER SERVING

Total calories: 280
Total fat: 9 g
Saturated fat: 2 g
Dietary fiber: 0 g
Carbohydrates: 11 g
Protein: 31 g
Cholesterol: 78 mg
Sodium: 595 mg

Chicken with Tomatoes and Parmesan

4 servings

2 chicken breasts, skinned and boned

1 tablespoon olive oil

Pinch paprika

Pinch powdered rosemary

⅓ cup dry white wine

1 tablespoon fresh lemon juice

1 cup chicken broth (page 143) or canned broth

¼ teaspoon salt

1 tablespoon arrowroot

3 tablespoons cold water

1 14-ounce can water-packed artichoke hearts, drained

½ cup sliced fresh mushrooms

1 large ripe tomato, cut into 1-inch chunks

¼ cup freshly grated Parmesan cheese

Rub chicken with olive oil, paprika, and rosemary. Arrange chicken in a single layer in an 8 x 8-inch ovenproof baking dish. Bake at 375°F 30 minutes or until chicken is cooked.

Meanwhile, in a 2-quart saucepan, combine wine, lemon juice, chicken broth, salt and bring to a boil. Reduce heat and simmer. When chicken is nearly cooked, bring mixture back to boiling. Combine arrowroot with cold water. Pour into broth; cook, stirring constantly, 2–3 minutes or until mixture thickens. Add artichokes and mushrooms.

Add tomatoes to chicken. Pour sauce over chicken and tomatoes. Sprinkle with cheese.

Serving Suggestion: Serve with tiny red potatoes, fresh green beans and, for dessert, Strawberry-Rhubarb Shortcake (page 395).

APPROXIMATE NUTRITIONAL INFORMATION PER SERVING

Total calories: 285
Total fat: 6 g
Saturated fat: 2 g
Dietary fiber: 2 g
Carbohydrates: 20 g
Protein: 35 g
Cholesterol: 78 mg
Sodium: 532 mg

Roast Chicken with Rosemary

4 servings

1 roasting chicken, about 3–4 pounds

Kosher salt

powdered rosemary

black pepper

1 large yellow onion, quartered

3 cloves garlic

1 tablespoon olive oil

Wipe inside of chicken with a damp paper towel; wash outside with cold water. Rub outside of bird and inside cavity with generous amounts of rosemary, salt, and black pepper. Put onions and garlic inside cavity. Skewer neck skin to back; tuck wing tips behind shoulder joints. Place chicken breast side up in a shallow roasting pan. Roast at 375°F. 60–75 minutes. Let stand 10 minutes before slicing.

APPROXIMATE NUTRITIONAL INFORMATION PER SERVING

Total calories: 315
Total fat: 13 g
Saturated fat: 2 g
Dietary fiber: 0 g
Carbohydrates: 4 g
Protein: 41 g
Cholesterol: 123 mg
Sodium: 124 mg

Roast Chicken Asian Style

12 servings

1 bunch leaf lettuce

1 roast chicken, thinly sliced (p. 335)

1 bunch green onions with tops

2 tablespoons rice wine vinegar

¼ cup reduced-sodium soy sauce

2 to 3 drops of hot chili oil

12 spring roll (lumpia) wrappers

¼ cup hot Chinese mustard

¼ cup toasted sesame seeds

Tear lettuce into bite-size pieces; arrange on a platter or tray. Layer chicken over lettuce. Slice green onions lengthwise and into 2-inch strips; arrange around edge of lettuce.

Combine rice wine vinegar, soy sauce, and hot chili oil in a small bowl; set aside.

Wrap spring roll wrappers in a damp paper towel, and steam 1 to 2 minutes in the microwave or warm in a tortilla warmer. Remove to a napkin-lined basket.

Everyone prepares his own: Lay each spring roll wrapper flat. Place a slice of chicken, some lettuce, and green onion lengthwise in center of each wrapper. Fold bottom edge up, left and right sides over, and roll as for crêpes.

Dip in hot Chinese mustard and sesame seeds and/or soy sauce and rice vinegar.

APPROXIMATE NUTRITIONAL INFORMATION PER SERVING

Total calories: 136
Total fat: 5 g
Saturated fat: 1 g
Dietary fiber: 1 g
Carbohydrates: 12 g
Protein: 13 g
Cholesterol: 30 mg
Sodium: 107 mg

Roasted Chicken with Garlic

6 servings

1 ½ teaspoons olive oil

3 whole skinned chicken breasts, halved (bone in)

40 garlic cloves (about 4 heads), unpeeled

1 ¼ cups dry white wine

1 tablespoon chopped fresh rosemary

1 tablespoon chopped fresh thyme

¼ cup fresh Italian flat-leaf parsley, chopped

salt and pepper to taste

6 1/4-inch-thick slices Tuscan-style bread

Double this recipe and use the leftovers for sandwiches. Encourage your family to enjoy every bit of flavor in this dish by dipping Tuscan bread in the sauce.

In a nonstick skillet, heat the oil. Add chicken and cook over medium-high heat 4 to 5 minutes. Turn chicken, add garlic, and cook 4 to 5 minutes longer, or until garlic cloves begin to brown. Transfer chicken and garlic to an ovenproof baking dish and set aside.

Pour the wine into the skillet to deglaze the pan; add rosemary and thyme and pour mixture over chicken. Cover tightly with foil. Bake at 350°F. for 30 minutes, or until chicken is done. Sprinkle with parsley. Season with salt and pepper; set aside.

Under a preheated broiler, toast the Tuscan bread slices until bread is golden-brown on each side. Pass bread for dipping with chicken.

APPROXIMATE NUTRITIONAL INFORMATION PER SERVING

Total calories: 315
Total fat: 5 g
Saturated fat: 1 g
Dietary fiber: 0 g
Carbohydrates: 27 g
Protein: 31 g
Cholesterol: 73 mg
Sodium: 338 mg

Roasted Turkey

Approximately 15 3-ounce servings

8 to 10-pound fresh turkey

fresh or ground sage to taste

**Kosher salt and black pepper
to taste**

3 celery stalks, cut into 2-inch pieces

2 onions, quartered

ROASTING CHART

WEIGHT	TIME
6-8 pounds	2¾ to 3½ hours
8-12 pounds	3¼ to 4 hours
12-16 pounds	3¾ to 5 hours
16-20 pounds	4¾ to 6½ hours
20-24 pounds	6¼ to 8 hours

ROASTING CHART FOR HALVES AND QUARTERS

WEIGHT	TIME
5-8 pounds	2½ to 3 hours
8-10 pounds	3 to 3½ hours
10-12 pounds	3½ to 4 hours

You can save fat and calories by choosing to eat white meat without skin instead of dark meat with skin. Save the dark meat and the skin for the soup pot.

Rinse inside and outside of turkey with cold water. Rub inside cavity with seasonings. Place celery and onions inside cavity. Skewer neck skin to back; tuck wing tips behind shoulder joints.

In a roasting pan, place turkey breast side up on a rack; roast at 325°F. Turkey is done when drumsticks move easily or twist out of joint. A meat thermometer should register 185°F. If turkey browns too quickly, cover it with a cap of aluminum foil. Remove skin before slicing.

Note: To be heart-healthy, the turkey should not be stuffed, as the fat from the turkey will drip into the dressing. Try Bread Stuffing (page 58).

To roast a half- or quarter-turkey: Season as for roast turkey. Place skin side up in a shallow roasting pan. Insert a meat thermometer so tip is in the thickest part of the thigh muscle or breast meat and does not touch bone.

APPROXIMATE NUTRITIONAL INFORMATION PER SERVING

Total calories: 143
Total fat: 4 g
Saturated fat: 1 g
Dietary fiber: 0 g
Carbohydrates: 0 g
Protein: 25 g
Cholesterol: 64 mg
Sodium: 59 mg

Roasted Herbed Turkey Breast

8 servings

3 pounds fresh turkey breast

1 tablespoon olive oil

1 tablespoon fresh rosemary

1 tablespoon chopped fresh sage

Kosher salt

black pepper

Pinch paprika

Serve this dish as an entrée. Use any leftover turkey for lunch-box sandwiches the rest of the week.

Rub breast on both sides with olive-oil. Rub turkey with rosemary, sage, salt, pepper, and a pinch of paprika for color. Position turkey breast on a rack in a roasting pan. Roast at 325°F. for 1-1½ hours, or until juices have no trace of pink; a meat thermometer should register 170°F.

APPROXIMATE NUTRITIONAL INFORMATION PER SERVING

Total calories: 196
Total fat: 2 g
Saturated fat: 0 g
Dietary fiber: 0 g
Carbohydrates: 0 g
Protein: 39 g
Cholesterol: 110 mg
Sodium: 68 mg

Turkey Meat Loaf

8 servings

⅓ cup barley

2 8-ounce cans tomato sauce

½ cup water

2 tablespoons dry mustard

3 tablespoons cider vinegar

¾ pound ground turkey breast

⅓ cup chopped sweet onion

1 egg

4 cloves garlic, finely minced

¼ teaspoon black pepper

In 1 cup of water, soak the barley overnight. Drain.

In a small bowl, combine tomato sauce, water, mustard, and vinegar. Set aside. Combine barley, ground turkey, onions, egg, garlic, pepper, and ½ cup of the sauce. Mix thoroughly. Arrange in a nonstick loaf pan. Pour an additional ½ cup sauce over top. Bake at 325°F. 1 hour. Serve with remaining sauce.

Note: It is not essential to soak the barley overnight, but it will be more tender if you do.

Serving Suggestion: Excellent for hot or cold sandwiches.

Add 6 calories for each additional tablespoon of sauce.

APPROXIMATE NUTRITIONAL INFORMATION PER SERVING

Total calories: 128
Total fat: 2 g
Saturated fat: 0 g
Dietary fiber: 2 g
Carbohydrates: 13 g
Protein: 16 g
Cholesterol: 62 mg
Sodium: 401 mg

Add 6 calories for each additional tablespoon of sauce.

Enchilada Casserole

8 servings

ENCHILADA SAUCE

1 8-ounce can tomato sauce

1 teaspoon ground cumin

¼ teaspoon chili powder

¼ teaspoon Koshersalt

½ teaspoon black pepper

SALSA

1 14-ounce can Italian plum tomatoes, diced

1 4-ounce can diced green chilies

⅛ teaspoon cayenne pepper

¼ teaspoon Kosher salt

1 teaspoon ground cumin

2 chicken breasts, skinned and boned

2 cups chicken broth (page 143) or canned broth

½ teaspoon olive oil or canola oil

¼ cup onion, chopped

½ teaspoon ground cumin

½ teaspoon chili powder

½ cup canned mushroom stems and pieces, drained

2 tablespoons diced green chilies

¾ cup freshly grated low-fat Cheddar cheese

¾ cup freshly grated part-skim mozzarella cheese

3 8-inch flour tortillas

In a covered jar, combine all enchilada sauce ingredients. Set aside.

In a bowl, combine all salsa ingredients. Set aside.

In a 2-quart saucepan, bring chicken and chicken broth to a boil. Reduce heat and simmer 20 minutes or until chicken is done. Remove chicken from broth. Dice.

In a nonstick skillet, heat olive oil. Add onion and sauté until onion is tender.

Toss chicken with onion. Sprinkle with cumin and chili powder. Toss with mushrooms and green chilies. Combine Cheddar and mozzarella cheese.

Cover the bottom of a nonstick 9-inch round cake pan with some of the enchilada sauce. Place one of the tortillas over the sauce. Top with half the salsa, half the chicken mixture, and a third of the cheese.

Top with a second tortilla, some enchilada sauce, remainder of salsa, chicken, and a third more cheese. Top with final tortilla. Pour remaining enchilada sauce over top and sprinkle with remaining cheese. Bake at 350°F. 40–45 minutes.

Serving Suggestion: Serve with Vegetable and Black Bean Antipasto (page 101), Sticky Rice (page 376) and orange or lemon sherbet with mangos and papayas.

APPROXIMATE NUTRITIONAL INFORMATION PER SERVING

Total calories: 204
Total fat: 6 g
Saturated fat: 3 g
Dietary fiber: 1 g
Carbohydrates: 14 g
Protein: 22 g
Cholesterol: 49 mg
Sodium: 587 mg

Meat

Grilled Veal with Mustard Sauce

4 servings

4 very thin veal scallops*

1 tablespoon Dijon Vinaigrette (page 207)

Prepare grill for direct grilling over medium-high heat. Grill veal 3-4 minutes on each side. Brush with vinaigrette during the last minute of cooking.

*The fat content of veal differs markedly with the cut. We recommend veal scallops cut from the rump roast, which is 13% fat. By comparison, veal cutlets are 48% fat and rib roast is 58% fat.

APPROXIMATE NUTRITIONAL INFORMATION PER SERVING

Total calories: 132
Total fat: 4 g
Saturated fat: 1 g
Dietary fiber: 0 g
Carbohydrates: 0 g
Protein: 23 g
Cholesterol: 91 mg
Sodium: 103 mg

Grilled Veal Tenderloins

4 servings

2 tablespoons olive oil

4 cloves garlic, crushed

¼ teaspoon Kosher salt

⅛ teaspoon black pepper

1 pound veal tenderloins

Combine olive oil, garlic, salt and pepper. Rub onto veal.

Prepare grill for direct grilling over medium-high heat. Grill tenderloins 5–6 minutes, turning once, or to desired doneness.

Serving Suggestion: Serve with Roast Potatoes with Rosemary (page 378), Asparagus with Lemon Vinaigrette (page 360) and fresh seasonal fruits.

APPROXIMATE NUTRITIONAL INFORMATION PER SERVING

Total calories: 189
Total fat: 7 g
Saturated fat: 5 g
Dietary fiber: trace
Carbohydrates: 1 g
Protein: 30 g
Cholesterol: 76 mg
Sodium: 195 mg

Grilled Veal with Tomatoes and Artichokes

4 servings

1 pound veal chops

1½ tablespoons olive oil

2 tablespoons fresh lemon juice

½ red onion

1 carrot diced

1 stalk celery, diced

1 16-ounce can plum tomatoes, diced

1 tablespoon fresh basil leaves

½ teaspoon kosher salt

¼ teaspoon black pepper

⅓ pound fresh mushrooms, sliced

1 8-ounce can artichoke hearts, quartered

½ fresh lime, cut into quarters

Arrange veal chops in a shallow dish. Combine ½ tablespoon olive oil with lemon juice. Pour over veal. Marinate in refrigerator 2 hours.

In a nonstick skillet, heat remaining tablespoon olive oil. Saute onions 2-3 minutes. Add carrots and celery. Saute 5-6 minutes longer or until vegetables are barely tender. Add diced tomatoes, salt, pepper, basil and mushrooms. Simmer 15-20 minutes. Add artichoke hearts and cook 5-10 minutes. Set aside tomato sauce.

Prepare grill for direct grilling over medium-high heat. Grill veal chops 6-8 minutes on each side. Remove to shallow serving dish. Squeeze lime juice over chops. Serve tomato sauce on the side

Serving Suggestion: Serve with a heavy-type pasta such as penne or rigatoni.

APPROXIMATE NUTRITIONAL INFORMATION PER SERVING

Total calories: 255
Total fat: 11 g
Saturated fat: 4 g
Dietary fiber: 3 g
Carbohydrates: 13 g
Protein: 25 g
Cholesterol: 90 mg
Sodium: 644 mg

Grilled Veal Burgers

4 servings

1 pound extra-lean ground veal

4 French rolls

1 sliced white onion

8 red lettuce leaves

1 sliced tomato

Press ground veal into 4 patties. Prepare grill for direct grilling over high heat. Grill patties for 4 to 6 minutes on each side. Turn when juices begin to form on top of meat. Place patties on French rolls with onion, lettuce, and tomato. Serve.

APPROXIMATE NUTRITIONAL INFORMATION PER SERVING

Total calories: 329
Total fat: 9 g
Saturated fat: 3 g
Dietary fiber: 2 g
Carbohydrates: 33 g
Protein: 27 g
Cholesterol: 88 mg
Sodium: 386 mg

Grilled Veal Steaks with Fresh Lemon and Mushrooms

4 servings

1 pound veal round steaks, pounded very thin

1 teaspoon olive oil

½ cup dry white wine

1 tablespoon fresh lemon juice

1 pound fresh mushrooms, thinly sliced

1 14-ounce can water-packed artichoke hearts, quartered

2 lemons, cut into quarters

Prepare the grill for direct grilling over medium-high heat. Grill veal for 5-7 minutes. Turn when juices begin to form on top of meat; cook 3 to 4 minutes longer, or to desired doneness.

While meat is cooking, combine olive oil, wine, and lemon juice; pour half of the mixture into a skillet and heat. Add mushrooms and sauté; add artichokes during the last few minutes of cooking. Remove mushrooms and artichokes to a platter; cover to keep warm. Quickly heat remaining sauce. Garnish veal with mushrooms and artichokes, squeeze lemon over; drizzle with wine sauce.

APPROXIMATE NUTRITIONAL INFORMATION PER SERVING

Total calories: 223
Total fat: 5 g
Saturated fat: 1 g
Dietary fiber: 2 g
Carbohydrates: 16 g
Protein: 29 g
Cholesterol: 88 mg
Sodium: 93 mg

Veal Chops with Lemon and Pepper

4 servings

4 small veal chops

1½ tablespoons olive oil

1½ tablespoons fresh lemon juice

1 tablespoon chopped fresh flat- leaf parsley

½ fresh lemon, cut into wedges

3 cloves garlic, minced

1 tablespoon fresh rosemary

Arrange veal chops in a shallow dish. Combine olive oil, lemon juice, garlic, rosemary, and parsley. Pour over veal. Marinate 2 hours.

Prepare the grill for direct grilling over medium-high heat. Grill for 5-7 minutes per side or untill nicely charred.

Serving Suggestion: Serve with Quinoa with Tomatoes and Parsley (page 351).

APPROXIMATE NUTRITIONAL INFORMATION PER SERVING

Total calories: 200
Total fat: 11 g
Saturated fat: 4 g
Dietary fiber: 1 g
Carbohydrates: 2 g
Protein: 22 g
Cholesterol: 110 mg
Sodium: 97 mg

Veal Piccata

4 servings

1 tablespoon olive oil

¾ pound veal scallops, very thinly sliced

juice of 1 lemon

¼ cup dry white wine

½ lemon, thinly sliced

black pepper

In a nonstick skillet, heat oil. Add veal and sauté 5–6 minutes. Turn. Add lemon juice. Cook 2–3 minutes, or to desired doneness. Remove veal to heated plates. Add wine to the skillet and deglaze over high heat, stirring constantly. Pour wine over veal. Top each scallop with a slice of lemon. Sprinkle with black pepper.

APPROXIMATE NUTRITIONAL INFORMATION PER SERVING

Total calories: 158
Total fat: 8 g
Saturated fat: 3 g
Dietary fiber: 1 g
Carbohydrates: 2 g
Protein: 16 g
Cholesterol: 67 mg
Sodium: 74 mg

Veal Italian-Style

4 servings

2 large tomatoes, preferably heirloom, diced

1 tablespoon extra-virgin olive oil

2 garlic cloves, finely minced

1 teaspoon fresh oregano leaves or ⅛ teaspoon dried

2 tablespoons fresh basil leaves or ¼ teaspoon dried

Kosher salt and coarsely ground pepper to taste

1 pound veal, sliced very thin and pounded extra-thin

2 ounces very thinly sliced part-skim mozzarella cheese

Prepare the grill for direct grilling over medium-high heat.

In a saucepan, combine tomatoes, olive oil, garlic, oregano and basil. Heat just to boiling (do not allow to boil). Remove from heat, add salt and pepper and adjust seasonings. Cover to keep warm.

Grill veal for 5-7 minutes total. Turn when juices begin to form on top of meat. Cover with cheese; grill until cheese melts and veal is done. Top with sauce.

APPROXIMATE NUTRITIONAL INFORMATION PER SERVING

Total calories: 235
Total fat: 10 g
Saturated fat: 4 g
Dietary fiber: 1 g
Carbohydrates: 5 g
Protein: 26 g
Cholesterol: 97 mg
Sodium: 155 mg

Roast Loin of Veal

8 servings

1 2-pound veal loin roast

1 teaspoon olive oil

Juice of ½ lemon

Pinch of fresh or dried thyme

Pinch of Kosher salt

Pinch of coarsely ground pepper

Let meat stand at room temperature for 1 hour; rub with olive oil. Sprinkle with lemon juice; season with thyme, salt, and pepper. Place fat side up on a rack in roasting pan. Insert a meat thermometer through outside fat into thickest part of meat. Roast uncovered at 325° F. for 15 to 30 minutes per pound; meat thermometer should register 170° F.

APPROXIMATE NUTRITIONAL INFORMATION PER SERVING

Total calories: 154
Total fat: 6 g
Saturated fat: 2 g
Dietary fiber: 0 g
Carbohydrates: 1 g
Protein: 22 g
Cholesterol: 89 mg
Sodium: 81 mg

Roast Veal with Rosemary and Garlic

8 servings

2 pounds veal loin roast, boned

Kosher salt and coarsely ground black pepper

8 cloves garlic

8 sprigs fresh rosemary

Rub roast with salt and pepper. Insert garlic at intervals over roast. Tuck sprigs of rosemary in with the garlic. Roast on a rack in a 325°F. oven about 30 minutes per pound or to desired doneness.

Serving Suggestion: Serve with Potatoes with Mushrooms and Tomatoes (page 373) and Green Beans with Pimiento (page 362).

APPROXIMATE NUTRITIONAL INFORMATION PER SERVING

Total calories: 176
Total fat: 5 g
Saturated fat: 2 g
Dietary fiber: trace
Carbohydrates: 1 g
Protein: 29 g
Cholesterol: 108 mg
Sodium: 55 mg

Steak and Onions

4 servings

1 pound beef tenderloin

1 tablespoon olive oil

6 cloves garlic, chopped

1 onion, halved and sliced

1 green or yellow pepper, seeded and cut into thin strips

1 red pepper, seeded and cut into thin strips

Slice the steak into thin, stir-fry strips.

In a nonstick pan, heat olive oil. Add steak and brown 1–2 minutes. Add onion and cook 3–4 minutes or until onion begins to soften. Add peppers and garlic and cook 2–3 minutes. Serve at once.

Serving Suggestion: Good with steamed rice and, for dessert, fresh strawberries with Vanilla or Chocolate Angel Food Cake (page 398-399).

APPROXIMATE NUTRITIONAL INFORMATION PER SERVING

Total calories: 218
Total fat: 9 g
Saturated fat: 3 g
Dietary fiber: trace
Carbohydrates: 5 g
Protein: 27 g
Cholesterol: 71 mg
Sodium: 55 mg

A NOTE ON RED MEAT

 ccording to the Beef Council, the "skinniest six" cuts of beef are top round, eye of the round, round tip, sirloin, top loin and tenderloin. The leanest cuts of beef are labeled "loin" or "round." The lowest-fat grade is "Select," followed by "Choice" and "Prime."

The leanest cuts of pork are labeled "loin" or "leg." With less than 5 grams of fat in a 3.5-ounce serving, pork tenderloin is the equivalent of skinless chicken breast.

The two leanest cuts of lamb are labeled "loin chop" and "leg."

Always trim all visible fat from meat before cooking—the difference between a 3-ounce trimmed T-bone steak and an untrimmed one of the same size is about 20 grams of fat.

Stir-Fried Beef and Asparagus

4 servings

1 pound fresh asparagus, trimmed

1 tablespoon sake

1 tablespoon reduced-sodium soy sauce

¾ pound eye of round steak, thinly sliced into stir-fry strips

1 tablespoon olive oil

SAUCE

1 tablespoon oyster sauce

2 tablespoons sake

¼ teaspoon granulated sugar

1 tablespoon reduced-sodium soy sauce

¼ cup water

½ teaspoon hot chili oil

½ teaspoon potato starch

Pour sake and soy sauce over beef and marinate at room temperature 20–30 minutes.

In a small bowl, combine sauce ingredients and stir well. Set aside. In a wok or nonstick skillet, heat olive oil. Add beef and stir-fry 4–5 minutes. Add asparagus and sauce. Cook, stirring constantly, 2–3 minutes.

Note: Oyster sauce is available in the Asian section of most supermarkets.

Serving Suggestion: Serve with sticky rice or Chinese soba noodles and fresh pineapple, papaya, and fortune cookies.

APPROXIMATE NUTRITIONAL INFORMATION PER SERVING

Total calories: 230
Total fat: 8 g
Saturated fat: 2 g
Dietary fiber: 1 g
Carbohydrates: 7 g
Protein: 27 g
Cholesterol: 62 mg
Sodium: 500 mg

Skewered Beef Kebabs

4 servings

1 tablespoon olive oil

¼ cup red wine vinegar

½ cup dry red wine

1 garlic clove, minced

¼ teaspoon pepper

1 pound extra-lean round steak, cut into 1-inch cubes

¾ pound fresh mushrooms

12 cherry tomatoes

12 artichoke hearts

1 white onion, cut into 2-inch cubes

2 red, green or yellow peppers, seeded and quartered lengthwise

Combine oil, vinegar, wine, garlic, and pepper; pour over meat and vegetables. Cover. Chill 1 to 4 hours. Drain. Put meat and vegetables on different skewers.

Prepare the grill for direct grilling over high heat. Grill skewers, basting and turning often, until the vegetable and meat are cooked. This is typically 8-12 minutes total for medium-rare meat.

APPROXIMATE NUTRITIONAL INFORMATION PER SERVING

Total calories: 264
Total fat: 9 g
Saturated fat: 2 g
Dietary fiber: 4 g
Carbohydrates: 19 g
Protein: 30 g
Cholesterol: 67 mg
Sodium: 89 mg

Grilled Steak Sandwich

1 sandwich

3 ounces cubed steak

2 slices French bread

1½ teaspoons light mayonnaise

2 white onion slices

2 tomato slices

2 lettuce leaves

young baby spinach leaves

Your kids will be pleasantly surprised to find a steak sandwich on the dinner menu.

Prepare the grill for direct grilling over whigh heat.

Grill steaks 3-5 minutes on each side or until meat is cooked to your liking. Serve on French bread with mayonnaise, onion, tomato, lettuce, and spinach leaves.

APPROXIMATE NUTRITIONAL INFORMATION PER SERVING

Total calories: 261
Total fat: 7 g
Saturated fat: 2 g
Dietary fiber: 1 g
Carbohydrates: 26 g
Protein: 23 g
Cholesterol: 52 mg
Sodium: 368 mg

Grilled Teriyaki Steak

6 servings

½ cup reduced-sodium soy sauce

½ cup dry vermouth

1 tablespoon brown sugar

1 tablespoon Worcestershire sauce

2 garlic cloves, minced

1 1-inch piece of fresh gingerroot, peeled and minced

1½ pounds flank steak, all visible fat removed

You can make leaner cuts of meat more tender by marinating them first in a lean marinade. Any leftover steak makes great lunch-box sandwiches.

In a small bowl, combine the soy sauce, vermouth, brown sugar, Worcestershire sauce, garlic, and gingerroot.

Arrange flank steak in a shallow glass casserole dish suitable for marinating; pour sauce over top. Cover with plastic wrap. Marinate in refrigerator 1 to 24 hours. Drain marinade.

Prepare the grill for direct grilling over high heat. Grill 6-8 minutes. Turn once, cook for another 3-5 minutes for medium rare, or until nicely charred and cooked to your liking. Remove to a cutting board. Cut beef across grain at a diagonal angle into thin slices.

APPROXIMATE NUTRITIONAL INFORMATION PER SERVING

Total calories: 194
Total fat: 9 g
Saturated fat: 4 g
Dietary fiber: 0 g
Carbohydrates: 1 g
Protein: 23 g
Cholesterol: 57 mg
Sodium: 244 mg

A NOTE ON REDUCED SODIUM SOY SAUCE

educed-sodium soy sauce contains 46% less sodium than regular soy sauce, with little or no difference in flavor. Reduced-sodium soy sauce has 80 milligrams of sodium per 1/2 teaspoon. By comparison, 1/2 teaspoon of salt has 1,150 milligrams of sodium.

Classic Grilled Burgers

8 servings

2 pounds ground chuck*

1 teaspoon salt

¼ teaspoon black pepper

8 large sesame hamburger buns

2 large firm ripe tomatoes, sliced

8 thin slices white onion

1 head Bibb lettuce, washed and crisped

Ground chuck is considered the best-tasting ground beef for burgers. Leaner cuts, such as round and sirloin, though more healthy (about 9% fat), dry out. Ask your butcher to select the leanest parts of a chuck roast and grind it especially for you. That way, the meat will be about 14% fat versus 25 to 30% fat in regular ground beef. Unfortunately, most commercial meat grinders are large so you need to buy a minimum of 2 pounds.

Prepare the grill for direct grilling over high heat.

Season meat with salt and pepper and shape into 8 patties. Grill 6 to 7 minutes per side for medium-rare and 10 to 11 minutes for well-done, turning meat when juices begin to form on top. Serve immediately on warm buns, French bread, or French rolls with tomato slices, onion slices, and lettuce.

*Remember, since ground chuck is not the leanest cut available, be sure to make low-fat choices for breakfast and lunch and always try to serve the burgers with low-fat accompaniments to keep the total fat content for the day in line.

APPROXIMATE NUTRITIONAL INFORMATION PER SERVING

Total calories: 318
Total fat: 17 g
Saturated fat: 1 g
Dietary fiber: 1 g
Carbohydrates: 17 g
Protein: 18 g
Cholesterol: 61 mg
Sodium: 365 mg

Grilled Round Steak

8 servings

2 teaspoons olive oil

3 tablespoons lemon juice

1 tablespoon red wine vinegar

2 garlic cloves, sliced

Pinch of fresh or dried thyme

½ teaspoon chili powder

2 pounds top round steak

1 large onion, sliced

Pepper to taste

Combine olive oil, lemon juice, vinegar, garlic, and seasonings; pour over steak. Top with onion. Cover. Marinate in refrigerator for 2 hours, turning several times to coat. Drain.

Prepare grill for direct grilling at high heat. Grill steak 7 to 8 minutes on each side, or to desired doneness. Sprinkle with pepper.

APPROXIMATE NUTRITIONAL INFORMATION PER SERVING

Total calories: 162
Total fat: 5 g
Saturated fat: 2 g
Dietary fiber: 0 g
Carbohydrates: 2 g
Protein: 25 g
Cholesterol: 67 mg
Sodium: 56 mg

Red-Hot Chili Steak

6 servings

1½ pounds top round steak

¾ cup Hot Chili Marinade (page 211)

½ cup Hot Chili Sauce (page 215)

Marinate round steak in Hot Chili Marinade in the refrigerator at least 2 hours and as long as overnight. Drain off marinade.

Prepare the grill for direct grilling over high heat.

Grill steak 6 minutes on each side, basting 2–3 times with reserved marinade. Cut steak on the diagonal into long strips. Accompany with Hot Chili Sauce.

Serving Suggestion: Serve with Black Beans and Rice.

APPROXIMATE NUTRITIONAL INFORMATION PER SERVING

Total calories: 200
Total fat: 6 g
Saturated fat: 2 g
Dietary fiber: trace
Carbohydrates: 8 g
Protein: 27 g
Cholesterol: 70 mg
Sodium: 434 mg

Sunday Night Steak and Onions

4 servings

1 tablespoon olive oil

2 cups Vidalia or Walla Walla onion, chopped

¾-pound beef tenderloin, cut into strips

Pinch of Kosher salt and black pepper to taste

This recipe is for another comfort food made easy—and lean!

Heat olive oil in a nonstick skillet. Add meat. Cook 3-4 minutes until beginning to brown. Add onions. Cook 4-6 minutes until onions are tender and meat is desired doneness. Serve.

APPROXIMATE NUTRITIONAL INFORMATION PER SERVING USING HOME-MADE GRAVY

Total calories: 250
Total fat: 7 g
Saturated fat: 17 g
Dietary fiber: 6 g
Carbohydrates: 17 g
Protein: 16 g
Cholesterol: 65 mg
Sodium: 70 mg

Beef Stew

8 servings

1 tablespoon olive oil

2 pounds chuck roast, cubed

1 28-ounce can plum tomatoes

½ teaspoon Kosher salt

¼ teaspoon black pepper

¼ cup red wine (optional)

4 celery stalks, sliced on the diagonal into quarters

1 onion, cut into eighths

5 carrots, peeled and quartered

½ pound fresh mushrooms, sliced

½ pound fresh green beans, cooked al dente

1 14-ounce can water-packed artichoke hearts

3 to 4 drops of hot chili oil

2 cups cooked macaroni

Heat olive oil in a nonstick skillet. Add chuck roast and brown the meat. Add tomatoes, salt, pepper, and wine. Bring to a boil but do not boil. Reduce heat.

Add celery, onion, and carrots. Simmer 35 minutes. Add mushrooms and artichoke hearts. Simmer 10 minutes longer. Add green beans, chili oil, and macaroni. Heat until warmed through.

APPROXIMATE NUTRITIONAL INFORMATION PER SERVING

Total calories: 397
Total fat: 14 g
Saturated fat: 5 g
Dietary fiber: 5 g
Carbohydrates: 32 g
Protein: 33 g
Cholesterol: 90 mg
Sodium: 281 mg

Beef Stroganoff

8 servings

¾ pound extra-lean ground round

¾ cup finely chopped onion

1 garlic clove, minced

½ pound fresh mushrooms, sliced

¼ teaspoon Kosher salt

⅛ teaspoon pepper

⅛ teaspoon dried rosemary

1½ cups Healthy Request Cream of Chicken Soup

1 cup nonfat sour cream

1 1-pound package bow tie pasta, cooked al dente

2 teaspoons poppy seeds

Fresh parsley for garnish

Sauté ground round, onion, and garlic; drain off any excess fat.

Add mushrooms; cook 3 to 5 minutes. Stir in salt, pepper, and rosemary; simmer, uncovered, 10 minutes.

Add soup and heat. Stir in sour cream; heat, but do not boil. Arrange pasta around edges of a large platter; spoon stroganoff into center.

Sprinkle pasta with poppy seeds. Garnish with fresh parsley.

APPROXIMATE NUTRITIONAL INFORMATION PER SERVING

Total calories: 331
Total fat: 6 g
Saturated fat: 2 g
Dietary fiber: 2 g
Carbohydrates: 51 g
Protein: 18 g
Cholesterol: 30 mg
Sodium: 288 mg

Country Pot Roast

6 servings

1 tablespoon olive oil

1 1½-pound chuck roast

1 28-ounce can plum tomatoes, diced

2 teaspoons caraway seeds

1 teaspoon Kosher salt

2 to 3 drops Tabasco sauce (optional)

1 bay leaf

¼ teaspoon pepper

12 fingerling potatoes

6 carrots, peeled and quartered

6 celery stalks, peeled and quartered

4 small chipotle onions

12 fresh mushrooms

Heat olive oil in a nonstick skillet. Add chuck roast and brown the meat. Add tomatoes and seasonings.

Cover and simmer ½ hour; add potatoes, carrots, celery, and onions. Cover and simmer about 1 hour, or until vegetables are crisp-tender. Add mushrooms and simmer 15 minutes.

APPROXIMATE NUTRITIONAL INFORMATION PER SERVING

Total calories: 381
Total fat: 12 g
Saturated fat: 4 g
Dietary fiber: 8 g
Carbohydrates: 38g
Protein: 32 g
Cholesterol: 90 mg
Sodium: 510 mg

Old-Fashioned Meat Loaf

8 servings

2 teaspoon extra-virgin olive oil

1 large yellow onion, finely chopped

2 pounds leanest (90% lean) ground beef

1½ cups bread crumbs

2 eggs, lightly beaten

1 teaspoon Kosher salt

½ teaspoon black pepper

1 teaspoon dry mustard

¼ teaspoon ground thyme

¼ cup finely chopped fresh parsley

½ cup evaporated skim milk

This recipe is an example of how buying the leanest ingredients possible makes a big difference. Finding 90% lean ground beef is worth the search! For an even leaner meat loaf, use a draining meat loaf pan available at most specialty kitchen stores. Serve leftover meat loaf slices on Kaiser rolls with Best Foods or Hellmann's light mayonnaise and lettuce.

In a nonstick skillet, heat olive oil over medium-high heat. Add onion and sauté until slightly soft, 4 to 5 minutes.

In a large bowl, combine ground beef, bread crumbs and sautéed onion. In a medium bowl, whisk together the eggs, salt, pepper, dry mustard, thyme, parsley and milk. Pour the egg mixture over the beef mixture. Using your hands, mix the ingredients together. Do not overmix or loaf will be too dry. Pat meat mixture into a 8-inch nonstick loaf pan. Bake at 350°F. for 1½ hours, or until meat loaf begins to shrink from sides of the pan. Cover pan with foil for the first 1/2 hour of baking. Then remove cover for the last hour. Remove from oven and let cool 5 to 10 minutes so the slices won't fall apart.

Cut meat loaf into thick slices.

APPROXIMATE NUTRITIONAL INFORMATION PER SERVING

Total calories: 317
Total fat: 14 g
Saturated fat: 5 g
Dietary fiber: 1 g
Carbohydrates: 19 g
Protein: 28 g
Cholesterol: 123 mg
Sodium: 556 mg

Dutch Meat Loaf

6 servings

1 15-ounce can tomato sauce

¼ cup water

2 tablespoons prepared mustard

1 tablespoon cider vinegar

1 pound extra-lean ground round

1 cup bread crumbs

1 egg

1 medium onion, chopped

¼ teaspoon pepper

Combine tomato sauce, water, mustard, and vinegar. Mix beef with bread crumbs, egg, onion, pepper, and a quarter of the tomato sauce mixture.

Shape into a nonstick loaf pan. Pour enough sauce over top of meat loaf to coat. Bake uncovered at 350° F. for 1 hour, basting often.

Warm remaining sauce; serve over sliced meat loaf.

APPROXIMATE NUTRITIONAL INFORMATION PER SERVING

Total calories: 218
Total fat: 8 g
Saturated fat: 3 g
Dietary fiber: 1 g
Carbohydrates: 19 g
Protein: 18 g
Cholesterol: 47 mg
Sodium: 431 mg

Beef and Veal Loaf with Red Pepper Sauce

10 servings

1 cup diced French bread with crust

½ cup nonfat milk

1 pound extra-lean ground round steak

1 pound extra-lean ground veal

2 eggs

¼ teaspoon black pepper

¼ teaspoon ground thyme

¼ teaspoon ground rosemary

¾ cup freshly grated Parmesan cheese

RED PEPPER SAUCE

1 red pepper, halved and seeded

1 tablespoon olive oil

1 teaspoon fresh lemon juice

¾ teaspoon balsamic vinegar

¾ teaspoon salt or to taste

¼ teaspoon cayenne pepper

Soften the bread in milk for 10–15 minutes. Meanwhile, combine ground round, veal, eggs, pepper, thyme, rosemary, and Parmesan cheese. Squeeze bread dry (discard milk), add to meat mixture and mix. Shape into a loaf and put into an 8-inch nonstick loaf pan.

Bake at 375°F. 1 hour.

A few minutes before meat loaf is cooked, in a microwave or a steamer basket over boiling water, steam red pepper 4 minutes or until softened. Put into a blender or food processor; add olive oil, lemon juice, vinegar, salt, and cayenne pepper. Purée. Pass the sauce with the loaf.

Serving Suggestion: Serve with Risotto Milanese (page 349). The leftovers make great sandwiches.

This dish is high in sodium. Keep a balance for the day by selecting low-sodium foods at other meals.

APPROXIMATE NUTRITIONAL INFORMATION PER SERVING

Total calories: 247
Total fat: 10 g
Saturated fat: 5 g
Dietary fiber: trace g
Carbohydrates:12 g
Protein: 27 g
Cholesterol: 114 mg
Sodium: 417 mg

Braised Meat Loaf

6 servings

6 fresh Shiitake mushrooms

2 cups water

1 slice white bread, crust removed

1 tablespoon nonfat milk

1 pound lean ground chuck

2 cloves garlic, chopped

½ teaspoon black pepper

3 tablespoons chopped white onion

2 eggs

½ cup bread crumbs

⅓ cup dry white wine

2 tablespoons tomato paste

1½ teaspoon Kosher salt

Coarsely chop mushrooms, discarding the tough bottom stems. In a small saucepan, combine bread with milk. Simmer 3–5 minutes, or until milk is absorbed and bread is soft. Dice.

In a mixing bowl, combine ground chuck, salt, garlic, and pepper. Knead in onions and diced bread, then eggs. Shape into a firmly packed ball. Roll into a baguette-type loaf, about $2^1/2$ inches thick. Roll loaf in bread crumbs.

In a nonstick skillet over medium heat, brown the meat loaf on all sides, turning carefully so the loaf will not break. When meat is browned, add wine and cook over medium-high heat 5–10 minutes, or until wine is reduced by $1/2$ (do not allow wine to boil).

In a small saucepan, warm two cups water. Stir in tomato paste. Simmer 5 minutes. Add to skillet along with chopped mushrooms. Cover and simmer 20 minutes, turning loaf twice. Adjust lid so it is slightly ajar and simmer 15 minutes longer. Remove loaf to cutting board and let stand 5 minutes before cutting. Place on serving platter. Ring with mushrooms. Pour remaining sauce over top.

Variation: For increased fiber, substitute oat bran for bread crumbs.

Serving Suggestion: The leftovers make great sandwiches.

APPROXIMATE NUTRITIONAL INFORMATION PER SERVING

Total calories: 234
Total fat: 5 g
Saturated fat: 5 g
Dietary fiber: 1 g
Carbohydrates: 10 g
Protein: 17 g
Cholesterol: 52 mg
Sodium: 143 mg

Shish Kebab

4 servings

- **2 teaspoons olive oil**
- **½ cup dry white wine**
- **1 teaspoon lemon juice**
- **¼ tablespoon Kosher salt**
- **1 pound lamb loin, cut into 1-inch cubes**
- **2 green or yellow peppers, seeded and quartered lengthwise**
- **12 cherry tomatoes**
- **8 water-packed artichoke hearts**
- **12 fresh mushrooms**
- **1 onion, cut into wedges**
- **2 cups fresh pineapple chunks**

Combine oil, wine, lemon juice, and salt; pour over lamb and vegetables.

Arrange lamb on skewers. Arrange vegetables and pineapple on separate skewers.

Prepare the grill for direct grilling over high heat.Grill 7-10 minutes, basting frequently and turning often, until lamb is done. Vegetables are done when crisp-tender.

Serving Suggestion: Accompany with steamed brown rice.

APPROXIMATE NUTRITIONAL INFORMATION PER SERVING

Total calories: 327
Total fat: 11 g
Saturated fat: 3 g
Dietary fiber: 4 g
Carbohydrates: 24 g
Protein: 29 g
Cholesterol: 80 mg
Sodium: 171 mg

Grilled Lamb Chops with Rosemary and Garlic

4 servings

4 extra-lean lamb chops

juice of ½ lemon

1½ tablespoons olive oil

6 cloves garlic, crushed

1 tablespoon fresh rosemary, chopped

Trim chops of all visible fat; score edges.

Place lamb in a shallow dish. Combine lemon juice, olive oil, garlic and rosemary. Pour over lamb. Marinate 30 minutes. Drain

Prepare grill for direct grilling over high heat. Grill chops 5-8 minutes per side for medium rare.

Serving Suggestion: Accompany with Sticky Rice (page 345) and skewered, grilled artichoke hearts, mushrooms, zucchini and cherry tomatoes.

APPROXIMATE NUTRITIONAL INFORMATION PER SERVING

Total calories: 170
Total fat: 7 g
Saturated fat: 3 g
Dietary fiber: 0 g
Carbohydrates: 0 g
Protein: 24 g
Cholesterol: 75 mg
Sodium: 78 mg

Grilled Lamb Roast

8 servings

1 3-pound leg of lamb, boned and butterflied

1 teaspoon fresh rosemary

1 teaspoon fresh thyme

3 cloves crushed garlic

¼ teaspoon Kosher salt

⅛ teaspoon ground black pepper

16 cherry tomatoes

16 mushroom caps, microwaved 2 to 3 minutes

16 asparagus spears, microwaved 3 to 5 minutes

Fresh Italian parsley for garnish

Fresh lemon wedges for garnish

Have butcher remove bone from leg of lamb and open roast; season with rosemary, thyme, garlic, salt, and pepper. Allow to stand at room temperature for about 1 hour before grilling.

Prepare grill for direct grilling over medium-high heat. Grill lamb, turning every 10 minutes, for 30 to 40 minutes for rare, 40 to 50 minutes for medium, and 50 to 60 minutes for well-done. Place on a carving platter and let set 10 minutes. Carve into diagonal slices.

Arrange tomatoes, mushrooms, and asparagus. Garnish with parsley and lemon wedges.

Variation: To oven roast, arrange lamb on rack in roasting pan. Cook 15 minutes at 450°F.; reduce heat to 350° and roast approximately 1¼ hours, or until lamb reaches desired doneness. Baste frequently.

APPROXIMATE NUTRITIONAL INFORMATION PER SERVING

Total calories: 254
Total fat: 10 g
Saturated fat: 4 g
Dietary fiber: 1 g
Carbohydrates: 2 g
Protein: 37 g
Cholesterol: 114 mg
Sodium: 90 mg

Butterflied Leg of Lamb

4 servings

1 3-pound boneless leg of lamb

1 teaspoon fresh rosemary

1 teaspoon Kosher salt

½ teaspoon black pepper

1 teaspoon fresh thyme

2 tablespoons olive oil

2 tablespoons red wine vinegar

1 tablespoon fresh lemon juice

3 cloves garlic, crushed

1 tablespoon Dijon mustard

Have butcher remove bone from lamb and cut meat into butterfly shape. Place lamb in a dish. Rub on both sides with generous amounts of rosemary, thyme, pepper and ½ teaspoon salt.

In a bowl, combine oil, vinegar, lemon juice, garlic, mustard, and salt. Pour over lamb. Marinate several hours or overnight, turning frequently. Remove lamb from marinade.

Prepare grill for direct grilling over medium-high heat. Grill lamb, turning every 10 minutes. Cook 30 to 40 minutes for rare, 40 to 50 minutes for medium, and 50 to 60 minutes for well done.

APPROXIMATE NUTRITIONAL INFORMATION PER SERVING

Total calories: 242
Total fat: 10 g
Saturated fat: 3 g
Dietary fiber: 0 g
Carbohydrates: 1 g
Protein: 34 g
Cholesterol: 105 mg
Sodium: 325 mg

Lamb with Garlic

8 servings

1 3-pound leg of lamb, boned and butterflied

1 tablespoon minced parsley

1 tablespoon ground sage

1 tablespoon powdered rosemary

2 tablespoons olive oil

2 tablespoons fresh lemon juice

½ teaspoon Kosher salt

¼ teaspoon black pepper

8 cloves garlic, thinly sliced

Rub lamb on all sides with parsley, sage and rosemary.

In a bowl, combine olive oil, lemon juice, salt and pepper. Pour over seasoned lamb and rub into meat.

Insert sliced garlic cloves in cracks and crevices.

Prepare grill for direct grilling over medium-high heat. Cover grill with foil Please lamb on the foil. Turn every 10 minutes for a total cooking time of about 30 minutes for rare and 45 minutes for well done. Rare will register 160°F. on a meat thermometer; well done, 175°F. Just before serving, cut lamb into slices ½ inch thick and arrange on a platter.

Serving Suggestion: Serve with Tabbouleh with Parmesan (page 354), Green Beans with Pimiento (page 362) and Grilled Herbed Tomatoes (page 383).

APPROXIMATE NUTRITIONAL INFORMATION PER SERVING

Total calories: 249
Total fat: 11 g
Saturated fat: 1 g
Dietary fiber: trace g
Carbohydrates: 3 g
Protein: 34 g
Cholesterol: 106 mg
Sodium: 192 mg

Medallions of Pork with Lemon

4 servings

1½ tablespoons olive oil

3 cloves garlic, crushed

½ teaspoon fresh rosemary

1 pound lean boneless pork tenderloins, thinly sliced

2½ tablespoons fresh lemon juice

¼ teaspoon Kosher salt

¼ teaspoon coarsly ground black pepper

Arrange pork ternderloins in a 8 x 8 x 2-inch casserole dish. Combine olive oil and garlic. Rub onto tenderloin. Sprinkle with rosemary. Marinate in refrigerator for 1-2 hours. Drain off marinade.

Heat a nonstick skillet. Add tenderloins and brown 2 minutes on each side. Reduce heat, add lemon juice and cook, turning often, 3–5 minutes more or until pork is cooked. Season with salt and pepper.

Serving Suggestion: Serve with Barley with Pine Nuts (page 355), Spinach-Stuffed Tomatoes (page 385) and sliced apples or applesauce.

APPROXIMATE NUTRITIONAL INFORMATION PER SERVING

Total calories: 205
Total fat: 11 g
Saturated fat: 3 g
Dietary fiber: 0 g
Carbohydrates: 2 g
Protein: 23 g
Cholesterol: 75 mg
Sodium:201 mg

Roast Pork Tenderloin

6 servings

1 extra-lean pork tenderloin roast, about 1½ pounds

Kosher salt

freshly ground black pepper

fresh rosemary

Rub roast with salt, black pepper, and rosemary. Place roast on wire rack in roasting pan. Roast at 350°F. 1 hour, or until meat is roasted to desired doneness.

Serving Suggestion: Brown Rice with Mushrooms (page 350), Grilled Herbed Tomatoes (page 383) and apple sauce.

APPROXIMATE NUTRITIONAL INFORMATION PER SERVING

Total calories: 157
Total fat: 6 g
Saturated fat: 2 g
Dietary fiber: 0 g
Carbohydrates: trace
Protein: 33 g
Cholesterol: 112 mg
Sodium: 70 mg

Beans, Rice & Other Grains

Refried Beans

4 cups

2 15-ounce cans kidney or pinto beans,* with liquid

2 cloves garlic

½ white onion, chopped

¼ teaspoon ground cumin

⅛ teaspoon oregano

1 teaspoon ground red chilies**

¼ teaspoon cayenne

½ teaspoon Kosher salt

½ cup grated part-skim mozzarella cheese

1 tablespoon olive oil

In a blender or food processor, purée beans and garlic until smooth. Add onion and seasonings, and process until smooth.

In a nonstick skillet over medium heat, heat olive oil. Add beans and cook, uncovered, 20–30 minutes, or until beans thicken; stir occasionally. Add cheese.

*To further reduce the sodium level of this recipe, when time permits, substitute homemade beans for canned beans.

**Ground red chilies are available in Spanish and Mexican markets, in gourmet kitchen stores and in the gourmet section of most supermarkets.

Serving Suggestion: Refried beans are great in tacos, taco salad or as a dip with fresh vegetables.

APPROXIMATE NUTRITIONAL INFORMATION PER ½-CUP SERVING

Total calories: 134
Total fat: 4 g
Saturated fat: 1 g
Dietary fiber: 4 g
Carbohydrates: 18 g
Protein: 8 g
Cholesterol: 4 mg
Sodium: 436 mg

Refried Black Beans

1 cup

1 15-ounce can black beans, drained, but not rinsed

1 tablespoon chili powder

½ teaspoon cumin

2 teaspoons extra virgin olive oil

In a blender or food processor, purée beans. Add chili powder and cumin. Blend.

In a nonstick skillet, heat olive oil. Add bean mixture and cook, stirring constantly, until beans are warm.

Serving Suggestion: Good with Chicken Enchiladas (page 282) or Chicken Fajitas (page 298).

APPROXIMATE NUTRITIONAL INFORMATION PER TABLESPOON

Total calories: 28
Total fat: 1 g
Saturated fat: trace
Dietary fiber: 1 g
Carbohydrates: 4 g
Protein: 1 g
Cholesterol: 0 mg
Sodium: 90 mg

Black Beans and Rice

7 cups

1 tablespoon olive oil

1 small onion, chopped

3 serrano chilies, halved and seeded

2 15-ounce cans black beans

⅛ teaspoon ground cumin

⅛ teaspoon cayenne pepper

1 cup uncooked long-grain white rice

1 ¾ cups chicken broth (page 143) or commercial broth**

3 cloves garlic, crushed

Pinch of Kosher salt (optional)

In a nonstick skillet over medium heat, heat olive oil. Add onion and chilies, and sauté 6–8 minutes or until tender. Drain beans, reserving ½ cup liquid. Add beans with ½ cup liquid to onions and chilies. Cook, uncovered, 20–30 minutes or until about half the liquid is absorbed. Season with cumin and cayenne pepper.

Meanwhile, in a medium saucepan, combine rice and chicken broth. Bring to a boil, sitr once. Cover and reduce heat. Simmer for 15 minutes. Remove from heat. Let stand covered 10 minutes longer.

Divide rice into individual serving bowls. Ladle black beans over rice. If desired, season with a pinch of Kosher salt.

**Canned broth is higher in sodium.

Serving Suggestion: Good with Grilled Chicken with Salsa (page 299).

APPROXIMATE NUTRITIONAL INFORMATION PER ½-CUP SERVING

Total calories: 116
Total fat: 1 g
Saturated fat: trace
Dietary fiber: 2 g
Carbohydrates: 21 g
Protein: 5 g
Cholesterol: trace
Sodium: 211 mg

Red Beans and Rice

7 cups

1 tablespoon olive oil

1 onion, finely chopped

2 15-ounce cans red kidney beans, drained

⅛ teaspoon cayenne

¼ teaspoon Tabasco, or to taste

½ teaspoon pepper

½ teaspoon Kosher salt

3 cups cooked Long Grain White Rice (p. 347)

Heat olive oil in a nonstick skillet; add onion and sauté until tender. Transfer to a 2-quart saucepan; add kidney beans, cayenne, Tabasco, pepper, and salt. Simmer over low heat for 20 to 30 minutes.

Prepare Long Grain White Rice according to recipe instructions.

Just before serving, ladle beans over rice.

Variation: Layer diced ham over the rice. Top with beans.

Be sure to choose low-sodium foods at other meals to help balance sodium intake for the day.

APPROXIMATE NUTRITIONAL INFORMATION PER 1-CUP SERVING

Total calories: 182
Total fat: 1 g
Saturated fat: 0 g
Dietary fiber: 5 g
Carbohydrates: 35 g
Protein: 8 g
Cholesterol: 1 mg
Sodium: 653 mg

Long-Grain Brown Rice

6 1/2-cup servings

1 cup chicken broth, preferably homemade (page 143)

1¼ cup water

1 cup brown basmati rice

1 tablespoon finely chopped fresh Italian parsley (optional)

In a 2-quart saucepan, bring chicken broth, water, and rice to a boil. Stir lightly with a fork. Reduce heat; cover and simmer for 45 minutes, or until rice is soft and moisture is absorbed. Remove from heat and let stand, covered, for 5-10 minutes longer. Stir in parsley.

APPROXIMATE NUTRITIONAL INFORMATION PER SERVING

Total calories: 115
Total fat: trace
Saturated fat: 0 g
Dietary fiber: 1 g
Carbohydrates: 23 g
Protein: 4 g
Cholesterol: 0 mg
Sodium: 41 mg

Sticky Rice

4 servings

1 cup short-grain rice

1 ¼ cups water

Short-grain rice is also called pearl or Japanese new-variety rice.

Pour rice into a 2-quart saucepan. Cover with cold water, stir and drain; repeat 2 to 3 times until water runs clear. Return drained rice to saucepan and add 1 ¼ cups cold water. Bring to a boil over high heat. Reduce heat to low, cover and simmer 20 minutes, or until rice is tender and liquid is nearly absorbed. Remove from heat and let stand, covered, for 5 to 10 minutes. Uncover; fluff with a fork.

Crushed Red Pepper Rice: Sprinkle cooked rice with dried crushed red peppers.

*We like the sticky rice served in Asain restaurants. Our favorite brand, Kokuho Rose No Talc Extra Fancy Rice, is available in Asian markets and some supermarkets.

APPROXIMATE NUTRITIONAL INFORMATION PER 1-CUP SERVING

Total calories: 170
Total fat: 1 g
Saturated fat: 0 g
Dietary fiber: 0 g
Carbohydrates: 39 g
Protein: 3 g
Cholesterol: 0 mg
Sodium: 5 mg

Wild Rice

5 cups

1 cup uncooked wild rice

2 cups chicken broth (page 143), preferably homemade

2 cups water

7 large fresh mushrooms, thinly sliced

2 tablespoons finely chopped fresh Italian parsley

½ ripe tomato, diced

In a 6-quart saucepan, bring broth and water to a boil. Add wild rice. Stir. Cover and reduce heat. Simmer 65-95 minutes, until rice becomes soft and fluffy. Add mushrooms. Remove from heat and let stand 10-15 minutes longer. Stir in parsley and tomatoes. .

APPROXIMATE NUTRITIONAL INFORMATION PER ⅔-CUP SERVING

Total calories: 145
Total fat: 1 g
Saturated fat: 0 g
Dietary fiber: 2 g
Carbohydrates: 26 g
Protein: 6 g
Cholesterol: 2 mg
Sodium: 225 mg

Wild and White Rice

Approximately 7 cups

2 cups beef broth (page 151) or commercial broth

2 cups water

1 cup wild rice

1 cup white basmati rice

1¾ cups chicken broth (page 143) or commercial broth

In a medium saucepan bring beef broth and water to a boil. Add wild rice. Stir and cover. Reduce heat. Simmer 65-95 minutes, until rice becomes soft and fluffy.

Meanwhile, in another medium saucepan or rice cooker combine basmati rice and chicken broth. Bring to a boil. Stir once and cover. Reduce heat and simmer 15 minutes. Remove from heat. Let stand covered 5-10 minutes.

Combine both kinds of cooked rice in a bowl and toss to make a colorful accompaniment to a main dish.

Variation: Use brown basmati rice in place of white. Increase chicken broth to 2¼ cups.

APPROXIMATE NUTRITIONAL INFORMATION PER 1/2 CUP

Total calories: 114
Total fat: trace
Saturated fat: trace
Dietary fiber: trace
Carbohydrates: 25 g
Protein: 2 g
Cholesterol: trace
Sodium: 57 mg

Wild Rice Stuffing

6 servings

1 tablespoon olive oil

½ medium yellow onion, chopped

3 stalks celery, chopped

8 fresh mushrooms, thinly sliced

2 cups bread cubes

½–¾ cup chicken broth (page 143) or commercial broth

¾ teaspoon sage

¼ teaspoon black pepper

¼ teaspoon Kosher salt

¾ cup cooked Wild Rice (page 345)

Heat olive oil in a nonstick skillet. Sauté onion and celery until tender. Add mushrooms. Sauté 3 minutes. Add bread cubes. Toss. Gradually add broth, a little less or a little more as needed to moisten. Season with sage, pepper, and salt. Add rice. Toss. Bake, covered, at 350°F. 30–35 minutes, or until hot.

APPROXIMATE NUTRITIONAL INFORMATION PER SERVING

Total calories: 70
Total fat: 1 g
Saturated fat: 0 g
Dietary fiber: 2 g
Carbohydrates: 14 g
Protein: 3 g
Cholesterol: 0 mg
Sodium: 180 mg

Long Grain White Rice

3 cups

1 cup basmati white rice

1¾ cups chicken broth (page 143) or commercial broth

In a saucepan, combine rice, chicken broth and bring to a boil. Stir. Reduce heat; stir once, cover, and simmer 15 minutes or until broth is absorbed and rice is tender. Remove from heat and let stand, covered, 5-10 minutes.

APPROXIMATE NUTRITIONAL INFORMATION PER 1/2 CUP

Total calories: 125
Total fat: trace
Saturated fat: trace
Dietary fiber: trace
Carbohydrates: 25 g
Protein: 3 g
Cholesterol: trace
Sodium: 152 mg

Rice with Chilies

6 cups

1 tablespoon olive oil

1 cup white basmati rice

1 small onion, chopped

3 cloves garlic, sliced

1 ¾ cups chicken broth (page 143) or commercial broth

1 4-ounce can diced green chilies

1 small tomato, diced

½ cup freshly grated reduced-fat Cheddar cheese

In a nonstick skillet, heat olive oil. Add onion and sauté 6-8 minutes until tender. Add garlic and sauté one minute longer. Set aside.

Meanwhile, in a 2-quart saucepan bring chicken broth and rice to a boil. Reduce heat. Cover. Simmer 15 minutes or until moisture is absorbed. Remove from heat. Let stand 5-10 minutes. Stir in onions. Add green chilies and tomatoes, and sprinkle with cheese. Cover and steam 2-3 minutes or until cheese is melted.

Serving Suggestion: Good with Chicken Black Bean Burritos (page 285).

APPROXIMATE NUTRITIONAL INFORMATION PER SERVING

Total calories: 155
Total fat: 3 g
Saturated fat: 1 g
Dietary fiber: 1 g
Carbohydrates: 22 g
Protein: 5 g
Cholesterol: trace
Sodium: 340 mg

Creole Rice

3 cups

1¾ cups chicken broth (page 143) or commercial broth

¾ cup water

⅛ teaspoon cayenne pepper

⅛ teaspoon ground cumin

⅛ teaspoon oregano

½ teaspoon Kosher salt

⅛ teaspoon white pepper

1 cup long-grain white rice

1 tablespoon olive oil

3 large cloves garlic

1 cup chopped white onion

¾ cup diced eggplant (optional)

¾ cup diced red, yellow, or green pepper

In a saucepan, bring chicken broth and water to a boil; add cayenne, cumin, oregano, and black and white pepper. Stir in rice. Reduce heat, cover and simmer 15-20 minutes or until broth is absorbed and rice is tender.

Meanwhile, in a nonstick skillet, heat olive oil. Add garlic, onion and eggplant, if using, and sauté 4–5 minutes or until onion is just tender and eggplant is softened. Add green pepper and cook 2–3 minutes. Toss with the cooked rice.

Serving Suggestion: Good side dish with Sauteéd Shrimp (p. 272)

APPROXIMATE NUTRITIONAL INFORMATION PER 1/2 CUP

Total calories: 176
Total fat: 2 g
Saturated fat: trace
Dietary fiber: 2 g
Carbohydrates: 29 g
Protein: 4 g
Cholesterol: trace
Sodium: 325 mg

Spicy Mexican Rice

6 ½-cup servings

½ teaspoon olive oil

½ cup finely chopped onion

1 cup chicken broth, preferably homemade (page 143)

½ cup water

1 cup Bloody Mary Mix

1 cup uncooked long-grain basmati rice

Heat olive oil in a nonstick skillet; add onion and sauté. In a medium saucepan, heat chicken broth, waterm and Bloody Mary mix to boiling; add onion and rice. Stir lightly. Cover; reduce heat, and simmer 15 to 20 minutes, or until rice is soft and moisture is absorbed. Remove from heat. Let stand, covered, 5-10 minutes longer.

Note: Although low in fat, this recipe is high in sodium due to the Bloody Mary mix. Be sure to limit your sodium in other meals to keep the sodium intake for the day in balance.

APPROXIMATE NUTRITIONAL INFORMATION PER SERVING

Total calories: 127
Total fat: 1 g
Saturated fat: 0 g
Dietary fiber: 1 g
Carbohydrates: 25 g
Protein: 4 g
Cholesterol: 0 mg
Sodium: 479 mg

Saffron Rice

4 servings

1 cup uncooked basmati white rice

1¾ cups chicken broth (page 143) or commercial broth

1 tablespoon olive oil

½ cup yellow onion, diced

½ teaspoon saffron threads, crushed

In medum saucepan, combine rice and chicken broth. Bring to a boil, stir once. Cover; reduce heat and simmer 15 minutes. Remove from heat and let stand covered 5-10 minutes longer.

Meanwhile, in a small nonstick skillet, heat olive oil. Add onion and saute 6-8 minutes until tender.

Toss onion with rice. Sprinkle with crushed saffron threads. Toss again, Serve

APPROXIMATE NUTRITIONAL INFORMATION PER SERVING

Total calories: 218
Total fat: 8 g
Saturated fat: 2 g
Dietary fiber: 1 g
Carbohydrates: 31 g
Protein: 6 g
Cholesterol: 1 mg
Sodium: 82 mg

Risotto Milanese

8 servings

6 cups chicken broth (page 143) or commercial broth

1 small onion, chopped

1 tablespoon olive oil

2 cups arborio rice

½ teaspoon saffron threads, crushed

¼ cup dry white wine

⅓ pound fresh mushrooms, sliced

Pinch Kosher salt

Pinch freshly ground black pepper

In a saucepan, bring chicken broth just to boiling; reduce heat and let simmer.

In a nonstick skillet, sauté onion in olive oil 4–6 minutes. When onion is tender, stir in rice; sauté 3–4 minutes, stirring often. Add saffron, wine and ¼ cup of the simmering broth. When the liquid is absorbed, add ½ cup additional broth. Stir and cook until liquid is absorbed, then add another ½ cup broth. Repeat the process until all the broth is used. Add mushrooms when last half-cup of stock is added. Remove from heat. Cover and let sit 5–10 minutes or until all the liquid is absorbed. Season with salt and pepper, if desired.

Note: It is important to add the risotto liquid very gradually and regulate the heat so that it does not evaporate too quickly. Total cooking time should be about 30 minutes. Arborio rice is found in the gourmet sections of many supermarkets and in Italian markets. It is what gives this dish its creamy texture.

APPROXIMATE NUTRITIONAL INFORMATION PER SERVING

Total calories: 272
Total fat: 3 g
Saturated fat: trace
Dietary fiber: 1 g
Carbohydrates: 54 g
Protein: 9 g
Cholesterol: 1 mg
Sodium: 250 mg

Brown Rice with Mushrooms

5 servings

1 cup uncooked basmati brown rice

1¼ cups chicken broth (page 143)

1 cup water

10 fresh Crimini mushrooms, thinly sliced

Kosher salt and coarsely ground-black pepper to taste

In a medium saucepan, bring rice, broth, and water to a boil. Stir once. Reduce heat to simmer. Cover and cook 45 minutes, or until most of the water has evaporated. Quickly lift lid and sprinkle mushrooms over top of rice (do not stir). Replace lid. Remove from heat. Let stand 5–10 minutes. Toss mushrooms with rice. Season.

APPROXIMATE NUTRITIONAL INFORMATION PER 2/3-CUP SERVING

Total calories: 113
Total fat: 1 g
Saturated fat: 0 g
Dietary fiber: 2 g
Carbohydrates: 29 g
Protein: 4 g
Cholesterol: 0 mg
Sodium: 145 mg

Wild Rice, Brown Rice and Mushrooms

7 1-cup servings

5 cups cooked Wild Rice (page 345)

3 cups cooked Brown Rice with Mushrooms (page 350)

1 tablespoon olive oil

1 cup yellow onion, diced

Prepare Wild Rice and Brown Rice with Mushrooms as directed. Fifteen minutes before serving heat olive oil in a nonstick skillet. Add onion and sauté 5-6 minutes until tender. Toss with wild rice and brown rice. Serve.

APPROXIMATE NUTRITIONAL INFORMATION PER SERVING

Total calories: 240
Total fat: 2 g
Saturated fat: 0 g
Dietary fiber: 2 g
Carbohydrates: 40 g
Protein: 11 g
Cholesterol: 0 mg
Sodium: 370 mg

Quinoa with Tomatoes and Italian Parsley

6 servings

1 cup chicken broth (page 143) preferably homemade

1 cup water

1 cup quinoa

1 tablespoon olive oil

½ cup yellow onion, diced

2 teaspoons fresh lemon juice

½ teaspoon Kosher salt

½ teaspoon black pepper

1 ½ teaspoons fresh thyme, finely chopped

1 medium tomato, diced

½ cup Italian parsley, chopped

Combine chicken broth, water and quinoa in a medium saucepan and bring to a boil. Reduce heat to simmer, cover and cook 10-15 minutes until water is absorbed and quinoa is soft.

Meanwhile, heat olive oil in a small nonstick skillet, add onion and sauté 6-8 minutes until tender. Toss with quinoa. Sprinkle with lemon juice, salt, pepper, and thyme. Toss. Add tomato and Italian parsley. Toss again.

APPROXIMATE NUTRITIONAL INFORMATION PER 2/3-CUP SERVING

Total calories: 140
Total fat: 4 g
Saturated fat: 0 g
Dietary fiber: 2 g
Carbohydrates: 22 g
Protein: 5 g
Cholesterol: 0 mg
Sodium: 480 mg

Rice with Grilled Garden Vegetables

10 servings

Balsamic Marinade

⅔ cup balsamic vinegar

3 tablespoons olive oil

2 garlic cloves, minced

2 tablespoons chopped shallots

3 tablespoons finely chopped fresh basil or 1½ tablespoons dried

1 teaspoon chopped fresh oregano or ¼ teaspoon dried

½ teaspoon chopped fresh rosemary or ½ teaspoon dried

1½ teaspoons fresh lemon thyme or ¾ teaspoon dried

2 Italian eggplants, halved lengthwise and then quartered

1 tablespoon salt (to be rinsed off)

⅔ cup wild rice

8 cups Wild Rice, Brown Rice, and Mushrooms (p. 350)

2 red onions, peeled and quartered

3 medium zucchini, cut diagonally into ½-inch slices

8 large mushrooms

1 red pepper, seeded and quartered

1 yellow pepper, seeded and quartered

1 green pepper, seeded and quartered

6 plum tomatoes, halved

Combine marinade ingredients in a covered jar. Shake well.

In a colander, toss eggplant with salt and allow to drain for 30 to 60 minutes. Rinse eggplant with water and drain well.

Prepare Wild Rice, Brown Rice, and Mushrooms according to directions.

Arrange vegetables in a 13 x 9 x 2-inch casserole. Toss with ½ of the marinade. When rice is nearly done, prepare the grill for direct grilling over medium heat. Place grill basket 4 to 6 inches above heat. Arrange onions and eggplant in grill basket, cook 5 to 10 minutes, turning often and basting frequently. Add remaining vegetables and continue cooking about 10 minutes longer, turning frequently and basting often until vegetables are tender.

To serve, mound rice in center of a serving platter. Ring with vegetables.

APPROXIMATE NUTRITIONAL INFORMATION PER SERVING

Total calories: 185
Total fat: 4 g
Saturated fat: 1 g
Dietary fiber: 1 g
Carbohydrates: 34 g
Protein: 6 g
Cholesterol: 1 mg
Sodium: 75 mg

Rice with Chicken, Prawns and Clams

8 servings

- **1 tablespoon olive oil**
- **2 cups chopped onion**
- **3 garlic cloves, chopped**
- **4 whole boneless, skinless chicken breasts, halved**
- **6 cups chicken broth, preferably homemade (page 143)**
- **2 cups uncooked, long-grain white rice**
- **¾ teaspoon saffron threads crushed**
- **½ teaspoon Kosher salt**
- **¼ teaspoon cayenne**
- **1 14½-ounce can water-packed artichoke hearts, drained and quartered**
- **2 cups frozen peas**
- **1 28-ounce can diced plum tomatoes, drained**
- **1½ pounds cooked prawns**
- **24 steamer clams, steamed (page 250)**
- **1 4-ounce jar pimientos, drained**

Heat olive oil in a nonstick skillet; add onion and garlic. Sauté 3 to 5 minutes. Add chicken breasts; brown 2 to 3minutes on each side. Set aside.

Bring chicken broth just to boiling; add rice. Reduce heat; cover and simmer 15 to 20 minutes. Add saffron; simmer 5 to 10 minutes longer, or until rice is tender and moisture is absorbed. Add salt and cayenne.

Transfer rice to a 4-quart casserole; add chicken, artichoke hearts, peas, and tomatoes. Reserve drained tomoato liquid for later use. Bake uncovered at 350°F. for 30 minutes. Arrange prawns and clams on top of casserole; cook 3 to 5 minutes longer. Garnish with pimiento.

APPROXIMATE NUTRITIONAL INFORMATION PER SERVING

Total calories: 448
Total fat: 6 g
Saturated fat: 1 g
Dietary fiber: 4 g
Carbohydrates: 53 g
Protein: 44 g
Cholesterol: 53 mg
Sodium: 599 mg

Shrimp Fried Rice

6 servings

1 tablespoon olive oil

2 eggs

2 tablespoons water

2 green onions, chopped

3 cups cooked basmati rice, prepared according to instructions on the box and cooled

½ pound cooked baby shrimp

1 tablespoon reduced-sodium soy sauce

Heat olive oil in a nonstick skillet; lightly stir eggs with water; pour egg mixture into skillet. Stir in green onion and scramble eggs with green onion. Just as eggs begin to set, stir in cooked rice. Gently toss eggs and rice until rice is coated and eggs are cooked. Toss with shrimp. Transfer to a serving dish. Sprinkle with soy sauce.

APPROXIMATE NUTRITIONAL INFORMATION PER SERVING

Total calories: 181
Total fat: 3 g
Saturated fat: 1 g
Dietary fiber: 1 g
Carbohydrates: 24 g
Protein: 13 g
Cholesterol: 128 mg
Sodium: 178 mg

Tabbouleh with Parmesan

4 servings

1½ cups beef broth (page 151) or commercial broth

¼ teaspoon Tabasco sauce

⅛ teaspoon Kosher salt

1 cup wheat bulgur

¼ cup freshly grated Parmesan cheese

In a large saucepan, combine beef broth, Tabasco sauce and salt, and bring to a boil. Stir in bulgur. Remove from heat and cover. Let sit until broth is absorbed and bulgur is tender. Add Parmesan and toss.

Variation: Substitute couscous for bulgur.

Serving Suggestions: Good with chicken, lamb and seafood.

APPROXIMATE NUTRITIONAL INFORMATION PER SERVING

Total calories: 156
Total fat: 2 g
Saturated fat: 1 g
Dietary fiber: 6 g
Carbohydrates: 27 g
Protein: 8 g
Cholesterol: 5 mg
Sodium: 264 mg

Barley with Pine Nuts

4 cups

1 cup pearl barley

2 cups water

1½ cups beef stock (page 150) or commercial broth*

1½ cups chicken broth (page 143) or commercial broth*

2 tablespoons leek, white part only

⅓ pound fresh mushrooms, sliced

⅓ cup pine nuts

2 tablespoons chopped fresh parsley

Soak barley overnight in water. About 45–60 minutes before dinner, in a saucepan bring beef and chicken stocks to a boil. Add barley along with soaking liquid and boil 1–2 minutes. Add leek. Reduce heat, cover and simmer 30–45 minutes or until most of liquid is absorbed.

Add mushrooms. Continue to simmer 5–10 minutes or until mushrooms are tender and liquid is absorbed. Stir in pine nuts and parsley.

*Canned broth is higher in sodium.

Serving Suggestion: Good with pork.

APPROXIMATE NUTRITIONAL INFORMATION PER 1/2-CUP SERVING

Total calories: 137
Total fat: 3 g
Saturated fat: 1 g
Dietary fiber: 4 g
Carbohydrates: 22 g
Protein: 5 g
Cholesterol: trace
Sodium: 225 mg

Barley and Mushroom Pilaf

8 cups

1¾ cups pearl barley

1 tablespoon olive oil

1 onion, chopped

½ pound fresh mushrooms, sliced

4 cups beef broth, preferably homemade (page 151)

Soak barley several hours or overnight in enough cold water to cover. Drain.

Heat olive oil in a nonstick skillet. Sauté onion and barley in oil until onion is tender and barley is toasted. Add mushrooms; cook 2 to 3 minutes longer. Spoon into a large casserole.

Heat broth to boiling; pour over barley. Stir. Bake, covered, at 350°F. for 1 hour. Uncover; bake 1 to 1½ hours longer, or until liquid is absorbed.

APPROXIMATE NUTRITIONAL INFORMATION PER 1-CUP SERVING

Total calories: 184
Total fat: 3 g
Saturated fat: 0 g
Dietary fiber: 2 g
Carbohydrates: 32 g
Protein: 8 g
Cholesterol: 1 mg
Sodium: 144 mg

Tabbouleh with Mushrooms

6 cups

1 tablespoon olive oil

1 medium onion, chopped

½ cup chopped celery

½ pound fresh mushrooms, sliced

1 cup uncooked cracked wheat bulgur

½ teaspoon minced fresh oregano or ½ teaspoon dried

¼ teaspoon Kosher salt

¼ teaspoon black pepper

2 cups chicken or beef broth, preferably homemade (page 143 or 151)

Warm olive oil in a nonstick skillet over medium heat; add onion and celery. Cook 5 minutes. Add mushrooms and bulgur; cook, stirring constantly, for 10 minutes, or until bulgur is golden brown and vegetables are tender. Add oregano, salt, pepper, and broth. Cover and bring to a boil; reduce heat and simmer 15 to 20 minutes, or until broth is absorbed.

Variation: Sprinkle with chopped fresh parsley just before serving. Or add ¼ teaspoon fresh dill weed to broth.

APPROXIMATE NUTRITIONAL INFORMATION PER 1-CUP SERVING

Total calories: 125
Total fat: 2 g
Saturated fat: 0 g
Dietary fiber: 2 g
Carbohydrates: 22 g
Protein: 6 g
Cholesterol: 1 mg
Sodium: 182 mg

Couscous

4 servings

2 cups chicken broth (page 143)

½ cup chopped yellow onion

1 cup uncooked couscous

In a medium saucepan, bring broth to a boil. Add onion and couscous. Cover and remove from heat. Let stand 6-10 minutes. Fluff with a fork.

APPROXIMATE NUTRITIONAL INFORMATION PER 2/3-CUP SERVING

Total calories: 169
Total fat: 1 g
Saturated fat: 0 g
Dietary fiber: 2 g
Carbohydrates: 32 g
Protein: 6 g
Cholesterol: 1 mg
Sodium: 145 mg

Vegetables

Fresh Artichokes

2 to 3 servings

2 to 3 fresh artichokes

Fresh lemon juice

3 tablespoons chopped onion

3 garlic cloves

1½ cups dry white wine

Dash of Kosher salt

⅛ teaspoon pepper

1 lemon, sliced

Wash artichokes. Cut 1 inch off the top; cut off stem and tips of leaves. Brush cut edges with lemon juice.

Combine remaining ingredients. Bring to a boil. Place artichokes upright in mixture; cover and simmer until bottom leaves pull off easily. Drain. Serve hot or cold.

Note: Artichokes are delicious cooked in the microwave. See following recipe.

To Microwave: Place artichokes upright in a microwave-proof baking dish. Pour 4 tablespoons lemon juice and 2 tablespoons water over each artichoke. Cover dish with premium microwave-safe plastic wrap; prick a hole in the top of plastic wrap to allow steam to escape. For 1 medium artichoke, allow 5 to 7 minutes cooking time at full power; for 2 medium artichokes, allow 7 to 9 minutes.

Variation: Add 2 teaspoons olive oil to the poaching mixture.

Serving Suggestion: Accompany with Dijon Vinaigrette (page 207) or light mayonnaise mixed with a touch of fresh lemon juice and some grated onion.

APPROXIMATE NUTRITIONAL INFORMATION PER ARTICHOKE

Total calories: 156
Total fat: trace
Saturated fat: 0 g
Dietary fiber: 7 g
Carbohydrates: 20 g
Protein: 5 g
Cholesterol: 0 mg
Sodium: 309 mg

Artichoke Hearts with Lemon, Garlic, and Olive Oil

4 servings

1 14½-ounce can water-packed artichoke hearts, drained

Juice of ½ lemon

3 garlic cloves, minced

1 tablespoon extra-virgin olive oil

Cut artichoke hearts into quarters. Squeeze lemon juice over. Heat garlic with olive oil in a nonstick skillet; add artichokes with lemon and toss gently to coat. Cook 3 to 5 minutes over medium-high heat, or just until warm.

APPROXIMATE NUTRITIONAL INFORMATION PER SERVING

Total calories: 56
Total fat: 3 g
Saturated fat: 0 g
Dietary fiber: 1 g
Carbohydrates: 6 g
Protein: 2 g
Cholesterol: 0 mg
Sodium: 181 mg

Artichoke Frittata

8 servings

3 eggs

1 15-ounce can artichoke hearts, drained and cut into quarters

¾ cup grated reduced fat Cheddar cheese

In a bowl, lightly beat eggs. Stir in artichokes and cheese. Pour into a 9-inch quiche or pie plate. Bake at 350°F. 45 minutes, or until eggs are set and cheese is melted. Cut into wedges. Serve hot.

APPROXIMATE NUTRITIONAL INFORMATION PER SERVING

Total calories: 70
Total fat: 4 g
Saturated fat: 1 g
Dietary fiber: 1 g
Carbohydrates: 3 g
Protein: 6 g
Cholesterol: 65 mg
Sodium: 155 mg

Vermicelli-Stuffed Artichokes

4 servings

4 fresh artichokes, cooked

½ pound vermicelli, cooked al dente

1 ripe tomato, diced

⅓ cup Pesto (page 213)

Remove small center leaves of each artichoke, leaving a cup; carefully remove choke. In a bowl, toss vermicelli with tomato and pesto; stuff artichokes.

APPROXIMATE NUTRITIONAL INFORMATION PER SERVING

Total calories: 226
Total fat: 2 g
Saturated fat: 0 g
Dietary fiber: 9 g
Carbohydrates: 41 g
Protein:11 g
Cholesterol: 2 mg
Sodium: 403 mg

Asparagus with Lemon Vinaigrette

4 servings

1 pound fresh asparagus

¼ cup fresh lemon juice

2 teaspoons extra-virgin olive oil

½ teaspoon Kosher salt

¼ teaspoon black pepper

Microwave or steam asparagus until crisp-tender. Combine lemon juice, olive oil, salt and pepper. Pour over asparagus while asparagus is still warm.

Variation: Substitute ½ pound fresh broccoli for asparagus.

APPROXIMATE NUTRITIONAL INFORMATION PER SERVING

Total calories: 52
Total fat: 2 g
Saturated fat: trace
Dietary fiber: 1 g
Carbohydrates: 6 g
Protein: 3 g
Cholesterol: 0 mg
Sodium: 221 mg

Pan-Steamed Asparagus

4 servings

½ pound fresh asparagus, trimmed

2 tablespoons water

1 fresh lemon, cut into wedges

Wash and trim asparagus. In a nonstick skillet, heat water to boiling.

Add asparagus spears. Cover tightly and steam over medium-high heat 3–5 minutes, or until asparagus is crisp-tender. Shake occasionally. Serve with lemon.

APPROXIMATE NUTRITIONAL INFORMATION PER SERVING

Total calories: 16
Total fat: trace
Saturated fat: 0 g
Dietary fiber: 1 g
Carbohydrates: 3 g
Protein: 1 g
Cholesterol: 0 mg
Sodium: 2 mg

Green Beans with Lemon

4 servings

1 pound fresh green beans

¼ cup fresh lemon juice

¼ teaspoon black pepper

½ teaspoon or less Kosher salt (optional)

Wash beans; remove ends and strings. In a covered vegetable steamer basket over boiling water, steam beans 5–15 minutes (depending on freshness of beans), or until just tender (do not overcook). Combine lemon juice, black pepper and salt, and pour over beans while beans are still hot.

APPROXIMATE NUTRITIONAL INFORMATION PER SERVING

Total calories: 39
Total fat: 0 g
Saturated fat: 0 g
Dietary fiber: 4 g
Carbohydrates: 9 g
Protein: 2 g
Cholesterol: 0
Sodium: 298 mg

Green Beans with Tomatoes and Peppers

8 servings

1 pound fresh green beans

1 16-ounce can plum tomatoes chopped

1 red pepper, cut into ½-inch julienne strips

½ cup chopped red onion

¼ teaspoon black pepper

1 teaspoon Kosher salt

Wash green beans; remove ends and strings. Bring water to boil in a saucepan. Add beans, bring back to a boil. Reduce heat. Cover and simmer 10-20 minutes, until just tender. Drain and remove to serving bowl.

Meanwhile, heat tomatoes, pepper, onion, pepper, and salt in saucepan on low heat. Pour over cooked beans.

APPROXIMATE NUTRITIONAL INFORMATION PER SERVING

Total calories: 36
Total fat: 0 g
Saturated fat: 0 g
Dietary fiber: 3 g
Carbohydrates: 8 g
Protein: 2 g
Cholesterol: 0 mg
Sodium: 84 mg

Green Beans with Mushrooms and Water Chestnuts

7 ½-cup servings

¾ pound fresh green beans

½ pound fresh mushrooms, sliced

1 8-ounce can sliced water chestnuts

2 tablespoons lemon juice

½ teaspoon Kosher salt

⅛ teaspoon coarsely ground black pepper

Place beans on a vegetable steamer rack over boiling water; cook 15 to 20 minutes, or until beans are nearly tender. Add mushrooms the last 5 minutes, add water chestnuts the last 3 minutes. Spoon beans into a serving bowl; toss with lemon juice, salt, and pepper.

APPROXIMATE NUTRITIONAL INFORMATION PER SERVING

Total calories: 38
Total fat: trace
Saturated fat: 0 g
Dietary fiber: 1 g
Carbohydrates: 9 g
Protein: 2 g
Cholesterol: 0 mg
Sodium: 130 mg

Green Beans with Pimiento

4 servings

½ pound fresh green beans

1 2-ounce jar pimiento strips, drained

Microwave or steam green beans until crisp-tender. Drain. Arrange in symmetrical bundles of three on a serving tray. Place a pimiento strip around the center of each bundle.

APPROXIMATE NUTRITIONAL INFORMATION PER SERVING

Total calories: 77
Total fat: trace
Saturated fat: trace
Dietary fiber: 0 g
Carbohydrates: 14 g
Protein: 4 g
Cholesterol: 0 mg
Sodium: 3 mg

Great Green Beans

6 servings

1 pound fresh green beans

1 15-ounce can water-packed artichoke hearts, drained and quartered

¼ cup fresh lemon juice

1 tablespoon extra-virgin olive oil

½ teaspoon Kosher salt

¼ teaspoon coarsely ground black pepper

Steaming is an easy, low-calorie way to prepare all sorts of vegetables. Steamed vegetables keep their color and nutrients—and they taste fantastic.

Wash beans; remove ends and strings. Place a metal vegetable steamer in a medium saucepan filled with 1 inch of water. Bring water to a boil.

Add beans; cover and steam 15 to 20 minutes, or until beans are just tender (do not overcook). Remove beans from steamer. Add artichokes. Toss with lemon juice, olive oil, salt, and pepper. Serve hot or cold.

APPROXIMATE NUTRITIONAL INFORMATION PER SERVING

Total calories: 63
Total fat: 3 g
Saturated fat: 0 g
Dietary fiber: 3 g
Carbohydrates: 9 g
Protein: 2 g
Cholesterol: 0 mg
Sodium: 404 mg

Green Beans, Italian Style

6 servings

1 pound fresh green beans

½ cup chicken broth, preferably homemade (page 143)

1 teaspoon olive oil

2 cups canned plum tomatoes

Dash of oregano

½ teaspoon Kosher salt

¼ teaspoon black pepper

Wash beans. Remove ends and strings; cut on the diagonal into 1-inch pieces. Set aside. Combine remaining ingredients and bring to a boil.

Add beans; cook covered for 15 to 20 minutes, or until beans are tender (do not overcook).

APPROXIMATE NUTRITIONAL INFORMATION PER SERVING

Total calories: 49
Total fat: 1 g
Saturated fat: 0 g
Dietary fiber: 3 g
Carbohydrates: 9 g
Protein: 2 g
Cholesterol: 0 mg
Sodium: 361 mg

Red Beets Vinaigrette

4 servings

4 medium-to-large beets

⅓ cup raspberry vinegar

pinch Kosher salt

pinch coarsely ground black pepper

Wash beets; trim stems and roots. Cut into julienne strips. In a covered vegetable steamer basket over boiling water, steam beets 10–20 minutes, or until barely tender. Remove to serving bowl. While beets are still hot, toss with raspberry vinegar. Season with salt and pepper.

Variation: While beets are still hot, toss with raspberry vinegar and 2 tablespoons walnut oil. (Walnut oil will increase the calories by 125 per tablespoon.)

APPROXIMATE NUTRITIONAL INFORMATION PER SERVING

Total calories: 49
Total fat: 0 g
Saturated fat: 0 g
Dietary fiber: 2 g
Carbohydrates: 6 g
Protein: 1 g
Cholesterol: 0 mg
Sodium: 64 mg

Stir-Fried Broccolini

4 servings

1 bunch broccolini

1 tablespoon extra-virgin olive oil

juice of 1 lemon

2 drops hot chili oil

pinch Kosher salt

pinch coarsely ground black pepper

In a nonstick skillet, heat olive oil. Add broccolini and stir-fry 2–3 minutes, or until crisp-tender. Squeeze lemon juice over broccolini. Toss with chili oil, salt, and pepper.

APPROXIMATE NUTRITIONAL INFORMATION PER SERVING

Total calories: 74
Total fat: 4 g
Saturated fat: 1 g
Dietary fiber: 5 g
Carbohydrates: 9 g
Protein: 5 g
Cholesterol: 0 mg
Sodium: 41 mg

Broccoli with Lemon Mustard Sauce

4 servings

1 bunch fresh broccoli, florets only

1 cup fresh lemon juice

1 tablespoon Dijon mustard

In a covered vegetable steamer basket over boiling water, steam broccoli 2–3 minutes, or until crisp-tender. Combine lemon juice with Dijon mustard and warm over low heat. Pour over broccoli. Toss and serve at once.

Variation: Substitute fresh asparagus or cauliflower for broccoli.

APPROXIMATE NUTRITIONAL INFORMATION PER SERVING

Total calories: 62
Total fat: 1 g
Saturated fat: 0 g
Dietary fiber: 5 g
Carbohydrates: 14 g
Protein: 5 g
Cholesterol: 0 mg
Sodium: 132 mg

Stir-Fried Broccoli and Cauliflower with Red Peppers

4 servings

1 tablespoon extra-virgin olive oil

1 teaspoon sesame oil

2 cups broccoli florets

2 cups cauliflower florets

¼ cup chicken broth, preferably homemade (page 143)

1 cup red pepper, seeded and cut into ¼ -inch strips

This recipe offers a variety of color (green, white and red) as well as a variety of vegetables (green leafy, cruciferous, and vitamin C-rich).

Place nonstick wok or skillet over high heat. When wok is hot, add olive oil and sesame oil. When oils are hot, add broccoli and cauliflower; stir-fry, uncovered for 1 minute. Add chicken broth. Cover and cook 2 minutes. Add red peppers. Cover and cook one minute longer, or until vegetables are crisp-tender.

APPROXIMATE NUTRITIONAL INFORMATION PER SERVING

Total calories: 72
Total fat: 5 g
Saturated fat: 0 g
Dietary fiber: 3 g
Carbohydrates: 6 g
Protein: 3 g
Cholesterol: 0 mg
Sodium: 82 mg

Little Green Trees

4 servings

2 tablespoons chicken broth, preferably homemade (page 143), or water

3 cups broccoli florets

juice of ½ lemon (optional)

When our niece and nephew Betsy and Guy Hedreen were young, they referred to broccoli as green trees. That is how we came up with the name for this recipe.

Stove Top: In a nonstick skillet, heat broth or water over medium-high heat. Add broccoli florets; cover tightly and steam 3 to 5 minutes, or until broccoli is crisp-tender. Shake pan occasionally during cooking. Drain. Squeeze lemon juice over broccoli.

Microwave: In a microwave-proof baking dish, arrange broccoli in a single layer, florets toward center. Cover with microwave-safe plastic wrap, and prick the plastic wrap to allow steam to escape. Cook at full power 3 to 4 minutes, or just until barely tender.

APPROXIMATE NUTRITIONAL INFORMATION PER SERVING

Total calories: 20
Total fat: 0 g
Saturated fat: 0 g
Dietary fiber: 2 g
Carbohydrates: 4 g
Protein: 2 g
Cholesterol: 0 mg
Sodium: 50 mg

Baby Carrots Vinaigrette

4 servings

12 baby carrots

2 tablespoons raspberry vinegar

black pepper

In a covered vegetable steamer basket over boiling water, steam carrots 3–4 minutes, or just until crisp-tender. Remove to serving bowl. While carrots are still hot, toss with raspberry vinegar. Season generously with black pepper.

Variation: Serve cold as part of an antipasto tray.

APPROXIMATE NUTRITIONAL INFORMATION PER SERVING

Total calories: 16
Total fat: 0 g
Saturated fat: 0 g
Dietary fiber: 1 g
Carbohydrates: 3 g
Protein: 0 g
Cholesterol: 0 mg
Sodium: 10 mg

Sautéed Baby Carrots

4 servings

2 teaspoons extra-virgin olive oil

1 large garlic clove, thinly sliced

20 baby carrots, peeled

¼ cup chicken broth, preferably homemade (page 143)

1 tablespoon chopped fresh parsley

1 tablespoon chopped fresh mint

⅛ teaspoon ground nutmeg

⅛ teaspoon Kosher salt

Carrots are a great vegetable choice because they are high in vitamin A.

Heat a nonstick wok or skillet over high heat. When wok is hot, add olive oil. When oil is hot, add garlic and carrots; stir-fry, uncovered, for 1 minute. Add chicken broth; cover and cook 3 to 5 minutes, or until carrots are crisp-tender. Sprinkle with chopped fresh parsley and mint the last minute of cooking. Season with nutmeg and salt.

APPROXIMATE NUTRITIONAL INFORMATION PER SERVING

Total calories: 54
Total fat: 3 g
Saturated fat: 0 g
Dietary fiber: 2 g
Carbohydrates: 8 g
Protein: 1 g
Cholesterol: 0 mg
Sodium: 145 mg

Grilled Corn in Husks

6 servings

6 ears corn, in their husks

Pull down husks on each ear of corn, leaving them attached at the base. Remove silky strands and throw away. Pull husks back up around each ear and secure with string. Soak the ears in cold water for 30 minutes. Drain. Prepare the grill for direct grilling over medium-high heat. Grill the corn, turning occasionally, for 25-30 minutes, charring husks.

Variation: Instead of using butter on corn, try lime juice or lemon juice, or even barbecue or stir-fry sauce.

APPROXIMATE NUTRITIONAL INFORMATION PER EACH 5 x 1¾ EAR OF CORN

Total calories: 83
Total fat: trace
Saturated fat: trace
Dietary fiber: 6 g
Carbohydrates: 19 g
Protein: 2 g
Cholesterol: 0 mg
Sodium: 13 mg

Eggplant Parmigiana

6 servings

1½ tablespoons olive oil

2 cloves garlic, sliced

1 onion, chopped

2 cups tomato, chopped

½ cup chicken broth (page 143) or canned broth

1 teaspoon basil

1 teaspoon parsley

1 teaspoon oregano

¼ teaspoon Kosher salt

¼ teaspoon black pepper

2 eggs, slightly beaten

⅓ cup Parmesan cheese

1 eggplant, cut into ⅛-inch slices

½ cup shredded part-skim mozzarella cheese

In a medium nonstick skillet, heat 2 teaspoons of the olive oil. Add garlic and onion, and sauté 6–8 minutes or until onion is tender; add tomato, chicken broth, basil, parsley, oregano, salt and pepper. Simmer, uncovered, over low heat 20 minutes, stirring often. Set aside.

Combine beaten eggs with 2 tablespoons of the Parmesan cheese. Dip eggplant into egg mixture. In a large nonstick skillet, heat remaining olive oil. Cook eggplant 1 minute on each side or until eggplant is lightly browned. Remove to platter as eggplant is cooked.

Pour ¼ of the tomato mixture on the bottom of an 8 x 8 x 2-inch ovenproof casserole dish. Layer eggplant over top. Sprinkle eggplant with ¼ more sauce, then with ⅓ mozzarella, then with ⅓ Parmesan. Repeat layers. Pour remaining sauce over top and sprinkle with remaining mozzarella and Parmesan. Cover with foil and bake in a 350°F. oven 30 minutes.

Serving Suggestion: Good with chicken and seafood.

APPROXIMATE NUTRITIONAL INFORMATION PER SERVING

Total calories: 189
Total fat: 10 g
Saturated fat: 3 g
Dietary fiber: 4 g
Carbohydrates: 13 g
Protein: 11 g
Cholesterol: 86 mg
Sodium: 360 mg

Roasted Garlic

4 servings

4 whole garlic heads

1 tablespoon extra-virgin olive oil

Leaving garlic head intact, remove outer layer of skin from the head.

Lay each head on the side and cut about ½ inch straight across the top. Arrange garlic in a small, shallow ovenproof casserole. Drizzle ½ teaspoon olive oil on top of each head, letting it run between the individual cloves. Cover pan with foil. Bake at 350°F. for 30 to 45 minutes, until garlic is tender when pieced with a toothpick. Serve the heads on individual bread or dinner plates.

To eat, peel off individual cloves and squeeze the roasted garlic onto bread, potatoes, or vegetables.

APPROXIMATE NUTRITIONAL INFORMATION PER SERVING

Total calories: 60
Total fat: 2 g
Saturated fat: 0 g
Dietary fiber: 0 g
Carbohydrates: 10 g
Protein: 2 g
Cholesterol: 0 mg
Sodium: 10 mg

Marinated Mushrooms

6 cups

1½ pounds fresh mushrooms

2 cups chicken broth (page 143), preferably homemade

1 cup rice vinegar

Wipe mushrooms with a damp paper towel. Trim stems. In a small stock pot, combine mushrooms with stock. Cook over medium heat, stirring frequently, 20–30 minutes. Remove from heat. Allow mushrooms to cool in the broth. Drain. Toss with rice vinegar. Serve or refrigerate for later use.

Serving Suggestion: Marinated mushrooms, cauliflower and artichoke hearts are nice additions to an antipasto or vegetable platter.

APPROXIMATE NUTRITIONAL INFORMATION PER 1/2-CUP SERVING

Total calories: 28
Total fat: 0 g
Saturated fat: 0 g
Dietary fiber: 1 g
Carbohydrates: 3 g
Protein: 2 g
Cholesterol: 0 mg
Sodium: 49 mg

Marinated Mushrooms with Artichoke Hearts

10 cups

1½ pounds fresh mushrooms

2½ cups chicken broth (page 143), or commercial broth

1–2 15-ounce cans artichoke hearts, drained

1½ cups rice vinegar

Wipe mushrooms with a damp paper towel. Trim stems. In a small stock pot, combine mushrooms with broth. Cook over medium heat, stirring frequently, 20–30 minutes. Add artichoke hearts. Cook 10 minutes. Remove from heat. Allow mushrooms and artichokes to cool in broth. Drain. Toss with rice vinegar. Serve or refrigerate for later use.

Serving Suggestion: Good as an antipasto or salad course, as part of a dinner buffet or with sandwiches on a picnic.

APPROXIMATE NUTRITIONAL INFORMATION PER CUP

Total calories: 45
Total fat: 0 g
Saturated fat: 0 g
Dietary fiber: 1 g
Carbohydrates: 5 g
Protein: 3 g
Cholesterol: 0 mg
Sodium: 207 mg

Sautéed Mushrooms

6 1/2-cup servings

2 tablespoons extra-virgin olive oil

1 garlic clove, minced

1 pound fresh mushrooms, caps or pieces

Heat olive oil and garlic in a heavy skillet. Add mushrooms. Cook uncovered over medium heat, stirring frequently, for 3 to 4 minutes.

APPROXIMATE NUTRITIONAL INFORMATION PER SERVING

Total calories: 55
Total fat: 4 g
Saturated fat: trace
Dietary fiber: 1 g
Carbohydrates: 4 g
Protein: 2 g
Cholesterol: 0 mg
Sodium: 3 mg

Roasted Sweet Peppers

8 peppers

8 large red and green sweet peppers

1 tablespoon olive oil

2 garlic cloves

2 teaspoons tarragon wine vinegar

3 teaspoons chopped fresh basil, or ½ teaspoon dried

½ teaspoon fresh rosemary or ¼ teaspoon dried

½ teaspoon minced fresh oregano or ¼ teaspoon dried

Prepare the grill for direct grilling over medium-high heat. Cook the peppers, turning as necessary, until skin is blistered and charred evenly, about 15-20 minutes. Place peppers in a paper bag, seal the top, and let sit for 5-10 minutes. Take out of bag. Remove skin, stems, and seeds; slice into strips. Combine remaining ingredients; pour over peppers.

Chill 24 to 48 hours. Serve with tomato slices or add to sandwiches or pizza.

APPROXIMATE NUTRITIONAL INFORMATION PER 1-PEPPER SERVING

Total calories: 42
Total fat: 2 g
Saturated fat: 0 g
Dietary fiber: 2 g
Carbohydrates: 7 g
Protein: 1 g
Cholesterol: 0 mg
Sodium: 2 mg

Grilled Peppers and Onions

4 servings

1 large red pepper

1 large yellow pepper

1 large green pepper

1 medium white onion

1 medium red onion

1½ tablespoons extra-virgin olive oil

Wash peppers and remove seeds. Cut into 2-inch strips. Peel onions and slice. Toss with olive oil and place in grill basket.

Prepare grill for direct grilling over medium-high heat. Place basket on grill. Close cover. Cook for 15-20 minutes, until skin on peppers chars.

APPROXIMATE NUTRITIONAL INFORMATION PER SERVING

Total calories: 42
Total fat: 2 g
Saturated fat: 0 g
Dietary fiber: 3 g
Carbohydrates: 8 g
Protein: 1 g
Cholesterol: 0 mg
Sodium: 3 mg

Pan-Fried Potatoes

4 servings

2 tablespoons olive oil

3 large Russet potatoes, unpeeled and diced or thinly sliced

pinch Kosher salt

pinch coarsely ground black pepper

In a nonstick skillet, heat oil. Add potatoes. Cook over medium-low heat for 5 minutes. Turn. Continue to cook for 20-25 minutes, turning frequently until nicely browned. Season with salt and pepper.
.

APPROXIMATE NUTRITIONAL INFORMATION PER SERVING

Total calories: 132
Total fat: 6 g
Saturated fat: 1 g
Dietary fiber: 7 g
Carbohydrates: 14 g
Protein: 6 g
Cholesterol: 0 mg
Sodium: 19 mg

Hash Brown Potatoes

2 servings

4 new potatoes, diced into ½-inch pieces

1½ teaspoons chopped onion (optional)

1½ tablespoons olive oil

pinch Kosher salt

pinch coarsely ground black pepper

Heat olive oil in a nonstick skillet. Add the potatoes and cook over medium-low heat for 5 minutes. Turn. Continue to cook 15-20 minutes until desired brownness. Season with salt and pepper.

APPROXIMATE NUTRITIONAL INFORMATION PER SERVING

Total calories: 180
Total fat: 7 g
Saturated fat: 1 g
Dietary fiber: 2 g
Carbohydrates: 28 g
Protein: 3 g
Cholesterol: 0 mg
Sodium: 273 mg

Country Fried Potatoes

4 servings

1½ tablespoons extra-virgin olive oil

1½ tablespoons minced garlic

4 medium red potatoes with skins (about 1 pound), very thinly sliced

In a nonstick skillet, heat olive oil over medium-low heat. Add garlic and sauté 2 to 3 minutes.

Add potatoes to skillet and sauté 4 to 5 minutes. Turn and cook 8 to 10 minutes longer, turning frequently until nicely browned.

APPROXIMATE NUTRITIONAL INFORMATION PER SERVING

Total calories: 124
Total fat: 6 g
Saturated fat: 1 g
Dietary fiber: 1 g
Carbohydrates: 16 g
Protein: 2 g
Cholesterol: 0 mg
Sodium: 6 mg

Potatoes with Mushrooms and Tomatoes

8 servings

⅓ cup beef consommé

2 tablespoons dry white wine

2 teaspoons chervil

1 tablespoon chopped Italian parsley

1 tablespoon extra-virgin olive oil

½ teaspoon Kosher salt

¼ teaspoon black pepper

1½ pounds tiny red potatoes, cooked and halved

**¼ pound fresh mushrooms, cooked and sliced, or
1 8-ounce can mushroom stems and pieces, drained**

1 large tomato, diced

In a small bowl, combine consommé, white wine, chervil, parsley, olive oil, salt and pepper.

Pour over potatoes while potatoes are still warm. Arrange in a low salad bowl. Toss with mushrooms and tomatoes.

Thoroughly drain excess marinade. Serve hot or cold.

APPROXIMATE NUTRITIONAL INFORMATION PER SERVING

Total calories: 100
Total fat: 2 g
Saturated fat: 0 g
Dietary fiber: 1 g
Carbohydrates: 18 g
Protein: 2 g
Cholesterol: trace
Sodium: 149 mg

Steamed Red Potatoes

4 servings

8 bite-size red potatoes
pinch Kosher salt
pinch coarsely ground black pepper

Select the smallest, most uniform bite-size (not dinner-size) red potatoes available. Scrub. In a covered vegetable steamer basket over boiling water, steam potatoes 15–20 minutes, or until just tender. Season

Variation: Chill. Toss with 1 red pepper that has been cut into julienne strips. Serve as a salad. Toss with Italian Vinaigrette.

APPROXIMATE NUTRITIONAL INFORMATION PER 2 BITE-SIZE POTATOES

Total calories: 88
Total fat: 0 g
Saturated fat: 0 g
Dietary fiber: 8 g
Carbohydrates: 18 g
Protein: 7 g
Cholesterol: 0 mg
Sodium: 24 mg

Steamed Red Potatoes Vinaigrette

4 servings

8 bite-size red potatoes
1½ tablespoons olive oil
¼ cup fresh lemon juice
¼ teaspoon coarsely ground black pepper
½ teaspoon Kosher salt

Select the smallest, most uniform bite-size (not dinner-size) red potatoes available. Scrub. In a covered vegetable steamer basket over boiling water, steam potatoes 15–20 minutes, or until just tender.

Remove potatoes to serving bowl. Combine oil, lemon juice, pepper and salt. Pour over potatoes while potatoes are still hot.

APPROXIMATE NUTRITIONAL INFORMATION PER 2 BITE-SIZE POTATOES

Total calories: 122
Total fat: trace
Saturated fat: 0 g
Dietary fiber: 8 g
Carbohydrates: 23 g
Protein: trace
Cholesterol: 0 mg
Sodium: 240 mg

New Potatoes with Sour Cream and Dill

4 servings

1 pound small new potatoes, unpeeled

1 small red onion, thinly sliced

1 green pepper, thinly sliced into rings

1 cup nonfat sour cream

1 tablespoon chopped fresh dill, or ¼ teaspoon dried

½ teaspoon Kosher salt

¼ teaspoon coarsely ground black pepper

Scrub potatoes; boil or steam until just tender. Place whole or sliced into a serving bowl; tuck onion and green pepper slices among potatoes. Combine sour cream, dill, salt, and pepper. Pass with potatoes.

APPROXIMATE NUTRITIONAL INFORMATION PER SERVING

Total calories: 150
Total fat: 2 g
Saturated fat: 1 g
Dietary fiber: 3 g
Carbohydrates: 29 g
Protein: 5 g
Cholesterol: 7 mg
Sodium: 250 mg

Parsleyed Potatoes

4 servings

4 new potatoes (approximately 1 pound)

1 tablespoon olive oil

Juice of ½ lemon

1 tablespoon chopped fresh Italian parsley

Scrub potatoes; steam in their jackets until just tender. Toss with olive oil. Drizzle with lemon juice. Sprinkle with parsley.

APPROXIMATE NUTRITIONAL INFORMATION PER SERVING

Total calories: 154
Total fat: 4 g
Saturated fat: 0 g
Dietary fiber: 2 g
Carbohydrates: 29 g
Protein: 3 g
Cholesterol: 0 mg
Sodium: 37 mg

Mashed Potatoes

4 servings

1½ pounds Yukon Gold potatoes

1 tablespoon Kosher salt

¼ -⅓ cup hot nonfat milk

Since these potatoes don't call for butter and cream, you save calories and fat grams And the best part is they taste just as delicious as their high-fat counterparts.

Wash potatoes, then pare and quarter. In a 4 -quart saucepan, bring 2 quarts of water and salt to a boil. Add potatoes and bring the water back to a boil. Lower the heat and simmer for 10-20 minutes until tender. Drain.

Using a potato masher or electric mixer, mash hot potatoes thoroughly until no lumps remain. Gradually beat in hot milk (amount depends on kind and age of potatoes used). Beat until potatoes are smooth and fluffy.

APPROXIMATE NUTRITIONAL INFORMATION PER SERVING

Total calories: 106
Total fat: 0 g
Saturated fat: 0 g
Dietary fiber: 2 g
Carbohydrates: 24 g
Protein: 3 g
Cholesterol: 0 mg
Sodium: 16 mg

Garlic Mashed Potatoes

4 servings

1½ pounds Yukon Gold potatoes

salt

10 large garlic cloves
(about 1 head), peeled

⅓–½ cup hot chicken broth,
preferably homemade (page 143)
or commercial broth

⅓ cup hot nonfat milk

The key to this lean version of mashed potatoes is the substitution of chicken broth for butter, and nonfat milk for the typical addition of cream.

Wash potatoes, then pare and quarter. In a 2½-quart saucepan, cover potatoes with water, adding ½ teaspoon salt per 1 cup water, and heat to boiling. Cover and boil 15 minutes. Add garlic. Continue boiling until potatoes are tender, 10 to 20 minutes; drain cooking water.

Using a potato masher or electric mixer, mash hot potatoes thoroughly until no lumps remain. Gradually beat in hot chicken broth (amount depends on kind and age of potatoes used). Gradually beat in hot milk. Beat until potatoes are smooth and fluffy.

APPROXIMATE NUTRITIONAL INFORMATION PER SERVING

Total calories: 120
Total fat: 0 g
Saturated fat: 0 g
Dietary fiber: 2 g
Carbohydrates: 26 g
Protein: 4 g
Cholesterol: 0 mg
Sodium: 103 mg

Roasted Red Potatoes with Lemon and Olive Oil

4 servings

1 pound tiny red potatoes, halved

¼ cup fresh lemon juice

2 tablespoons olive oil

½ teaspoon Kosher salt

¼ teaspoon coarsely ground black pepper

In a 13 x 9 x 2-inch ovenproof casserole dish, arrange potatoes.

Combine lemon juice, olive oil, salt, and pepper; pour over potatoes. Roast in a 350°F. oven 30–40 minutes or until potatoes are tender, turning 3–4 times to baste.

APPROXIMATE NUTRITIONAL INFORMATION PER SERVING

Total calories: 187
Total fat: 6 g
Saturated fat: 19 g
Dietary fiber: 3 g
Carbohydrates: 30 g
Protein: 2 g
Cholesterol: 0 mg
Sodium: 249 mg

Garlic Roasted Red Potatoes

4 servings

1 pound small red potatoes

1½ tablespoon extra-virgin olive oil

½ cup peeled and minced garlic (about 8 large cloves)

2 tablespoons chopped fresh rosemary sprigs or 1 teaspoon powdered rosemary

pinch Kosher salt

pinch coarsely ground black pepper

1 tablespoon minced fresh parsley

The fresh rosemary and garlic add a whole new level of taste to these roasted potatoes.

Preheat oven to 400°F. Scrub potatoes and cut into quarters. Toss will olive oil, garlic, and rosemary until coated. Arrange potatoes on a baking sheet in a single layer.

Bake 15 minutes, or until potato tops begin to brown. Turn potatoes and continue baking 20 to 30 minutes more, turning frequently, until potatoes are tender and golden brown. Season with salt and pepper. Sprinkle with parsley.

APPROXIMATE NUTRITIONAL INFORMATION PER SERVING

Total calories: 144
Total fat: 7 g
Saturated fat: 1 g
Dietary fiber: 1 g
Carbohydrates: 17 g
Protein: 2 g
Cholesterol: 0 mg
Sodium: 8 mg

Baked Potatoes with Sour Cream and Chives

2 servings

2 medium Russet potatoes

1 teaspoon olive oil

½ cup nonfat sour cream

¼ cup chopped chives or green onions

¼ cup Tomato Salsa, preferably homemade (page 214) (optional)

Scrub potatoes in their jackets. Rub with olive oil. Prick with a fork. Bake at 425°F. for 40 to 60 minutes, or at 350°F. for 60 to 80 minutes. Cut potatoes open and top with sour cream, chives, and salsa.

APPROXIMATE NUTRITIONAL INFORMATION PER SERVING

Total calories: 286
Total fat: 2 g
Saturated fat: 0 g
Dietary fiber: 3 g
Carbohydrates: 58 g
Protein: 8 g
Cholesterol: 1 mg
Sodium: 362 mg

Roast Potatoes with Rosemary

4 servings

4 new potatoes, scrubbed and halved

2 tablespoons olive oil

fresh rosemary

pinch Kosher salt

pinch coarsely ground black pepper

¼ cup water

Brush potatoes with olive oil. Sprinkle with salt, rosemary, salt, and pepper.

Arrange cut side up in shallow roasting pan. Pour ¼ cup water in bottom of pan. Roast at 375°F. 40–60 minutes, or until tender.

APPROXIMATE NUTRITIONAL INFORMATION PER POTATO

Total calories: 169
Total fat: 4 g
Saturated fat: 0 g
Dietary fiber: 1 g
Carbohydrates: 25 g
Protein: 3 g
Cholesterol: 0 mg
Sodium: 4 mg

Stuffed Potatoes

4 servings

2 large Russet baking potatoes

1 tablespoons extra-virgin olive oil

8 sprigs fresh rosemary

1 small white onion, finely chopped

2 tablespoons finely chopped pickled jalapeño nacho rings

¼ cup low-fat (1%) buttermilk

½ cup nonfat sour cream

2 tablespoons chopped green onions

¼ cup shredded reduced-fat cheddar cheese

¼ cup shredded part skim mozzarella cheese

There's more to potato toppings than sour cream and chives! If the potato shells fall apart when you scoop out the insides, just piece them together as best you can before placing the mashed potatoes on top. Once the cheese melts, they'll look perfect.

Scrub potatoes; cut in half lengthwise. Lay each potato half, cut side down, on a piece of aluminum foil. Drizzle ½ teaspoon of the olive oil among the potato halves and rub each half on all sides with the oil. Tuck 2 sprigs of rosemary under each potato half. Wrap potato in aluminum foil. Bake at 425°F. for 30 to 40 minutes, or until tender.

In a nonstick skillet, heat remaining 1 teaspoon olive oil. Add onion and sauté until golden, 3 to 5 minutes. Toss with jalapeños.

Carefully scoop the insides of each potato half into a large bowl, leaving a thin shell. Using a potato masher or electric mixer, mash hot potatoes thoroughly until no lumps remain. Gradually beat in buttermilk until potatoes are smooth and fluffy. Gently stir in the sour cream, green onions, sautéed onions and jalapeños. Divide the potato mixture among the 4 potato shells. Top with cheddar and mozzarella cheeses. Rebake the potatoes at 350°F. until the cheese melts, about 10 minutes.

APPROXIMATE NUTRITIONAL INFORMATION PER SERVING

Total calories: 140
Total fat: 2 g
Saturated fat: 0 g
Dietary fiber: 2 g
Carbohydrates: 23 g
Protein: 7 g
Cholesterol: 23 mg
Sodium: 162 mg

Jumbo Oven Fries

4 servings

2 tablespoons extra-virgin olive oil

2 pounds new potatoes

salt to taste

Roasting the potatoes actually brings out their flavor. You won't miss the deep fat.

Preheat oven to 400°F. Move oven rack to highest position. Place a nonstick baking sheet on rack and heat at least 5 minutes.

Meanwhile, scrub potatoes. Cut each potato lengthwise into fourths. Cut each fourth lengthwise into ¼-inch strips. Toss with olive oil.

Arrange potatoes on nonstick baking sheet. Bake for 15 to 20 minutes. Turn with a fork or tongs and bake 15 to 20 minutes until they are tender and evenly browned on all sides. Season with salt.

APPROXIMATE NUTRITIONAL INFORMATION PER SERVING

Total calories: 157
Total fat: 3 g
Saturated fat: 0 g
Dietary fiber: 3 g
Carbohydrates: 31 g
Protein: 4 g
Cholesterol: 0 mg
Sodium: 11 mg

Variation: For Rosemary Oven Fries, prepare as directed above and after tossing the potatoes with olive oil, sprinkle them with 2 to 3 tablespoons chopped fresh rosemary sprigs, Kosher salt, and coarsely ground pepper to taste.

Loaded Baked Potatoes

4 servings

2 large Russet potatoes
1 teaspoon extra-virgin olive oil
8 sprigs of fresh rosemary
pinch Kosher salt
pinch coarsely ground black pepper
¼ cup nonfat sour cream
¼ cup nonfat cottage cheese

You won't miss the butter when you discover how much flavor is added by the fresh rosemary! And we think you'll find this sour-cream-cottage-cheese mixture just as pleasing as full-fat sour cream.

Preheat oven to 425°F. Scrub potatoes. Cut in half lengthwise.

Lay each potato half, cut side down, on a piece of aluminum foil; rub on all sides with olive oil. Tuck 2 sprigs of rosemary under each potato half. Wrap each half in aluminum foil.

Bake at 425°F. for 30 to 40 minutes, or until tender. Season with salt and pepper. Combine sour cream and cottage cheese; pass with potatoes.

APPROXIMATE NUTRITIONAL INFORMATION PER SERVING

Total calories: 102
Total fat: 1 g
Saturated fat: 0 g
Dietary fiber: 1 g
Carbohydrates: 17 g
Protein: 7 g
Cholesterol: 1 mg
Sodium: 118 mg

Snow Peas

4 servings

1 pound snow peas
¼ cup chicken broth (page 143)
2 tablespoons Wasabi Sauce, optional

Snap ends of snow peas and remove strings. Heat broth in a wok; stir in snow peas. Cover and cook 2–3 minutes, or until peas are deep green and crisp-tender.

APPROXIMATE NUTRITIONAL INFORMATION PER SERVING

Total calories: 49
Total fat: 0 g
Saturated fat: 0 g
Dietary fiber: 4 g
Carbohydrates: 8 g
Protein: 3 g
Cholesterol: 0 mg
Sodium: 22 mg

Ratatouille

10 servings

1 medium eggplant, cut into 1-inch cubes

1 tablespoon Kosher salt (to be rinsed off)

1 large onion, sliced into rings

3 medium zucchini, cut into ½-inch slices

2 green peppers, seeded and cut into ½-inch pieces

3 large tomatoes, chopped

1 cup minced fresh Italian parsley

½ teaspoon Kosher salt

1 tablespoon chopped fresh basil, or ½ teaspoon dried

4 garlic cloves, pressed

1 tablespoon olive oil

pinch Kosher sal

pinch ground pepper

In large colander, toss eggplant with salt and allow to drain for 30 to 60 minutes. Rinse eggplant with water and drain well.

Layer vegetables in a deep ovenproof casserole; sprinkle with parsley, salt, basil, and garlic. Drizzle with olive oil. Chill overnight. Bake, covered, in a 350°F. oven for 1½ hours. Sprinkle with salt and pepper.

APPROXIMATE NUTRITIONAL INFORMATION PER SERVING

Total calories: 43
Total fat: 2 g
Saturated fat: 0 g
Dietary fiber: 2 g
Carbohydrates: 7 g
Protein: 1 g
Cholesterol: 0 mg
Sodium: 69 mg

Stir-Fried Snow Peas

4 servings

1 tablespoon olive oil

1 teaspoon finely minced garlic

1 teaspoon minced fresh ginger

¼ teaspoon crushed red pepper

½ pound snow peas or sugar snap peas

In a nonstick skillet, heat olive oil, garlic, ginger, and red pepper, sauté 2–3 minutes. Add snow peas. Stir-fry 2–3 minutes or just until crisp-tender.

APPROXIMATE NUTRITIONAL INFORMATION PER SERVING

Total calories: 55
Total fat: 3 g
Saturated fat: 0 g
Dietary fiber: 1 g
Carbohydrates: 45 g
Protein: 2 g
Cholesterol: 0 mg
Sodium: 3 mg

Lemony Spinach

4 servings

2 pounds fresh spinach

juice of ½ lemon

pinch Kosher salt

pinch coarsely ground black pepper

The lemon in the spinach recipe will help the body absorb the iron in the spinach.

Remove spinach stems and wash. Place a metal steamer in a medium saucepan filled with 1 inch of water. Bring water to a boil. Add spinach, cover, and steam for 3 to 4 minutes, or until just wilted. Remove from steamer; season with lemon juice, salt and pepper.

APPROXIMATE NUTRITIONAL INFORMATION PER SERVING

Total calories: 43
Total fat: 0 g
Saturated fat: 0 g
Dietary fiber: 4 g
Carbohydrates: 7 g
Protein: 5 g
Cholesterol: 0 mg
Sodium: 126 mg

Popeye Spinach

4 servings

1 tablespoon extra-virgin olive oil

2 garlic cloves, peeled and minced

1 pound fresh spinach, trimmed and washed

2 tablespoons water

salt and pepper to taste

1 teaspoon balsamic vinegar

Check your produce market for baby spinach leaves. They are often tastier and more tender than regular spinach leaves.

Place a nonstick skillet over medium-low heat. When skillet is hot, add olive oil. When olive oil is hot, add garlic; sauté until golden, about 1 minute. Add spinach.

Cover and cook over medium heat until spinach is wilted, 2 to 3 minutes. Remove spinach, shaking off excess moisture, and place on a serving platter. Season with salt and pepper. Sprinkle with balsamic vinegar and toss gently to mix.

APPROXIMATE NUTRITIONAL INFORMATION PER SERVING

Total calories: 81
Total fat: 5 g
Saturated fat: 1 g
Dietary fiber: 3 g
Carbohydrates: 4 g
Protein: 3 g
Cholesterol: 0 mg
Sodium: 89 mg

Variation: For Parmesan Spinach, omit the balsamic vinegar and sprinkle the cooked spinach with 2 tablespoons freshly grated Parmesan cheese.

Sesame Spinach

2 servings

1 bunch fresh spinach

1 teaspoon sesame oil

4 teaspoons lemon juice

⅓ teaspoon Kosher salt

**2 teaspoons toasted
sesame seeds**

Wash spinach in ice water; remove thick stems. Pat dry; tear into bite-size pieces. In a small bowl, combine sesame oil, lemon juice, and salt. Pour over spinach. Sprinkle with sesame seeds.

APPROXIMATE NUTRITIONAL INFORMATION PER SERVING

Total calories: 48
Total fat: 3 g
Saturated fat: 0 g
Dietary fiber: 2 g
Carbohydrates: 5 g
Protein: 3 g
Cholesterol: 0 mg
Sodium: 66 mg

Baked Squash

4 servings

1 pound hubbard or butternut squash

1 tablespoon extra-virgin olive oil

½ teaspoon Kosher salt

½ teaspoon pepper

Wash squash; cut into halves or squares; remove seeds and rinds. Toss with olive oil. Place cut side down in a shallow pan. Bake at 350°F. for 20 minutes; turn. Bake 10 minutes longer, or until tender. Season with salt and pepper.

APPROXIMATE NUTRITIONAL INFORMATION PER SERVING

Total calories: 54
Total fat: 2 g
Saturated fat: 0 g
Dietary fiber: 3 g
Carbohydrates: 11 g
Protein: 1 g
Cholesterol: 0 mg
Sodium: 252 mg

Grilled Herbed Tomatoes

6 servings

3 large ripe tomatoes, halved

¼ teaspoon extra-virgin olive oil

**1 teaspoon fresh rosemary or
½ teaspoon powdered rosemary**

¼ teaspoon Kosher salt

¼ teaspoon black pepper

3 cloves garlic, slivered

Brush tomato halves with olive oil, then sprinkle with rosemary, salt, and pepper. Divide slivered garlic among tomatoes, pushing each sliver all the way into the tomato. Prepare grill for direct grilling over medium-high heat. Grill herb side up 5–8 minutes. Turn often until charred and tomatoes start to soften.

APPROXIMATE NUTRITIONAL INFORMATION PER HALVED TOMATO

Total calories: 16
Total fat: trace
Saturated fat: trace
Dietary fiber: 1 g
Carbohydrates: 3 g
Protein: trace
Cholesterol: 0 mg
Sodium: 78 mg

Vera Cruz Tomatoes

4 servings

¼ cup chopped onion

1 tablespoon extra-virgin olive oil

6 cups trimmed fresh spinach (1 bunch), chopped

½ cup nonfat sour cream

Dash of Tabasco sauce

4 medium tomatoes

3 tablespoons grated part-skim mozzarella cheese

Sauté onion in olive oil until tender; add spinach and cook 3 to 4 minutes. Cool, drain, and squeeze excess water from spinach. Mix spinach and onion with sour cream and Tabasco sauce. Cut tops from tomatoes and remove centers, leaving shells. Fill shells with spinach mixture. Place in a baking dish. Bake at 375° F. for 20 to 25 minutes. Top with cheese.

APPROXIMATE NUTRITIONAL INFORMATION PER SERVING

Total calories: 100
Total fat: 5 g
Saturated fat: 1 g
Dietary fiber: 2 g
Carbohydrates: 10 g
Protein: 5 g
Cholesterol: 7 mg
Sodium: 82 mg

Tomatoes Stuffed with Snow Peas

4 servings

4 ripe tomatoes

¾ pound snow peas

Cut tops from tomatoes. Using a curved grapefruit knife, hollow centers. Stand tomatoes upside down to drain. In a covered vegetable steamer basket over boiling water, steam snow peas 1–2 minutes, or until crisp-tender. Drain.

Arrange vertically in tomato shells.

Variations: Hollow cherry tomatoes from each end. Thread 3–4 snow peas through center of each tomato.

Substitute steamed green beans for snow peas.

APPROXIMATE NUTRITIONAL INFORMATION PER SERVING

Total calories: 62
Total fat: 1 g
Saturated fat: 0 g
Dietary fiber: 4 g
Carbohydrates: 2 g
Protein: 3 g
Cholesterol: 0 mg
Sodium: 14 mg

Baked Tomatoes with Spinach and Parmesan

4 servings

2 bunches fresh spinach leaves

2 cloves garlic, minced

1 egg, beaten

2 tablespoons bread crumbs

1 teaspoon olive oil

⅛ teaspoon powdered thyme

½ teaspoon black pepper

⅛ teaspoon cayenne pepper

2 tablespoons fresh Parmesan cheese

1 large tomato, cut into 4 thick slices

Microwave or steam spinach with garlic 2–3 minutes or until spinach is just wilted. Cool. Wring out excess moisture. Chop. Add egg, bread crumbs, olive oil, thyme, black pepper, cayenne pepper, and Parmesan cheese, and toss. Arrange tomato slices in an 8 x 8-inch ovenproof casserole dish. Top with spinach mixture. Bake at 350°F. 20 minutes or until spinach is hot.

APPROXIMATE NUTRITIONAL INFORMATION PER SERVING

Total calories: 87
Total fat: 4 g
Saturated fat: 1 g
Dietary fiber: 1 g
Carbohydrates: 8 g
Protein: 6 g
Cholesterol: 55 mg
Sodium: 183 mg

Spinach-Stuffed Tomatoes

4 servings

4 large ripe tomatoes

6 cups fresh spinach leaves

1 teaspoon Tabasco sauce

Scoop pulp and seeds from tomatoes (reserve for soup). Drain tomatoes upside down for a few minutes.

In a nonstick skillet or in a microwave, steam spinach leaves, covered, 1–2 minutes or just until leaves begin to soften. (It is not necessary to use additional moisture or oil since there is already enough moisture in the spinach.) Set aside.

Arrange tomatoes in an 8 x 8 x 2-inch ovenproof casserole dish. Place under broiler 5–10 minutes or until tomatoes are hot. Drizzle cavity of each tomato with ¼ teaspoon Tabasco. Fill each tomato with spinach. Serve at once.

Variation: Just before serving, sprinkle with freshly grated Parmesan cheese.

APPROXIMATE NUTRITIONAL INFORMATION PER SERVING

Total calories: 42
Total fat: trace
Saturated fat: 0 g
Dietary fiber: 8 g
Carbohydrates: 8 g
Protein: 3 g
Cholesterol: 0 mg
Sodium: 81 mg

Vermicelli-Stuffed Tomatoes

4 servings

8 large ripe tomatoes

½ pound vermicelli, cooked al dente

½ cup Pesto (page 213)

fresh basil, for garnish

Cut tops from tomatoes. Using a curved knife, hollow centers. Stand tomatoes upside down to drain. Toss vermicelli with pesto and spoon into centers of tomatoes. Garnish with fresh basil.

APPROXIMATE NUTRITIONAL INFORMATION PER SERVING

Total calories: 226
Total fat: 4 g
Saturated fat: 0 g
Dietary fiber: 9 g
Carbohydrates: 41 g
Protein:14 g
Cholesterol: 2 mg
Sodium: 345 mg

Holiday Yams

8 servings

2 large Red Delicious apples, sliced

⅓ cup chopped pecans

⅓ cup brown sugar

½ teaspoon cinnamon

1 28-ounce can yams, drained

1 cup miniature marshmallows

These yams are lean due to no cream and butter. And your kids will love the apples and the marshmallow topping.

Preheat oven to 350°F.

Put apples and pecans in a medium mixing bowl. Combine brown sugar with cinnamon in a small bowl. Pour over apples and gently toss until apples are coated. Arrange yams in a 1½-quart ovenproof casserole. Poke apples in between yams. Cover with aluminum foil. Bake 35 to 40 minutes. Sprinkle with marshmallows. Broil 6 to 8 minutes, or until marshmallows are lightly browned.

APPROXIMATE NUTRITIONAL INFORMATION PER SERVING

Total calories: 206
Total fat: 4 g
Saturated fat: 0 g
Dietary fiber: 3 g
Carbohydrates: 45 g
Protein: 0 g
Cholesterol: 0 mg
Sodium: 32 mg

Zucchini with Garlic and Tomatoes

6 servings

1 16-ounce can plum tomatoes, diced

½ medium yellow onion, chopped

2 cloves garlic, minced

3 small zucchini, sliced ½ inch thick

2 tablespoons chopped fresh parsley

½ teaspoon dried basil or 4–6 leaves fresh

In a medium saucepan, simmer tomatoes, onion and garlic 30 minutes. Add sliced zucchini; simmer 10–15 minutes, or just until zucchini begin to soften but are still crisp-tender. Sprinkle with parsley and basil.

APPROXIMATE NUTRITIONAL INFORMATION PER 1/2 CUP SERVING

Total calories: 28
Total fat: 0 g
Saturated fat: 0 g
Dietary fiber: 2 g
Carbohydrates: 6 g
Protein: 2 g
Cholesterol: 0 mg
Sodium: 109 mg

Zucchini with Onions and Tomatoes

10 servings

1 large white onion, chopped

3 cloves garlic, peeled

¾ cup white wine

1 16-ounce can plum tomatoes, diced

1 cup chicken broth (page 143), preferably homemade

½ teaspoon fresh or ⅛ teaspoon dried thyme

¼ teaspoon fresh or ⅛ teaspoon dried oregano

¼ teaspoon fresh or ⅛ teaspoon dried marjoram

¼ teaspoon fresh or ¼ teaspoon dried basil

¼ teaspoon black pepper

1½ teaspoons Kosher salt

3 medium zucchini, thinly sliced

In a nonstick skillet, heat olive oil. Add onion and sauté 4-6 minutes, just until onions begin to soften. Reduce heat and add garlice and zucchini. Cook over low heat 10-15 minutes.

In a saucepan, combine wine, tomatoes, broth, thyme, oregano, marjoram, basil, salt, and black pepper.

Bring to a boil; reduce heat to simmer. Add onions, garlic and zucchini.

APPROXIMATE NUTRITIONAL INFORMATION PER 1/2 CUP SERVING

Total calories: 38
Total fat: trace
Saturated fat: 0 g
Dietary fiber: 1 g
Carbohydrates: 5 g
Protein: 1 g
Cholesterol: 0 mg
Sodium: 94 mg

Grilled Zucchini

4 servings

4 small zucchini

2 teaspoons olive oil

Slice zucchini in half lengthwise. Brush zucchini with olive oil. Prepare grill for direct grilling over medium-high heat. Grill, turning often, 12-14 minutes, or until the zucchini are tender when pierced with a knife.

APPROXIMATE NUTRITIONAL INFORMATION PER SERVING

Total calories: 37
Total fat: 2 g
Saturated fat: 0 g
Dietary fiber: 1 g
Carbohydrates: 3 g
Protein: 1 g
Cholesterol: 0 mg
Sodium: 4 mg

Grilled Vegetables

8 servings

1 large white onion

2 small pattypan squash or zucchini

1 summer squash

8 bite-size (not dinner-size) red potatoes

8 large fresh mushrooms

1 Japanese eggplant

1 zucchini

1 red pepper

1 green pepper

4 hot peppers

2 teaspoons olive oil

8 cherry tomatoes

Horseradish Sauce (page 212)

Cut onion, squash, eggplant and peppers into 2-inch cubes. Toss with olive oil. Alternate on skewers with whole mushrooms and cherry tomatoes.

Prepare grill for direct grilling over medium-high heat. Cook, turning once or twice, until tender or tender-crisp, about 6-12 minutes, depending on the vegetable. Arrange on serving platter. Serve with Horseradish Sauce.

APPROXIMATE NUTRITIONAL INFORMATION PER SERVING WITHOUT SAUCE

Total calories: 115
Total fat: 2 g
Saturated fat: 0 g
Dietary fiber: 7 g
Carbohydrates: 20 g
Protein: 6 g
Cholesterol: 0 mg
Sodium: 20 mg

Stir-Fried Vegetables

4 servings

1 tablespoon extra-virgin olive oil

2 teaspoons sesame oil

3 medium carrots, cut diagonally into slices ⅛ inch thick

3 large garlic cloves, thinly sliced

¼ cup chicken broth, preferably homemade (page 143)

1 teaspoon peeled, minced fresh gingerroot

½ pound snow peas, ends and strings removed

1 red pepper, seeded and cut into ½-inch-wide strips

1 tablespoon reduced-sodium soy sauce

Investing in a nonstick skillet or wok will allow you to sauté in minimal fat with ease.

Place a nonstick wok or skillet over high heat. When wok is hot, add olive oil and sesame oil. When oils are hot, add carrots and garlic; stir-fry, uncovered, for 1 minute. Add chicken broth. Cover and cook 3 minutes. Add ginger, snow peas, and red pepper. Cover and cook 1 minute longer, or until vegetables are crisp-tender. Drizzle with soy sauce.

APPROXIMATE NUTRITIONAL INFORMATION PER SERVING

Total calories: 113
Total fat: 6 g
Saturated fat: 1 g
Dietary fiber: 4 g
Carbohydrates: 13 g
Protein: 3 g
Cholesterol: 0 mg
Sodium: 235 mg

Chinese Vegetable Stir-Fry

6 servings

2 cups chicken btock (page 143), preferably homemade

1 6-ounce package soba noodles

1 teaspoon sesame oil

1 tablespoon olive oil

2-3 drops hot chili oil

8-10 fresh black forest (Shiitake) mushrooms

1 8-ounce can sliced water chestnuts

1 red, yellow, or green pepper, cut into julienne strips

1 bunch fresh asparagus, steamed until crisp-tender

10 cherry tomatoes, halved

¼ cup reduced-sodium soy sauce

2 tablespoons rice vinegar

In a saucepan, heat chicken stock just to boiling (do not boil). Add buckwheat noodles and cook until just tender, 3 to 4 minutes. Drain. Set aside.

In a wok or heavy skillet, heat sesame oil, olive oil, and chili oil. Add Shiitake mushrooms and stir-fry 4-5 minutes. Add water chestnuts and green pepper and stir fry 2-3 minutes. Toss with noodles, asparagus and tomatoes.

This stir-fry is not low in sodium, so be sure to choose lower-sodium foods at your other meals to balance out the day..

APPROXIMATE NUTRITIONAL INFORMATION PER SERVING

Total calories: 216
Total fat: 3 g
Saturated fat: 0 g
Dietary fiber: 3 g
Carbohydrates: 40 g
Protein: 8 g
Cholesterol: 1 mg
Sodium: 753 mg

Asian Stir-Fry

4 servings

SAUCE

1 cup chicken broth (preferably homemade, page 143)

1 tablespoon plus 1 teaspoon cornstarch

2 tablespoons reduced-sodium soy sauce

1 teaspoon spicy Thai chili sauce* (2 teaspoons for extra spicy flavor)

1 15-ounce can chicken broth or 2 cups homemade (page 143)

2 cups water

1 6-ounce package soba noodles

1 tablespoon sesame oil

1 10-ounce package firm Chinese tofu

1 tablespoon extra-virgin olive oil

2 tablespoons peeled and minced fresh ginger

2 cups broccolini florets

¼ pound shiitake mushrooms, sliced

½ cup chopped green onions

2 cups snow peas, ends and strings removed

4 cups baby bok choy leaves, chopped

This dish comes together in minutes once the vegetables are cut up. Soba noodles are a great way to get your kids to eat whole grains.

To make the sauce, combine the 1 cup chicken broth with cornstarch in a small bowl; stir until smooth and no lumps remain. Stir in soy sauce and Thai chili sauce. Set aside.

In a medium saucepan, bring chicken broth and water to a boil. Add soba noodles and cook until just tender, 3 to 4 minutes. Drain. Transfer to shallow serving bowl. Toss with sesame oil. Set aside.

Drain tofu in a colander for 30 minutes. Cut into ½-inch squares.

Heat a nonstick wok over medium-high heat. When wok is hot, add olive oil. When oil is hot, add ginger and stir-fry for 30 seconds. Add broccolini and stir-fry, uncovered, for 2 minutes. Add mushrooms, green onions, snow peas, and bok choy and stir-fry 1 to 2 minutes. Cover and cook 1 minute. Uncover, add tofu and sauce. Stir gently and cook 2 to 3 minutes or until sauce thickens. Pour vegetables over noodles and toss.

*Available in the Thai section of the supermarket.

This stir-fry is not low in sodium, so be sure to choose lower-sodium foods at your other meals to balance out the day..

APPROXIMATE NUTRITIONAL INFORMATION PER SERVING

Total calories: 336
Total fat: 12 g
Saturated fat: 2 g
Dietary fiber: 6 g
Carbohydrates: 41 g
Protein: 18 g
Cholesterol: 0 mg
Sodium: 898 mg

Antipasto Vegetables

6 servings

4 small carrots, peeled and thinly sliced on the diagonal

1 small zucchini, peeled and sliced on the diagonal into matchstick strips

¼ pound broccoli florets

6 baby red potatoes, quartered

⅓ pound fresh green beans

1 clove garlic, minced

¼ cup fresh lemon juice

2 tablespoons olive oil

½ teaspoon salt

¼ teaspoon black pepper

In a steamer rack over boiling water, steam vegetables one type at a time until crisp-tender: carrots, zucchini and broccoli about 2 minutes each; potatoes and green beans about 6–10 minutes. As each vegetable is cooked, remove to a large, low serving bowl.

While vegetables are steaming, in a small saucepan, combine garlic, lemon juice, olive oil, salt, and pepper, and simmer 5–10 minutes. Pour sauce over cooked vegetables.

Serving Suggestion: Great with grilled entrées.

APPROXIMATE NUTRITIONAL INFORMATION PER SERVING

Total calories: 146
Total fat: 4 g
Saturated fat: trace
Dietary fiber: 4 g
Carbohydrates: 24 g
Protein: 3 g
Cholesterol: 0 mg
Sodium: 199 mg

Raw Veggies in a Basket

6 servings

16 baby carrots or 4 larger carrots, peeled and cut into thirds

4 stalks celery, trimmed and cut into thirds

1 bunch green onions, trimmed

1 small bunch radishes, rinsed and trimmed

1 small summer squash, cut crosswise into rings

1 English cucumber, cut crosswise into rings

8 cherry tomatoes, halved

2 cups sugar snap peas

1 small bunch fresh spinach, rinsed and trimmed

Keep your kids' interest by experimenting with different dips for your vegetables. It will make eating them more fun. These fresh vegetables are particularly good with saucy entrées such as Classic Lasagna (page 241) and Macaroni & Cheese (page 226). Encourage your family to dip the vegetables into the sauce

Chill vegetables. Arrange in a spinach-lined basket.

Variation: Other options include blanched green beans or asparagus, red or green pepper strips, daikon radish, and jicama strips.

As an after-school snack, you may want to experiment with various dips, including Black Bean Dip (page 91), White Bean and Garlic Dip (page 92), Artichoke Dip (page 93), Avocado Dip (page 94) and Sour Cream Dip (page 94).

APPROXIMATE NUTRITIONAL INFORMATION PER SERVING

Total calories: 55
Total fat: 0 g
Saturated fat: 0 g
Dietary fiber: 3 g
Carbohydrates: 10 g
Protein: 2 g
Cholesterol: 0 mg
Sodium: 52 mg

Roasted Mixed Vegetables

6 servings

2 tablespoons extra-virgin olive oil

2 pounds selected vegetables, such as asparagus, broccoli, carrots, cauliflower, or green beans

1 tablespoon balsamic vinegar (optional)

Kosher salt and coarsely ground pepper to taste

Preheat oven to 425°. Trim and wash vegetables. Pat with paper towels to remove all excess moisture. Toss with olive oil. Arrange vegetables in a single layer on hot baking sheet. Roast vegetables until tender, about 5 to 7 minutes depending on size and freshness. Turn vegetables with tongs 2 to 3 times during cooking. Transfer cooked vegetables to serving dish. Drizzle with balsamic vinegar, if desired. Season with salt and pepper.

Variation: For Roasted Baby Vegetables, select a combination of baby eggplants, baby zucchini, patty pan squash, red, green or yellow pepper cut into squares, and small white cremini or portobello mushrooms. Cook as directed above.

APPROXIMATE NUTRITIONAL INFORMATION PER SERVING

Total calories: 77
Total fat: 3 g
Saturated fat: 0 g
Dietary fiber: 4 g
Carbohydrates: 10 g
Protein: 2 g
Cholesterol: 0 mg
Sodium: 35 mg

Desserts

Strawberry Shortcake

8 servings

6 biscuits made from reduced-fat biscuit mix

4 cups hulled strawberries

2 cups light vanilla ice cream

To make a fun Valentine's Day dessert, cut the biscuits with a 3-inch heart-shaped cookie cutter.

Prepare biscuit batter and bake according to package directions; let sit 20 minutes.

Reserve a few whole berries for garnish. Place remaining berries in a bowl and slightly crush them.

Split the still-hot biscuits and put them on individual dessert plates. Add crushed berries and a dollop of ice cream to the bottom half. Cover with the other half. Add more ice cream and crushed berries. Garnish with reserved whole berries.

APPROXIMATE NUTRITIONAL INFORMATION PER SERVING

Total calories: 180
Total fat: 4 g
Saturated fat: 2 g
Dietary fiber: 1 g
Carbohydrates: 31 g
Protein: 5 g
Cholesterol: 3 mg
Sodium: 336 mg

Strawberry-Rhubarb Shortcake

12 miniature servings

**1 24-ounce container
nonfat Greek vanilla yogurt**

2 cups sliced rhubarb

**3 cups strawberries,
hulled and halved**

2 tablespoons water

2 tablespoons cornstarch

½ cup granulated sugar

1 cup all-purpose flour

1½ teaspoons baking powder

½ teaspoon salt

**3 tablespoons olive oil
or canola oil**

⅓ cup nonfat milk

Pour yogurt into an ice-cream freezer. Process according to manufacturer's directions.

In a 2-quart saucepan, combine rhubarb, strawberries, water, cornstarch, and sugar. Bring to a boil. Reduce heat, cover and simmer, stirring often, about 10 minutes or until rhubarb is tender.

Meanwhile, in a mixing bowl, combine flour, baking powder, and salt. In a small jar, combine olive oil and milk; add all at once to flour mixture. Stir with a fork until dough forms. Pour into miniature nonstick muffin tins and bake at 475°F. 10–12 minutes.

To serve, cut biscuits in half. Ladle warm strawberry-rhubarb sauce over biscuit. Top with a scoop of frozen yogurt, then top biscuit with other half. Ladle additional sauce over top.

Variation: Use angel food cake in place of biscuits.

Shortcut: Substitute Vanilla Angel Food Cake (page 399) or a heart-healthy brand of angel food cake mix for homemade, and a heart-healthy commercially prepared frozen yogurt or low-fat ice cream for the vanilla yogurt.

**APPROXIMATE
NUTRITIONAL
INFORMATION
PER SERVING**

Total calories: 186
Total fat: 5 g
Saturated fat: 1 g
Dietary fiber: 2 g
Carbohydrates: 32 g
Protein: 4 g
Cholesterol: 3 mg
Sodium: 174 mg

Cobbler Batter

8 servings

1 cup all-purpose flour, sifted

½ teaspoon salt

1½ teaspoons baking powder

⅓ cup nonfat milk

3 tablespoons canola oil

Combine flour, salt, and baking powder. Mix milk with oil; add to flour. Using a fork or pastry blender, work dough into a ball. Drop by spoonfuls onto fruit cobbler (recipes follow).

APPROXIMATE NUTRITIONAL INFORMATION PER SERVING

Total calories: 106
Total fat: 5 g
Saturated fat: 0 g
Dietary fiber: 1 g
Carbohydrates: 13 g
Protein: 2 g
Cholesterol: 0 mg
Sodium: 139 mg

Berry Cobbler

8 servings

¾ cup water

2 tablespoons cornstarch

½ cup granulated sugar

3 cups strawberries, raspberries, blueberries or blackberries

1 recipe Cobbler batter (see above)

In a medium saucepan, combine water, cornstarch, and sugar, and bring to a boil. Cook 1 minute, stirring constantly. Add berries and remove from heat. Pour into a 9- or 10-inch pie plate.

Combine flour, salt, and baking powder. Mix milk with oil and add to flour. Using a fork or pastry blender, work dough into a ball. Drop by spoonfuls onto fruit cobbler.

Bake at 425°F. 25–30 minutes or until topping is lightly browned.

APPROXIMATE NUTRITIONAL INFORMATION PER SERVING

Total calories: 172
Total fat: 5 g
Saturated fat: 1 g
Dietary fiber: 2 g
Carbohydrates: 29 g
Protein: 2 g
Cholesterol: trace
Sodium: 202 mg

Cherry Cobbler

8 servings

2 14.5-ounce cans pitted red tart pie cherries with liquid

½ cup + 1 tablespoon sugar

1 tablespoon minute tapioca

1 drop almond extract (optional)

1 recipe cobbler batter (page 396)

Drain the cherries and reserve the juice from one can. Combine cherries, sugar, and tapioca in a medium saucepan; cook, stirring constantly, until sugar is dissolved and syrup is clear. Pour into a 9-inch pie plate. Dot with cobbler batter. Bake at 425°F. for 25 to 30 minutes, or until topping is lightly browned.

APPROXIMATE NUTRITIONAL INFORMATION PER SERVING

Total calories: 191
Total fat: 5 g
Saturated fat: 1 g
Dietary fiber: 1 g
Carbohydrates: 34 g
Protein: 4 g
Cholesterol: 0 mg
Sodium: 141 mg

Pudding Cake

12 servings

1 Vanilla Angel Food Cake (page 399)

¾ cup freshly squeezed orange juice

1 tablespoon gelatin

¼ cup all-purpose flour

⅔ cup granulated sugar, plus 3 tablespoons

¼ teaspoon salt

2 cups nonfat milk

3 pasturized eggs, separated*

1 tablespoon grated orange zest

Prepare and bake the cake according to package instructions.

Combine orange juice and gelatin; set aside. In a double boiler over boiling water, combine flour, ⅔ cup of the sugar, salt, and milk. Cook and stir until thickened, about 10 minutes. Stir in gelatin, egg yolks, and orange zest. Remove from heat at once and cool. Cut cooled cake into bite-size pieces.

Beat egg whites to soft peaks. Add the remaining 3 tablespoons sugar and beat 2–3 minutes. Fold into custard. Alternate layers of cake and custard in a nonstick bundt pan. Refrigerate at least 6 hours. Unmold.

*Uncooked eggs have been the source of salmonella. The American Egg Board recommends using only pasturized eggs to eliminate the risk. They are available in many supermarkets.

Variation: Garnish with raspberries. This is also beautiful served in a glass dish. And it can be turned into an English trifle by layering with fruit and sherry or other spirits.

APPROXIMATE NUTRITIONAL INFORMATION PER SERVING

Total calories: 245
Total fat: 1 g
Saturated fat: 0 g
Dietary fiber: 0 g
Carbohydrates: 51 g
Protein: 8 g
Cholesterol: 54 mg
Sodium: 224 mg

Angel Food Cake and Fresh Strawberries with Strawberry Sauce

12 servings

1 Angel Food Cake (page 399)

4 cups strawberries, sliced

1 Strawberry Sauce, chilled (page 426)

Prepare and bake the cake according to package instructions. Arrange cake on a platter lined with a paper doily. Surround with bowls of sliced strawberries and Strawberry Sauce. Top cake slices with sliced berries, then sauce.

Variation: Substitute sliced peaches for strawberries and Peach Sauce (page 426) for Strawberry Sauce.

APPROXIMATE NUTRITIONAL INFORMATION PER SERVING

Total calories: 174
Total fat: trace
Saturated fat: trace
Dietary fiber: 2 g
Carbohydrates: 39 g
Protein: 4 g
Cholesterol: 0 mg
Sodium: 143 mg

Chocolate Angel Food Cake

12 servings

1 package angel food cake mix (choose a one-step mix; Betty Crocker is good)

⅓ cup unsweetened cocoa powder (Ghirardelli and Dröste are good)

Prepare cake mix according to package directions. After ingredients are moistened, begin to beat and add cocoa powder gradually, 1 tablespoon at a time. Do not overbeat the mixture; stay within the time limit designated on the package. Scrape sides and bottom of bowl with a spatula to mix in any extra cocoa powder. Pour into a nonstick bundt or angel food cake pan. Bake according to package directions.

Serving Suggestion: Good with Orange or Chocolate Glaze (page 399).

APPROXIMATE NUTRITIONAL INFORMATION PER SERVING

Total calories:158
Total fat: 1 g
Saturated fat: trace
Dietary fiber: trace
Carbohydrates: 35 g
Protein: 5 g
Cholesterol: 0 mg
Sodium: 142 mg

Angel Food Cake with Seven-Minute Icing

12 servings

1 box angel food cake mix

FROSTING
2 pasturized egg whites*
1¼ cups granulated sugar
dash of salt
½ cup water
¼ teaspoon cream of tartar
1 teaspoon vanilla extract

Angel food cake is the cake of choice at our house because it's so low in fat.
Prepare angel food cake according to package instructions. When cake has thoroughly cooled, prepare frosting.

In bottom of a double boiler, bring 2 cups water to a boil. In the top of the double boiler, combine egg whites, sugar, salt, ½ cup water, and cream of tartar; beat 1 minute. Place over boiling water. Using highest speed of electric mixer, beat constantly for 5 to 7 minutes, or until frosting stands in stiff peaks. Remove from heat. Stir in vanilla. Spread frosting over top and sides of cake.

Chocolate Glaze: In a small bowl, combine 1 cup confectioners' sugar, sifted, and 2 tablespoons cold nonfat milk; stir until smooth. Add 1 teaspoon unsweetened cocoa powder (Ghirardelli and Dröste are good); stir until smooth. Spread the glaze over the top of the cake and allow it to drizzle down the sides.

Orange Glaze: In a small bowl, combine 1 cup confectioners' sugar, 2 tablespoons chilled, freshly squeezed orange juice, and 1 tablespoon orange zest. Stir until smooth. Spread the glaze over the top of the cake and allow it to drizzle down the sides.

With Fresh Strawberries: Crush or slice 2 pints of strawberries. Top each slice of cake with berries, a dollop of light vanilla ice cream or frozen yogurt and one whole berry for garnish. If desired, substitute raspberries or peaches for strawberries. With this variation I like to use mini angel food cake pans, which are available at kitchen stores. They are on the order of muffin tins; each tin makes six mini angel food cakes.

*Uncooked eggs have been the source of sal-monella. The American Egg Board recommends using only pasturized eggs to eliminate the risk. They are available in many supermarkets.

APPROXIMATE NUTRITIONAL INFORMATION PER SERVING

Total calories: 214
Total fat: 0 g
Saturated fat: 0 g
Dietary fiber: 0 g
Carbohydrates: 51 g
Protein: 4 g
Cholesterol: 0 mg
Sodium: 224 mg

WITH CHOCOLATE GLAZE

Total calories: 170
Sodium: 172 mg

Other amounts remain the same.

WITH ORANGE GLAZE

Total calories: 170
Sodium: 170 mg

Other amounts remain the same.

EACH MINI CAKE WITH FRESH STRAWBERRIES

Total calories: 340
Fat: 2 g
Sodium: 359 mg

Other amounts remain the same.

Black Bottom Cupcakes

24 cupcakes

FILLING

1 8-ounce package reduced-fat cream cheese, softened

1 egg

1⅓ cups granulated sugar

⅝ teaspoon salt

1 6-ounce package semisweet chocolate chips

½ cup sifted all-purpose flour

1 teaspoon baking soda

⅓ cup Hershey's unsweetened cocoa powder

1 cup water

1 2½ -ounce jar baby food prunes

2 tablespoons canola oil

1 tablespoon cider vinegar

1 teaspoon vanilla extract

With no frosting, these cupcakes are convenient to pack in a lunch box or send along to the Brownie meeting or class picnic.

Preheat oven to 350°F.

With an electric mixer on medium speed, combine cream cheese, egg, ⅓ cup of the sugar, and ⅛ teaspoon of the salt in a mixing bowl. Stir in chocolate chips. Set cream cheese mixture aside.

In a small bowl, combine flour, remaining 1 cup sugar, baking soda, cocoa, and remaining ½ teaspoon salt with a wire whisk. Add water, prunes, canola oil, vinegar, and vanilla; whisk together until blended and smooth.

Fill 24 paper-lined muffin cups one-third full with batter. Top each with a heaping teaspoon of the cream cheese mixture. Bake for 25 minutes.

APPROXIMATE NUTRITIONAL INFORMATION PER CUPCAKE

Total calories: 120
Total fat: 5 g
Saturated fat: 2 g
Dietary fiber: 1 g
Carbohydrates: 20 g
Protein: 2 g
Cholesterol: 10 mg
Sodium: 160 mg

Chocolate Cake

12 slices

2 eggs, separated

1¼ cups sugar

1¾ cups cake flour

¾ teaspoon baking soda

¾ teaspoon salt

½ cup canola oil

**1 cup nonfat milk plus
1 tablespoon vinegar**

¼ cup unsweetened cocoa powder

½ teaspoon vanilla extract

Beat egg whites until frothy. Gradually beat in ½ cup of the sugar; beat until egg whites are stiff. Set aside.

In a large mixing bowl, sift together remaining sugar, flour, baking soda, and salt; add oil and half the milk and vinegar. Beat 1 minute on medium speed; add remaining milk, egg yolks, cocoa powder, and vanilla. Beat 1 minute longer. Fold in egg whites.

Pour in 2 nonstick 9-inch round cake pans or 24 paper-lined muffin cups. Bake at 350°F. for 30 to 35 minutes, or until a toothpick inserted near the center comes out clean. Cool on wire racks for 10 minutes. Remove from pans. Cool thoroughly on racks.

Serving Suggestion: Frost with Seven-Minute Icing (page 399), if desired.

APPROXIMATE NUTRITIONAL INFORMATION PER SLICE

Total calories: 251
Total fat: 10 g
Saturated fat: 1 g
Dietary fiber: 1 g
Carbohydrates: 37 g
Protein: 4 g
Cholesterol: 36 mg
Sodium: 234 mg

Easy Pastry Crust

2 9-inch crusts

2 cups cake or pastry flour

¼ teaspoon salt

⅓ cup canola oil

½ cup very cold nonfat milk, plus 1 tablespoon

Pies are a "special occasion" treat, not to be eaten too often. The recipes in the book use this crust, which is made without lard. You may prefer to use a commercial mix or ready-made pie crust. If so, be sure to check the ingredients list and avoid ones with lard, palm oil, and hydrogenated oils.

In a mixing bowl, combine flour and salt. Pour canola oil and milk into a small bowl (do not stir); add all at once to flour mixture. Stir lightly with a fork or pastry blender. Using hands, form dough into two balls.

Place each ball between two sheets of waxed paper; press into a thick, flat disk about 5 inches in diameter. Place into zip-lock bags and chill 15 minutes.

Roll each disk of dough into a circle on a well-floured pastry cloth. Place in a 9-inch pie plate. Adjust crust. Flute edges.

If a baked shell is needed, prick bottom and sides generously with tines of a fork (prick where bottom and sides meet all around pie shell). If filling and crust are to be baked together, do not prick crust. Bake at 450°F. 8–10 minutes or until golden. Cool on wire rack.

For single-crust recipes: place one of the flattened 5-inch disks in the freezer. It will keep several weeks.

Note: Oil-based pastry crusts do not have the same rich flavor nor the same light, flaky texture as shortening-based crusts. Crusts made with oil, however, are a great improvement from a heart-healthy standpoint. For example, this homemade oil-based recipe has 794 calories and 37 grams of fat. A shortening-based crust has 900 calories and 60 grams of fat.

APPROXIMATE NUTRITIONAL INFORMATION PER CRUST

Total calories: 785
Total fat: 37 g
Saturated fat: 5 g
Dietary fiber: 3 g
Carbohydrates: 96 g
Protein: 15 g
Cholesterol: 1 mg
Sodium: 1,194 mg

Old-Fashioned Apple Pie

8 servings

6 cups apples, pared and sliced*

1¼ tablespoons lemon juice

¼ cup granulated sugar

⅛ teaspoon salt

½ teaspoon cinnamon

2 tablespoons all-purpose flour

2 Easy Pastry Crusts, unbaked (page 402) or prepared from a mix such as Krusteaz

In a bowl, toss apples with lemon juice. Combine sugar, salt, cinnamon, and flour, and mix with apples. Spoon into pastry-lined pie plate. Adjust top crust, flute edges, and prick. Bake at 450°F. 10 minutes. Reduce heat to 375°F. and continue baking 40–50 minutes.

*The tart and sweet tart flavors of Braeburn Jonathan, McIntosh, and Granny Smith are our favorite apple choices for this recipe.

APPROXIMATE NUTRITIONAL INFORMATION PER SERVING

Total calories: 293
Total fat: 10 g
Saturated fat: 1 g
Dietary fiber: 3 g
Carbohydrates: 50 g
Protein: 4 g
Cholesterol: trace
Sodium: 110 mg

Apple-Cranberry Pie

8 servings

3 large Red Delicious apples, peeled, cored and cut into eighths

1 cup fresh cranberries, picked over and rinsed

½ cup fresh raisins

½ tablespoon sugar

1½ tablespoons cornstarch

1 teaspoon cinnamon

2 Easy Pastry Crusts, unbaked (page 402) or prepared from a mix such as Krusteaz

1 egg, slightly beaten

1 tablespoon water

In a bowl, combine apples, cranberries, and raisins; toss with ½ cup of the sugar, cornstarch and cinnamon. Pour into a 9-inch pastry-lined pie plate. Arrange crust over top and flute edges. Using a sharp knife, make slits in top of crust to create steam vents. Combine egg with water and brush over pie crust. Sprinkle with remaining 1 tablespoon sugar. Bake at 400°F. for 20 minutes. Reduce heat to 350°F. and bake 30 minutes more. Remove to rack to cool. Serve warm or cold.

APPROXIMATE NUTRITIONAL INFORMATION PER SERVING

Total calories: 229
Total fat: 5 g
Saturated fat: 1 g
Dietary fiber: 2 g
Carbohydrates: 44 g
Protein: 3 g
Cholesterol: 27 mg
Sodium: 47 mg

Fresh Berry Pie

8 servings

2 Easy Pastry Crusts, unbaked (page 402) or prepared from a mix such as Krusteaz

2 tablespoons all-purpose flour

½ cup granulated sugar

⅛ teaspoon salt

4 cups fresh raspberries, strawberries, or blackberries

1 teaspoon lemon juice

Line a 9-inch pie plate with pastry. Mix together flour, sugar, and salt; sprinkle ¼ of the mixture on uncooked bottom crust. Coat berries with lemon juice and toss with remaining sugar mixture. Spoon into pie plate. Adjust top crust, flute edges, and prick. Bake at 450°F. 15 minutes. Reduce heat to 350°F. and continue baking 25–30 minutes.

APPROXIMATE NUTRITIONAL INFORMATION PER CRUST

Total calories: 281
Total fat: 9 g
Saturated fat: 1 g
Dietary fiber: 4 g
Carbohydrates: 45 g
Protein: 5 g
Cholesterol: trace
Sodium: 110 mg

Fresh Strawberry Pie

8 servings

1 Easy Pastry Crust (page 402), or prepared from a mix such as Krusteaz

2 quarts big fresh strawberries (the bigger the berries, the more outstanding the pie), stemmed

¾ cup granulated sugar

3 tablespoons cornstarch

½ cup water

2 cups light vanilla ice cream

This is a quick and easy dessert for the summer when strawberries are fresh.

Prepare and bake 9-inch pie shell according to instructions. Let stand until cool.

Arrange 1½ quarts of the strawberries, pointed tips up, in pie shell. Crush remaining berries. Mix sugar and cornstarch in a 2-quart saucepan. Gradually stir in water and crushed berries. Place pan over medium heat and cook, stirring constantly, until mixture thickens and boils. Boil and stir 1 minute. Pour over berries in pie shell. Chill at least 2 hours. Serve with vanilla ice cream.

APPROXIMATE NUTRITIONAL INFORMATION PER SERVING

Total calories: 289
Total fat: 7 g
Saturated fat: 1 g
Dietary fiber: 2 g
Carbohydrates: 53 g
Protein: 7 g
Cholesterol: 2 mg
Sodium: 233 mg

Strawberry-Rhubarb Pie

8 servings

½ **cup granulated sugar**

¼ **cup all-purpose flour**

¼ **teaspoon salt**

¼ **teaspoon nutmeg**

3 **cups rhubarb, cut into**
½-**inch pieces**

1 **cup sliced strawberries**

2 **Easy Pastry Crusts, unbaked**
(page 402) or prepared from a mix
such as Krusteaz

In a bowl, combine sugar, flour, salt, and nutmeg. Add fruit and toss to coat. Let stand 20 minutes. Spoon into pastry-lined pie plate. Adjust top crust, flute edges, and prick. Bake at 400°F. 40–45 minutes.

APPROXIMATE NUTRITIONAL INFORMATION PER SERVING

Total calories: 274
Total fat: 10 g
Saturated fat: 1 g
Dietary fiber: 2 g
Carbohydrates: 43 g
Protein: 5 g
Cholesterol: trace
Sodium: 145 mg

Pumpkin Pie

8 servings

1 **Easy Pastry Crust (page 402),**
or prepared from a mix such as
Krusteaz

1 **1-pound can pumpkin**

¾ **cup firmly packed brown sugar**

3 **lightly beaten eggs**

¼ **teaspoon salt**

1 **teaspoon cinnamon**

½ **teaspoon ground ginger**

½ **teaspoon nutmeg**

¼ **teaspoon ground cloves**

1 **12-ounce can evaporated**
skim milk

This pie saves calories and fat-grams because it's made with nonfat milk instead of whole milk. Best of all, you never taste the difference.

Preheat oven to 400°F.

Prepare pie shell according to instructions. Line a 9-inch pie plate with crust.

Measure remaining ingredients into a medium mixing bowl. Mix with wire whisk or spoon until well-blended. Pour into pie shell. Cover edges of crust with a 3-inch strip of aluminum foil to prevent excessive browning. Bake for 50 minutes, or until knife inserted in center of pie comes out clean.

APPROXIMATE NUTRITIONAL INFORMATION PER SERVING

Total calories: 274
Total fat: 8 g
Saturated fat: 2 g
Dietary fiber: 0 g
Carbohydrates: 44 g
Protein: 8 g
Cholesterol: 81 mg
Sodium: 257 mg

Lemon Chiffon Pie

10 servings

⅓ cup fresh lemon juice

⅔ cup water

1 envelope unflavored gelatin

¼ cup granulated sugar, plus 2 tablespoons

3 pasturized egg yolks, slightly beaten*

1 tablespoon lemon zest

5 pasturized egg whites*

½ teaspoon cream of tartar

1 Easy Pastry Crust, baked (page 402) or prepared from a mix such as Krusteaz

10 strawberries, thinly sliced (optional)

In a saucepan, combine lemon juice, water, gelatin, ¼ cup of the sugar, and egg yolks. Heat just to boiling, stirring constantly. Remove from heat. Stir in lemon zest. Place saucepan in a larger saucepan filled with ice and water. Refrigerate 20 minutes or until mixture mounds when dropped from a spoon.

Beat egg whites and cream of tartar to soft peaks; gradually add remaining 2 tablespoons sugar and beat to stiff peaks. Fold in lemon mixture. Mound into pie shell and chill at least 3 hours.

Just before serving, layer top of each piece with sliced strawberries, if desired.

*Uncooked eggs have been the source of salmonella. The American Egg Board recommends using only pasturized eggs to eliminate the risk. They are available in many supermarkets.

APPROXIMATE NUTRITIONAL INFORMATION PER SERVING

Total calories: 133
Total fat: 5 g
Saturated fat: 1 g
Dietary fiber: trace
Carbohydrates: 17 g
Protein: 5 g
Cholesterol: 64 mg
Sodium: 61 mg

Lemon Meringue Pie

10 servings

¼ cup all-purpose flour

5 tablespoons cornstarch

1 teaspoon salt

1¼ cups granulated sugar

2¼ cups boiling water

3 pasturized egg yolks, lightly beaten*

½ cup freshly squeezed lemon juice, plus 1 tablespoon

1 teaspoon lemon zest

1 Easy Pastry Crust, baked (page 402) or prepared from a mix such as Krusteaz

MERINGUE

7 pasturized egg whites*

½ teaspoon cream of tartar

½ teaspoon vanilla extract

⅓ cup granulated sugar

In the top of a double boiler, combine flour, cornstarch, salt, sugar, and boiling water. Cook over simmering water 10–15 minutes or until thickened and clear, stirring constantly. Add egg yolks and cook 2 minutes more. Remove from heat. Add lemon juice and lemon zest. Cool. (Do not stir filling while it is cooling.) Turn into cooled baked pie shell.

To make meringue, beat egg whites until fluffy. Add cream of tartar and vanilla. Continue beating, gradually adding sugar. Beat until stiff peaks are formed. Spoon meringue over filling. Mound in peaks, covering filling completely. Bake at 400°F. 6–12 minutes or until peaks are golden.

*Uncooked eggs have been the source of salmonella. The American Egg Board recommends using only pasturized eggs to eliminate the risk. They are available in many supermarkets.

APPROXIMATE NUTRITIONAL INFORMATION PER SERVING

Total calories: 253
Total fat: 5 g
Saturated fat: 1 g
Dietary fiber: trace
Carbohydrates: 48 g
Protein: 5 g
Cholesterol: 64 mg
Sodium: 288 mg

Peanut Butter Cookies

3 dozen cookies

¾ cup creamy peanut butter
2 tablespoons butter
1¼ cups all-purpose flour
½ cup granulated sugar
½ cup brown sugar
2 eggs
1 teaspoon baking soda
¼ teaspoon baking powder
dash of salt

Preheat oven to 350°F.

With an electric mixer on medium speed, combine peanut butter and butter in a mixing bowl. Add remaining ingredients and mix well.

Drop tablespoons of dough 3 inches apart on nonstick cookie sheets. Bake until golden, about 10 to 12 minutes. Transfer to a wire rack to cool.

APPROXIMATE NUTRITIONAL INFORMATION PER COOKIE

Total calories: 80
Total fat: 3 g
Saturated fat: 1 g
Dietary fiber: 0 g
Carbohydrates: 10 g
Protein: 2 g
Cholesterol: 10 mg
Sodium: 75 mg

Gingersnaps

4 dozen cookies

2 cups all-purpose flour
¼ teaspoon salt
1 teaspoon baking powder
1 teaspoon baking soda
½ teaspoon ground cloves
1¼ teaspoons ground ginger
1¼ teaspoons cinnamon
⅔ cup canola oil
¼ cup molasses
1 egg
1 cup firmly packed brown sugar
¼ cup granulated sugar

Sift together flour, salt, baking powder, baking soda, cloves, ginger, and cinnamon. Set aside. Using lowest speed of an electric mixer, blend oil, molasses, and egg; add brown sugar. Blend. Gradually add flour mixture; mix well.

Chill dough for 2 hours. Form into 1-inch balls. Roll each ball in granulated sugar. Place on nonstick baking sheets. Sprinkle each cookie with 2 to 3 drops of water. Bake at 375° for 8 to 10 minutes, or until set and tops are crackled. Remove cookies immediately from cookie sheet. Cool cookie on a wire rack.

APPROXIMATE NUTRITIONAL INFORMATION PER COOKIE

Total calories: 74
Total fat: 3 g
Saturated fat: 0 g
Dietary fiber: 0 g
Carbohydrates: 11 g
Protein: 1 g
Cholesterol: 4 mg
Sodium: 41 mg

Rice Krispies Cookies

24 cookies

3 tablespoons butter

40 regular marshmallows

½ teaspoon vanilla

5 cups Rice Krispies cereal

Melt butter in a 6-quart stock pot. Add marshmallows and cook over medium heat until marshmallows are melted, stirring constantly. Add vanilla. Pour in cereal. Mix well. Using a large piece of waxed paper, press mixture evenly into a waxed paper-lined 13 x 9 x 2-inch pan. Cut into 24 2 x 2-inch squares when cool.

APPROXIMATE NUTRITIONAL INFORMATION PER COOKIE

Total calories: 70
Total fat: trace
Saturated fat: 0 g
Dietary fiber: 0 g
Carbohydrates: 12 g
Protein: 0 g
Cholesterol: 0 mg
Sodium: 24 mg

Almond Macaroons

1 ½ dozen

½ pound almond paste (Bordon's Red-E is good; so is Solo Brand)

⅔ cup granulated sugar

¼ cup pasturized egg whites (about 2–3 eggs)

In a mixing bowl, cut almond paste into small pieces. Blend with sugar. Add egg whites and beat 4–5 minutes or until mixture is smooth. Drop by tablespoons or use a pastry bag with star tube (tablespoon size) and pipe cookies onto baking sheets lined with brown paper or parchment paper. Leave about 1-inch space between each cookie.

Bake at 350°F. 18–20 minutes or until golden. Allow to cool 5 minutes. Remove from pans and cool on wire racks. If cookies stick, dampen the back of the paper with a moist cloth; after a few minutes, remove the cookies from the paper.

APPROXIMATE NUTRITIONAL INFORMATION PER COOKIE

Total calories: 88
Total fat: 3 g
Saturated fat: 0 g
Dietary fiber: 1 g
Carbohydrates: 13 g
Protein: 1 g
Cholesterol: 0 mg
Sodium: 7 mg

Pain Au Chocolat

4 sandwiches

8 ¼ -inch-thick slices of a 2 x 3-inch French baguette

16 small squares (¼ x 1-inch) Lindt Swiss Milk Chocolate Bar (½ of a 3-ounce bar)

Pain au chocolat was the simple forerunner of the fancy chocolate croissant.

Place 4 chocolate squares on a baguette slice. Top with a second baguette slice. Wrap sandwich in a paper napkin. Cook in microwave for 1 minute, just until chocolate melts. Cut sandwich in half. Serve with milk.

Variation: Use eight 2 x 2-inch graham crackers in place of baguette slices.

APPROXIMATE NUTRITIONAL INFORMATION

PER SANDWICH

Total calories: 137
Total fat: 4 g
Saturated fat: 2 g
Dietary fiber: 0 g
Carbohydrates: 21 g
Protein: 3 g
Cholesterol: 0 mg
Sodium: 201 mg

PER GRAHAM CRACKER SANDWHICH

Total calories: 114
Total fat: 5 g
Saturated fat: 2 g
Dietary fiber: 0 g
Carbohydrates: 16 g
Protein: 2 g
Cholesterol: 0 mg
Sodium: 86 mg

Lemon Custard

6 servings

3 egg whites

2 egg yolks

⅔ cup nonfat milk

¼ cup freshly squeezed lemon juice

1 teaspoon grated lemon zest

¼ teaspoon salt

¾ cup granulated sugar

¼ cup all-purpose flour

In a bowl, beat egg whites until stiff peaks form; set aside. In another bowl, lightly beat egg yolks; beat in milk, lemon juice, and lemon zest. Add salt, sugar and flour, and beat until smooth. Fold yolk mixture into egg whites. Pour into six individual 1-cup custard cups. Place the cups in a 9 x 13 x 2-inch baking pan. Pour boiling water into baking pan to a depth of about 1 inch. Bake at 350°F. 20–30 minutes or until golden and top springs back. Serve warm at the height of the meringue.

APPROXIMATE NUTRITIONAL INFORMATION PER SERVING

Total calories: 149
Total fat: 2 g
Saturated fat: trace
Dietary fiber: trace
Carbohydrates: 30 g
Protein: 4 g
Cholesterol: 71 mg
Sodium: 133 mg

Spanish Flan

Six ½-cup servings

⅓ cup granulated sugar, plus 6 tablespoons

4 whole eggs

4 egg whites

1 teaspoon vanilla extract

2 cups nonfat milk

Sprigs of fresh mint (optional)

In a small nonstick skillet, spread ⅓ cup of the sugar. Cook over medium heat, stirring constantly, just until sugar is completely melted and forms a caramel syrup that is clear amber in color. Pour syrup immediately into 6 individual 1-cup custard cups. Tilt so syrup coats bottom of each cup. Set cups on a baking rack.

In a large bowl, using a whisk, beat eggs, additional egg whites, the remaining 6 tablespoons sugar and vanilla until well blended but not frothy. Add milk and stir. Pour egg mixture into custard cups.

Arrange custard cups in a 9 x 13 x 2-inch pan. Pour boiling water into the pan, filling bottom to a depth of about 1 inch. Bake at 350°F. 40 minutes or until knife inserted near edge of cup comes out clean. Cool on wire rack 30 minutes. Serve at once or chill.

To serve, run a knife around edge of flan; invert cup onto dessert plate. Caramel syrup will flowover flan. Garnish with mint sprig or small fresh flower.

Serving Suggestion: Good with Mexican and Cajun dishes.

APPROXIMATE NUTRITIONAL INFORMATION PER SERVING

Total calories: 177
Total fat: 3 g
Saturated fat: 1 g
Dietary fiber: 0 g
Carbohydrates: 27 g
Protein: 9 g
Cholesterol: 143 mg
Sodium: 121 mg

Easy Chocolate Pudding

5 servings

¼ cup unsweetened cocoa powder

½ cup granulated sugar

2 tablespoons cornstarch

⅛ teaspoon salt

2 cups nonfat milk

1 egg, beaten

½ teaspoon vanilla extract

In a medium saucepan, blend cocoa, sugar, cornstarch, salt, and milk. Cook over medium heat, stirring constantly, until mixture comes to a boil and begins to thicken. Remove from heat.

Mix ¼ cup of the mixture with beaten egg. Gradually stir egg mixture into hot mixture. Cook over low heat, stirring constantly, 5–10 minutes, or until mixture comes to a boil. Remove from heat. Stir in vanilla extract. Pour into custard cups. Chill.

APPROXIMATE NUTRITIONAL INFORMATION PER 1/2-CUP SERVING

Total calories: 148
Total fat: 2 g
Saturated fat: 1 g
Dietary fiber: 1 g
Carbohydrates: 30 g
Protein: 5 g
Cholesterol: 39 mg
Sodium: 122 mg

Tapioca Pudding

6 servings

1 egg, well beaten

2½ cups nonfat milk

3 tablespoons quick-cooking tapioca

¼ cup sugar

1 teaspoon vanilla extract

In a medium saucepan, combine egg, milk, tapioca, and sugar; let stand 5 minutes. Cook tapioca over medium heat, stirring constantly, until mixture comes to a full boil, 6 to 8 minutes. Add vanilla. Stir only enough to mix. Pour into bowl or individual serving cups. Let cool for 20 minutes. Chill.

Variation: For chocolate tapioca, add 3 tablespoons semisweet cocoa powder along with the vanilla to completed recipe.

APPROXIMATE NUTRITIONAL INFORMATION PER SERVING

ORIGINAL RECIPE	CHOCOLATE TAPIOCA
Total calories: 130	Total calories: 136
Total fat: 1 g	Total fat: 1 g
Saturated fat: 1 g	Saturated fat: 1 g
Dietary fiber: 0 g	Dietary fiber: 0 g
Carbohydrates: 22 g	Carbohydrates: 23 g
Protein: 9 g	Protein: 9 g
Cholesterol: 37 mg	Cholesterol: 37 mg
Sodium: 63 mg	Sodium: 64 mg

Cold Raspberry Soufflé

10 servings

2 envelopes unflavored gelatin

½ cup fresh lemon juice

4 pasturized egg yolks*

½ cup granulated sugar

2 cups raspberries, puréed

¼ cup Crème de Cassis liquor

8 pasturized egg whites*

¼ teaspoon cream of tartar

2 cups plain non-fat yogurt

In a saucepan, soften gelatin in lemon juice. Simmer over low heat, stirring frequently, until gelatin is dissolved and liquid is clear. In a bowl, beat egg yolks with sugar about 5 minutes, or until light and fluffy.

In top of a double boiler, combine puréed raspberries and Crème de Cassis. Stir in egg yolks and gelatin. Cook over boiling water until mixture thickens, stirring constantly. Cool to room temperature, about 40–45 minutes.

Beat egg whites until soft peaks form. Add cream of tartar. Beat until stiff peaks form. Fold egg whites, then yogurt, into raspberry mixture. Pour into a 2-quart soufflé dish with a waxed-paper collar extending 2–3 inches above rim of dish. Chill 3 hours. Remove paper collar. Serve.

*Uncooked eggs have been the source of salmonella. The American Egg Board recommends using only pasturized eggs to eliminate the risk. They are available in many supermarkets.

APPROXIMATE NUTRITIONAL INFORMATION PER SERVING

Total calories: 134
Total fat: 2 g
Saturated fat: 1 g
Dietary fiber: 2 g
Carbohydrates: 17 g
Protein: 8 g
Cholesterol: 86 mg
Sodium: 84 mg

Cold Lemon Soufflé

8 servings

1 cup fresh lemon juice

3 pasturized egg yolks*

¼ cup granulated sugar

2 tablespoons honey

3 envelopes unflavored gelatin

⅔ cup hot water

grated peel of 1 lemon

1 tablespoon Grand Marnier

1¼ cups plain non-fat Greek yogurt

5 pasturized egg whites

¼ teaspoon cream of tartar

⅛ teaspoon salt

In top of a double boiler, combine lemon juice, egg yolks, sugar, and honey. Cook 5–7 minutes over hot (not boiling) water, beating constantly with electric mixer until thick and frothy. Remove from heat.

Dissolve gelatin in ⅔ cup hot water; gradually add to egg mixture. Stir in grated lemon. Place mixture over ice water and beat 5–10 minutes, or until mixture begins to gel. Add Grand Marnier. Beat 5–10 minutes. Set aside.

Combine remaining ingredients. Beat until egg whites form stiff peaks. Fold into egg mixture. Spoon into an 8-inch soufflé dish or individual parfait glasses. Chill 2–3 hours.

*Uncooked eggs have been the source of salmonella. The American Egg Board recommends using only pasturized eggs to eliminate the risk. They are available in many supermarkets.

APPROXIMATE NUTRITIONAL INFORMATION PER SERVING

Total calories: 114
Total fat: 2 g
Saturated fat: 1 g
Dietary fiber: 0 g
Carbohydrates: 16 g
Protein: 8 g
Cholesterol: 80 mg
Sodium: 106 mg

Fresh Lemon Ice Cream

1 1/2 quarts

⅓ cup fresh lemon juice

1½ teaspoons lemon zest

1⅓ cups evaporated skim milk, chilled

1 pasturized egg*

1½ cups granulated sugar

¾ cup nonfat milk

4 cups Raspberry Puree (page 417)

1 cup fresh blueberries or raspberries (optional)

Combine lemon juice and lemon zest. Chill in refrigerator. Beat chilled milk with egg on high speed until it is the consistency of heavy cream, about 5 minutes. Gradually add sugar and beat until mixture thickens. Add lemon juice and lemon zest; beat 2 minutes. Add nonfat milk and beat 1 minute more.

Pour into ice-cream freezer and process according to manufacturer's directions.

Scoop into stemmed glasses. Top with Raspberry Puree. Sprinkle with blueberries or raspberries.

*Uncooked eggs have been the source of salmonella. The American Egg Board recommends using only pasturized eggs to eliminate the risk. They are available in many supermarkets.

APPROXIMATE NUTRITIONAL INFORMATION PER 1/2-CUP SERVING WITH 1/4-CUP SERVING OF RASPBERRY PUREE

Total calories: 147
Total fat: 0
Saturated fat: 0
Dietary fiber: 0
Carbohydrates: 35 g
Protein: 3 g
Cholesterol: 19 mg
Sodium: 39 mg

Strawberry Sherbet with Strawberry Sauce

1 1/2 quarts

3 egg yolks, beaten

¾-1 cup granulated sugar

3 cups nonfat milk

¼ teaspoon salt

4 cups fresh strawberries

1 teaspoon vanilla extract

In a 2-quart saucepan, combine egg yolks, ½ cup of the sugar, 1 cup of the nonfat milk, and salt. Cook over medium heat, stirring often, until bubbles form around edges, about 15 minutes. Chill at least 4 hours.

In a blender or food processor, purée berries. Remove half the puréed berries to a small serving bowl and chill in refrigerator. To remaining puréed berries, add remaining ½ cup sugar and whirl 1 minute to blend.

Pour chilled egg mixture, sugared berries, vanilla and remaining 2 cups milk into ice-cream freezer. Process according to manufacturer's directions.

Serve in bowls. Top with remaining puréed berries.

APPROXIMATE NUTRITIONAL INFORMATION PER 1/2-CUP SERVING

Total calories: 112
Total fat: 1 g
Saturated fat: trace
Dietary fiber: 1 g
Carbohydrates: 22 g
Protein: 3 g
Cholesterol: 54 mg
Sodium: 78 mg

Vanilla Nonfat Frozen Yogurt

3 cups

1 24-ounce container Greek vanilla nonfat yogurt, chilled

Pour chilled yogurt into ice-cream freezer. Process according to manufacturer's directions. Enjoy as is or top with Strawberry, RHUBARB, or Raspberry Puree.

Note: This is so simple and yet so good, as well as heart-healthy. I have tried several recipes for frozen non-fat yogurt, and none is as good or as easy as this.

APPROXIMATE NUTRITIONAL INFORMATION PER 1/2-CUP SERVING

Total calories: 100
Total fat: trace
Saturated fat: trace
Dietary fiber: 0 g
Carbohydrates: 20 g
Protein: 4 g
Cholesterol: 3 mg
Sodium: 63 mg

Frozen Yogurt Parfait with Fruit Sauces

4 servings

¼ **cup Strawberry Sauce (page 426)**

2 cups Vanilla Nonfat Frozen Yogurt (page 415)

¼ **cup Peach Sauce (page 426)**

Sprigs of mint

Spoon a dab of strawberry sauce in a narrow parfait or champagne glass. Top with a small scoop (use a melon baller or very small ice-cream scoop) of frozen yogurt; then, in order, peach sauce, frozen yogurt, and strawberry sauce. Garnish with mint.

APPROXIMATE NUTRITIONAL INFORMATION PER SERVING

Total calories: 127
Total fat: trace
Saturated fat: trace
Dietary fiber: 1 g
Carbohydrates: 27 g
Protein: 5 g
Cholesterol: 3 mg
Sodium: 62 mg

Frosty Lemon Supreme

8 servings

½ cup crushed graham cracker crumbs

2 pasturized egg whites*

⅓ cup very cold water

⅓ cup nonfat dry milk

1 pasturized egg yolk*

1 teaspoon grated lemon zest

¼ cup fresh lemon juice

¼ cup granulated sugar

Line a 9-inch pie plate with ¼ cup of the graham cracker crumbs. Beat egg whites, water, and milk to stiff peaks. Add egg yolk, lemon zest, and lemon juice; beat 1 minute, gradually adding sugar. Spoon into pie plate. Sprinkle remaining crumbs over top. Freeze at least 2 hours.

Note: When selecting a brand of graham crackers, be sure to read the label. Heart-healthy brands use unsaturated oils such as safflower, soybean, cottonseed, rapseed or canola. Do not buy a brand that uses saturated fat such as lard, palm oil or coconut oil.

*Uncooked eggs have been the source of salmonella. The American Egg Board recommends using only pasturized eggs to eliminate the risk. They are available in many supermarkets..

APPROXIMATE NUTRITIONAL INFORMATION PER SERVING

Total calories: 61
Total fat: 1 g
Saturated fat: trace
Dietary fiber: trace
Carbohydrates: 11 g
Protein: 2 g
Cholesterol: 27 mg
Sodium: 47 mg

Raspberry Purée

4 cups

2 pints fresh or frozen raspberries

1 tablespoon fresh lemon juice

2 tablespoons granulated sugar

dash Kirsch liqueur (optional)

Wash fresh berries. In a blender or food processor, combine ingredients and purée until smooth. Chill.

Serving Suggestions: Serve fruit purées as a sauce with fresh berries, melons, apricots and peaches, as a sauce over ice cream, and as a syrup over pancakes waffles or French toast. Great on Vanilla Frozen Yoghurt.

APPROXIMATE NUTRITIONAL INFORMATION PER 1/4-CUP SERVING

Total calories: 20
Total fat: 0 g
Saturated fat: 0 g
Dietary fiber: trace
Carbohydrates: 6 g
Protein: 0 g
Cholesterol: 0 mg
Sodium: 0 g

Strawberry Purée

4 cups

2 pints fresh or frozen strawberries

¼ –½ teaspoon almond extract

¼ –½ teaspoon vanilla extract

1–2 tablespoons granulated sugar (optional)

Wash and hull fresh berries. In a blender or food processor, purée the berries. Add almond and vanilla extracts. Sweeten with sugar.

Note: You may want to vary the amount of almond and/or vanilla extract, as well as the sugar, depending on the sweetness of the berries.

Serving Suggestion: Serve fruit purées as a sauce with fresh berries, melons, apricots and peaches, as a sauce over ice cream and as a syrup over pancakes, waffles or French toast.

APPROXIMATE NUTRITIONAL INFORMATION PER 1/4-CUP SERVING

Total calories: 12
Total fat: 0 g
Saturated fat: 0 g
Dietary fiber: 1 g
Carbohydrates: 3 g
Protein: 0 g
Cholesterol: 0 mg
Sodium: 0 mg

Creamy Banana Purée

1 1/2 cups

3–4 ripe bananas, peeled

Wrap bananas in plastic wrap. Freeze. Just before serving, purée bananas in a blender or food processor.

APPROXIMATE NUTRITIONAL INFORMATION PER 1/4-CUP SERVING

Total calories: 63
Total fat: 0 g
Saturated fat: 0 g
Dietary fiber: 2 g
Carbohydrates: 16 g
Protein: 1 g
Cholesterol: 0 mg
Sodium: 1 mg

Fresh Pineapple Purée

2 cups

1 fresh pineapple, peeled and cored

Cut pineapple into quarters. Purée in a blender or food processor.

Rhubarb Purée

6 cups

6 cups rhubarb, sliced into 1-inch pieces

½ cup orange juice

2 tablespoons granulated sugar

In a saucepan, combine rhubarb and orange juice. Cover and cook slowly 10 minutes. Add sugar. Cook 5–10 minutes, or until rhubarb is tender.

Serving Suggestion: Serve warm over sliced bananas or fresh strawberries.

Papaya Purée

1 cup

1 ripe papaya, peeled and seeded

Cut papaya into quarters. Wrap in plastic wrap and freeze. Just before serving, purée papaya in a blender or food processor.

APPROXIMATE NUTRITIONAL INFORMATION PER 1/4-CUP SERVING

Total calories: 29
Total fat: 0 g
Saturated fat: 0 g
Dietary fiber: 1 g
Carbohydrates: 7 g
Protein: 1 g
Cholesterol: 0 mg
Sodium: 1 mg

Fresh Peaches with Strawberry and Creamy Banana Purées

4 servings

½ cup Creamy Banana Purée (page 418)

½ cup Strawberry Purée (page 418)

4 ripe peaches, sliced

fresh blueberries for garnish

Chill 4 deep-lip dessert plates. Ladle 2 tablespoons Banana Purée and 2 tablespoons Strawberry Purée onto each plate. Arrange peaches symmetrically around sauces. Garnish with blueberries.

APPROXIMATE NUTRITIONAL INFORMATION PER SERVING

Total calories: 81
Total fat: 0 g
Saturated fat: 0 g
Dietary fiber: 2 g
Carbohydrates: 23 g
Protein: 1 g
Cholesterol: 0 mg
Sodium: 1 mg

Fresh Peaches in Raspberry Sauce

4 servings

1 10-ounce package frozen raspberries with sugar, thawed

2 tablespoons freshly squeezed orange juice

1 teaspoon cornstarch

½ cup cold water

4 fresh peaches, pitted and thinly sliced

For a "hands-on" after-school snack, in place of the peaches substitute 4 cups Tropical Fruit Salad (page 429) or Hawaiian Fruit Salad (page 429). Arrange the fruits in symmetrical piles on a serving plate with a cup-size bowl of the raspberry sauce in the center. Your kids will love the presentation, and dipping the fruit in the sauce adds to the fun.

In a 2-quart saucepan, combine raspberries and orange juice; heat to boiling. In a small bowl, combine cornstarch with cold water and stir until smooth; gradually add to boiling raspberries. Heat and stir until sauce thickens slightly. Pour mixture into a blender. Blend until smooth and frothy, about 2 minutes. If desired, pour mixture through a strainer to remove raspberry seeds. Chill. Serve in 4 chilled deep-lip dessert plates. Ladle ¼ cup sauce onto each plate. Arrange peaches symmetrically over sauce.

APPROXIMATE NUTRITIONAL INFORMATION PER SERVING

Total calories: 143
Total fat: 1 g
Saturated fat: 0 g
Dietary fiber: 5 g
Carbohydrates: 35 g
Protein: 1 g
Cholesterol: 0 mg
Sodium: 1 mg

Fresh Raspberries with Strawberry Purée

6 servings

1 cup Strawberry Purée (page 418)

3 pints fresh raspberries, washed and hulled

Chill 6 deep-lip dessert plates. Ladle ¼ cup of Strawberry Purée onto each plate. Arrange raspberries over sauce.

Variations: Substitute strawberries for raspberries, or use Raspberry Purée (page 417) in place of Strawberry Purée.

APPROXIMATE NUTRITIONAL INFORMATION PER SERVING

Total calories: 87
Total fat: 0 g
Saturated fat: 0 g
Dietary fiber: 11 g
Carbohydrates: 20 g
Protein: 2 g
Cholesterol: 0 mg
Sodium: 0 mg

Fresh Fruit with Raspberry, Banana and Pineapple Purées

8-10 servings

1 fresh pineapple

4 apricots, pitted and cut into quarters

4 peaches, pitted and cut into quarters

½ cantaloupe, peeled and cut into wedges

1 pint strawberries, hulled

1 papaya, peeled and cut into julienne strips

¼ watermelon, peeled and cut into wedges

1 cup Fresh Pineapple Purée (page 419)

¾ cup Creamy Banana Purée (page 418)

2 cups Raspberry or Strawberry Purée (pages 417)

sprigs of fresh mint (optional)

Cut pineapple in half horizontally, leaving the stem end intact. Using a curved grapefruit knife, carefully remove pineapple from shell. Cut pineapple flesh into cubes and return to shell.

Arrange pineapple shell with pineapple cubes in center of a large platter. Ring with apricots, peaches, cantaloupe, and watermelon. Garnish with strawberries and papaya. Pour purées into small custard cups. Garnish with fresh mint, if desired. Tuck purées among fruits or arrange separately next to fruit platter.

Variation: During the winter months, use sliced pears and Granny Smith apples, fresh figs and Mandarin oranges. Accompany with Creamy Banana Purée, Papaya Purée and Rhubarb Purée (page 418).

Serving Suggestion: This makes a spectacular dessert for any occasion.

APPROXIMATE NUTRITIONAL INFORMATION PER CUP OF FRUIT WITHOUT PURÉES

Total calories: 131
Total fat: 0 g
Saturated fat: 0 g
Dietary fiber: 4 g
Carbohydrates: 31 g
Protein: 2 g
Cholesterol: 0 mg
Sodium: 9 mg

Fresh Pineapple with Berries

8 servings

1 ripe pineapple

2 ripe papayas

1½ cups strawberries, raspberries, or blueberries

The papaya purée adds a nice touch to the presentation.

Cut off the top and bottom of the pineapple. Peel off the brown skin, cutting fairly deep. Remove any brown "eyes" that may remain. Cut into rings. Cut rings into quarters.

Pare papayas; cut in half and remove seeds. Place papaya halves in food processor and purée. Divide purée among individual dessert plates. Arrange pineapple quarters over the top. Garnish with berries.

APPROXIMATE NUTRITIONAL INFORMATION PER SERVING

Total calories: 86
Total fat: 1 g
Saturated fat: 0 g
Dietary fiber: 4 g
Carbohydrates: 21 g
Protein: 1 g
Cholesterol: 0 mg
Sodium: 3 mg

Fresh Pineapple with Papaya Purée

4 servings

1 large ripe papaya, peeled, halved and seeded

1 small fresh pineapple, peeled and cut into cubes

1 banana, sliced

1 mandarin orange, sectioned

In a blender or food processor, purée papaya. Chill. Divide papaya purée equally among dessert plates; arrange pineapple cubes, banana slices, and orange sections over top.

APPROXIMATE NUTRITIONAL INFORMATION PER SERVING

Total calories: 79
Total fat: trace
Saturated fat: trace
Dietary fiber: 2 g
Carbohydrates: 20 g
Protein: trace
Cholesterol: 0 mg
Sodium: trace

Strawberries and Papaya with Raspberry Purée

4 servings

1 cup Raspberry Purée (page 417)

2 pints fresh strawberries, washed and hulled

1 ripe papaya, peeled and cut into julienne strips

Chill 4 deep-lip dessert plates. Ladle ¼ cup of Raspberry Purée onto each plate. Arrange strawberries and papaya symmetrically over sauce.

Variation: Substitute cantaloupe for papaya.

APPROXIMATE NUTRITIONAL INFORMATION PER SERVING

Total calories: 88
Total fat: 1 g
Saturated fat: 0 g
Dietary fiber: 7 g
Carbohydrates: 21 g
Protein: 2 g
Cholesterol: 0 mg
Sodium: 4 mg

Bananas and Fresh Strawberries with Rhubarb Purée

4 servings

1 cup Rhubarb Purée (page 419)

1 pint fresh strawberries, washed and hulled

2 bananas, cut on the diagonal into 2-inch slices

Chill 4 deep-lip dessert plates. Ladle ¼ cup Rhubarb Purée onto each plate. Arrange strawberries and bananas symmetrically over the sauce.

APPROXIMATE NUTRITIONAL INFORMATION PER SERVING

Total calories: 89
Total fat: 1 g
Saturated fat: 0 g
Dietary fiber: 4 g
Carbohydrates: 22 g
Protein: 1 g
Cholesterol: 0 mg
Sodium: 4 mg

Strawberries with Sour-Cream Topping

4 servings

1½ pints fresh strawberries, hulled

4 sprigs fresh mint (optional)

4 tablespoons brown sugar

½ cup nonfat sour cream

Arrange strawberries in a pretty serving bowl. Garnish with mint, if desired. Accompany with small, custard-size bowls of brown sugar and sour cream.

APPROXIMATE NUTRITIONAL INFORMATION PER SERVING

Total calories: 99
Total fat: 0 g
Saturated fat: 0 g
Dietary fiber: 2 g
Carbohydrates: 24 g
Protein: 3 g
Cholesterol: 0 mg
Sodium: 27 mg

Apple-Pear Sauce

2 quarts

6 large Granny Smith apples, peeled and quartered

2 large pears, peeled and quartered

¾ cup water

2 tablespoons brown sugar

1 teaspoon cinnamon

In a heavy saucepan, combine apples, pears and water. Cover and cook over low heat, stirring often, about 45–60 minutes, or until apples and pears soften and become saucy. Add sugar and cinnamon. Simmer 20–30 minutes.

APPROXIMATE NUTRITIONAL INFORMATION PER 1/2-CUP SERVING

Total calories: 69
Total fat: 0 g
Saturated fat: 0 g
Dietary fiber: 3 g
Carbohydrates: 18 g
Protein: 0 g
Cholesterol: 0 mg
Sodium: 1 mg

Strawberry Sauce

1 cup

2½ cups strawberries

2 tablespoons granulated sugar

1 teaspoon fresh lemon juice

In a blender or food processor, combine strawberries, sugar, and lemon juice. Purée until very smooth.

Variation: Substitute raspberries for strawberries.

Serving Suggestion: Good as a sauce with peaches, apricots, melons and berries, and also on Vanilla Angel Food Cake (page 398), Strawberry Sherbet (see page 415) or any flavor frozen yogurt.

APPROXIMATE NUTRITIONAL INFORMATION PER TABLESPOON

Total calories: 13
Total fat: trace
Saturated fat: trace
Dietary fiber: trace
Carbohydrates: 3 g
Protein: trace
Cholesterol: trace
Sodium: trace

Peach Sauce

1 1/2 cups

4 ripe peaches, peeled and pitted

1½ teaspoons fresh lemon juice

¼ cup granulated sugar

1 teaspoon almond extract

In a blender or food processor, combine peaches, lemon juice and sugar. Purée until very smooth. Add almond extract.

Serving Suggestion: Good as a sauce with fresh peaches, apricots, melons or berries. Excellent with sliced peaches over Vanilla Angel Food Cake (page 398).

APPROXIMATE NUTRITIONAL INFORMATION PER TABLESPOON

Total calories: 14
Total fat: trace
Saturated fat: trace
Dietary fiber: trace
Carbohydrates: 3 g
Protein: trace
Cholesterol: 0 mg
Sodium: trace

Peaches Supreme

4 servings

½ cup Peach Sauce (page 426)

4 fresh ripe peaches

½ cup fresh raspberries

½ cup fresh blueberries

Divide peach sauce among 4 chilled dessert plates. Slice peaches into quarters only deep enough to remove the pits and still leave sections attached. Center 1 peach on each plate. Sprinkle with raspberries and blueberries.

APPROXIMATE NUTRITIONAL INFORMATION PER SERVING

Total calories: 83
Total fat: trace
Saturated fat: trace
Dietary fiber: 3 g
Carbohydrates: 21 g
Protein: 1 g
Cholesterol: 0 mg
Sodium: 1 mg

Amaretto Oranges with Strawberries

4 servings

3 large navel oranges, peeled, sliced into thin rings and then torn or cut into sections

2 tablespoons amaretto liqueur

6 strawberries, thinly sliced

4 whole strawberries

Arrange oranges in a shallow bowl; pour amaretto over oranges and toss. Chill 2 hours or overnight. Just before serving, line the edges of 4 small dessert plates with sliced strawberries. Arrange orange sections in center. Top with whole strawberries.

APPROXIMATE NUTRITIONAL INFORMATION PER SERVING

Total calories: 81
Total fat: trace
Saturated fat: trace
Dietary fiber: 2 g
Carbohydrates: 16 g
Protein: 1 g
Cholesterol: 0 mg
Sodium: trace

Chilled Anisette Melons

6 servings

½ **cantaloupe**

7 tablespoons anisette liqueur

3½ **tablespoons water**

¼ **watermelon**

Sprigs of fresh mint

Using a melon baller, form balls from cantaloupe. Combine 3 tablespoons of the anisette with 1½ tablespoons of the water; pour over cantaloupe balls. Cover and chill 1–2 hours.

Remove rind from watermelon. Cut melon into wedges. Combine remaining 4 tablespoons anisette with remaining 2 tablespoons water; pour over melon. Chill 1–2 hours.

To serve, arrange watermelon triangles symmetrically on chilled individual dessert plates. Top each triangle with a melon ball. Garnish with remaining melon balls and mint.

APPROXIMATE NUTRITIONAL INFORMATION PER SERVING

Total calories: 117
Total fat: trace
Saturated fat: trace
Dietary fiber: 1 g
Carbohydrates: 19 g
Protein: 1 g
Cholesterol: 0 mg
Sodium: 6 mg

Berry-Filled Melon Rounds

4 servings

½ **cantaloupe, peeled, seeded and cut crosswise into rounds 1 inch thick**

1½ **cups fresh raspberries**

½ **lime, cut into wedges**

Arrange melon rounds on chilled dessert plates. Fill with berries. Garnish with lime wedges.

Variation: Freeze raspberries. Just before serving, purée raspberries in a blender or food processor. The berries will taste almost like sorbet when blended.

APPROXIMATE NUTRITIONAL INFORMATION PER SERVING

Total calories: 28
Total fat: trace
Saturated fat: trace
Dietary fiber: 2 g
Carbohydrates: 7 g
Protein: trace
Cholesterol: 0 mg
Sodium: 1 mg

Tropical Fruit Salad

8 servings

½ grapefruit

½ cantaloupe

¼ watermelon

½ honeydew

½ pineapple

1 papaya

2 cups peach or raspberry sorbet

fresh mint for garnish

A great Sunday salad. Double the recipe and your fruit will be cut up and ready for the whole week. This fruit salad is especially high in vitamins A and C and in folic acid, a B vitamin.

Peel and section grapefruit and remove membrane. Remove rind and seeds from melons and cut into 2-inch pieces. Peel pineapple; remove core and cut into 2-inch pieces. Peel and seed papaya and cut into 2-inch pieces. Arrange fruits in uniform rows on individual salad plates. Serve with sorbet garnished with mint.

APPROXIMATE NUTRITIONAL INFORMATION PER SERVING

Total calories: 157
Total fat: 1 g
Saturated fat: 0 g
Dietary fiber: 3 g
Carbohydrates: 39 g
Protein: 1 g
Cholesterol: 0 mg
Sodium: 13 mg

Hawaiian Fruit Salad

10 servings

1 fresh pineapple

1 cup strawberries, stemmed and halved

1 cup blueberries

½ small cantaloupe, peeled and cut into 1-inch cubes

1 papaya, peeled, seeded and cut up

1 cup seedless green grapes

fresh mint for garnish

Presentation is so important to the whole eating experience. Add to your family's pleasure by serving this fruit salad in a pineapple boat.

Cut pineapple in half horizontally, leaving the stem end intact. Using a curved grapefruit knife, carefully remove pineapple flesh from shell and cut into cubes. Place ½ of the pineapple cubes in a salad bowl (reserve remaining half for later use). Add remaining fruit and toss. Transfer fruit to pineapple shells. Garnish with mint.

APPROXIMATE NUTRITIONAL INFORMATION PER SERVING

Total calories: 60
Total fat: 0 g
Saturated fat: 0 g
Dietary fiber: 2 g
Carbohydrates: 15 g
Protein: 1 g
Cholesterol: 0 mg
Sodium: 5 mg

Berries and Ice Cream

4 servings

1½ cups sliced fresh strawberries

2 cups light slow-churned, ½ the fat vanilla ice cream

1½ cups fresh blueberries

fresh mint for garnish

The good news: you can definitely have dessert with calories this few.

Divide strawberries among 4 stemmed dessert or champagne glasses. Add a scoop of vanilla sorbet and yogurt. Top with fresh blueberries. Garnish with fresh mint.

APPROXIMATE NUTRITIONAL INFORMATION PER SERVING

Total calories: 150
Total fat: 4 g
Saturated fat: 2 g
Dietary fiber: 2 g
Carbohydrates: 27 g
Protein: 3 g
Cholesterol: 15 mg
Sodium: 35 mg

Strawberry Sundaes

6 servings

1½ pints light slow-churned, ½ the fat vanilla ice cream, softened

1½ cups Strawberry Sauce (p. 426) or Strawberry Puree (p. 418)

You won't miss "real" ice cream when you flavor light ice cream with delicious seasonal fruits.

Scoop ice cream into 6 parfait glasses. Top with strawberries.

APPROXIMATE NUTRITIONAL INFORMATION PER SERVING

Total calories: 167
Total fat: 4 g
Saturated fat: 3 g
Dietary fiber: 2 g
Carbohydrates: 29 g
Protein: 3 g
Cholesterol: 25 mg
Sodium: 35 mg

Homemade Applesauce

8 servings

8 to 10 large tart cooking apples, such as Granny Smith

½ cup water

½ cup granulated sugar

1 teaspoon ground cinnamon

1 tablespoon red-hot cinnamon candies (optional)

Your family will never be able to face another jar of commercial applesauce once they have tasted your homemade variety. Sprinkling red-hot cinnamon candies on top adds a kid-friendly touch to this nutritious dessert.

Wash and peel apples. Core and cut into quarters. Put in a medium saucepan, add water and bring to a boil. Reduce heat, cover and simmer, stirring frequently, until apples are barely tender, 8 to 10 minutes. Add sugar and continue cooking until apples are tender and sugar is dissolved, about 10 minutes. Remove from heat. Stir in cinnamon. Serve in bowls. Sprinkle with red-hot cinnamon candies, if desired.

APPROXIMATE NUTRITIONAL INFORMATION PER 1/2-CUP SERVING

Total calories: 130
Total fat: 0 g
Saturated fat: 0 g
Dietary fiber: 3 g
Carbohydrates: 34 g
Protein: 0 g
Cholesterol: 0 mg
Sodium: 1 mg

Baked Apples

4 servings

4 tart cooking apples, such as Granny Smith or McIntosh

⅓ cup brown sugar

zest of 1 orange

1 tablespoon butter

½ cup dried cranberries or raisins

¾ cup water

2 tablespoons granulated sugar

4 scoops light slow-churned, ½ the fat vanilla ice cream, optional

Dried cranberries are plumper and sweeter than raisins. Your kids will love them.

Preheat oven to 375°F.

Wash apples and remove core to ½-inch of the bottom. Arrange apples in an 8 x 8 x 2-inch ovenproof baking dish. Using a fork, combine brown sugar, orange zest and margarine; stir in the cranberries. Fill each apple center with the mixture.

In a small container, combine water and granulated sugar; pour around apples. Bake about 30 minutes, or until apples are tender but not mushy. Remove from oven and baste the apples several times with the pan juices. If the juices are thin, remove the apples to individual serving bowls and reduce the pan juices before glazing the apples. Serve warm with ice cream.

APPROXIMATE NUTRITIONAL INFORMATION PER SERVING

Total calories: 346
Total fat: 6 g
Saturated fat: 3 g
Dietary fiber: 4 g
Carbohydrates: 75 g
Protein: 3 g
Cholesterol: 9
Sodium: 99 mg

Baked Caramel Pears

4 servings

½ cup water

½ cup brown sugar

1 vanilla bean, split open

4 ripe firm Bosc or Anjou pears

¼ cup caramel dessert topping

This dessert is sure to satisfy the cravings of even the most serious sweet tooth.

In a small saucepan, combine water, brown sugar and vanilla bean. Simmer 5 minutes to dissolve sugar.

Meanwhile, carefully peel pears. With apple corer, remove cores. Slice a small piece off the bottom so each pear will stand alone. Arrange pears in a shallow ovenproof casserole. Pour brown sugar mixture over top. Cover casserole with aluminum foil and bake at 425°F., for 30 to 40 minutes, or until pears are tender, occasionally basting pears with syrup in casserole. Serve pears on deep-lip dessert plates. Warm caramel topping and drizzle 1 tablespoon over each pear.

APPROXIMATE NUTRITIONAL INFORMATION PER SERVING

Total calories: 243
Total fat: 1 g
Saturated fat: 0 g
Dietary fiber: 4 g
Carbohydrates: 60 g
Protein: 1 g
Cholesterol: 0 mg
Sodium: 111 mg

Poached Pears with Raspberry Purée

4 servings

2 cups dry white wine

2½ cups water

1 cinnamon stick

1 vanilla bean

zest of 1 lemon

4 firm, ripe pears

1 cup Raspberry Purée (page 417)

In a deep saucepan, combine wine, water, cinnamon stick, vanilla bean and lemon zest. Bring to a boil. Peel pears, leaving stems intact. Gently drop pears into poaching liquid, adding water or wine, if necessary, to completely cover the fruit. Cover and simmer 25–30 minutes, or until pears are tender. Remove from heat. Cool pears in the poaching liquid until ready to serve.

Serve pears on deep-lip dessert plates. Pour ¼ cup of Raspberry Purée over each pear.

Note: The poaching liquid will keep several weeks in the refrigerator and may be reused.

Variations: Substitute champagne for wine. Or use puréed strawberries or blueberries in place of Raspberry Purée.

APPROXIMATE NUTRITIONAL INFORMATION PER SERVING

Total calories: 194
Total fat: 1 g
Saturated fat: 0 g
Dietary fiber: 6 g
Carbohydrates: 30 g
Protein: 1 g
Cholesterol: 0 mg
Sodium: 6 mg

Index

A

B

Metric Guidelines

These guidelines were developed to simplify the conversion from Imperial measures to metric. The numbers have been rounded for convenience. When cooking from a recipe, work in the same system throughout the recipe: do not use a combination of the two. *

METRIC SYMBOLS

Celcius: C
Liter: L
Milliliter: ml.
Kilogram: kg
Gram: g
Centimeter: cm
Millimeter: mm

OVEN TEMPERATURE CONVERSIONS

IMPERIAL	METRIC
250° F	120° C
275° F	140° C
300° F	150° C
325° F	160° C
350° F	180° C
375° F	190° C
400° F	200° C
425° F	220° C
450° F	230° C
475° F	240° C
500° F	260° C

LENGTH

IMPERIAL	METRIC
¼ inch	5 mm
⅓ inch	8 mm
½ inch	1 cm
¾ inch	2 cm
1 inch	2.5 cm
2 inches	5 cm
4 inches	10 cm

VOLUME

IMPERIAL	METRIC
¼ teaspoon	1 ml.
½ teaspoon	2 ml.
¾ teaspoon	4 ml.
1 teaspoon	5 ml.
2 teaspoons	10 ml.
1 tablespoon	15 ml.
2 tablespoons	25 ml.
¼ cup	50 ml.
⅓ cup	75 ml.
½ cup	125 ml.
⅔ cup	150 ml.
¾ cup	175 ml.
1 cup	250 ml.
4 cups	1 L
5 cups	1.25 L

MASS (WEIGHT)

IMPERIAL	METRIC
1 ounce	25 g
2 ounces	50 g
¼ pound	125 g
½ pound (8 ounces)	250 g
1 pound	500 g
2 pound	1 kg
3 pounds	1.5 kg
5 pounds	2.2 kg
8 pounds	3.5 kg
10 pounds	4.5 kg
11 pounds	5 kg

SOME COMMON CAN/PACKAGE SIZES

IMPERIAL	METRIC

VOLUME

IMPERIAL	METRIC
4 ounces	114 ml.
10 ounces	284 ml.
14 ounces	398 ml.
18 ounces	540 ml.
28 ounces	796 ml.

MASS

IMPERIAL	METRIC
4 ounces	113 g
5 ounces	142 g
6 ounces	170 g
7 ounces	220 g
15 ounces	425 g

*Developed by the Canadian Home Economics Association and the American Home Economics Committee.